ALEISTER CROWLEY
IN PARIS

ALEISTER CROWLEY IN PARIS

SEX, ART, AND MAGICK
in the
CITY OF LIGHT

TOBIAS CHURTON

Inner Traditions
Rochester, Vermont

Inner Traditions
One Park Street
Rochester, Vermont 05767
www.InnerTraditions.com

Text stock is SFI certified

Cataloging-in-Publication Data for this title is available from the Library of Congress

ISBN 978-1-64411-479-7 (print)
ISBN 978-1-64411-480-3 (ebook)

Printed and bound in the United States by Lake Book Manufacturing, Inc.
The text stock is SFI certified. The Sustainable Forestry Initiative® program
promotes sustainable forest management.

10 9 8 7 6 5 4 3 2 1

Text design by Debbie Glogover and layout by Virginia Scott Bowman
This book was typeset in Garamond Premier Pro and Gill Sans with Kepler used as
the display typeface

To send correspondence to the author of this book, mail a first-class letter to the
author c/o Inner Traditions • Bear & Company, One Park Street, Rochester, VT
05767, and we will forward the communication.

This book is dedicated with love
to the memory of Mindy Branstetter,
companion on a road paved with books.

Contents

Foreword

Aleister Crowley in Paris is a book that opens new vistas. Reader, be warned: it is a book that whets the appetite for more and invites further research. It is also an open-ended book. Like nobody else, Tobias Churton knows how to assess Aleister Crowley's thought in all its ambiguity, bringing new perspectives to the history of his time. Churton evokes the transformative power of magick and art, as envisioned by Crowley around the turn of the century, in a new age in which the magic tradition, too, assumed new forms in reaction to a dominant technological rationality. Angels and demons or electromagnetic fields and gamma rays: they were two sides of one and the same invisible cosmic energy.

Aleister Crowley spent a considerable part of his life in Paris, though at intervals. He was shaped by the city when he visited it in 1899, convinced that he was the incarnation of Éliphas Lévi, the French innovator of the occult sciences. In addition, he strongly identified with Baudelaire and translated the first part of *Les paradis artificiels* (1860) as *The Poem of Hashish*. Tradition and renewal: *Il faut être absolument moderne!*

As the Order was also open to women, absolutely modern was also the Paris lodge of the Golden Dawn, into which Crowley was initiated. Its founder, S. L. MacGregor Mathers, leaned on the spiritual feminism of Anna Kingsford, which may also explain the fascination for the Egyptian goddess Isis. Mathers's wife, Moina Bergson, decorated the temple with symbolistic representations. Having studied at the Slade School of Art, she continued her studies at the Académie Colarossi in

Montparnasse, a private art academy that admitted women. The female art students were even permitted to paint from the nude male model. Many young English women attended this academy or the Académie Julian, a similar institution. It was an irresistible artistic milieu for the *homme à femmes* Aleister Crowley.

Tobias Churton offers an engrossing picture of some of the women in these so far hardly explored English enclaves as well as the psychology of English girls of a certain standing and a strict upbringing who, guided by a female chaperone, took their first artistic steps in libertine Paris. Naturally they are situated in Crowley's direct environment, though the networks of these often less-well-known women certainly stretched to the leading figures of the Paris avant-garde. *Aleister Crowley in Paris* provides numerous opportunities for the kind of art-historical research that is nowadays trending. The book highlights not only female artists but also, above all, forgotten women who were active as intermediaries in a male-dominated art world and as a result received the recognition they deserved only later. In Crowley's circle of female friends and lovers there is the painter and poet Mina Loy, who exhibited at the Salon d'Automne in 1905 and subsequently joined the Italian futurists. In Florence in 1914 she wrote her "Feminist Manifesto," which was only published long after her death. Sculptor Kathleen Bruce was a student of Rodin, but nowadays she is better known as the widow of Antarctic explorer Robert Falcon Scott. Nina Olivier, who, according to Crowley in his *Confessions* "I loved and loved so well and sang so passionately," was only a few years ago identified by Crowley specialist William Breeze as "Nina de Montparnasse," or Eugénie Auzias, friend and future wife of the collector and art critic Leo Stein, elder brother of the famous Gertrude. With Nina and the Steins, Crowley moved in the inner circle of the French avant-garde.

Crowley admired Rodin. He met the artist through Kathleen Bruce and Stephen Haweis, Mina Loy's husband, who photographed Rodin's work. He passionately defended Rodin's sculpture of Balzac, which had been dismissed by critics in 1898 as too rough, too unfinished, and totally unlike Balzac himself. Crowley for his part saw in the statue the expression of the creative will, a manifestation of the power in nature. Was not this what art and magick were all about? Not to imitate nature but to evoke its energy and so live the life inspired? The alchemical imperative to "fix the volatile" was the blueprint for every creative act. However expressed, it represented the incarnation of the mind, force, or will: the power of Aiwass, who had dictated *The Book of the Law* in Cairo in 1904. As in every creative act, this revelation, too, was mediated by a woman, Crowley's then wife, Rose Kelly.

Aleister Crowley in Paris is a vibrantly written, evocative book, as we have come to expect of Tobias Churton. He probes deep into the distortions of the *Confessions* and once again shifts the boundaries of accepted interpretations and *idées reçues*. As such, this book is an expression of the creative will.

FRANK VAN LAMOEN

FRANK VAN LAMOEN is a researcher and assistant curator of Visual Arts at the Stedelijk Museum Amsterdam. Coauthor (with Geurt Imanse) of *Russian Avant-Garde; The Khardzhiev Collection,* he has published articles on alchemy and Hermetic philosophy and has been a principal contributor to more than thirty years of prestigious publications of the *Bibliotheca Philosophica Hermetica* in Amsterdam.

Acknowledgments

First, I should like to thank William Breeze, Outer Head of Ordo Templi Orientis, for his generous cooperation in making this, the final volume of my six-volume biography of Aleister Crowley, possible. His eagle-eyed proofreading of the text has proved vital, not only in correcting numerous errors and misconceptions but also for contributing greatly from the immense store of his own research to the up-to-date content and breadth of the work.

Thanks again to Assistant Librarian Philip Young and the staff of the Warburg Institute, London University, for their help in providing courteous access to the Yorke Collection of Crowleyana.

For kind assistance regarding illustrations I wish to express my gratitude to Steve Brachel of the 100th Monkey Press; Geraldine Beskin of the Atlantis Bookshop, London; Anton Liss of the Modern British Art Gallery, Paris; Sigurd Bune (Perdurabo ST) of Denmark; and Clare McNamara, Image Library Officer, Decorative Arts and History, National Museum of Ireland.

I am particularly grateful to Thomas Jamet for kindly introducing me to Philippe Pissier, who has recently translated into French Crowley's novel *Moonchild* (2021) and *Rodin in Rime* (*Le dit de Rodin,* 2018), together with André Murcie's fascinating accompanying essay "49 toasts pour un siècle qui s'éloigne" ("49 toasts for a century that drifts away: Rodin/Crowley: an exemplary encounter"), which is a model of insight and originality rarely found in English-speaking writers on the subject, for "a prophet is not without honor, except in his own country" (Mark 6:4).

Philippe Pissier has also provided me with additional generous assistance in clarifying aspects of Crowley's life in Paris, best known to one intimately familiar with the city and its traditions.

As ever, I am thankful for the friendship over many years of Christopher McIntosh, who has never failed to encourage and enlighten my efforts to get to the many truths of Aleister Crowley obscured by ignorance and all-too-human frailty.

To the fabulous staff at Inner Traditions International, my ardent thanks: to Ehud Sperling, Jeanie Levitan, Jon Graham, Mindy Branstetter, Jamaica Burns Griffin, Erica Robinson, Patricia Rydle, Ashley Kolesnik, and everyone at Vermont's golden beehive.

To all who have helped me on this long but in some ways too short a journey—and especially to my wife, Joanna, and daughter, Merovée, for their love, understanding, and patience—my hearty and sincere "Thank you!"

ONE

Sir Aleister Crowley Will Be Expelled from France Tomorrow

Ninety-three years ago . . . April 1929. Despite disarmament in Germany, a sporadically peaceful world still has its dangers; some emerge from unpredictable quarters.

In mid-April, following a deadly smallpox epidemic in London, the British government, after initial protest, accepts French demands that travelers from Britain be vaccinated. Weeks later, 100 miles north of London, Birmingham experiences an outbreak of "great parrot fever." Transmitted via a bacterial species in South American birds dormant until the birds are caged or frightened, their importation as pets triggers a pandemic. The psittacosis pandemic will afflict nearly a thousand people worldwide with up to three weeks of persistent coughing, headaches, insomnia, chronic fatigue, fever, or pneumonia. More unfortunate sufferers experience delirium and semiconsciousness followed by protracted recovery periods; 15 percent of infected victims die.

A Turkish delegation, meanwhile, submits radical disarmament proposals to the Geneva-based League of Nations disarmament commission as American-directed negotiations to reschedule the Allies' imposed war debt responds to a stricken Germany's (now) three million unemployed. Hitler's rising Nazi Party (NSDAP) opposes the American plan; Hitler wants revenge and rearmament, not accommodation.

In China, Nationalist republican leader Chiang Kai-shek imposes martial law following mutiny in his army, while in the Soviet Union, Stalin arrests hundreds of Leon Trotsky's supporters. Paris rejects Trotsky's asylum plea as Red Army units enter China in retaliation for Chinese aggression against Soviet consulates. In Italy, dictator Mussolini claims his single-party *fascisti* government has secured 99 percent of votes in a general election. Across the Atlantic, newly inaugurated President Hoover sends warplanes to the Mexico-Arizona border after American troops suffer cross fire between Mexico's Catholic rebels and federal forces in Sonora.

Plus ça change, plus c'est la même chose . . .

But wait! Something different . . .

On Tuesday, April 16, 1929, stark beneath an account of German Reichsbank president Dr. Hjalmar Schacht's "conditional acceptance" at the Hotel Georges V of the American plan for Germany's war reparations debt, the *Paris-Midi* newspaper informs Parisians that

SIR ALEISTER CROWLEY
WILL BE EXPELLED FROM FRANCE TOMORROW

*It's the epilogue of a curious tale of German
espionage in the United States during the war*

That's decided. Next Wednesday they're expelling Sir Aleister Crowley. One of the most picturesque and mysterious figures of the contemporary international landscape, this English baronet, who lives in Paris's avenue Suffren, is, in effect, the world's most celebrated mage (you know, the famous Master Therion). He's crossed China on foot, he's tried and almost succeeded in conquering the Himalayas; he's been received in Tibet by sacred lamas. . . . American newspapers reproach him for having burnt women alive and having drunk the blood of young infants. This, Sir Aleister Crowley denies. His native government reproaches him only for having been, during the war, one of Germany's most active agents in America, and the French police reproach him for his intimate relations with a too celebrated child of Spain and several other chaps. This, Sir Aleister Crowley disputes. For him, Magic alone is important.

—She raises the soul above these petty contingencies, he asserts.

Fig. 1.1. Paris-Midi, *Tuesday, April 16, 1929; Crowley headline, below center.*

The baronet, to defend himself told us . . .

One of us has visited Sir Aleister Crowley. Bedridden with an infirmity, our last interview was yesterday. An extraordinary figure emerges from the white sheets. The height of his face is that of an Asiatic illuminate. The eyes jump from their sockets. The bulk of the figure is of childlike softness, with a tender feminine mouth.

—They want to expel me. I protest. Besides, I am ill, very ill. They'd have to transport me. . . . They've already seen out my fiancée—a Nicaraguan divorced from a Frenchman—Mme Ferrari de Miramar, as well as my secretary, Israel Regardie, a twenty-one-year-old American, and already a master of Kabbalah. . . .

—What are they accusing you of?

—of being a spy. They understand nothing. Yes, to be exact, I very actively participated in German counterespionage in America during the war, but I was in accord with the Naval Intelligence Service of my own country! I've counterbalanced, by my influence, the formidable German organization that hit the USA from 1914 to 1917. I was myself close to the Germans, and particularly encouraged the ambassador Von Bernsdorf to support an Irish revolution. In doing so I was obliged to publish violent articles against my own country in *The Fatherland*. That's how on 3 January 1917 I suggested England become a German colony. That's also how I wrote in your language, the "Call to French good sense" where I proclaimed that England toyed with her ally and toiled to extract the maximum profit from the conflagration.*

—I remember. This article had a formidable resonance. You've counselled a separate peace to us. Weren't you going a bit far in . . . your game? And a bit strong?

—I had to do it to gain the confidence of the Germans. I had my goal. . . .

America-Germany "Intelligence Service"

—this goal?

—to get German submarines to sink the still neutral American ships.

—What! I don't understand!

—Yes, by this means the Americans were obliged to enter the war on our side.† I was, besides, always in accord with Captain Gaunt, chief of the [British Naval] Intelligence service in America. Today, Gaunt is lord-admiral and I have telegraphed him to send me a letter to exonerate me with respect to your government.

—You've lived in France for how long?

—For twenty-six years. But I traveled. Lived in Paris without interruption for the past six years.

---

*"Appel au bon sens Français" ("Call to French good sense") first appeared in pro-German George Sylvester Viereck's New York–based arts and culture magazine, *The International* (IX.10), in October 1915. After expressing his longstanding love for Paris and its virtues of liberty, toleration, and humanity, Crowley's propaganda paean asked how such a country could find itself tricked into cordial alliance with Britain, alleged enemy of these virtues. France had more in common with Germany than with "perfidious Albion," alliance with whom was, the piece alleged, sole cause of conflict. Germany was for science, peace, progress, and resistance to the "Tartars" of Russia. I'm grateful to Philippe Pissier for bringing the original article to my attention.

†In a letter from Brussels (April 23, 1929; YC OSD3, 242), Crowley alerted Gerald Yorke to inaccuracies in the *Paris-Midi* article: "The fact that you [Yorke] really missed about the 'unlimited submarine campaign' was that Wilson had been re-elected in 1916 purely and solely on the slogan 'He kept us out of War.' I heard on all sides that the cause of the allies was desperate, and I don't believe that any other move would have solved the problem."

—There must have been a new factor then, recently?

—Not at all. It was promised that no more would any sanction be held against me over facts of war. But there've been stories of private life and incomprehension of my magical rites. That's another story. . . .

Because Sir Aleister Crowley has a lot more surprising things to recount, we've given him leave to speak; we leave to him responsibility for his affirmations.

Appearing at midday, France's first news concerning Crowley's "expulsion" was written by Pierre Lazareff and Claude Dhérelle.* A follow-up appeared on *Paris-Midi*'s front page two days later:

BLACK MAGIC SOON MENTIONED WHEN SPEAKING OF CROWLEY!

Under the vigilant eye of the Sûreté générale, Sir Aleister Crowley took the 11:30 train to Brussels, yesterday morning.

On the platform at the Gare du Nord, a very gay Sir Aleister Crowley, supported by his inseparable English nurse, speaks to us.

—I leave because I'm obliged to, but I shall return. I go to Brussels to retrieve my fiancée, Mlle Ferrari de Miramar—whom I shall doubtless marry over there—and my secretary Regardie who's waiting for me. . . . But I wish to return to France to ascertain on what basis they accuse me, and to obtain openly information used against me so I can exonerate myself. Because it's certain some tales told by an Austrian-turned-American journalist in Paris—and who was in my employ—have provided the basis for this unjustified decision. . . .

As the noble Englishman cites to us the name of this well-known colleague [Carl de Vidal Hunt] in connection with [Alexander]

---

*Dhérelle was a staff journalist at *Paris-Midi*. The *New York Times* (April 21, 1972) obituary of Pierre Lazareff (1907–1972) informs us that Lazareff would become publisher and director of *France-Soir*, Paris's largest circulation newspaper. He also directed the Sunday newspaper *Journal du Dimanche* and the women's periodical *Elle*. Esteemed a French press giant, Lazareff earned the epithet "the Napoleon of Journalists," having, among other achievements, challenged French journalistic ethics while typifying pre–World War II French journalism as venal and treasonous. In such hands was Crowley's reputation in April 1929.

Zubkoff, the kaiser's famous brother-in-law,* who lodged with him when Zubkoff recently lived in Paris, the train pulled out.

But we are not leaving it there. Our enquiries led us also to Auteuil, to a calm, often deserted street where for a long time the mage possessed a bachelor flat. And from the lips of his best companions, of his neighbors, we have learnt that Sir Aleister Crowley did not respect all of the obligations of theosophical rites: he was a joyous lover of life who loved well and drank much, who ate spicy food and enjoyed pretty women.

—about black magic! said one of his most faithful commensals to us, American papers asserting that are very naïve! Crowley created books, paintings, cinema scenarios, and even some poems so *légère* that someone has burnt them, in London, in a public place!

—And the black masses?

—Crowley, I told you, loved pretty women and wasn't against the company of young chaps. The Bois [de Boulogne] was close, the opportunities numerous. But black masses! Crowley, whilst he'd reported on strange things during his travels to India and China, always preserved the manners of the most civilized European.

Our police, for their part, confirm it:

—The Aleister Crowley affair? Simply an affair of customs.

Indeed!

A glance to the article's left records an unusual stroke of Crowleyan luck, or fate, if you will, regarding Crowley's exit to Brussels by train. Three hours and thirty-two minutes before Crowley's departure (10:00 a.m., April 17), an earlier Paris–Brussels express collided with a goods train at Hal in Belgium, killing eleven people, seriously injuring fifteen, and wounding thirty-one others. It was perhaps good manners that prevented *Paris-Midi* journalists from connecting the two events . . . for *Black Magic is soon mentioned when speaking of Crowley.*

So, at least, we find on the front page of *Le Journal,* published

---

*A scandal would erupt in 1931 when Zubkoff, widower of the former kaiser's sister Princess Victoria, was found serving beer and dancing for patrons of a Luxembourg café. The former kaiser, through Countess von Spach, offered Zubkoff a small house and income, but Zubkoff, fearing entrapment into a lunatic asylum insisted on staying put.

Fig. 1.2. Paris-Midi, *Thursday, April 18, 1929; column on right,* MAGIE NOIRE C'EST BIENTÔT DIT EN PARLANT DE CROWLEY!

6:00 a.m. Wednesday, April 17, 1929, around the time of the crash. Next to the announcement that "tomorrow all English visitors to France must be vaccinated," we find a less scientific message:

> The high priest
> of black magic
> will today be
> expelled from France

In the Middle Ages, they burnt sorcerers in the Place de Grève. Nowadays they're content to expel them. This punishment, evidently less grave than times past, does not in the least take away lively protests over Sir Aleister Crowley, whose punishment is about to be applied today.

We've paid a call on one who pretends, rightly or wrongly, to be one of the masters of modern Kabbalah.

On the fifth floor of luxury apartments in the avenue de Suffren, a furnished apartment with all the refinements of elegance and most

Fig. 1.3. Le Journal, *Wednesday, April 17, 1929; center column,* LE GRAND PRÊTRE DE LA MAGIE NOIRE SERA AUJOURD'HUI EXPULSÉ DE FRANCE.

demanding concerns of modern comfort. A bright room. Double curtained windows filter a pale light that emphasizes the geometrical design of a thick Moroccan carpet.

A man is seated at a vast writing desk overloaded with books, his blue eyes, candid and surprised, pierce the lines of one approaching fifty.

—Yes, someone wants to expel me from France—me, French to the heart—who's lived in Paris for twenty years.

—What have they got against you?

—I don't quite know. They reproach me vaguely—oh! very vaguely—for spying in America, during the war. In fact, during the period 1914–17 I belonged to England's Naval Intelligence Service. I'd allied myself to the German counterespionage service, to be better able to perceive close-up, their plans. That's how I was led to write in an American paper an article unfavorable to France. But I repeat, this was only to gain the confidence of our enemies. I acted with the plain consent of Captain Gaunt, since lord of the Admiralty, then my chief of service direct to Naval Intelligence.

—And that's all?

—Peuh! All the rest is stories. . . . I've numerous enemies. They make arrows out of any wood. They accuse me of intimacy with young men. The best proof I can give to counter that is my engagement to Mlle Ferrari de Miramar. . . .

A slight shrug of the shoulders.

—What rot hasn't been laid at my door? The old popular hatred against those engaged in magic is smeared over their lips. They accuse me of eating little children, of burning women alive. Doesn't it go as far as treating me as "grand priest of black magic"?

Whilst we make ourselves at home, Sir Aleister chants, with well-measured tones and a light British accent:

—I've taken Monsieur Paul-Boncour as my advocate.* Make it clear I only ask for one thing: what are the precise accusations made against me. I don't want *toleration,* I want a *vindication.* —S.F.

The late edition of *Le Petit Parisien* ("the most powerful draw of world news in the world") ran Crowley's interview with Yves Dautun (1903–1973) next to a recent headshot of the mage:

Fig.1.4. Le Petit Parisien, *front page, Wednesday April 17, 1929; right column with Crowley headshot,* Le mystérieux visage d'Aleister Crowley qui va être "refoulé" de France.

---

*Advocate Joseph Paul-Boncour, of the Republican Socialist Party, became prime minister 1932–1933.

Magician? Spy?

THE MYSTERIOUS FACE OF ALEISTER CROWLEY WHO'S TO BE "TURNED OUT" OF FRANCE

Today they're going to "turn out" of France a singular personality, Aleister Crowley, of British nationality, who's reproached for suspect relations with foreign intelligence services, and for surrendering himself to obscure magical practices, barely compatible with modern civilization.

This "turning out" is not an expulsion order, only the withdrawal of identity card, without which a foreigner cannot live in France.

Aleister Crowley received us serenely.

—I don't like the papers saying I'm a baronet, he declared to us. I have the title of chevalier. Now I permit you to publish that I am duke, marquis, or prince.

This dark personality, would he be pure joker? Here he is sat on his bed, legs crossed under the sheets, chubby and formidable in his precious undress. From a pyjama of champagne silk, the monstrous neck emerges, which supports the strangest imaginable head. The enormous bare front adorned by a lock in the Tartar mode; his eyes, clear blue, go you know not where before focusing on you with a cruel insistence. The voice is fat, with a very pronounced accent.

In the bedroom, a sickroom, a bizarre perfume floats, something unnatural, like an oriental drug.

That for which he is reproached he recounts while defending himself:

—First, I do black masses. Women. I crucify them, and then I eat them. That's convenient. I am a spy also. Finally, I've stolen the towers of Notre-Dame. There!

He laughs. But it doesn't seem commodious to laugh with him. One rather wishes to hide in a corner. This laugh has something funerary about it. And the grin that accompanies it is no more reassuring.

—Magic? Of course. I believe in it. Magic, that's all, that's life. If you're there, interrogating me, that's magic. Yes, monsieur. But the black masses, no. To profane a mystery, it's necessary to believe in the mystery. But I don't believe in anything. As for women, I don't eat them. I am besides, very gentle [or kind].

His spying role, finally, he defends vigorously. He was made part of German counterespionage organized by England in America during the war, this certainly; he served his country; he's nothing to reproach himself for.

—I very much want specificity regarding the accusations. Up to now it's been a tale from *1001 Nights*. It's all the same to me if I go to prison. They must accuse me formally; then I can justify myself.

In a confident tone, he speaks of a shady businessman who wanted to roll it and who proposed to him an affair "not very proper."

—Think about it, he wanted me to matchmake a marriage between the Prince Sixtus de Bourbon* and a rich American. I wouldn't act. These kinds of adventures frighten me. I'm a very modest petit bourgeois. I like to stay in my corner, well-fed, and I play chess admirably. That's the bottom of things.

Paris, I adore. It's my *quartier*. I only know the good restaurants, and my chess circle, where I'm respected. I'm not happy to go. Brussels is sad, they say. Still, I must rejoin my secretary, who's very kind, and my fiancée, who's from Nicaragua, whom the police have already expedited.

I'm going to get married. And straightaway I'll demand to return to France to turn on the light. I've given Monsieur Paul-Boncour my case. Justice must be done by me.

Shall we soon know the true face of Aleister Crowley?

Appearing the day after Crowley's departure, Crowley's "true face" seemed no mystery to "Paris's only daily socialist paper," *Le Populaire* (April 18, 1929):

---

*Prince Sixtus of Bourbon-Parma (1886–1934) married Hedwige de la Rochefoucauld (1896–1986) in 1919. The marriage, however, went unauthorized by Sixtus's elder half brother Elias, Duke of Parma. The "rich American" was Mabelle Corey (see pages 318–19). The *New York Times* (February 25, 1929) reported Corey's expected marriage to disgraced Don Luis de Bourbon-Orléans was "unavoidably delayed" due to King Alfonso of Spain's mother's death; they never married. The reference to Sixtus rather than Don Luis could be Crowley's or Yves Dautun's error.

Fig. 1.5. Le Populaire, *Thursday, April 18, 1929; column center-right with portrait,* UNE ETRANGE FIGURE—ALEISTER CROWLEY MAGE, POETE ET, DIT-ON, ESPION—*Ce personnage compliqué vient d'être expulsé de France.*

A strange figure

ALEISTER CROWLEY MAGE, POET AND, SOME SAY, SPY

This complicated personality comes to be expelled from France

---

Strange personality, without any doubt, but to which our sympathy refuses itself without hesitation. This you'll understand easily when you know what the question of Sir Crowley is about.

French police have "turned out" this less than desirable personality. You've probably read they expelled him yesterday morning.

There were good reasons for it. But I understand that we don't make of it a shining gift to the country where Sir Crowley is intent on and which only he currently knows. Unless he is himself as little aware as ourselves.

Sir Aleister Crowley gives himself the title of English baronet. Of its legitimacy, nothing is less certain.

What's more certain is that his past is full of mystery. Shaking it a bit, a stack of stories more or less turbulent appear incontinently on the surface of a vessel of depths.

To believe many American papers, Aleister Crowley spied during the war to the profit of Germany. Defending himself, Crowley retorts, not without cynicism, that he served England in the same honorable conditions. Testifying to a unique vanity he flatters himself to the hilt with having been one of the Naval Intelligence Service's best agents.

Each takes his certificates where he can!

The Strange Life of Aleister Crowley

But nothing is lost to his glory. It's also said he's allied to a sect of Kabbalists. Multiple and astonishing initiations of sorcery are attributed to him. His name is bound to incredible scenes of black magic.

It seems however that that these facts alone were insufficient for the police to proceed against him the expulsion measure.

Sir Crowley would have brought on himself official attention and hostility for failure to observe the rules of morality.

Sir Crowley was educated. He enjoyed in England a good reputation as a poet. He once frequented divers reputable salons in Paris—so it's said.

Tall, completely shaven, his nose lost in his face, the look of Aleister Crowley shone with singular flame.

He had, once, founded a luxurious revue of occultism: *The Equinox*. But, it was too many times taken for a state of impotence, his gifts of sorcery considered a vast joke.

Sir Crowley has therefore been expelled. Bon voyage all the same.

Adjacent to the front-page news that Reichsbank president Dr. Schacht had presented the American "Young memorandum" to the Reich (*Paris-Soir,* Thursday, April 18, 1929), was a photo taken of a calm, determined Crowley at the Gare du Nord wrapped in a warm overcoat, sporting a homburg:

Hit by an expulsion order

THE MAGE CROWLEY HAS LEFT FOR BRUSSELS WHERE HE'LL MARRY

He will return to Paris to vindicate himself

It's done: Aleister Crowley's been "turned out." The singular personality accused of magic, and more gravely, of relations with

Fig. 1.6. Paris-Soir, *Thursday, April 18, 1929; right column,* Le mage Crowley est parti pour Bruxelles où il se mariera *Il reviendra à Paris pour se justifier.*

foreign intelligence services, left this morning at ten o'clock for Brussels.

We assisted his embarkation in a modest taxi. As several suitcases were slid into the vehicle, Crowley appeared. This man with a huge, round, pale face has already passed the Franco-Belgian border.

In a blue jacket, smoking a long, straight, round pipe, he responds to our questions from one corner of his thin lips to the other:

—I've already said everything. I admit all that one wants: magic, theft, espionage, assassination. . . . Does that suffice? Before trying to vindicate myself of all that, I'm getting married in Brussels. Yes, I don't hesitate before another crime!

—*Parbleu!* . . . Justice will have to defend me.

Whilst the car moves off without the cobbles bursting into flames or clouds enveloping the humble car, the likeable proprietor of the mage's avenue Suffren apartment gave us her impression:

—An *illuminé*, perhaps crazy, but a very polite tenant, very correct, very "old France". . . even though British. Certainly he's occupied with magic, but though my floorboards were burnt by his incense, I believe these practices do evil to no one. Several months ago, I gave a soirée to which he was invited. That funny man scared my friends when they learnt their worst catastrophes.

—that have come to pass?

—None. . . . An inoffensive man, I tell you. Evidently, if they expel him, they're reproaching him for serious things, but I'm not concerned with politics, I've heard nothing of it.

Happy woman!—*Morency.*

To Crowley's sorrow, he would never again reside in Paris, perhaps the nearest place to an intellectual and spiritual home he would ever know. As so often after 1914, he simply couldn't raise the money either for his distinguished advocate in Paris or the "backhanders" required to secure cooperation from people with influence. Furthermore, employees, or former employees, of Britain's security services never publicly defended any part of his American disinformation campaign. There was too much potential embarrassment and ambiguity in his case for official exposure, and he was, anyway, regarded as too unpredictable and independent to accommodate; his outsider stance invited prejudice and wariness. No terrestrial intelligence service is *all*-knowing. While Britain's intelligence services did not echo the frequently mendacious accusations of the gutterpress, Crowley was nevertheless left to deal with the weight of opprobrium by himself. While it was easy to regard him as provocateur of his own misfortunes, newspapers of record never broached the issue in his lifetime.

From the Parisian newspaper reports translated in this chapter, one might be as perplexed as they were in assessing Crowley's true character, motives, and actions. We should not expect too much from newspaper

Fig. 1.7. Crowley, as depicted in Paris-Soir *the day after quitting Paris.*

stories cooked up for the late or morning edition. For that we shall need to trace Crowley's long, intimate association with France's capital. Never before attempted, this biographical focus will enable us to see clearly how and why Aleister Crowley found himself on the 10:00 a.m. Paris–Brussels train on Wednesday, April 17, 1929.

TWO

※

One Flame 1883–1898

Crowley first glimpsed Paris in 1883 as parents Edward and Emily alighted at the Gare du Nord for a family holiday to France and Switzerland. Seven-year-old "Aleck" (as he was called) was doubtless oblivious to the spiritual dawn kissing the capital's horizon. Twenty-five-year-old critic Joséphin Péladan (1858–1918) had just declared his life's mission to spiritualize and idealize French art with a broadside against convention in *L'Artiste* to which even *young* Crowley might have assented: "I believe," announced Péladan, "in the Ideal, in Tradition, in Hierarchy." At the same time, Péladan's friend-to-be, Marquis Stanislas de Guaita, published his first poetry book, *La Muse Noire* ("The Black Muse") while fellow Symbolist Catulle Mendès introduced de Guaita to the magical works of Éliphas Lévi.* Attraction to Lévi and Lévite magus "Mérodack" in Péladan's hit novel, *Le Vice Suprême* (1884), would bring de Guaita to Péladan, and both men to the center of that "French Occult Revival" to which fellow Decadent Aleister Crowley would owe so much.

Indeed, it took less than a decade for Crowley's identification with Éliphas Lévi to lead him to believe Lévi was *his* former incarnation, attributing his finding parts of Paris weirdly familiar to déjà vu. Crowley also shared much in common with de Guaita, and they might have met had de Guaita not died so tragically young in 1897, a few months after Crowley's inward poleaxing by what he'd call the "Trance of Sorrow": a crushing sense of life's impotence against ultimate futility. De Guaita

---

*Alphonse-Louis Constant, 1810–1875.

Fig. 2.1. Joséphin Péladan *(1858–1918), by Alexandre Seon, Museum of Fine Arts, Lyon.*

had long before come to magic through similar nihilistic despair, rebelling, like Crowley, against religious austerity. Fellow poet of the symbol, Crowley would also experiment with hashish, not as decadent appurtenance, but to explore mystical consciousness. Both men became scholars of "the occult."

The year 1888 was one of ignition. Péladan and de Guaita joined forces in the *Ordre Rose+Croix+Kabbalistique* while Paris's Hermetic movement of Symbolist-inspired artists, composers, and writers open to magic and mysticism coalesced inside Edmond Bailly's Librairie de l'Art Indépendant at 11 rue de la Chaussée d'Antin. Further impetus came from Lucien Mauchel and Gérard Encausse's Librairie du Merveilleux at 29 rue de Trévise, center for the Groupe Indépendant d'Études Ésotériques. Calling himself "Papus" after a late-antique demon (*génie*) of medicine (he was training to be a doctor), Encausse and enthusiastic associates embraced every aspect of esotericism, from tarot to a revived Martinism. When Jules Doinel's Gnostic Church was consecrated in 1890 at Lady Caithness's mansion at 124 avenue de Wagram (Theosophist epicenter), its members met at the back of the Librairie du Merveilleux. The year 1888 also saw the first issue of *L'Initiation*, Papus's monthly journal of esoteric commentary,* through whose pages in 1890, Péladan announced his demitting from de Guaita's Rose-Croix Order in favor of his *own* revived Order of the Catholic Rose Cross, the Temple and the Grail, dedicated to establishing his idealist, spiritual aesthetic in all arts, to save the Latin world, as he saw it, from Germanic barbarity and spiritual decay, or if not to save it, then at least to furnish a spirited last stand before the end. Erik Satie was Order "chapelmaster," composing music for, and inspired by, Péladan's ideal.†

Links with Britain came through Freemason and inspirer of the Hermetic Order of the Golden Dawn Kenneth Mackenzie (1833–1886),

Fig. 2.2. Papus's chair, beloved of Parisian Martinists today. The sign reads: "Armchair still occupied by Gérard Encausse—Papus—the morning of his 'death'" (October 25, 1916).

---

*Placed on the Papal Index in 1891 for alleged Gnostic heresy.
†For the story of the movement, see my *Occult Paris*.

who interviewed Éliphas Lévi in 1861, and Lady Caithness's close friend, Anna Kingsford (1846–1888), who inspired Golden Dawn cofounder Samuel Mathers, and whose death in 1888 probably influenced Mathers and Masonic colleagues to build on Mackenzie's "Brothers of the Light" Order, honoring Kingsford's dynamic spiritual feminism by opening their Hermetic Order of the Golden Dawn equally to women.

By the time Crowley again passed through Paris—en route, aged eighteen, to climbing in the Austrian Tyrol in 1894—the spiritual movement had passed its zenith, though new actors were still emerging. While Crowley's entrance proper (if we except his former life as Lévi) did not occur until 1899, the magnet that drew him to Paris was already ensconced.

MATHERS IN PARIS

S. L. MacGregor Mathers, as Samuel Liddell Mathers called himself, explored Paris in July 1891, shortly after Papus and Augustin Chaboseau established the Martinist Order Supreme Council. Doubtless perceiving a potential clash of interests, Mathers "recognized" Papus's Order, on the spurious basis that the Golden Dawn was *chief* line of Rosicrucian succession with authority to recognize or disregard other Orders. Mathers's Order, however, owed some core doctrines to Paris. Its amalgam of astrology, Kabbalah, alchemy, Theurgy, Hermetic Egyptianism, Germanic neo-Rosicrucianism with the angel magic of Elizabethan Dr. John Dee and alchemist-seer Edward Kelley was centered around Éliphas Lévi's identification of the tarot's twenty-two trump cards with the twenty-two letters of the Hebrew alphabet, a speculation developed further by de Guaita and friends Oswald Wirth and Papus toward an initiatory system entwined about the numerical speculations of the Sefer Yetzirah applied to the sephiroth-bearing "Tree of Life" glyph from the kabbalist Sefer HaBahir ("Book of Illumination, or Brightness"). However, Crowley's study of the tarot, *The Book of Thoth* (part 1, I; 1944), asserts that the attributions of the twenty-two tarot trumps in Éliphas Lévi's *Dogma and Ritual of the High Magic* (two volumes, 1854; 1856) contained deliberate errors of correspondence; that is to say, the volumes "Dogma" and "Ritual" (meaning Theory and Practice), each arranged in twenty-two chapters, intentionally misaligned chapter numbers to trumps. Crowley believed Lévi did this to conceal the initiated doctrine from the profane. Crowley derived this view from Golden Dawn sources: something today's Outer Head of Ordo Templi Orientis, William Breeze, clarified for me recently: "The English taught that the French attributions were blinds. But the French went on to build entire systems on their different attributions. The systems are almost non-interoperable as a result."[1]

Walking in the Bois de Boulogne in 1891, Mathers allegedly encountered his Order's "Secret Chiefs," their presence so "electric" he felt drained of vitality, a description redolent of the recorded invocation of spirits of thirteenth-century Cathars at Lady Caithness's mansion in 1889 that initiated Doinel's Gnostic Church.* Mathers believed "his" chiefs included a French initiate linked to Scottish royalty. Lady Caithness (1830–1895) believed Mary Queen of Scots to be her guardian angel (her mansion was called Holyrood). Mathers believed he was himself alchemy-patron King James IV of Scotland reincarnated, identifying with the clan MacGregor, whose clan name was forbidden by James VI of Scotland (fearing magic) in 1603.† Neo-Jacobite Legitimist Mathers also conspired to place Stuart survivors on Britain's throne. Note also that Martinists with authority to initiate were called "Supérieurs Inconnus" (S.I.), a title given by eighteenth-century "Strict Observance" Masons to mysterious, even preternatural adepts to God's will: "unknown superiors" behind manifest Orders.

MINA MATHERS AND ANNIE HORNIMAN

Mathers first discovered Mina Bergson studying Egyptian art at the British Museum in 1887, a year before London's first G.D. temple was chartered. Born of British and Polish Jewish stock in Geneva in 1865, Mina's talented family (music and medicine) moved to Paris in 1867, settling in 1873 in London, where in 1880 Mina distinguished herself in drawing at Bloomsbury's Slade School of Art, on Gower Street. She met lifelong friend Annie Horniman there in 1882. Marrying Mathers in 1890, Mina changed her name to the Celtic *Moina* ("gentle") while Mathers curated Annie's father, Frederick J. Horniman M.P.'s, Forest Hill

---

*See *Occult Paris,* 358–61.
†Until reemergence, MacGregor clansmen were dubbed "children of the mist."

Fig. 2.3. Mina (also "Moina") Mathers (1865–1928).

museum. When Mathers was dismissed, Annie, now a Golden Dawn officer, subvented the couple's move to Paris in 1892, offering continued support. Now able to see her Paris-based brother, doctor of philosophy Henri Bergson (1859–1941), Moina pursued painting at the Académie Colarossi, 10 rue de la Grande-Chaumière, Montparnasse.

Near the Hôtel des Invalides on January 6, 1894, with Annie Horniman and cofounder William Wynn Westcott assisting, Imperator Mathers consecrated 1 avenue Duquesne (the Mathers's apartment), Ahathoor Number 7 Temple.

The Golden Dawn's center moved in early 1895 to 87 avenue Mozart, an attractive villa in sedate Auteuil, close to the Bois de Boulogne. The villa had two other addresses: 43 rue Ribéra, a narrow back street, and 41 rue de la Source, another pleasant residential road. Via back roads, visitors could enter the garden, then the temple: a large hall by a marble staircase serving as dais for adepts and the way to the Mathers's apartments. Partially blocked by a new structure, the former rue Ribéra back entrance is still visible. The rue de la Source entrance around the corner is gone, modern tenements replacing the villa's former gardens.

Here, on March 23, 1895, with Moina's impressive paintings of Egyptian deities looming around him, Papus was ceremonially admitted

*Fig. 2.4.
Present-day
87 avenue
Mozart.*

*Fig. 2.5.
Present-day
43 rue Ribéra.*

Neophyte into the Golden Dawn (in French). Years later, Crowley regarded *his* initiation as life defining. It's unlikely Papus felt that way about it, declining further initiations in the Outer Order. Perhaps Papus felt he deserved admission straight into the exclusive Second Order, or maybe he was simply curious. Papus's colleagues at the Librairie du Merveilleux and its adjuncts (including the Gnostic Church) mostly ignored the Golden Dawn.* Papus may have been suspicious, especially since he hoped to bring all esoteric bodies under the unifying banner of the Martinist Order, with a Christian emphasis obscured in the G.D.

A few months later, traveling alone through Paris, Crowley headed for the 2,061-meter Kleine Schiedegg mountain pass in the Bernese Oberland. After a guideless ascent of the Eiger, an urgent cable summoned him back for Cambridge University entrance examinations.

Crowley took up residence at Trinity College in October 1895, entering for the Moral Science Tripos, which by 1870 consisted of moral and political philosophy, mental philosophy (psychology), and logic and political economy. In the event, Crowley balked at the subjects offered, particularly political economy, which, as he joked in *Confessions* (chapter 12), was said by a professor to be very difficult "because there was no reliable data."[2] Crowley successfully persuaded his understanding tutor, classics scholar (with an interest in "psychic" phenomena) Professor A. W. Verrall, that he preferred to devote his studies to English literature. In fact, Crowley spent his time at Trinity studying pretty much what interested him at any given time, assembling an impressive library in the process. A recommended reading list for his magical Order (the A∴A∴) offers perhaps a hint that his literary studies may have extended to some French literature: *Le Comte de Gabalis* by Abbé Nicolas-Pierre-Henri de Montfaucon de Villars; *The Golden Verses of Pythagoras* by Fabre d'Olivet (a Martinist favorite); Balzac's *Le Peau de Chagrin* (regarded as magical allegory); and François Rabelais's *Gargantua and Pantagruel,* which described an imagined libertarian, chivalrous "Abbey of Thelema" guided by the sole rule: "Do What

---

*Notable exceptions were Jules Bois and astrologer Ely Star (Eugène Jacob). Initiated Neophyte on August 22, 1896, raised to Adeptus Minor on February 25, 1898, Star became temple Hierophant on September 1899, just in time for Aleister Crowley's second visit to the suburb for *his* Adeptus Minor raising into the Second Order, January 1900.

Thou Wilt" (*fay çe que vouldras*). In later life Crowley would translate Baudelaire's *Les Fleurs du Mal,* which, like a good Decadent, he adored. Apart from Lévi, Crowley also enjoyed J. K. Huysmans's Symbolist-occult novels *Là Bas* (1891) and *À Rebours* (1884).

On October 12, 1896—his twenty-first birthday—Crowley inherited some £45,000. Given his upbringing's peculiarity, this windfall presaged disastrous results, for as Crowley would repeat frequently after its exhaustion, he'd been raised without any sense that money could be earned or knowledge of how to make it.

Less than two months after acquiring his fortune, a penurious Mathers begged a loan from Golden Dawn member F. L. Gardner:

> We have been in *terrible* monetary anxiety of late, and have *immediate and urgent* need of *£100* (one hundred pounds); could you let me have the sum?
>
> I have no security worth the name to offer you. Of course, there is the furniture here, but it is worth very little, and there are several paintings and drawings of Vestigia's [Moina Mathers's Golden Dawn name/motto], most of which have been exhibited, but I know the value of pictures depends almost entirely on circumstances.[3]

Annie had ended her subvention in September, hence the desperate letter to Gardner. The day before sending it, Mathers wrote to Annie, now Sub-Praemonstratrix of London's Isis-Urania temple;

> In my letter to you in answer to your reply to my manifesto I insisted upon your complete and absolute submission to my authority as regards *the management as well as the teaching* of both the First and Second Order [of the Golden Dawn].[4]

In characteristically autocratic response, Mathers removed Annie's name from the Order rolls. Annie's offense, in Mathers's estimation, lay in suppressing Order member Edward Berridge's support for Thomas Lake Harris's sexual theories. Berridge circulated a paper that apparently suggested sexual relations with "elemental" spirits. The coincidence of Horniman's expulsion and her having ceased subventing the Mathers's life in Paris hardly seems coincidental.

Some weeks later, Crowley's *Confessions* informs us, a hankering for mysterious, dark places to the north led to Crowley's being entertained by "the stuffy old British minister"* at ice-cold Stockholm's British Embassy during his end-of-term Christmas vacation. For many years Crowley's account of New Year's Eve 1896 suggested magical or mystical illumination, an intimation of unsuspected magical power. This romanticism obscured Crowley's willing seduction by Hampshire-born family man, James Lachlan Dickson (1855–1927), cotton salesman of Scottish descent. Despite Dickson's emotional indifference, the thrill of homosexual sex came as a profound shock to Crowley's sensorium; he'd never imagined such ecstasy existed.

While the empire got excited over Queen Victoria's diamond jubilee, Crowley visited St. Petersburg in June 1897 to glean a working knowledge of Russian for an intended diplomatic career. During his return, the diplomatic dream crashed. He claimed nihilistic despair overwhelmed him. For how long would even the finest ambassador be remembered?

The *Confessions* offers as trigger the sight of "non-entities" gathered for a Berlin chess tournament suddenly looking distant, absurd, tawdry, vacant of meaning—despite youthful dreams of chess mastery. Another account has him waking from a dental operation, experiencing a world of pure pain, before anesthetic took hold: two parables perhaps obscuring an unknown third story.

Crowley made an interesting leap. He now sought a material that did not rot, decay, or fade. The stuff of the world could only ever be instrument, tool, weapon, salve, or mirror of the soul. This realization, he asserted, drove him to embrace a philosophy of spiritual causation.

Returning to Cambridge, Crowley says he fell ill. By Michaelmas term's end 1897, God and the Devil, as he put it, fought for his soul. *God won;* "but," he added, "which of the twain was God?"† This suggests something of a nervous breakdown.

Nevertheless, some rather effective poetry ("Astray in Her Paths"),

---

*From a fictionalized description in Crowley's private, comedic account of homosexual adventures, *Not the Life and Adventures of Sir Roger Bloxam,* begun in the United States 1916–1917.

†From Crowley's *Aceldama, A Place to Bury Strangers In* (1898), describing a night visiting Cambridge don, Charles George Lamb (1867–1941) on December 7, 1897.

written January 8, 1897, at Copenhagen, Denmark, nearly six months *before* his trip to St. Petersburg shortly after the Dickson experience, suggests that alienation from the world in favor of spiritual sublimity was already intensified—after *Stockholm:*

> . . . because we love,
> Are not of earth, but, as the immortals, stand
> With eyes immutable; our souls are fed
> On a strange new nepenthe from the cup
> Of the vast firmament. Nor do we dream,
> Nor think we aught of the transient world,
> But are absorbed in our own deity.
>
> But now I turn to thee, whose eyes
> Blaze on me with such look as flesh and blood
> May never see and live; for so it burns
> Into the inmost being of the spirit
> And stains its vital essence with a brand
> Of fire that shall not change; and shuddering I
> Gaze back, spirit to spirit, with the like
> Insatiable desire, that never quenched,
> Nor lessened by sublime satiety,
> But rather crescent, hotter with the flame
> Of its own burning, that consumes it not,
> Because it is the pure white flame of God.
> I shudder, holding thee to me; thy gaze
> Is still on me; a thousand years have passed,
> And yet a thousand thousand; years they are
> As men count years, and yet we stand and gaze
> With touching hands and lips immutable
> As mortals stand a moment. . . .
> The universe is One: One Soul, One Spirit,
> One Flame, One infinite God, One infinite Love.*

---

*From *Mysteries: Lyrical and Dramatic,* 1898, in *The Collected Works of Aleister Crowley,* vol. 1.

Fig. 2.6. Herbert Charles Pollitt (1871–1942), by Frederick Henry Evans.

While sexual bliss and material-transcendence are clearly combined in the poem, his relations with another man between October 1897 and his final term at Trinity College in 1898 would make him definitively choose the latter at the expense of the former.

Cambridge University theatrical star Herbert Charles Pollitt (1871–1942), four years Crowley's senior and star of E. F. Benson's novel *The Babe, B.A.,* had returned to the Cambridge Footlights Revue to perform his famous drag act as "Diane de Rougy," a skit on Parisian bisexual courtesan Liane de Pougy, decadent star of the Folies Bergère and darling-to-be of lesbian poet Natalie Clifford Barney. Lightweight, casually artistic Pollitt was doubtless a tonic for Crowley's spiritual crisis, a kind of curious mirror of his anxieties. Pollitt introduced Crowley to Decadent literature and the art of Aubrey Beardsley (who designed a bookplate for Pollitt), James McNeill Whistler, and devilish Belgian Félicien Rops, illustrator of Péladan's novels. These influences informed Crowley's visual aesthetic sense, pre-accommodating him to aspects of Parisian art and attitudes. Pollitt also knew Beardsley's publisher Leonard Smithers, canny purveyor of erotica and risqué poetry, including Oscar Wilde, Ernest Dowson, and Crowley's *Aceldama.*

By Michaelmas term's end, Crowley, in love with Pollitt, went alone to Amsterdam to explore his soul.* Writing fevered letters to Pollitt,

---

*Smithers had erotic works printed in Amsterdam, such as Crowley's *White Stains,* printed by Binger Brothers, May 1898.

he composed poetry of his physical and mixed metaphysical love yearnings. On Christmas Day came *The Nativity,* in which he imagined Jesus's mother cursing God from the pain of childbirth until, much relieved, she was delivered of "the Christ." Crowley kissed his silver crucifix, as though in farewell, choosing for himself another testing destiny of fire and ice, as his boots crunched frosty cobbles by the freezing docks of old Amsterdam.

Back in England before New Year, Crowley booked himself, for some reason, into the Queen's Hotel, Stephenson Street, Birmingham (one of many grand victims of postwar demolition). Pollitt arrived. They dined, talked, and retired. Pollitt then entered Crowley's room and seduced him, precisely one year after "initiation" with Dickson in Stockholm.

Returning to Cambridge, Crowley lived as wife to Pollitt: the "purest" love relationship he'd known. Nevertheless, apart from sex, Decadent art, and pleasure in entertaining, the relationship lacked empathy either for Crowley's mountaineering or spiritual world-transcendence. While committed, like many Symbolists in Paris, to a

Fig. 2.7. Queen's Hotel, Stephenson Street, Birmingham.

kind of spiritual androgyny, Crowley was also sensitive to general presumptions that homosexuality entailed degenerate effeminacy.

At Easter, Pollitt joined Crowley and climber Oscar Eckenstein at a Wasdale hotel in the Lake District. The contrast was stark. Pollitt could hardly blend in. Crowley was reading von Eckartshausen's *Cloud upon the Sanctuary* (1804), recommended by Golden Dawn member A. E. Waite, to whom Crowley had written for advice. Eckartshausen's account of a body of saints directing human destiny through chosen adepts made sense to Crowley, but not to Pollitt. Crowley intuited an end to the affair.

The poet booked a room at the Bear Hotel, Maidenhead, Berkshire, during his final term to concentrate on writing *Jezebel*. Seeking solitude with his muse, he confided his whereabouts to one: perhaps new friend old Etonian Gerald Festus Kelly (1879–1972)—about to complete his first year at Trinity Hall. Pollitt appeared. Incensed by interruption, Crowley angrily informed Pollitt that he intended to devote himself to religion, not *him*.

At the summer term's end, Crowley repented, whereupon, accord-

Fig. 2.8. The Bear Hotel (on right), High Street, Maidenhead.

ing to *Not the Life and Adventures of Sir Roger Bloxam** (chapter 29, in which Pollitt is the much loved "Hippolytus"), he posted an ameliorative letter from the Gare de Lyon, Paris, en route to Zermatt, Switzerland: "Did I say '*Always*'?" he wrote. Perhaps the letter went astray, or "did he [Pollitt] interpret it amiss?" Later on, oblivious, Crowley passed Pollitt in London's Bond Street. Believing himself cut, Pollitt took it as final. Crowley would twice return to Maidenhead; first, in 1909 when approaching divorce from first wife, Rose, and second, during World War II after a near-death experience in Torquay.

It wasn't just sex, after all. Crowley had known love.

---

*Written by Crowley in 1916–1917 as a "novelissim," it remained unpublished and unfinished in his lifetime. A manuscript and typescript in the Yorke Collection formed the basis for a 76-page, privately printed publication in 1989, *NOT the Life and Adventures of Sir Roger Bloxam* (Fairfax, California), subsequently serialized in "The Magical Link" (O.T.O., 1990–1994).

✠

THREE

The Road to Auteuil 1898–1900

Crowley's Swiss mountaineering in summer 1898 marked both end and new beginning. At Wasdale at Easter, he'd issued a spiritual call to the Secret Chiefs for guidance. At Zermatt's Hotel Mont Rose in June, guidance came. Crowley was spouting about alchemy over evening drinks when chemist Julian Levett Baker (1873–1958) introduced himself. Realizing Baker's superior knowledge, Crowley glimpsed the path he sought. Baker, it transpired, had experimented with alchemical recipes when he was chief chemist for the Sugar Association. Like his friend George Cecil Jones (also a chemist), Baker was a member of the Hermetic Order of the Golden Dawn. In due course Baker and Jones suggested Crowley's joining the Order might resolve his spiritual quest.

By November, Crowley was experimenting with astral travel with Jones in Basingstoke and, on Monday, November 14, with Julian Baker at the Hotel Cecil on London's Strand, close to Crowley's lawyers, Todd, Dennes & Lamb, at 22 Chancery Lane. Four days later, at the Mark Masons' headquarters, a mile west on St. James's Street, Crowley was initiated Neophyte into the Golden Dawn's Outer Order.

Seeking to accommodate his magical experiments, Crowley's lawyer, Mr. Dennes, recommended a rental advantageous to a nearby business client. That's how Crowley moved into upper rooms at 67 and 69 Chancery Lane, close to one of London's busiest thoroughfares, the Strand! Despite the noise, Crowley contrived two experimental temples, one for evocation (lower spirits, demons), and one for invocation (higher beings, angels). In the meantime, he'd become acquainted with Mrs. Lilian Horniblow (née Horsham), whose husband, Lieutenant Colonel (later Brigadier General) Frank Horniblow of the Royal Engineers, served in India. *Confessions* calls the colonel's wife a "seductive siren." She knew an eligible argonaut when she saw one.

In Crowley's manuscript "Notes of [Astral] Travel 1898–1899" we read that at the temple, Chancery Lane, 10–11:00 p.m. December 31, 1898, Crowley performed a ceremony "to exorcise my Qliphoth," described as "black and deformed."[1] *Qliphoth* in Kabbalah means "shells" or "husks"; that is, cast-offs: bad or misleading waste products emitted in process of creation, believed to cling to the human aura. Such, it was believed, caused "obsessions." Crowley performed the "Lesser Banishing Ritual"—required learning for the grade of Zelator he'd taken that month—to clear the temple of unclean spirits. He then occupied his magic circle. The document refers to "L.G.," almost certainly Laura Grahame, Mrs. Horniblow's name for assignations. Crowley asked for "the spirit governing their relations." In a diary entry from the 1920s, Crowley noted this lady's preference for anal sex, but I cannot say what spirit governs that.

Having taken the Theoricus grade in February 1899, Crowley had to wait three months before proceeding to the final grade of the Outer or "First" Order: Philosophus 4° = 7□ This he duly took in May. Shortly afterward, Crowley went to Paris, meeting Mathers in Auteuil for the first time. Introduction probably came through Crowley's new friend, poverty-stricken electrical genius Allan Bennett. Mathers was Bennett's adoptive father;* hence, despite sometimes uneasy relations between them, Bennett called himself Allan MacGregor. Invited to live with Crowley at Chancery Lane, Bennett passed on all he'd learned of magic.

The immediate circumstances necessitating the visit to Paris involved an intermediary grade between the Outer and Inner Order: the Portal grade, a "completing" of the elemental grades, requiring a symbolic ritual of the four elements, a testing of the secrets of the Philosophus grade,

---

*I am grateful to William Breeze for this information.

delivery of the Portal's meaning, and the swearing of an oath. It made sense to make the oath before Mathers himself, since a minimum of seven months had to pass before admission to the Second Order of the Ruby Rose and Cross of Gold via the Adeptus Minor grade. Admission required *invitation*. Doubtless aware Crowley was supporting Allan, Mathers probably saw advantages for himself in assisting Crowley.

There were other issues. Crowley may have come to Mathers through Legitimism, rather than through Bennett. *Confessions* recounts Crowley's involvement with Lord Ashburnham's Legitimist plot to arm an uprising to put pretender Don Carlos de Borbón on the Spanish throne. Crowley claimed a knighthood (including a night's lonely vigil) from one of Don Carlos's lieutenants while learning marksmanship, tactics, and strategy. Ashburnham did have a training area reserved on his Welsh estates.* Crowley knew members of the so-called Thames Valley Legitimist Club, with its explicit Jacobite sympathies. Mathers's involvement soon alarmed Annie Horniman's sympathizers in London's Second Order. Anyhow, Crowley's active Legitimist enthusiasm must have been brief indeed, since by Crowley's own admission, the capture of Ashburnham's Spain-bound steam yacht *Firefly* at Arachon by alerted French customs authorities in July 1899, and their discovery of its cargo of German rifles, quashed the plot. Crowley said mysteriously in his *Confessions* that he could not "yet" tell the full story, but given the timescale, there may not have been all that much more to tell.

When, in 1949, Crowley's younger Cambridge friend Gerald Kelly (knighted 1945), read the *Confessions* account of Crowley as rifle-toting knight, he attributed it to Crowley's imagination. Kelly was familiar with Crowley during this period; they'd met during Crowley's last term. Crowley was not, as was once suggested, on Ashburnham's fated steam yacht.† He was climbing at Beachy Head at the time.‡

Of the services Crowley *did* perform for Mathers, none were politi-

---

*See my *Aleister Crowley in America* for more detail.

†This suggestion was made by Sharon Lowenna in "Noscitur A Sociis: Jenner, Duncombe-Jewell and Their Milieu." *Cornish Studies* 12 (2004): 61–87.

‡It's difficult not to recall a 1980s BBC spoof documentary about the Spanish Civil War where an imaginary Oxbridge don (played by comedian Griff Rhys Jones), claiming a youthful part in that war, evoked his Republican service with the straight-faced admission: "It was the most exciting *weekend* of my life."

cal. When not in the temple or in the Bois de Boulogne, Mathers walked miles across Paris to the Bibliothèque de l'Arsénal where, seeking long-unpublished magical texts, he found a version of the "Sacred Magic of Abra-Melin the Mage," probably composed in Germany in the early seventeenth century, purporting to be fifteenth century in origin. Translating it (Moina executed a fine drawing for its title page), Mathers sought income from publishing. In a letter of October 28, 1899 (more than two months before Crowley joined the Second Order), we find the following chit signed by Mathers:

> I the undersigned do hereby Authorise my Friend the Count Vladimir Svareff to act as my Representative in all matters relating to the Copyright of my book called the "Sacred Magic of Abra-melin."[2]

"Count Vladimir Svareff" was Crowley's disguise, chosen to avoid potential family interference as suggested by Abra-Melin's "Sacred Magic," whose aim might provide a shortcut to the crown of Golden Dawn aspiration: the Higher Genius. While Crowley contemplated Abra-Melin's promise of "knowledge and conversation with the Holy Guardian Angel," Mathers collaborated with Martinist (S.I.) and Golden Dawn initiate Jules Bois (1868–1943). Avid supporter of Paris's 1896 feminist congress, Bois recognized Samuel and Moina's usefulness to his own spiritualized feminist agenda.

In the year Bois lost a duel with Stanislas de Guaita at the Tour Villebon near Fontainebleau, he'd published *The Little Religions of Paris* (1894). Describing Paris's Cult of Isis, Bois cited Lady Caithness as devotee because of her claim to have manifested the feminine divine Sophia of Alexandrian gnosis and Antoine de la Rochefoucauld due to his inspired painting—La Rochefoucauld underwrote Péladan's first Rose-Croix (Art) Salon of 1892 and supported the Nabi artist "prophets." For Bois, Isis constellated a spiritual project to relate political equality to eternity. In 1893 he'd commissioned composer Erik Satie for an analogous theatrical mission, *La Porte héroïque du ciel*. Samuel and Moina undertook an Isis cult revival, with themselves as high priests Rameses and Anari, replete with striking costumes, poetic ritual, and polytheist rationale.

Launched in the avenue Mozart, Bois suggested the rites move to the Théâtre de la Bodinière (the Théâtre d'Art International), 18 rue St. Lazare on the Montmartre *butte,* where he'd been busy in the 1898/99 season with a Buddhist religious ceremony and lecture. Reticent to perform publicly, Moina was reassured by a dream wherein Isis requested Moina revive her worship in the city.*

Crowley would later write to Gerald Kelly of witnessing the Mathers perform Isis rituals "semi-publicly" at La Bodinière—semi-publicly because in addition to theatrical student performances and those of distinguished performers, founder Charles Bodinier provided for educational lectures at the theater. Robert de Montesquiou, for example, lectured there January 17, 1894, assisted by Sarah Bernhardt. In January 1900, *L'Écho de Paris* advertised the Mathers's events only as "Conférences," which is what made them semi-public. Invitations were probably required, or at least educational interest. After the Mathers's talk and Isiac performance, theater lovers could see *L'Huissier des Traditions* ("The Usher of Traditions"), and the popular shadow show, *La Marche au Soleil* ("March to the Sun"), based on Léon Durocher's poem, with music by Georges Fragerolle.

Fig. 3.1. Poster for the "March to the Sun" shadow show at La Bodinière, 1900.

Paris, Moina believed, was derived from the Greek *baris,* "a boat": symbol of Isis.

Fig. 3.2. Moina Mathers as Anari, priestess of Isis; La Bodinière, 1900.

Crowley's first sight of the performances may have occurred during another visit to Paris Alpine mountaineering with Eckenstein after summer 1899. *Confessions* refers to a Parisian visit to mollify "Laura Grahame," their having parted some time in 1899 on account of Abra-Melin's requiring "chastity."

Meanwhile, aware that Allan Bennett's asthma—exacerbated by London's sooty air—could prove fatal, and mindful of Bennett's wish to go East to ease the condition while studying raja yoga and Buddhism (abandoning magic), Crowley and George Cecil Jones performed an evocation of Buer, a demon adept in healing. Amid the incense the magicians discerned part of a leg and a helmeted head, and to that partial vision Crowley attributed a helpful dénouement.

Unable to surrender Crowley, Mrs. Horniblow pleaded he visit her at her hotel (possibly the Cecil). There, Laura promised anything he wanted if he'd take her back. Taking this offer, apparently, as inspired by Buer's semimanifested spirit, mischievous Crowley said her selfishness could be overcome by altruism serving a universal benefit. If agreeable, she could give him one hundred pounds, not for himself, but for another; he had reasons for not using his own money (which reasons are not obvious). She should expect nothing in return, nor hope of it. "Laura Grahame,"

COUNCIL OF THE BUDDHASASANA SAMAGAMA.

Fig. 3.3. Allan Bennett "Ananda Metteya" (seated center), with fellow councillors of the International Buddhist Society (Buddhasasana Samagama); a photo taken for Bennett's pioneering journal, Buddhism, *published in Rangoon, 1904.*

at least, agreed, her generosity paying for Allan's ticket to India, resulting, eventually, in the first Buddhist sangha's attempt to evangelize Britain.* Thank Mrs. Horniblow; thank the tremors of adultery!

"Laura" visited Crowley again. While promising not to distract his Abra-Melin magic, would he at least give her something as a "living memory of our love"? This implies a baby. Her plea, Crowley related, made him reconsider. Somewhat ludicrously, Crowley pondered the question: Was *he* not selfish for putting his "spiritual welfare above her happiness"? Deciding on a reciprocally generous gesture, he says he took her to Paris. Later in Crowley's narrative, we find the following:

---

*See my *Aleister Crowley in India* (2019).

The lady previously mentioned was now made happy as a result of the fortnight we had spent together in Paris. I therefore thought it my duty to take care of her until the following spring. The fulfilment of her hopes [pregnancy?] would end my responsibility before the beginning of my Operation. [He planned to start the main Abra-Melin operation at Easter 1900.][3]

When, on November 17, 1899, Mary Rose Burton of Boleskine House, Loch Ness, Foyers, received £2,300 for a property worth half that, the purchaser was identified as Aleister MacGregor of 87 "Rue Mozart," Paris: suggestive of some degree of identification with Mathers. Long after falling out definitively, Crowley still praised Mathers for inspiring confidence by his never doubting himself—an expression perhaps of Crowley's paradoxically sarcastic overstatement. Mathers's authoritarianism would soon lose him the confidence of most of the Golden Dawn. I suspect a father-figure projection kept Crowley, temporarily, loyal, but in the end, according to the Oedipus complex, he would have to destroy him, or the Secret Chiefs would, or Mathers would accomplish it himself.

From around this time emerges an undated letter from Boleskine to Gerald Kelly, still at Trinity Hall but now co-opted into the Golden Dawn as Frater Eritis Similis Deo. Crowley advised Kelly to contact Mrs. Rosher (wife of member Charles Rosher) of Helvain Road, Wealdstone, for a robe and nemyss, while a Masonic Rose-Croix sword from Kenning's shop, Great Queen Street (opposite Grand Lodge, London), would do. "Or," Crowley suggests, "we might trot over to Paris for a few days or weeks. I have to go there anyway, and would like you to meet the Chief; the Gregarach [Clan MacGregor], the Imperator of Isis-Urania and his wife [Moina] whose painting makes you wild. Adieu! The Gods watch over you! Until we meet. Yrs f[raterna]lly. . . ."[4]

As Crowley prepared Boleskine in early December for the Abra-Melin experience, putting himself, as he put it in his *Magicall Diarie* on December 3, "in harmony with the movement of the Reign of Light," he felt it valuable to have on hand an adept in case things got out of hand. Abra-Melin demons apparently came without evocation, and he feared "obsession" if left alone. Charles Rosher came up initially but disappeared without explanation one morning, so Crowley asked William

Evans Hugh Humphrys (1876–1950), described in *Confessions* as "an old Cambridge acquaintance," as professional houseguest. From a well-heeled family, Downing College science graduate Humphrys was initiated Golden Dawn Neophyte, November 21, 1899, some five months after graduation.*

While Mr. and Mrs. Mathers performed Isiac rites in Paris, preparing for the great "Universal Exhibition" to be opened in April 1900, ructions stirred Golden Dawn adepts, including Crowley's opponent, poet W. B. Yeats, aimed at checking Mathers's—and Crowley's—progress. Crowley's expectation of invitation into the Second Order was dismissed, despite the chief's having invited him. Laura had warned Crowley in November of a danger from the police. Claiming it came from "the Astral" (plane), it came supported by an anonymous, terrestrial letter insisting her lover "was about to be in trouble" and was to be avoided. According to *A Magicall Diarie 1899,*[5] Laura was probably at Boleskine on December 12 when Humphrys served as Crowley's assistant in a magical ceremony to "obsess Gardner"; that is, Frederick Leigh Gardner (1857–1930), who had lent Mathers money in 1896 and never got it back, and with whom Crowley (as Svareff), representing Mathers, had exchanged bellicose letters in October. Gardner, Crowley was convinced, was party to the mudslinging. As to the operation, the diary reveals: "LG [Laura Grahame] sees the success of the op." She may not necessarily have been at Boleskine; she may have observed its effect on Gardner or experienced some "astral" intuition of its success. To be "obsessed" in this context means to be unwillingly affected in mind by another agency. Showing symptoms

---

*According to researcher Sally Davis (see her webpage, "Hermetic Order of the Golden Dawn," online at WrightandDavis.co.uk, 2015), Humphrys (Frater Gnothi Seauton = "Know thyself") was an enthusiastic performer in university theatricals, penning reviews for university papers, even rushing to Cambridge station for scoop interviews when theatrical troupes or popular sportsmen arrived. As editor and publisher of the latest version of *The Cambridge Magazine,* Humphrys would certainly have known, or known about, Pollitt. During the 1900s, Humphrys became a motor enthusiast and motor journalist. He may have been interested in the university's first car, owned by Hon. Charles Stewart Rolls (1877–1910; cofounder of Rolls Royce), Crowley's contemporary at Trinity, or indeed in Crowley's own car; cars were rare in Cambridge. Humphrys drove to the south of France in winter 1902/03, where he met Crowley again in Nice. See page 120.

Fig. 3.4. Samuel Liddell
Mathers *(1854–1918),*
oil painting by Moina
Mathers, ca. 1895.
Courtesy of the Atlantis
Bookshop, London

of "panic fear," a nervous Humphrys made his excuses and left.

When Crowley alerted Mathers to Second Order members revolting against their leader in Paris, Mathers invited him for initiation as Adeptus Minor (5° = 6$^\square$) in the Second Order Rosae Rubeae et Aureae Crucis (Rose of Ruby and Cross of Gold). Leaving Laura at Boleskine (!), Crowley traveled to Paris by night boat on January 15, 1900. After eight days in Paris, during which he (again?) saw the Isis rituals performed, Crowley was symbolically bound to the "cross of suffering" at 87 avenue Mozart according to G.D.'s interpretation of primary Fraternity R.C. document the *Fama Fraternitatis* (first published in Kassel, Germany, 1614): "We are born of God, we die in Jesus, we live again through the Holy Spirit."

Entitled to the grade documents, Crowley suspected Yeats and his Inner Order friends in London would refuse. Mathers insisted that Crowley demand the grade documents, then advised Crowley to avoid London and keep an intended Cambridge visit short; the stars were unpropitious. As Crowley left the Gare du Nord, *L'Initiation* carried an announcement from Papus that the Martinist Order was preparing a special lodge to offer spiritual insight to visitors to Paris in honor of the forthcoming Universal Exhibition. Leading Martinist, poet Victor-Émile Michelet would give a talk on the Esoteric in Art.

Mathers should perhaps have watched his own stars more closely, for he was about to be deceived within a net he'd partially woven himself. In February 1900, a couple from America calling themselves Mr. and Mrs. Horos arrived in Auteuil promising to help establish the Isis cult, which they'd heard about in America, even offering to fund a regular temple: irresistible to cash-strapped Mathers. Mrs. Horos then confided to her credulous prey that *she* was the adept from the fraternity of Nuremberg Rosicrucians who'd fostered authority for the Golden Dawn in the first place! She knew all and could teach him. Mathers was completely taken in by the con artists who'd done their homework and knew how to inflate further the vanity of an ego like his. Or was it promise of funds that netted him?

As fate had it, their arrival coincided with correspondence from Mrs. Emery (actress Florence Farr), who, as Annie Horniman's replacement, was trying bravely to maintain harmony among overstimulated London members. Here was Mathers's moment!—or so he thought. He wrote to Mrs. Emery that the Second Order had no alternative to accepting his authority since he was in personal contact with the enterprise's source of authority (Mrs Horos!), who validated his position wholly. He then lobbed the bombshell: cofounder William Westcott knew alleged correspondence with Anna Sprengel (the name given to the Nuremberg adept) had been forged. What Mathers *thought* he was doing by this devastating revelation was to show all concerned that *he* was the sole reliable authority—the vital link with the Secret Chiefs and thus with the real essence and future of the Order. What Mathers achieved, however, was to sow every kind of doubt that the Order possessed any trustworthy authority at all. Instead of showing there was no alternative to his authority, he presented doubters with little alternative but to oppose him.

Meanwhile, Crowley returned to Boleskine ten days after leaving to find, as *Confessions* puts it, "that my protégée [Laura] had also taken fright, fled to London and hidden herself." The pressure mounted as Crowley tried to persist with Abra-Melin preparations amid a sense of encroaching spiritual darkness attributed to the operation. He must, he prayed, be strong, despite having heard from girlfriend Evelyn Hall in London that the police had been watching Chancery Lane, and he was suspected of something illegal connected with a Cambridge friend. Gardner had been busy, and finding Laura Grahame through Humphrys (who appears to have fancied the lady himself), persuaded her to go to the police over the matter of money Crowley allegedly extracted. Concerned her husband might find out, Mrs. Horniblow didn't press charges.

In March, a committee of London's Second Order resolved on secession from Paris. On April 2, Mathers declared their resolutions void and looked to Crowley to assert authority. Proud of the chief's summons, Crowley made the momentous decision of leaving Abra-Melin aside to offer his fortunes to a cause he identified with the supernal Order.

In London on Monday, April 9, Crowley ascertained the loyalty of girlfriend Elaine Simpson (Soror Fidelis). She was loyal, despite (or perhaps because of) her mother's suspicions of Crowley astrally visiting her daughter's boudoir. Crowley took the overnight ferry to France.

That day, Paul Ulrich Villard presented a paper to Paris's Academy of Sciences describing gamma ray penetration for the first time: a subject interesting to Crowley, for whom invisible forces always held mystery's key. Had he read of it, one can imagine him wanting to identify with a gamma ray, an invisible force to penetrate a shield.

Meeting Mathers and Vestigia, a long discussion ensued. One, at least, of Crowley's proposals was accepted: members should wear masks to reduce interpersonal conflicts and foster essential business (a somewhat literal and impractical notion). Committed heavily to the Isis project, Mathers was content to use Crowley as shield and sword, literally if necessary, for Mathers suspected Mr. and Mrs. Horos of fomenting trouble, having, he alleged, stolen Order documents useful to a takeover. Crowley left Paris as Envoy Plenipotentiary at 11:50 a.m. on Friday, April 13, 1900—the day before President Émile Loubet officially opened Paris's Universal Exhibition, an event whose clamor forced sculptor Rodin to move beyond the city.

Events crowded in. Unwilling to buckle and play Gulliver to Lilliputian cords, twenty-four-year-old Crowley engaged a "chucker-out" from a Leicester Square pub to effect, in Mathers's name, reappropriation of Order premises in Blythe Road, Hammersmith, where a wooden reproduction of Christian Rosenkreuz's tomb was installed for ceremonies. A scuffle over locks and keys occurred; a policeman arrived, and the whole silly business wound up in an abortive legal case. Crowley had worn MacGregor tartan, dagger, and face mask for the occasion, ready to resist and slay dark forces, achieving naught for either cause or reputation.

A previously unpublished note to Gerald Kelly survives, postmarked April 18, 1900, sent from the Savoy Hotel, Embankment Gardens, London. It adds perspective to the unfolding cartoon:

Die ☾ [Monday]

Dear Kelly . . .

There's a bloody row. I'm in town with the Laura [Grahame] for some time. *Make an appointment & keep it you bugger!* Am v[ery]. drunk
Y[ou]rs truly Chateau Yquem[6]

Here is another card to Kelly, written a few weeks later with letterhead "Hotel Cecil, The Strand" crossed out and replaced by "c/o. T.D.L. [Todd, Dennes, and Lamb, solicitors] 22 Chancery Lane":

Dear G[erald],

Have assayed with Eckenstein after all to go to Wales [mountaineering]. Return May 4–10 for NibelungenRing [Wagner's *Ring* cycle] at C.G. [Covent Garden] & then Paris. Explain my delay to the Caruso. Ever A.C.[7]

I imagine "the Caruso" (opera singer Enrico Caruso was flush with success in the Florence Opera at the time) refers to New York opera singer Lucile Hill,* who understudied soprano Susan Strong in *Tannhäuser* at Covent Garden Opera House in May 1900. Lucile's glamour had smitten Crowley in Paris at one of the Mathers's semipublic performances. They enjoyed an affair, and in May, in London, Crowley arranged conferral of a Golden Dawn grade upon her with seven hard-to-assemble, nonrebellious Golden Dawn officers, including Gerald Kelly. As Crowley intimated she was a member of the Order when he'd met her in Paris with the Matherses, it may be the grade conferred was Zelator, even though he describes her in a letter to Kelly as "our 0° = 0▫" (Neophyte). Crowley, incidentally, planned to arrive at Covent Garden in his motor car, having driven from Cambridge—a marvelous sight in 1900!

---

*See *Aleister Crowley in America,* 24–26, 54–56.

Returning to Paris in early summer to report on the Isis-Urania Temple rebellion, Crowley realized there was nothing more to do. *Confessions* recounts his hearing some Order members at the Mathers's house discussing a recent sojourn in Mexico. The picture painted to his highly suggestible imagination of a largely untamed, volcanic, and very sunny country conjured a spontaneous resolve to go. He swung Eckenstein into joining him later to pocket some world records in mountaineering.

It was now July 4, 1900. Aboard a steamship to New York, thoughts of America's Independence Day inspired a prophetic poem, *Carmen Saeculare,* about the destinies of the world's great nations and dedicated to Moina, priestess to Isis, Queen of Heaven. The Mathers's Isiac rites in Paris had clearly impressed him, because six months later, his January–April 1901 Mexican diary begins: "*In Nomine Dei* [Hebrew letters Aleph Mem Nun = AMN], *Inspiret Naturae Regina Isis*"*: "In the Name of God AMN, Queen Isis inspires of Nature."[8]

---

*Note the capitals make "INRI," the acronym placed above Jesus on the cross.

FOUR

Toward the City of Light

He certainly was an Artist.
NANCY CUNARD (1894–1965), WRITING ABOUT
HER FRIEND ALEISTER CROWLEY, 1954

Crowley's return to Paris in November 1902 followed a two-and-a-half year search around the world for truth, inspiration, pleasure, and respite from mediocrity. In that time, he opened his soul to experience the United States, Hawaii, Japan, China, India, and Egypt.

Opportunity for Crowley to explore Paris for himself, rather than as an adept on business, came thanks to younger friend Gerald Kelly's invitation to visit his rented studio at 17 rue Campagne Première in Montparnasse, south of the Seine.

Crowley had been busy exploring Mexico when Gerald Festus Kelly (1879–1972), son of Rev. Frederick Festus Kelly of Camberwell Rectory, graduated B.A. from Trinity Hall, in 1900. Freed from academe to paint in earnest, Kelly, like Moina Bergson Mathers and many other aspiring artists, looked to Paris as pharos to artistic fulfillment.

Kelly greatly admired American painter James McNeil Whistler (1834–1903). Whistler had immersed himself in Paris's bohemian haunts in 1855, in good time for the shock of Baudelaire's sex-and-death drenched *Fleurs du Mal* (Flowers of Evil). Baudelaire's daring revelation of new poetic territory enticed Whistler's style into a period of unsentimental realism, later touched by Symbolism's emerging spirit in the 1880s. Symbolist concern with spiritual unity in all arts is perhaps reflected in Whistler calling his paintings "arrangements," "symphonies," and "harmonies." Wagner's "total-art" captured the imaginations of many French artists.

Inheriting Symbolist concern with a universal magic of creativity, Crowley would convey to Kelly his belief that poetry should literally *sound* like the images projected in word. Seeking a magical effect through verbal arrangement, Crowley's rather literal approach to musical values would too often exhale a self-conscious surfeit of alliteration, an approach identifying his style as securely nineteenth century, influenced heavily by Swinburne's rhythmic blasphemies and Browning's roughness and often obscure intensity. Crowleyan humors, however, when not reminiscent of cavalier Sir John Suckling, or of a Restoration dramatist's rumbustious bawdiness, can also be modern, transcendentalist, idiosyncratic. The combination sometimes suggests originality, if disconcertingly so. Versification often befogs Crowley's complex thoughts like an ill-fitting suit. Building his longer poems in stages, he was often indifferent to refining results, creating many a curate's egg. Crowley's verse can, sporadically, take you high, but the implied peak is too often elusive, and an adolescent bathos often dampens enthusiasm. Perhaps Crowley's metrical—even explosively chemical—approach to experimentation in strict verse was too close in spirit to that of his inventive, clock-making maternal great-grandfather, a mechanical genius known to Samuel Taylor Coleridge and William Wordsworth as Conjuror Cole,* a brilliant star who declined into mental breakdown.

GERALD KELLY

When Crowley wrote of Kelly for *Confessions* in 1922–1923, the two men had long parted with much bitterness and little if any sorrow, so comments about his onetime close friend are unreliable as to the facts at the time, if indeed he could, or chose to, remember them accurately. By the 1920s, Kelly was a successful portraitist, a success Crowley considered a shameful reward for accurate, even pedantic copying from nature, earning Kelly unkind dismissal as "painter, according to the telephone

---

*His name was James Cole; see my *Aleister Crowley: The Biography,* 17–19.

book." Crowley would hardly have been surprised when, in the 1940s, his sometime brother-in-law became favored artist to Britain's royal family, or that *Sir* Gerald Kelly (knighted in 1945) would become Royal Academy president in 1950. In Crowley's view, Kelly had taken what Parisian Decadents in the 1880s dubbed ironically, the "way of the cross"—not the cross borne in suffering on the *Via Dolorosa,* but any one of the crosses pinned as medals by an approving French state. Thus Erik Satie would decry the greater success of onetime close friend Claude Debussy by calling him a "coupolade"; that is, someone with his eye on the "coupole" or domed roof of the Académie des Beaux Arts, the French Establishment's department of art.* As Crowley in 1927 would wittily opine in the precise spirit of Parisian Decadence: "Some people are respectable, and some are respected: but you can't have it both ways."

Crowley goaded sarcastically in *Confessions* that Kelly had truly fought hard to become an artist, almost to the point of accomplishment, but alas, while many were deceived by his facility, the vulgar world had surely captured him, and he would have to settle for the disgrace of success.

Art, to Crowley, was of its essence, *contra mundum,* indifferent to opinion. For materialists, truth is simply a commodity. He wrote of how in England the genius of the future could always be recognized early by his having automatically invited mediocrity's instinctive, irrepressible drive to persecute and ridicule him. The great artist in England was almost sure to die of neglect, unless he was the superior type of solitary temper. This attitude, or insight, nascent in Crowley's personal idea of full-blooded chivalrous aristocracy, received a major spiritual boost from the leaven of the artistic struggles that had made Paris such a creative mecca. They were attitudes with little meaning in the country of his birth, where an artist was either "successful" (i.e., pleased the people who ruled) or worthless. Thus Crowley would opine that the English poet, if he wished to be true, must either suffer ignominy and rejection at home or make a successful exile. Crowley counted his own manifold "failures"

---

*While Crowley was in Paris in January 1903, Claude Debussy was made Chevalier de la Légion d'Honneur—while Satie languished in relative obscurity, composing cabaret tunes in the cheapest lodgings in Arceuil, three and a half miles from Paris's center.

as inevitable results of attempting "the impossible." For according to him, attempting the impossible constituted the sole road to that greatness that makes for progress, such "failure" being honorable and educative.

Crowley was at heart pure Decadent, and it was, he confessed, Pollitt who made a poet of him. However, Crowleyan decadence was balanced by abundant, virile common sense in judgment of practically everything but his own conduct.

When *Confessions* was written, amid persecution by popular British newspapers and their global satellites, and painful exile from Sicily by order of Mussolini, it was vital to project an image of the "rejected one," the martyr stoically suffering for truth, art, and timeless virtues. Thus, in *Confessions,* Crowley becomes the shameless exemplar of farsighted genius, and Gerald Kelly a bourgeois mediocrity whose art held merit only to a blind and stupid world. I very much doubt if he believed that this dichotomy embodied the whole truth or indeed anything like it.

And it is Crowley's alleged cavalier approach to truth that is the question raised in Gerald Kelly's never-before-published comments of 1949 on the two volumes of *Confessions,* published in 1929, presumably written by Kelly for a publisher's reader, or perhaps for John Symonds, who was at the time preparing his 1951 biography, *The Great Beast.* Kelly would have been justifiably incensed by what he read about himself, his friends, and his family in Crowley's "autohagiography," and this, coupled with past bitterness, doubtless colored his comments. We might also bear in mind that Crowley was then dead, and in no position to question whether Kelly knew as much about him as some of his woundingly skeptical remarks might suggest.

The following examples give an idea of Kelly's enflamed assessment of Crowley's autobiographical skills, beginning, somewhat contrarily, with Crowley's flattering estimation of Kelly's knowledge, as printed on page 202 of the *Confessions:**

G[erald].K[elly].'s knowledge of both Art and Literature was "encyclopaedic." It's embarrassing to read such a foolish word about

---

*Kelly is reacting to page 202 of volume 1 of Crowley's *The Spirit of Solitude, An Autohagiography, Subsequently re-Antichristened THE CONFESSIONS OF ALEISTER CROWLEY.*

oneself. I was saturated with English lyric poetry, remembered a lot if it, and we used to cap each other's quotations.

p. 245: G.K[elly]. and Ivor [Back] magical experiment is all a lie. It may be an exquisitely amusing incident—but it was invented by A.C. Neither Ivor nor I took the slightest interest in "magic"—which was humbug to us. [Arguably contradicted by Kelly's brief relations with the Golden Dawn.]

p. 160: The faults in A.C.'s prose are *lushness*—the tawdriness of too many epithets, no rhythm—and his conceit, vanity really would spoil any. [*sic*]

p. 305: "Whistler's quarter tones of grey"—I've long since learned to distrust any criticism which mixes technical vocabularies (¼ tone is for music).*

p. 307: "my persistent search for dangerous adventure"—dangerous? His mountaineering may have been so—and the worse he did it the more so. But A.C. never seemed to run real risks. His earlier acquaintances (self, Guy Knowles, etc) rather thought he backed out of trouble with much prudence.

p. 318: A.C. deceived people—did things that it is difficult to believe were actuated by the highest motives. He seemed, often, not to be devoted to truth. He certainly hadn't the gift to see himself as others saw him.

p. 352: He always dressed in such a way as to attract attention. The MacGregor tartan is very conspicuous. Huge, unwieldy rings, enormous pipes, huge fur coats, etc. I remember a waistcoat of green satin spotted with yellow—I painted him in this astounding garment. All this in 1903, etc.

p. 395: I believe that A.C. really believed that he was above money. Did he sponge on the credulous neophytes—I know of one old lady out of whom he squeezed a goodish sum on several occasions.

---

*From this point forward Kelly's page numbering refers to volume 2 of the 1929 *Confessions.*

p. 396: All that about persecution of eminent artists is thin conventional credulous stuff.

p. 403–4: This story strikes me as improbable—I suspect the paragraph (bottom of 404) is by A.C.

p. 410: Modest A.C.—so the only rival to his little poem is the Bhagavad-Gita!

p. 471: Hollow sounding stuff. I think he'd have made more money if he could.

p. 478–79: I cannot believe this version of what took place. It is so completely similar in colouring to all the incidents in which I or my friends figure. With A.C. the wish was father.[1]

Sir Gerald Kelly gave no quarter because he received none. His denigration of Crowley's art and character gains in perspective when we read reflections conveyed to two British authors some fifteen and twenty years later.

During the early sixties, Jean Overton Fuller (1915–2009) wrote the biography of sometime Crowley acolyte, poet Victor B. Neuburg (1883–1940). She'd wondered what "so conventional a person as Sir Gerald" had made of his "extraordinary brother-in-law." She was a little surprised by what he had to say:

"When I first knew him he was an utterly delightful person. I met him at Cambridge during his last term there. We just overlapped. I didn't feel anything in the slightest degree sinister."

The portrait Sir Gerald gave me [Fuller] was of an almost extrovert type: sunny humorous, athletic, good at everything, good looking. "He was very well read, and he wrote verses which he didn't pretend were poetry. He was a very rich man. The only thing was—" here, Sir Gerald caught himself, hesitated, and then took the plunge—"this dates me, but I'll say it—he was not a *gentleman*. He had certain vulgarisms. But he was very good company. When he invited me to his house in Scotland, Boleskine, I enjoyed every minute of it! I thought he was a quite wonderful personality. My sister married him and for about two years I believe they were wonderfully happy. Then he began turning so peculiar she had to get rid of him."[2]

Ms. Fuller considered it obvious Kelly "had at no time even an inkling of Crowley's inner life."

My friend, fellow author, and Western esotericist Christopher McIntosh tried to make a film about Crowley for the BBC in the late sixties. He wrote Sir Gerald requesting assistance. Kelly's reply suggests his recollection of Crowley had long set in a familiar mold. Still, Kelly was ninety when he replied to Christopher:

Sir Gerald Kelly, K.C.V.O., P.P.R.A.
117 Gloucester Place
Portman Square, W.1

25 November 1969

Dear Mr. McIntosh,

There is nothing more I can say about Crowley.

He was very good looking and gay. He was making a wonderful collection of first editions and a bookseller introduced me to him. I liked him very much.

He went down from Cambridge at the end of my first term, and I saw him in London. He then took a house in Scotland—near Strathpeffer, where my mother was having a cure, and I went to stay with him there. It was all great fun.

He and my sister fell in love and rushed away and got married. She lived three or four years with him, but by that time he was behaving so badly that I was very glad she divorced him.

I am an old man, and I don't think you will gain any advantage by stirring up the dusty past.

Anyhow, I can't or won't help you.

Gerald Kelly

Well, let's stir up the dusty past and return to the days, not quite of "nursery freshness," but to happier times when Gerald and Aleister were friends.

Throughout his travels, whether in Ceylon, Mexico, New York, San Francisco, Baltistan, Yokohama, or Honolulu, Crowley issued a stream of warm, witty letters to his younger friend in England. The letters frequently echo discussions between the men on art, aesthetics, and structural problems in Crowley's burgeoning poetic oeuvre. A letter from Madras, for example, scribbled to Gerald on December 6, 1901, while he was packing bags for Calcutta, concerns poetic effects in recent poems, particularly *Orpheus* (an epic that took months and months, and eventually contained an entire play!) and Crowley's cleverly wrought "Ascension Day," and "Pentecost": both ingenious semiparodies of Browning's style that simultaneously addressed Browning's outlook, as well as Crowley's own shortcomings.* The correspondence demonstrates the seriousness and humor with which Crowley approached his work, as well as Kelly's evident enthusiasm (at the time). Crowley sought and trusted Kelly's views. The letter reveals Crowley's frequent use of alliteration embodied a belief in the power of onomatopoea; thus in book 3 of "Orphy" (*Orpheus*) he wished to "onomatopoeize the rush and airiness of his [Orpheus's] flight":

You know my idea that all poetry should suggest its subject by its sound, as music does. Perhaps Wagner's leitmotif is even more allowable in poetry. [Dante Gabriel] Rossetti utterly misunderstood the refrain and destroyed its use. See Browning "Sucked along in the flying wake / Of the luminous water-snake" in *Xmas Eve*.

Crowley elaborates with an intense discussion concerning wordplay in Swinburne and the odd "trick" he learned from Swinburne's use of onomatopoeias in *Atalanta in Calydon* (1865):

"cling to her—spring to her—wing to her"—spring—wing—cling—and two indifferent rhymes. See my "Light of the Sea" now in *Argo*[*nauts*] IV for an extreme of this—almost touching the ballade complexity. . . . You are quite right my art has been totally changed. . . . (I broke off to pack.)
. . . Note that A[scension].D[ay]. and P[entecost]. required much

*See the new edition of Crowley's *The Sword of Song,* edited by Richard Kaczynski (London: Kamuret Press, 2021).

work. You can't trace in the MS. how much building up has been done already. I began as a deliberate riposte to Browning—and found new points of view obtruding at every moment. I hope to get every aspect in: not of course explicit but suggested.

So long
Ever Loving
Aleister Crowley [3]

Crowley moves lightning fast, and intuitively, from techniques of poetry to techniques of painting, as here in a letter hastily written December 13, 1901, from Calcutta to his friend's temporary digs in Paris:

Dear Gerald,

Here's your letter from Rue Vaugirard.* I think your ménage absurd: never mind: you will get to understand by-&-bye. There is a life beyond Cambridge: there *is* beauty in Bohemianism & the "unpaid-for-w[oman]'s c[unt]. . . ."

On *W.[aikiki] Beach.*† Your raptures, justifiable perhaps, [Crowley adds above the line:] But absurd—addressed to *me*!

You are of course *very very nice.* (O me!) and rather contradictory—your letter and your notes to typed pome [poem] disagree. I return your letter with one or two alterations. But I must explain *On W.[aikiki] Beach* was written on "The 3rd Day." "She was more graceful than the royal palm" &c.‡ See the connection?

. . . What I want is you to take whole responsibility of Intro: & Criticism and to give me your detailed views on the text. . . . Send me some of your studies and photos of your pictures (if you have the

---

*Rue de Vaugirard, running southwest from the Latin Quarter through Montparnasse to the Porte de Versailles.
†"On Waikiki Beach," an effective poem written at Honolulu in 1901.
‡Reference to "The Third Day" section of *Alice: An Adultery* (1903), a poem describing Crowley's affair with Alice Rogers (née Mary Sarah Alice Beaton) conducted passionately between Honolulu and Japan: *She was more graceful than the royal palm; / Tall, with imperial looks, and excellence / Most simply swathed in spotless elegance, / And holy and tuneful like some stately psalm. / Her breath was like a grove of myrrh and balm, / And all the sight grew dim before the sense / Of blind attraction toward; an influence / Not incompatible with her own calm.*

latter) I shall be art-sick in Kashmir. . . . Seen G∴D. [Golden Dawn] in newspapers?* You should call on MacGregor of Paris [Mathers]. Allan [Bennett] only cares for the "sublime by me" I don't think I showed him *On W.B.* [Waikiki Beach]

Ever as ever, Aleister Crowley

P.S. The Picture. Portrait of course! Cf *On W. Beach.* You *can not* imitate Nature you *must* beat her. Nature is nearly always marred (surely I know who have lived with her in so many aspects) by incongruities in the soul of her. e.g. a windmill canal scene in sunset (Holland)— "Melancholy"? And there's a laughing girl in the foreground! But the artist must make everything subservient to his one idea.[4]

The only way to become an artist, Crowley insisted, was to undertake an intense self-opening to *all* senses: "a slut for a mistress, a gamine for your model: a procuress for your landlady, and a whore for your spiritual guide. That is the only way to become a great artist," as he put it to Gerald from Kandy in summer 1901. Kelly was coming to the right place for all that, and Crowley urged him to take full, but meaningful, advantage of that position. Crowley himself left Calcutta, first to explore the jungle between Prome and the Arakans in Burma, second to locate Buddhist bhikkhu Allan Bennett in an Akyab monastery, where he found him revered for sanctity by local Burmese. Returning to Calcutta, he crossed India, eventually joining expedition leader Oscar Eckenstein at Delhi in March 1902 for the world's first major assault on K2, the second-highest mountain in the world, where the team's intrepid efforts, without oxygen, took Crowley above the Baltoro Glacier, amid appalling conditions, to about 22,000 feet, a height not exceeded for another thirty-seven years.[†]

Disappointed by failure to conquer the mountain, Crowley left Bombay aboard SS *Egypt* on September 30, 1902. Indulging himself in Cairo's fleshpots, he wrote to Kelly from the famous Shepheard's Hotel on October 22, impatient to exchange Cairo for Paris:

---

*Confidence tricksters Mr. and Mrs. Horos had been sentenced to imprisonment. See page 42.
†See *Aleister Crowley in India.*

I come via Marseilles to Paris: I have business also with the chiefs of the Order of which I have recently heard so much and seen so little.

But I do not wish my presence in Paris known till the Hour of Triumph, or some how like that: and I will accept your kindness in the same spirit in which I have always received your insults and drive straight off to Montparnasse. I know the Boulevard M[ont]-P[arnasse], not your street though. I am not likely to get to England until certain arrangements are made—tell you what later. As you say, there is lots to do. Get and cram up Michelet* "Histoire des Templiers."[5]

Three days later, thoroughly bored with Cairo, Crowley addressed another letter to Kelly's apartment at 17 rue Campagne Première, Montparnasse (above what is today the *À bout de souffle* restaurant/bar). Had Kelly copies of his earlier work? For he was now "half writing, half compiling a book called (?) 'The Lovers' Alphabet' all lyrics of rural love." He could hardly contain his excitement at returning:

Dear Gerald,

. . . I expect to see any amount of good work [painting] when I arrive. You must fulfil your ancient promise to paint me. I fancy you will find me a good deal changed, even in looks! And I expect ditto of you. We must have a great dinner to celebrate my return. I shall perhaps write S.R.M.D. and Vestigia.† I suppose you see them occasionally.

Are you still *en famille* with a sister?‡ Or has the need of solitude got you? Or are you bold with lust?

I most probably leave Port Said November 3 to Paris via Marseilles. How I look forward to civilisation! The Opera! The Louvre! The everlasting nonchalant charm of the Boulevards! Art! And the sub-

---

*Jules Michelet (1798–1874), *Le Procès des Templiers, publié par Monsieur Michelet*, Book 1, Imprimérie Royale, 1841; later editions under the title *Les Templiers*.
†G.D. motto of Samuel Mathers: *'S Rioghail Mo Dhream* = Gaelic: "Royal is my Blood"; Moina's motto: *Vestigia Nulla Retrorsum* = "Never a Step Backward."
‡The "sister" was Gerald's widowed sister Rose Edith Skerrett (1874–1932). Within a year, Rose and Crowley would be married.

tlety of festal Festus! Here everyone says "cunt" right out loud and calls a spade a bloody shovel. How I hate it! Cairo is a filthy low place with no beauty at all, unless you go to the Nile. Maison dine. And that's something when you think that three months back I over-ate myself badly because the taste of coarse badly cooked mountain sheep was so delicious! Fly, loathèd days, until I can get to you.

Yours ever,
Aleister Crowley[6]

One can only feel regret at the fading of the light of boyish empathy that illuminated this relic of the dusty past. It is also interesting to note from the references to the Opéra, the Louvre, and the boulevards that at this stage Crowley's touristy feeling for Paris could have been culled from a Baedeker travel guide! One wonders if young Gerald found Crowley's language "vulgar" then . . .

Given that it took about four and a half days to sail by steam-ship from Port Said to Marseille, and that the ship left some time on November 3, Crowley likely arrived in Paris on Saturday, November 8, or Sunday the ninth, if, that is, he spent a night in Marseille before taking the train to Paris.

Paris hadn't seen Crowley for two and a half years.

Fig. 4.1. Montparnasse, rue de l'Arivee and avenue du Maine, ca. 1900.

FIVE

Paris, November 1902

Le Figaro lightened its dense print on Friday, November 7, with news that the city was adorned by exceptional, springlike weather, with the Bois de Boulogne speckled into new life by the gaiety of "cavaliers and amazons," flattered by the sunshine, beaming smiles, openly enjoying what the paper called "le high life." Many of those out to be seen, rather than to labor, would have delighted the eye: varied and colorful fabrics and sculpted hats familiar to anyone who has seen *Gigi*—a superabundance of beautifully tailored dress, ladies like sprigs of fresh flowers with men in gracefully cut suits of gray or pastel, sporting a variety of top hats, with accessories of canes, beards, and mustaches thick and thin amid a visual splendor blending imperial classicism with Art Nouveau.

La Presse observed how Paris's superb weather drew large crowds to the races at Auteuil's hippodrome, a short stroll to the west of the Mathers's house on the avenue Mozart. The big event was the Prix Montgomery Steeplechase on Saturday. While horses dominated the sports page as they did ordinary transport, the 1902 Mors Z racing car's four-cylinder engine could, for its part, muster 60 horsepower at 1400 rpm, sufficient to have just smashed the world's land-speed record set in August by American William K. Vanderbilt. Frenchman Henri Fournier achieved a top speed of 123 km per hour (76.4 mph) at Dourdon in Brittany; proud Frenchmen were agog.

While the nifty Mors Z resembled nothing so much as a low-slung antique tractor with a snub nose, upper-class motorists could sate their

Fig. 5.1. Period advertisement in Le Figaro *for ladies' dresses and coats in the Samaritaine department store, central Paris, 1902.*

urge for modernity with a stately Maison Boyer. Though it might look to us like two plush sofas mounted on a landau chassis with a down-turned fire hood for a bonnet, this enviable monster of gracious living was pictured in *La Presse* with the caption "Valeur; 6,000 Francs" (approximately $28,000 today). This was the newspaper's "big prize" for a segregated competition whose "feminine contest" tested ladies' knowledge with questions such as *What are the six essential virtues for women?* A tough one . . . but should competitors offer satisfaction on that burning issue, they next had to ponder *What are the six most remarkable cyclists in the world?*—remarkable cyclists being *men,* naturally—there to be admired in a world in which women stooped to conquer, though conquer they often did.

We like to think, when not busy chasing novelties, that there's nothing new under the sun, but vegetarianism is no fad of the supermarket era. *L'Écho de Paris*'s sporting news that Friday noted how vegetarianism might affect sports after *Revue Scientifique* published experimental findings of a walk from Dresden to Berlin. The first six (men) to arrive were all vegetarian; they included a Frenchman, German, Russian, and Englishman. The diet knew no borders.

After France lost her emperor (Louis-Napoléon) to the German

Fig. 5.2. For 6,000
francs you could
buy this Maison
Boyer automobile in
November 1902.

Fig. 5.3. Described as "the Latest Scientific Triumph" and "the Ideal at
Last!" the "New Minstrel Interchangeable" big-cylinder wax "phono" with
twenty-five free cylinders of music could be yours for only 23 centimes a
day with twenty-one months of credit. Advertisement in Le Petit Parisien,
November 1902: the Belle Époque in sound!

invasion of 1870, the Third Republic, which succeeded him, gained an
empire. Now in existence for fifteen eventful years, French Indochina's
southeast Asian colonies had, like most bureaucracies, a tendency
to expand. French incursions over the borders of Siam (Thailand)
inflamed the Siamese government, and Monsieur Deloncle, responsible
for Indochina, was negotiating a treaty with the only country in the
region not to be colonized.

While sensitive readers were shaken by news of a devastating volcanic eruption in French colony Martinique, Monsieur Cogordan, director of political affairs at the foreign ministry, retraced Crowley's journey, leaving Marseille for Egypt to deliver letters of recall to the Khedive ʿAbbās II, regulating French affairs at a court anxious to reduce British influence in Egypt; Crowley would in part have shared the concern. Meanwhile, Parisians took an interest in the latest from New York, where congressional elections looked set to deliver a Republican majority for Theodore Roosevelt, who'd taken the reins after President McKinley's assassination in 1901.

The United States had only recently come to an end of protracted, bitter strikes led by the United Mine Workers of America when France was hit like hammer on anvil by miners' strikes to the north of Paris in the "Black Country," between the Pas de Calais, Lille, and Dunkerque, where dockers refused to deal with shipping and rioters erected barricades and pillaged shops in sympathy with the miners. In the Chamber of Deputies, famous Socialist Jean Jaurès urged government to follow Roosevelt in conciliating between owners and miners. As the Republic moved to arbitrate, deputy Jaurès visited the region. Paris's radical *L'Intransigeant* declared on Sunday, November 9, that French President Loubet's arbitration maneuvers did nothing but "mock the miners." Tempers ran high. On Friday, November 7, page 3 of *La Presse* reported a duel to be fought the next day. A series of defamatory articles by Monsieur Lagrillère-Beauclerc, director of the journal *Le Progrès du Nord,* accused a Monsieur Basly of fomenting trouble in Dunkerque. Monsieur Basly's seconds were Messieurs Delesalle of Lille's town hall, and Monirt, editor of *Réveil du Nord:* two northern journals, one claiming its "awakening," the other its "progress."

Duels made news, and that was deplorable, asserted Monsieur Maxime Leconte, who called on the Republic to make dueling an "offence," proposing that calling a duel be punished by imprisonment from one month to a year and a 500 to 1,000 franc fine. In cases of wounding: two months to two years imprisonment and a fine from 200 to 2,000 francs; in the event of death, one to three years imprisonment, plus a fine of 500 to 5,000 francs. Having already attempted to establish the measure in June 1892, Leconte insisted on its urgency—but how *then* might editors settle their differences?

Most Parisian newspapers reported the Republic's moves against "congrégationalistes": religious schools with simple, not solemn vows. French progressive secularists were often anticlerical, loathing a Vatican that was dogmatically ultramontane and decidedly opposed to liberalism, belief in science, and social democracy. A law of 1901 required religious schools to apply for documents of authorization; many were expelled. The Vatican condemned the law but left congregations to decide whether to request them. With the Leftist bloc in the Chamber of Deputies triumphing in May 1902, Grand Orient Freemason Émile Combes and Jaurès's Socialists applied themselves to further restriction of Catholic influence in education. As Crowley arrived in Paris, investigating judge Monsieur André interrogated several Frères de St. Paul on the rue de Dantzig. The following year, while more than 1,900 applications for authorization were submitted, only five "congregations" were commended to the Senate for toleration. It's difficult to assess whether Crowley would have found such measures unnecessarily restrictive or a triumph for rationalism in a progressive country.

One Frenchman with an instinct for fair play was moderate Republican President Émile Loubet. It earned him bitter opposition and subtle lampooning in *La Presse* on November 7, under the punning headline SA GRÂCE; that is, "His Grace." Assumption of a pontifical role was implied in the ducal honorific, for the president had the right of pardon and commutation in criminal cases.

La Presse was outraged that the man who'd pardoned "traitor" Alfred Dreyfus (the army officer controversially court-martialed for alleged spying in 1894, whose case was prejudiced by determined anti-Semites) might even commute the death sentence just passed on "Jack the Ripper of the south," Henry Vidal, who had murdered three wholly innocent women and was suspected of more. Vidal, thirty-five, had tuberculosis; his mother pleaded he was weak witted. The paper was incredulous at the prospect of an "assassin and degenerate" escaping the guillotine. President Loubet eventually commuted the sentence to penal servitude for life. Perhaps there was a link with the secular liberalism of the Grand Orient de France, the country's leading, and most politically engaged, Masonic organization. It was reported in *La Presse* on Friday, November 7, that the Paris Grocery Association, protesting against the prefect of the Seine's new taxes, met at the Grand Orient de France (also accommodating of "Dreyfusades"). This was the year the Grand Orient expressed support for abolishing the death penalty; Loubet is believed to have been a Freemason.* Crowley would join a Parisian lodge of rival, the Grande Loge de France, the next year.

Under the headline HUSBANDS WHO KILL, Sunday's *La Presse* told of a different kind of murderer: one driven there through jealousy. At a pleasant villa in St. Cloud, an outer suburb 5.6 miles west of Paris's center, Monsieur Gaston Eugène Aubry poured three revolver shots into his wife's head and breast as she lay in bed. He then walked to the commissariat and informed the police commissioner. The victim, a pretty woman of about thirty-two, was a singing teacher. Aubry was a sober man, a good employee of the town hall, of good family. The paper described the act as a "moment of madness," prejudging any verdict by calling it a "drame passionel." If judged unpremeditated with no malice aforethought, Aubry would avoid the death penalty.

Some have it imposed upon them, others upon themselves. On Saturday, November 8, the suicide was reported of young "demi-mondaine" (courtesan or habitué of immoral or risqué nightlife) "Mlle Joséphine B . . ." who "amused herself under the name Suzanne de Livry," a resident of 29 rue de Naples. The cause was given as despair: having had the honor of an "audience particulière" with an Asiatic sovereign who'd recently visited the capital, the "joy of this favour had turned the already weak head of Suzanne," and truly remarkable beauty notwithstanding, she poisoned herself. That was *their* story.

Le Matin of Friday, November 7, gave the twenty-seven-year-old demi-mondaine known as "Suzanne de Livry" a surname and a different

---

*Livre Rare-Book website offered for sale at 2,300 euros for a Lyon antiquarian bookseller a folio dated Lisbon, October 27, 1905, signed by the Grand Master, the President of the Council, and the Secretary General of the Lusitanian United Grand Orient, with dry seals: a text welcoming Émile Loubet, President of the French Republic, before the Supreme Council of Portuguese Masonry during his trip to Portugal, October 1905. "Émile Loubet's secret of belonging to Freemasonry has always been well kept and contemporary Masonry historians do not speak of it, whether it is Serbanesco, Alec Mellor, Ligou or Lantoine; Pierre Chevalier simply indicates that Émile Loubet's membership has not been established: 'there is doubt.' Only Henry Coston presents this membership as certain after a Belgian source circa 1935. Émile Loubet's membership in Freemasonry sheds new light on the history of the end of the nineteenth century and the beginning of the twentieth century (Dreyfus Affair, Rome Affair, etc.)."

Christian name. Mademoiselle *Jeanne* Bienfait, we are informed, suffered a history of "mental instability." She'd been linked "very closely" with café-concert artist Marguerite Duclerc, who'd recently died. Duclerc had secured Jeanne/Joséphine a job at a Champs Élysées theater in July, but on the fifteenth, while visiting her protectress at 15 rue de Turin, Mademoiselle Bienfait became mad. Duclerc tried to stop her throwing herself out of the window. Interned at the Saint-Anne asylum, she left twenty days later. Appearing quite sane, she again performed in music halls and *cabarets de nuit*. The night before her death, she'd dined with friends in a state of "exhuberant gaiety." Departing at one o'clock in the morning, her friends asked if she'd instructions for tomorrow. She replied, "No, nothing. . . . Who knows where I'll be tomorrow!" She left two letters: one to the police, one to her father, writing, "I put an end to my days that I may suffer no more." Her parents were honest workers.

This terribly sad, rather confused, story makes one think of the very different fate of no less beautiful demi-mondaine Folie Bergères star Liane de Pougy, who only the previous year had released *Idylle Saphique* (1901), a fictionalized account of her lesbian affair with American Salon hostess, poet, and talent magnet, Natalie Clifford Barney. Barney's infidelities in Paris compelled British Symbolist poet and cross-dresser Renée Vivien (1877–1909) to split painfully with her that same year. A reconciliation attempted in 1904 on Lesbos failed. Suffering from chronic debt and deeply depressed, Vivien drank laudanum in a suicide attempt in 1908. Where suicide failed, self-neglect, alcoholism, drug abuse, and anorexia brought her swiftly to interment in Passy Cemetery, aged thirty-two.

In *Souvenirs indiscrets* ("Indiscreet Memories," Paris, 1960), Barney wrote of Vivien: "She could not be saved. Her life was a long suicide. Everything turned to dust and ashes in her hands." No one troubled to write about Jeanne—or was it Joséphine?—Bienfait . . . until now.

The rich were noticed; aristocracy and royalty gained column space. The front page of Friday's *L'Écho de Paris* reported the king of Portugal and Queen Amélie were going to stay at the chateau de Sandricourt, north of Paris, with Marquis and Marquise de Beauvoir, with whom the queen had been very friendly since childhood. The honored marquis, himself attached to the royal family of France, would provide a spot of hunting. The royal couple, accompanied by Portugal's ambassador and

Prince Joachim Napoléon Murat, a member of the Bonaparte-Murat family, left Paris's Gare du Nord for Sandricourt in a train specially composed of beautiful coaches set to stop at one of the chateau avenues. Strewn with Portuguese flags, Sandricourt village echoed to cries of "Vive le roi!"

What other aristocrats were (officially) up to was reported respectfully in the paper's *Carnet Mondain* (Social Register). Le Comte Robert de Montesquiou-Fézensac (1855–1921), described as a "delicate Symbolist poet," had installed himself at his pavilion in Neuilly-sur-Seine. He'd just published *Prières de tous: Huit dizaines d'un chapelet rythmique* (Maison du Livre, 1902). The count, famed art collector and dandy, was considered to have inspired Jean des Esseintes, Symbolist eccentric, in Joris-Karl Huysmans's *À Rebours,* which in turn inspired Oscar Wilde's *Dorian Gray* and, we may suspect, an aspect of Aleister Crowley's social pose in this period. Rather like Crowley, the count preferred the company of bright young men but lacked Crowley's enthusiasm for women. No wonder Crowley wanted to be seen as an aristocrat! It was one way of being a poet and *noticed.*

Manuel Maria de Medina Pomar y Mariategui, Duke of Medina Pomar, was another literary aristocrat. He authored five "society" novels in the 1870s (including one about reincarnation, *Through the Ages*) and was reported in *L'Écho de Paris* as about to leave for a big tour of India but would finish winter in Nice at the Tiranti palace, to return to his mansion in the avenue de Wagram in the spring. The duke, born in 1854, was only son to Maria née Mariategui, Countess of Caithness and Duchess of Pomar, whose house in the 1880s until her death in 1895 was such a radiant center of Theosophical society, bringing most stars of the French occult revival into social contact to meet luminaries like Madame Blavatsky and Anna Kingsford. Crowley had missed that boat, and the loss showed, but one wonders, as he went to Nice in the late winter, whether he met the Duke of Medina Pomar there. We have no diaries for this period so it is quite possible, especially in view of shared interests (psychic research, India, Blavatsky, spiritual evolution, a New Age, writing). It would also appear that Crowley would take at least one of his cardinal beliefs from, or in tune with, the Duchess of Pomar's writings. In 1884—when the Theosophical Society suffered the blow of the Society for Psychical Research's exposure of Blavatskyan trickery—the duchess wrote a two-part book (first part, "Christian Theosophy"; second part, "Buddhist Theosophy"), *Théosophie universelle*. Essential doctrines include the following, as described by Joscelyn Godwin: The Jewish Messiah is the mystic and divine being represented by the Initiates of all nations. The historical Christ is the precursor of the mystic and esoteric Christ. For the universal Theosophist, Jesus is a Christ, whereas for the Christian Theosophist, he is *the* Christ. *The Sun, of which the visible sun is an emblem, sends an avatar or messenger-savior, every six hundred years. The third such since Christ is imminent.*[1] Interestingly, the Duchess of Pomar claimed to have originated the phrase "the Higher Self" in an 1895 interview.

On Friday, November 7, *Le Figaro* reported that Kaiser Wilhelm II (Guillaume II)—said to be "in very good humour"—would arrive in London Sunday. Diplomacy regarding the occasion was eased slightly by the ending of the Boer War on May 31, for, to Britain's intense chagrin, Germany had exported Mauser rifles to the Boers, who'd employed them with deadly effect ambushing British soldiers. Crowley had one: the Mauser 1893/95, five-shot 7X57 bolt rifle; he used it for hunting. In Mexico in 1900, Crowley criticized his government's war conduct, asserting British people were misled about costly military failures.

La Presse reported the kaiser's ship, the *Hohenzollern,* arriving at Port Victoria (now gone) on the Medway, was saluted by British ships. Wilhelm was taken by special train to Shorncliffe, near Folkestone. Wearing an English admiral's uniform, the kaiser was welcomed by Lord Roberts, army commander Sir Evelyn Wood, several generals, and the First Regiment of Dragoons. A special train then took him to Sandringham to meet uncle and King-Emperor Edward VII, whom President Loubet would soon cultivate in Paris, sealing the famous Entente Cordiale in spring 1904.

L'Écho de Paris opined on Saturday, November 8, that, "like the majority of his subjects, Guillaume II has never liked the English, and several times has expressed his feelings with absolute freedom." He once said to someone about a nosebleed, "It's nothing, I lose the last drops of English blood in my veins." *Le Matin* noted on the Friday that the kaiser "will be treated [by British newspapers] with respect for his rank and as grandson of Victoria, but we cannot pretend he will be welcomed with enthusiasm." It was more than suspected in Britain that Germany was preparing for war and using negotiations with Russia to weaken both Russia and England via Russia.

Friday's *L'Écho de Paris* evinced the fact that Germany was in no better odor with the French. Actress Sarah Bernhardt, the paper reported, was making 77,000 marks performing in Berlin. After her triumph in *Phèdre,* however, *L'Écho* could only bemoan her "downfall" in *Hamlet,* described as "mortally boring" despite Sarah's talent. *Hamlet* was translated into French for her by Eugène Morands and Marcel Schwob, the latter of whom would render a similar service for Crowley. Germans, the paper reported, "say how dare a French troupe put on *Hamlet* before a nation of 'profound thinkers.'" "No," declared *L'Écho,* "you *were* a people of profound thinkers, but are now a people of *savants appliqués,* commercialists, chemists, and big industry. France has Bergson, Renouvier, Fouillé, Lachelier. You still have von Hartmann, but as *he* said: not ten people read him in Germany! A people of 'profound thinkers'? No. Very superficial." The article also noted the German *Vorwärts* paper publishing an ominous warning from the Russian Ministry of War that revolutionary propaganda was being spread in the army. We are in the period when alliances were being sought. Once sealed, they would eventually turn a Balkan conflict in the Austro-Hungarian Empire into the Great War. Crowley was not alone in seeing dark clouds on the horizon of Edwardian England's imperial sunset: a coming era of "Force & Fire," as Crowley prophesied, coalesced. Easy to see in retrospect, of course.

On Sunday, November 9, *La Presse* was indignant at German treatment of the great Sarah Bernhardt: they mentioned Sarah's age "with all the lightness of an elephant," respecting neither her sex nor her artistry. Emperor Guillaume, however, had showed superiority to his subjects by "responding with gracious attention to Sarah." Sarah should have known, the paper concluded, that she didn't belong in Prussian theaters where German papers even made jokes about her body!

What about French theaters? What did they offer Aleister Crowley that November weekend? Since there's no indication of theatrical visits during his near two and a half years of exploring, it may be the last show he saw was *Tannhäuser* at Covent Garden in May 1900, when lady-love Lucile Hill understudied Susan Strong.

On Saturday, November 8, *La Presse* offered as "spectacles de ce soir" Gounod's *Faust* at the Opéra at 8:00 p.m., and *Le Roi d'Ys* by the Opéra Comique. A three-act opera of 1875 by Édouard Lalo and Édouard Blau (libretto), *Le Roi d'Ys* was based on Breton legend of the city of Ys, capital of Cornouaille, which sank beneath the waves, possibly inspiring Claude Debussy's magnificent *La Cathédrale Engloutie* (1910), which took as its symbol an ancient cathedral rising again from beneath the waves amid voices of sacred song emanating from watery cloisters. It could equally symbolize the waxing and waning of spiritual movement through the depredations of time.

It is always interesting, even haunting, to see in past newspapers that figures and works we might expect to see being hailed as significant gain little or no notice, while stars forgotten by history—either through incapacity, change of fashion, or awaiting rediscovery by seekers of rare jewels—spring up from ghostly interment to our gaze; the seas of print and time give up their dead.

Debussy had long considered writing an opera based on the Spanish

Fig. 5.4. Le Roi d'Ys: *poster by Auguste François-Marie Gorguet for the opera's first performance by the Opéra Comique in May 1888.*

legend *Le Cid,* but Symbolist poet Henri de Régnier persuaded him to engage with Maurice Maeterlinck's Merovingian period story *Pelléas et Mélisande.* The rest, you might say, is history; but in fact, when first performed in April in the Opéra Comique's Salle Favart, *Pelléas* caused no sensation, save among student aficionados from the Conservatoire. Such was not the fate of Debussy's breakthrough work, the orchestral *Prélude à l'après-midi d'un faune,* based on Stéphane Mallarmé's exquisite Symbolist poem. Well received in 1894, it now dignified popular music programs. *Le Matin,* for example, reported that at the Nouveau Théâtre on Saturday, November 8, the fourth *concert Lamoureux,* conducted by Monsieur Chevillard, would feature Schumann's second symphony, followed by *Prélude à l'après-midi d'un faune;* Gluck's *Air du Sommeil* from *Armide;* Handel's Concerto in D minor; Mendelssohn's *Cavatina* from *Paulus;* and the Overture from Wagner's *Tannhäuser:* quite a collection! The Salle Favart, dedicated to innovative works—and we all know what that can mean—was now hosting *Pelléas et Mélisande*'s return, and despite initial indifference, this winter season would, by its end, confirm *Pelléas* as a great work. Indeed, such acclaim had gathered by New Year 1903 that Debussy would ascend the "way of the cross," being duly appointed Chevalier of the Légion d'honneur. What is less known is that during that same period, while Crowley familiarized himself with the Paris art scene, seeking with true Decadent taste the *unacceptable,* Debussy and Victor-Émile Michelet sketched ideas for an opera based on Michelet's *Le pélerin d'amour* (Pilgrim of Love). A fine poet, Michelet was prominent in Parisian Martinism, being the first to write explicitly about Esotericism in art, and about Paris's Hermetic movement from the 1880s to World War I. Michelet is a gem worth discovering.

Pelléas et Mélisande was performed on Friday, November 7, at the Opéra Comique. On Monday, the theater presented Léo Delibes's opera *Lakmé,* with its now ubiquitous "flower song," used to disconcerting effect as a lesbian love theme in the Ridley Scott movie *The Hunger* (1983) starring Catherine Deneuve and Susan Sarandon as sapphic vampires. I expect Debussy would have loved it. On Tuesday, Jules Massenet's *Manon* delighted its audience, becoming a mainstay of the Opéra Comique, receiving its 2,000th performance there in 1952!

The Sarah Bernhardt Theatre (yes, she was *that* big) presented Edmond Rostand's *L'Aiglon* (*The Eaglet*) on Saturday evening. This

1900 play concerned the life of Napoléon II and Empress Marie Louise. Sarah (as the French called Bernhardt) played the empress at its first Parisian run and again in London in 1901: a pleasure Crowley missed, being abroad.

Le Journal on Friday announced the Vaudeville Theatre was presenting "lyric play" *Sapho,* which also had music by Jules Massenet, based on an 1884 novel. Jules Bois's lady friend (and fellow Martinist) opera star Emma Calvé had played Fanny Legrand in its first perfor-

Fig. 5.5. Poster by Jean de Paleologu (1855–1942) for the Opéra Comique's premiere of Massenet's Sapho *at the Théâtre Lyrique, Paris, November 27, 1897.*
Courtesy of Adam Cuerden

mance in 1897. "Sapho" is not a lesbian but an artist's model of notorious past whose real name is Fanny. Enough already.

The big hit of the time, according to most newspapers, was Jewish playwright Pierre Wolff's *Le Cadre* (The Frame). *L'Écho de Paris* raved, praising its bald author's wit and topical realism, adding up to "a triumphant success." It began with a portrait of a loved one whose *frame* is changed, which changes the main character's point of view. Perhaps it was a skit on Symbolism. This three-act comedy could be enjoyed at L'Athénée Theatre at 9:00 p.m.

Always happy to go down-market, one wonders if Crowley took time to look into the Théâtre des Capucines, where he could have witnessed what look like fairly brief cabaret shows, going by the titles *Chonchette, En Famille,* and *Au Temps des Croisés*—"At the time of the Crusades"—the mind boggles!

The Théâtre Rabelais at 43 boulevard de Clichy showed *Vertu de Nini* (Nini's Virtue), *La Ceinture de Chastité* (The Chastity Belt), *La Revue a l'Envers* (The Backward Revue), Suzette Nellson (attractive actress and cabaret singer), and *Philippon,* a member of the Antient and

Fig. 5.6. Suzette Nellson, long forgotten actress and singer. To make a bit of extra cash, Suzette's publicity photographs came with her hand-written message: Pour conserver ma voix / comme un cristal de roche / chaque matin je bois / du bon "Quina-Laroche" *(To preserve my voice / like a rock crystal / each morning I drink / from good "Quina-Laroche"). Quina-Laroche was a French wine tonic. Containing Peruvian bark, it purported to cure wasting diseases, poor blood, fever, ague, and exhaustion: ideal for a cabaret act.*

Primitive Rite of Memphis-Misraim (according to historian of the rite, Serge Caillet).

Talent and beauty cavorted at the renowned Folies Bergère that weekend in the shape and sound of Ada Colley and Emilienne d'Alençon, as well as the first performance of *Pierrot, Don Juan*.

Recently founded by first chanteuse of the *chanson réaliste* genre, Eugénie Buffet (1866–1934), La Purée at 75 boulevard de Clichy glittered briefly. That weekend, she presented veteran French singers Xavier Privas, Marcel Legay (fifty-one-year-old famously long-haired composer of nearly nine hundred songs; doyen of the 1880s *Hydropathes* and *Chat Noir* Montmartre scene), herself, and piano singer and songwriter Léo Daniderf. Perhaps veterans were not in vogue, for the cabaret closed the following year.

Montmartre's Moulin Rouge, as we all know, offered nightly concert-balls, and on Wednesdays and Saturdays "grandes fêtes de nuit," gaudy events that suffer in translation to the morning after.

Le Matin reported how the Thursday before Crowley's arrival, electricity in the center of Paris was cut off, a hazard that might have proved embarrassing for two entertainment venues in particular.

Louis Jean Lumière and brother Auguste are now renowned for inventing realist cinema, or documentary, and being first to shock audiences with reality filmed. Radical *L'Intransigeant* of Sunday, November 9, included in its theatrical roundup the Cinématographe Lumière, open daily at 6 boulevard Saint-Denis, and in the festive hall of department store Grands Magasins Dufavel. The "cinématograph" on the boulevard Saint-Denis apparently resembled more of a shop front than the kind of cinema we now know, for while cinema had been invented, cinemas hadn't. One man who saw the genius of Lumière's movie equipment was magician-filmmaker Georges Méliès. Had Crowley a mind to it, he could have found Méliès at his Théâtre Robert-Houdin at 8 boulevard des Italiens. Méliès performed prestidigitation matinées Thursdays, Sundays, and holidays, while every night at the theater: *cinématographe*. Stage conjuror Méliès made his own magical films and exhibited them there, as well as arranging distribution with his brother in the United States, where many of his works were pirated. One might have thought Crowley would have wanted to see what magic Méliès was performing, especially as Crowley enjoyed

Fig. 5.7. Advertisement for the 1896 Cinématographe Lumière presentation,
L'Arroseur arrosée *("The Sprinkler sprinkled," meaning "the joke's on you").*

H. G. Wells's novel *The First Men in the Moon,* published the previous
year, which he read for inspiration before the K2 attempt in 1902, the
year Méliès began experimenting with camera movement to create the
illusion of a figure or object changing size. In May—just seven months
before Crowley's arrival—Méliès committed imagination and humor
to *A Trip to the Moon,* with Jules Verne's *From the Earth to the Moon*
in mind. Nobody who's seen this masterpiece can forget the spacecraft
shot from a cannon poking the man in the moon in his eye: a charming
comic blasphemy. The film lasted all of fourteen minutes—exceptional
at the time—and cost a mighty wedge of 10,000 francs. Friday's *La
Presse* reported controversial discussions over extending the boulevard
Haussmann. The Théâtre Robert-Houdin was demolished to rebuild
the boulevard in 1923. Is nothing sacred?

The book section of Sunday's *L'Intransigeant* should have interested Crowley: first French version of Swinburne's *Nouveaux Poèmes et*

ballades, translated by Albert Savine with a note on each poem's background. The reviewer gushed, "These poems and ballads, so beautiful and of such pure feeling, appear here for the first time in the French language." They were "for all men of taste, for everyone artistic and concerned with literary tradition." Such would have gladdened Crowley's heart, whose style owed so much—probably too much—to Swinburne.

On the weekend Crowley arrived, *L'Écho de Paris* indicated punters could attend matinées and soirées of *Alleluia* at La Bodinière (Théâtre d'Art International) at 18 rue St. Lazare, Montmartre—where Crowley witnessed the Mathers's Isiac rites nearly three years before. *L'Écho de Paris* praised *Alleluia* to the skies, recounting how people were astonished to see the word *Alleluia!* daubed over posters in the ninth arrondissement. This was not, said the paper, a presentiment of a new messiah or religion but rather encouragement to see a new play by Italian Marco Praga (1862–1929), whose main character's name was "Alleluia." Praga had collaborated on the libretto for Puccini's *Manon Lescaut* (1894), written eleven years after Massenet's version of the original novel.

Given Crowley and Mathers's Carlist Legitimist enthusiasms of 1899, he might also have noted a story in Sunday's *La Presse,* telegraphed from Cerbère on the Pyrenean French-Spanish border: numerous arrests after another Carlist plot was foiled. Two brothers of "General Moore" were found "seeking refuge" in Perpignan on the coast. Banker Jean Buco, compromised in the plot, had disappeared. Two detainees were released on denouncing the plot's existence to the civil governor and having revealed names of the compromised. "Carlist circles denied any participation in the plot." *Plus ça change. . . .* One wonders if Mathers had anything to do with it, for it was to Mathers, once he'd settled into Gerald Kelly's studio at 17 rue Campagne Première, Montparnasse, that Crowley made his way.

SIX

Old Threads and New 1902–1903

Something of Crowley's mood at the time found expression in song-poem "Summa Spes," a testament to disillusionment, soaked in Nietzschean nihilism with none of Nietzsche's flip side of joy. Failure to conquer Chogo Ri (K2) had thoroughly disheartened Crowley. *Summa spes* means "summit hope" or the "sum of hope," an ironic double meaning suggesting hope summed up or the heights of hope, or even all the hope there is, combining a bitter peak, a Buddhistic estimation of human futility, and Crowley's naturalist imperative to sensual pleasure, or plain, earthy physiological satisfaction:

VERSE 3
As far as reason goes,
There's hope for mortals yet:
When nothing is that knows,
What is there to regret?
Our consciousness depends
On matter in the brain;
When that rots out, and ends
There ends the hour of pain.

(*Chorus*)
Let me die in a ditch,
Damnably drunk,

Or lipping a punk,
Or in bed with a bitch!
I was ever a hog;
Dung? I am one with it!
Let me die like a dog;
Die, and be done with it!

If we can trust to this,
Why, dance and drink and revel!
Great scarlet mouths to kiss,
And sorrow to the devil!
If pangs ataxic creep,
Or gout, or pox, annoy us,
Queen Morphia, grant thy sleep!
Let worms, the dears, enjoy us!
(*Chorus*)

VERSE 5
But since a chance remains
That "I" survives the body,
(So talk the men whose brains
Are made of shit and shoddy.)
I'll stop it if I can.
(Ah Jesus, if Thou couldest!)
I'll go to Martaban
To make myself a Buddhist.

(*Chorus*)

And yet; the bigger chance
Lies with annihilation.
Follow the lead of France,
Freedom's enlightened nation!
Off! Sacerdotal stealth
Of faith and fraud and gnosis!
Come, drink me: Here's thy health,
Arterio-sclerosis!

Printed in red with green art nouveau borders by T. Spicer Simpson in London in early summer 1903, friends in Paris received it with a treated photograph by the Montparnassian photographic partnership of Stephen Haweis and Henry Coles, and a cartoon of a demiurgical monster (the world), colored green, gobbling a hapless poet (?) with the words (in red) "And so—Farewell!"

Fig. 6.1. "And so— Farewell!" Vignette from "Summa Spes" (1903). Courtesy of 100th Monkey Press and Ordo Templi Orientis

Samuel and Moina Mathers were busy moving from avenue Mozart to new (cheaper) accommodation in Montmartre when Crowley reappeared in November 1902. By that time the Isis performances probably felt to Mathers like a lost paradise. Since then, his world had fallen about his ears; Crowley's, despite despairs, had grown.

According to *Confessions,* Mathers still commanded allegiance as "representative of the Secret Chiefs,"[1] but having mulled over Bennett's doubts regarding "integrity," with added suspicion that Mathers was either temporarily "obsessed" by forces emanating from the book of the Sacred Magic of Abra-Melin, or had permanently "fallen," Crowley's Order commitment was inertial, partially compensated for by an intellectual Buddhism. Still, having consulted with Mathers last time he'd been in Paris, it seemed logical to rejoin the thread, and so he went, ostensibly to recover bags and books left when leaving for America two and half years before.

Surrounded by turmoil, Mathers appeared reticent, which Crowley attributed to embarrassment. Mathers had almost certainly sold Crowley's bags, including an "almost new fifty-guinea dressing case."[2] Mathers handed over the books but said the bags he'd have to search for. Crowley watched as Mathers did to him what he knew he'd done to others: taken and not returned. But if the chiefs *had* discarded Mathers, Crowley (he says) knew no replacement; the issue rankled.

It was probably Kelly who introduced Crowley to former Peterhouse, Cambridge student Hugh Stephen Haweis (1878–1969), son of Rev. Hugh Reginald Haweis (author of *Music and Morals,* 1871) and artist Mary Eliza Haweis. Ensconced in Montparnasse's English artist colony, Haweis, like Moina Mathers nearly a decade earlier, attended the Académie Colarossi where in 1902 he met artist Mina Loy and, venturing into forested Meudon on Paris's southwestern outskirts, acquainted himself with controversial sculptor Auguste Rodin. Rodin invited Haweis to photograph his work. Haweis's application of Steichen's gum-bichromate process to the images captivated the sixty-two-year-old: "Mieux que Steichen," Rodin exclaimed.[3] Crowley noted some two decades later, "the youth"—in fact Haweis was less than three years his junior *and* a Cambridge contemporary—had achieved "a certain delicate eminence,"[4] which, whatever Crowley may have thought it meant, sounds patronizing, with a hint of envy. In 1904, Rodin made Haweis and Coles his official photographers.

According to *Confessions,* desire for an independent view on Mathers made Crowley ask Haweis to visit Montmartre, which he did, only to return with a tale of Mathers boring him with a disquisition on the gods of Mexico. Recognizing this as something Mathers picked up from the people who'd first "induced me to go out to Mexico," Crowley smelled "charlatan," "exploiting *omne ignotum pro magnifico* like the veriest quack."[5] Crowley here exploits a phrase uttered by Conan Doyle's Sherlock Holmes in "The Red Headed League" (*Strand* magazine, August 1891) that liberally transliterated means "everything unknown seems magnificent (to the ignorant)." Again, the implication is that Mathers aggrandized himself with stolen goods, which worked for him until someone recognized "the trick." *Confessions* states that the

Fig. 6.2. Auguste Rodin, *by William Rothenstein (1872–1945), chalk on paper, 1906 (Metropolitan Museum of Art; gift of Roger E. Fry, 1907).*

"moment" he realized it, he came into contact with Mathers's "forces." Using Captain Fuller's account written eight years later (*Equinox* 1, no. 4 (1910): 174–77), Crowley removed himself from whatever facts, if any, underlay what allegedly happened next.

According to Fuller, Crowley found Kelly perturbed. Inquiry revealed that vampire sorceress "Mrs M," was manipulating a "Miss Q."* Crowley asked to visit Miss Q where Mrs M was living. Alone with Mrs M while Miss Q made tea, Crowley examined a bronze head of Balzac. While examining it, he felt dreamy and noticed Mrs M no longer appeared worn by middle age but as a bewitching beauty leaning over him, hair dangling seductively. Crowley allegedly got up, calmly replaced the bronze, and talked normally while mentally confronting her wiles with magical resistance. She tried harder, approaching with obsessing lust. Crowley's resistance apparently confronted her with the hell of her own future decrepitude. She tried an obscenity and a kiss, but Crowley held the siren at arm's length, netted in her own evil energy. Blue-greenish light seemed to envelop her head as what was now a hideous hag hobbled hopelessly from the room. Wanting to know if the

---

*According to William Breeze, "Mrs M" was Bertie Longworth, an American woman sculptor, and "Miss Q" was Marie Preble, an American-born painter.

vampire worked alone or was directed, Crowley supposedly asked Kelly if he knew a clairvoyant. He said he did: the "Sibyl." The Sibyl eventually envisioned a house Crowley recognized as Mathers's. Entering the vision, Crowley found within it not Mathers and wife but what looked like Theo and Mrs. Horos: "Their bodies were in prison; but their spirits were in the house of the fallen chief of the Golden Dawn."[6]

Crowley couldn't tell whether to direct a hostile will-current against Mathers and Moina for inviting the spirits into themselves or to see the figures as disguised Abra-Melin demons. Should he warn Mathers of evil done about him? The Sibyl responded to an inner voice: *Leave it alone.* Crowley reflected years later in *Confessions* that this "story" was typical of his magical state at the time. He could function as a "Master of Magick" but wasn't really interested. He thought he might complete Abra-Melin, but the mess over Mathers soured the proposal.

Inclined to Buddhism, Crowley published in Paris an edition of *Berashith,* written in India. *Berashith* portrayed Buddhism as essentially a science of mind elaborated into moralistic dogma. Years later, Crowley wondered if he hadn't become rather big-headed on the strength of his adventures; he implies he had. Anyhow, "the big people in the artistic world in France accepted me quite naturally as a colleague."[7]

Gerald Kelly's comments of 1949 on Crowley's Parisian reminiscences drew attention to a passage on page 3 of the 1929 *Confessions* edition that Kelly considered was intended to excuse distorted or fanciful scenes:

> A further difficulty is introduced by the nature of the mind, and especially of the memory, of the man himself [A.C.]. We shall come to incidents which show that he is doubtful about clearly remembered circumstances, whether they belong to "real life" or to dreams, and even that he has utterly forgotten things which no normal man could forget. He has, moreover, so completely overcome the illusion of time (in the sense used by the philosophers, from Lao Tzu and Plotinus to Kant and Whitehead) that he often finds it impossible to disentangle events as a sequence.

Kelly's summary: "Incidents can be invented, happenings put in the wrong order. They certainly were."[8] Kelly's comments confirm that Miss Q was Marie Preble, but as for the rest:

The story of Miss Q (Miss Prebble [*sic*]) and Mrs. M. is all rot: invented from beginning to end. At least G.K. [Kelly] has no knowledge of it, and he is supposed to have called in A.C., and to have provided the Sibyl. Why did he invent this improbable story?[9]

I imagine it served to justify Crowley's eventual assumption of Mathers's claim to be chosen by the Secret Chiefs with authority to absorb the Golden Dawn into his own system. It reads like an opium dream-blend of the Mr. and Mrs. Horos deception with the magical melodrama of the Wilkie Collins type. Thus we find an image of Balzac's head while sculptor Rodin was being attacked for misrepresenting Balzac (Crowley purchased bronzes from Rodin through Kelly), while the Sibyl surely derives from Kelly's artist friend Sibyl Meugens, who, according to Crowley, had become Kelly's mistress after switching from Haweis when the latter went to Brussels. "What dreadful days those were!" wails Crowley in *Confessions,* as if merely an observer: "They worked themselves up into such a state that Kelly actually proposed to marry Sibyl, and his sister [Rose] bustled over post haste to prevent it by threatening that his allowance would be stopped if he did anything so foolish. I had of course no sympathy whatever for the fatuity of the young people [!], but I have always felt with Shelley [note!] that parental tyranny is the most indefensible kind. I offered to make Kelly an allowance equal to what he was receiving, which rather took the wind out of the sails of the old wooden three-deckers in Camberwell vicarage. The gesture was sufficient. The threat was withdrawn; Gerald on his side had cooled off sufficiently to see the folly of throwing himself away on a half-caste."[10] Charming stuff, as Kelly might have said. As for Crowley's claim that "the big people in the artistic world in France accepted me quite naturally as a colleague," Kelly's sarcastic comment: "Delicious!!"

Indeed, and Crowley's dismissal of Sibyl Meugens (ca. 1877–1942) as "Sibyl Muggins" further displays Crowley's more uninviting characteristics. Born Harriet Sibyl Meugens to an English mother and father of Belgian extraction—a chartered accountant of Meugens, King and Simpson, Calcutta—Sibyl studied with Stephen Haweis, and at the Académie Colarossi, living, like Haweis, in the same building as Kelly. An accomplished still-life artist, Sibyl exhibited at the third and fourth

*Fig. 6.3. A 1903 drawing
by Gerald Kelly, thought to
be of Sibyl Meugens.*
Courtesy of Anton Liss, the
Modern British Art Gallery

Salons d'Automne (1905 and 1906, along with Mina Loy), established
in 1903 by Eugène Carrière, Frantz Jourdain, Félix Vallotton, Hector
Guimard, George Desvallières, Édouard Vuillard, and Eugène Chigot to
counter the dominance of the official Salon des Beaux Arts. Marrying
artist and theatrical designer George Sheringham (1884–1937) in 1912,
they had their own show at the Ryder Gallery, London, in 1914. Mystical
author C. G. Harrison dedicated his *The Creed for the Twentieth Century*
(1923) to the couple, calling them "my dear friends" without whom the
book "might never have seen the light."*

Confessions fails to furnish a reliable picture of events in Paris at
the time. Fortunately, there are other sources, apart from Kelly's "post-
judiced," sometimes jaundiced, critique. We start with a verse from *The
Star and the Garter*, Crowley's poem about love in Paris, published in
1903 by Watts & Co. of Johnson's Court, London. In the second verse,
the poet attempts to understand the silence of "my Queen," model for
the ideal "Star" of the work:

You are silent. That we always were.

---

*Crowley, incidentally, read Harrison's *The Transcendental Universe* (1895) in 1913.

The racing lustres of your hair
Spelt out its sunny message, though
The room was dusk: a rosy glow
Shed from an antique lamp to fall
On the deep crimson of the wall,
And over all the ancient grace
Of shawls, and ivory, and gems
To cast its glamour, till your face
The eye might fall upon and rest,
The temperate flower, the tropic stems.
You were silent, and I too. Caressed
The secret flames that curled around
Our subtle intercourse. Profound,
Unmoved, delighting utterly,
So sat, so sit, my love and I.

The "deep crimson of the wall" refers to Crowley's newly rented rooms at 8 bis rue Campagne Première, between boulevard du Montparnasse and boulevard Raspail, almost opposite Kelly's studio at number 17. And lo! Fortune offers a piece of the crimson wallpaper alluded to, for on it Crowley wrote an undated (Wednesday, probably 1903) letter to Gerald Kelly, then in London on account of his mother's having an operation:

My dear Gerald,

I am not in a state to write. The crimson paper is being put up to-day. V.H. Soror Perseverantia 6=6* is coming at 2, Sibyl [Meugens] at 5, E [probably Eileen Gray] at 8. And many of her fearful destinies are on me.

I wrote to your poor mother a letter purely to take her mind away from the Operation, as you used the word "disturb." It would have been worse than useless to have written a letter of condolence. I asked E[ileen] and she approved of what I did write. T'was a difficult task you set me, and I hope didn't strike as being callous. All

---

*Alice Isabel Simpson (1852–1935), Mathers loyalist, expelled from London's Golden Dawn in 1900.

the Quarter, like the good Quarter it is, is frightfully concerned. Anyone would give their best painting to the flames if thereby they could secure a successful [outcome?] for ♄ [Saturday]. Thanks for writing about [the?] poetry: I can do no better than [reply?] in same strain. [Crowley then gives authorization for Kelly to obtain from publishers Kegan Paul the Zaehnsdorf-bound versions of *The Mother's Tragedy* and *The Soul of Osiris* (both 1901)—probably gifts for Eileen Gray] Will you show them [publishers] A.D. ["Ascension Day"] & P ["Pentecost"; both written in India] and find if they decline to publish on grounds of blasphemy: if so, the name of a good but "notoriously infidel" publisher.

I will fulfil all your commissions. The Haweis letter is characteristic!

Yours very disturbedly—the best of wishes and luck to all!
Aleister Crowley[11]

Twenty years later, from Olympian height, Crowley castigated Kelly for getting engaged to Sibyl, but then, somewhat hypocritically, confessed he was affianced to Eileen Gray! What was going on?

EILEEN GRAY AND FRIENDS

One figure towered over all ambition in Montparnasse's English artistic colony: Auguste Rodin. Rodin made friends in the early 1850s with fellow drawing student Alphonse Legros (1837–1911), who in 1863 was encouraged by Rodin's friend James McNeil Whistler to seek fortune in England. Teaching at South Kensington's School of Art (now the Royal College of Art), Legros was appointed Slade professor at University College, London, in 1876. Ladies attending his art school became known as Slade Girls, and from their number Crowley found numerous girlfriends, for students had a Bohemian reputation as "new women," a reputation not always earned, in Crowley's view. One of them was the Hon. Eileen Gray, born at Brownswood House, Enniscorthy, County Wexford, August 8, 1878, daughter of Baroness Gray and James McLaren Smith, painter from Lancashire. Eileen Gray would in due course become an important figure in the history of twentieth-century

Fig. 6.4. Aleister Crowley in Paris 1902–1901, photographed and treated by Haweis & Coles for twelve copies of "Summa Spes" (1903). He sent the portrait to some of his friends in Paris when departing for England in 1903. It was also reproduced in volume 2 of the vellum edition of The Works of Aleister Crowley *(1906).*
Courtesy of 100th Monkey Press and Ordo Templi Orientis

art and design, a gifted innovator in architecture, furniture, interior and public space design. Gray's remarkable house, called E-1027, at Roquebrune-Cap-Martin, drew intense admiration from Le Corbusier and Jean Badovici.

Enrolling at the Slade in 1900, Eileen studied fine art until 1902, when she followed her teachers' example and found a pension at 7 rue de Joseph Bara with artist friends Kathleen Bruce (1878–1947) and Eileen's cross-dressing lover, Jessie Gavin,* some 220 yards from Kelly's studio, across the boulevard Montparnasse.[12]

While Gray attended the Académie (sometimes "École") Colarossi

---

*Born in England in 1876, Jessie was daughter of Ann Sophia Lord and Crichton Strachan, merchant. In 1915 she would marry senior civil engineer of mines René Raoul-Duval, who died for France on December 11, 1916. Jessie died in 1939, interred in Père-Lachaise, Paris.

Fig. 6.5. Eileen Gray, 1902.
© *National Museum of Ireland*

at nearby 10 rue de la Grande-Chaumière, before switching to the Académie Julian in the passage des Panoramas off the boulevard Montmartre in 1903, Kelly took informal lessons from Canadian artist James Wilson Morrice (1865–1924), studying closely works by Whistler, Velasquez, Sickert, and Dégas. Acquaintance with Dégas came through leading art-dealer Paul Durand-Ruel (1831–1922), in whose gallery Péladan mounted the first successful Salon Rose-Croix in 1892.

Through Durand-Ruel, Kelly was introduced to Rodin, Pierre-Auguste Renoir, Claude Monet, Paul Cézanne, and sculptor Aristide Maillol.

After Kelly introduced Eileen to Rodin in 1902, she wrote to him about purchasing the bronze *Danaid*.[13] Crowley followed her lead, with Kelly as purchasing intermediary. Kelly also took Eileen to the Île

St. Louis, to meet Jewish writer and critic Marcel Schwob (1867–1905) and his beautiful actress wife, Marguerite Moreno (1871–1948), whose hands Kelly drew. Concerned over Kelly's poor French, Marguerite arranged for him to dine twice weekly with irascible, rough-talking theater critic and pro-Symbolist *Mercure de France* journal writer Paul Léautaud (1872–1956). Gray met Léautaud with Kelly at the Schwobs' in 1904, which led a smitten Léautaud to join the queue of Eileen's fervent, unsuccessful admirers.[14]

Startlingly attractive Eileen could count Kelly as admirer and friend.* According to Gray's biographer Peter Adam: "To Eileen he [Kelly] seemed someone quite extraordinary, and she took to this talkative Irishman [*sic*; Etonian Kelly was born in London], he was good company."[15]

Fig. 6.6. Eileen Gray, ca. 1903.
© *National Museum of Ireland*

---

*Gray's biographer Peter Adam's belief that Kelly and Gray were Slade contemporaries is mistaken; Jennifer Goff apparently follows this error.

Haweis was another friend. He'd enrolled at the Académie Julian in 1899, getting to know Irishman Paul Henry and Scottish artist Francis Cadell. Henry would recall Haweis's dark eyes, small stature, and eccentric dress: brown corduroy suit, long dark hair cut straight across the forehead topped by a black beret. He would also wear beads or a live green snake that slithered about the easels.[16] Leaving in 1900, Haweis returned for night sessions at the Colarossi in 1902, meeting Gray and Mina Loy, whom he later married and whose life he made a misery. Paul Henry's *An Irish Portrait* (1951) informs us that the Académie Julian "was not in any sense of the word a teaching institution. It was not a school with regular classes and teachers, it granted no degree, and there were no prizes. As long as you paid up, behaved properly and did not steal the easels, you were free."[17]

Fig 6.7. Mina Loy, by Stephen Haweis, 1905.

Crowley would get to know artist Mina Loy (née Lowy), who contacted him again in the twenties for advice (see page 277). Haweis's memoirs speak of her and Gray's beauty in the same paragraph:

There were several amazingly beautiful girls in our Paris of the early 1900s. Mina (Loy) was half-English, half-Jewish Hungarian, whose complexion was so perfect that the students betted upon its truth, and would not believe their eyes when a scrub on the studio towel left it . . . perfectly white. Her mouth was an incredible wonder and almost plum coloured. It was as beautiful as Eileen's shoulders, which were the most perfect I ever saw . . . things beautiful which live forever in memory and for which to be grateful. Of course there are always beauties when many young people of different nationalities are gathered together, yet some remain like planets among the stars, more radiant than others. . . . It is not only for their beauty that these girls are to be remembered, nor for their talent, though some of them were talented enough and one was a genius. They marked the end of an era, and created a new one without knowing very much about it. To repeat, ad nauseam, most of the girls were as poor as the men, but they cared for "beauty" and were not content to be dull echoes of the prevailing fashion.[18]

Eileen Gray also attracted—and still attracts—female admiration. Kathleen Bruce, who proceeded to establish herself as a monumental sculptor, was fair enamored with Eileen, writing in her posthumous autobiography *Self-Portrait of an Artist* (1949):

She was fair, with wide-set pale blue eyes, tall and of grand proportion, well born and quaintly and beautifully dressed. But for a rather vague look and an absent-minded manner, she would have been wonderful, when, one night she told me that she lived her whole life in terror because there was madness in her family. I thought her not only wonderful to look at, but also the most romantic figure I had ever seen.[19]

Fig. 6.8. Portrait of Kathleen Bruce in 1907, titled Souvenir of an "International Ball" *by Charles Hasslewood Shannon (Cleveland Museum of Art; Mr. and Mrs. William H. Marlatt Fund).*

Jasmine Rault's *Eileen Gray and the Design of Sapphic Modernity: Staying In* (2016) takes this and other indices of Gray's sexuality considerably further than either Peter Adam or Jennifer Goff. Rault examines Gray's postwar interior designs and architecture as expressive of an implicate subtext of lesbian erotic pleasure, of sensual freedom in the home, and criticizes Adam's biographical treatment for sidestepping potent sapphic suggestions by concentrating on her many male admirers, marginalizing evidence of nonheterosexual attachments. Rault sees Kathleen Bruce's autobiographical narrative as particularly telling, long before Gray became familiar with Paris's lesbian artistic scene before and after the Great War, dominated by figures Gray knew personally, such as sometime lovers Colette and Natalie Clifford Barney. Rault notes how Bruce introduces Jessie Gavin as tall, dark, and pretty, while Gray is remote, vague, wonderful, and potentially mad. The former Miss Bruce then gives away the game:

> I was never at all at ease with them, but it was many years before I discovered why. . . . One evening a tall, thin, shy, nice-looking youth in corduroys and a Norfolk jacket came in. This was [Gavin], with a wig and a slightly blackened moustache. "We'll go and play chess in a café. I can take you to places where you can't go without a man."[20]

Jasmine Rault takes Peter Adam to task for suppressing investigation of gender transgression, emphasizing instead a jealousy reaction involving a *man* as the cause for a rift between Gray and Bruce. Kathleen was in love with her cousin Henry, but *he* fell for Eileen, and it remains for Rault to lament the loss of biographical insight into "the potential lesbian story of Gray's early years in Paris."[21] Rault implies it was Gray's lesbian leanings that led her to reject so many male admirers, Gerald Kelly among them. This view, however, may not have fully taken into account Crowley's self-confessed folly (with hindsight) of becoming engaged to Eileen, culminating, according to Goff, in Crowley's (uncharacteristic) gift of a diamond brooch, which Eileen accepted, even while going, as Rault writes, "dancing all night with her partner Jessie Gavin."[22]

Before examining Crowley's relationship with Eileen—which, contrary to his sardonic *Confessions* account, was real and meaningful—we need to consider the position of many of the young women who came to

Paris to study art. Writing in early middle age, amid barely suppressed bitterness, Crowley displayed contemptuous attitudes for their plight, as if proverbial British moral "hypocrisy" was their own fault. I wonder if he was so *entirely* unsympathetic at the time, despite world experience having demonstrated graphically that sin in Kensington might be virtue in Kashmir.

When Eileen first attended the Slade in 1900, it was only relatively recently that its predominantly middle- and upper-class ladies could sketch from a partially covered model. Life classes were segregated, though other classes were mixed, with women outnumbering men by more than two to one in a total class of some 228 students.[23] Before relaxation of rules, women had to file out of class when male teachers entered to inspect student work. Parents expected the manners of home to be respected in institutions, that their daughters would be unsullied by unchaperoned male attention. In Paris, of course, relaxation was de rigeur. It was observed that male art students were as focused on female art students as upon the art they aspired to; pressure must have been great, with undraped male and female models commonplace. Male students wanted to know if women could be classed as "kind" or not. Frenchmen did not have the same inhibitions Englishwomen expected of suitors or potential suitors; they were frequently forward—a young Englishwoman marked as "kind" (*gentille*) was fair game. A club was formed for American female students for socializing without interference, but outside the club was . . . *Paris,* and whatever else Paris might have been, it did not harmonize with puritanism. Of course, that was also the great attraction for those women who'd already acquired a taste for London-style Bohemia-*lite.*

Temptation was ever present, with plenty of artistry and poetry appealingly curled about the portals of the flesh, but if a girl succumbed, she could quickly find herself socially finished, or trapped in premature marriage with attendant misery and social prejudice. Virginity was a prized and protected social asset, and for most women, admissible attraction simply *had* to be an affair of the heart, of noble feelings, high and remote romance that might find expression in very subtle sensual signals, though should sensuality predominate, a perilous cliff edge appeared, fatal for a casual tip-toe in the "wrong" direction. What would a politely raised young Englishwoman think or feel in the presence of a professional Parisian courtesan of great beauty, knowingness, and poise?

The Symbolist movement had assisted women's spiritual aspirations, for they could claim that all art was for the *Ideal,* and any love or romance worth the name must aspire to the ideal, and fleshly, material, sensual vision was not the ideal, which was spiritual and transcendent: exaltation of spirit might be expressed poetically in language redolent of ecstasy of orgasm, but joyous surrender worth the name involved sacrifice of lust and worship of ideal, not corruptible, form. Crowley's peculiar poetry must have been problematic for women readers because he freely crossed all these lines, failing to distinguish, or choosing not to distinguish, between spiritual transcendence and physical release. In contradistinction to Walter Scott's famous paean to love, Crowley had found it was *Nature* that "rules the court, the camp, the grove, and men below, and saints above." For (to Crowley) sex is heaven, and heaven is sex, for those who *know.* One might also note that in this period, a poet printed in sumptuous volume invited the same awe a student of predownload days reserved for revered pop stars promoting a new album—and *this* poet had ascended Chogo Ri and entered the soul of the "mystic orient": strong dope in Paris in 1902!

We should also note that with so much sexual repression typical of Anglo-Saxon and Celtic worlds, some students of art and the ideal might find themselves fixating interior longings upon members of their own sex, for as Keats's "Ode on a Grecian Urn" intoned, "beauty is truth, truth beauty," and while the heart's longing could find beauty enough in itself, there was more possibility for fulfillment, when contrasted with restrictions dividing men and women, for physical intimacies between females, which, acquiring the invisibility of the unexpected or unsought, could pass relatively unnoticed.

All indications suggest Eileen Gray's nature was bisexual, as we currently understand the word:

> The love-taught magus, the hermaphrodite,
> Knows how to woo the Mother, and awake her;
> Beholding, in the very self-same sight,
> The self-illumined image of the Maker.*

---

*Crowley, "The Adept," vv. 12–13, sec. 6 in *Clouds without Water* (pub. 1909); inspired by Kathleen Bruce.

Crowley shared bisexual sensibilities, and one may speculate whether experience imparted secret empathy to relations both with Eileen and, later, with Eileen's (perhaps at the time frustrated) admirer Kathleen Bruce for, in 1907, Crowley himself, by now married to Kelly's sister Rose, entertained a passionate affair with sculptress Kathleen, who, he wrote, initiated him into the "torturing pleasures of algolagny on the spiritual plane," invoked luridly in sections 6 and 7 of *Clouds without Water,* directly inspired by Kathleen, and completed in Paris in July 1908.

Algolagnia is a condition of physical pleasure induced by inflicting pain, particularly on erogenous zones. That Crowley refers to such occurring "on the spiritual plane" suggests Kathleen was denying him something he physically craved, while she teased the craving to intense levels. While they clearly kissed with fervor, the poem suggests an ultimate, hyperintense frustration that Crowley found agonizing but strangely delicious. Kathleen is described with arch, and likely misleading hindsight in *Confessions* as "an old friend. I had known her in Paris in 1902. She was one of the intimates of my fiancée. She was studying sculpture under Rodin and was unquestionably his best woman pupil."[24]

One of the intimates of my fiancée . . . the fiancée being Eileen Gray.

Crowley continues in frivolous terms:

She [Bruce] was strangely seductive. Her brilliant beauty and wholesome Highland flamboyance were complicated with a sinister perversity. She took delight in getting married men away from their wives, *and the like* [my italics]. Love had no savour for her unless she was causing ruin or unhappiness to others. I was quite ignorant of her intentions when she asked me to sit for her, but once in her studio she lost no time. . . . She showed me how to intensify passion by self-restraint. . . . She made me wonder, in fact, if the secret of puritanism was not to heighten the intensity of love by putting obstacles in its way. . . . To her I dedicated *Rodin in Rime* and *Clouds without Water* itself—not openly; our love affair being no business of other people, and in any case being too much ginger for the "hoi polloi," but in such ways as would have recommended themselves to Edgar Allan Poe.*[25]

Sir Gerald Kelly's acerbic comments on this passage and earlier reference to Kathleen being Rodin's pupil (repeated in every biographical treatment of Kathleen) are interesting:

> He's referring to K.B. [Kathleen Bruce] who afterwards married twice and very well. She was a pretentious creature and a very bad sculptress. She was not a pupil of Rodin. What a tawdry mind A.C. had. Everything had to be "improved"—[i.e., made] more interesting. His home should have been Hollywood.[26]

I presume what Kelly meant concerning Rodin was that while Kathleen studied and followed his work, she was not apprenticed or taken on by him personally or professionally. Otherwise, Kelly might say, he could himself be called "pupil of Velasquez." Kelly objects to Crowley making Kathleen sound more significant than Kelly thinks she was. Kelly's acquired disdain for Crowley, however, and his snobbery, seem frequently to distort his picture of the past. In fact, as William Breeze informs the author, Rodin came to London in 1908 to attend Kathleen's wedding to Captain Robert Falcon Scott, a courtesy clearly indicating a friendly relationship. A teacher-pupil relationship ought not to be excluded. Besides, the lady whom Kelly judged "a very bad sculptress" would receive numerous prestigious commissions still on public display today. As for Crowley overcooking the egg of Kathleen's unusual approach to sex and relationships, a recent study by Janice Cavell suggests Crowley's presentation may not have been *all* personal

---

*Crowley refers to Edgar Allan Poe's poem "The Acrostic," in which the first letter of each line, reading downward, spells the name ELIZABETH. Likewise, the terzain opening *Clouds without Water* has an acrostic spelling KATHLEEN BRUCE. Unable to marry one "explorer" (Crowley) and bear a child, *Confessions* confides she married another: Antarctic explorer Robert Falcon Scott (unnamed) married Kathleen in September 1908. A brother officer and rival for Kathleen's love sent the acrostic to a member of Scott's team to give Scott after departing for his fated dash to the South Pole, whereafter, beaten to the prize by Norwegian Roald Amundsen, courageous Scott and companions perished in relentless blizzards in March 1912.

fantasy, rather adding nuance to the picture of intimate relations in the Montparnasse Quarter in 1902–1903.

Cavell's primary interest is Kathleen's first husband, Captain Scott, whom Kathleen is shown to have pursued but not truly loved until *after* she bore his "toy-child" (as her diary puts it) and realized she'd attained her goal. While Baroness Kennet (as she became in 1935) was widely admired, publication of memoir and diary extracts in 1949, two years after her death, showed both unconventionality and how she'd manipulated the "Scott of the Antarctic" image after Scott's death.

Captain Scott himself was very fond of *Peter Pan* author J. M. Barrie. Barrie told Kathleen that she "wasn't made up like most people," being "half man and half woman, but the woman-half was more womanish than the average woman."[27] According to Cavell, "for Barrie, the masculine half only added piquancy to that unusually intense womanliness. But in retrospect, Kathleen Scott has been perceived not only as dauntingly masculine but as emasculating. Strong-willed, egotistical, and given to flirtation even after her marriage, she does not seem to be the wife a truly manly man would have chosen. Neither a conventionally feminine woman nor an early feminist, she has little appeal for any constituency of writers or readers today."[28] *I wonder . . .*

Despite a painful early life—her mother died at forty-two after bearing eleven children in fifteen years of marriage—Kathleen arrived in Paris with a vitalistic desire to be open to experience, establishing her studio at 22 rue Delambre.* Kathleen and Eileen Gray's mutual friend (in the 1920s), dancer Isadora Duncan, described Kathleen as "a magnetic person, filled with life and health and courage."[29] By contrast, interior designer Sibyl Colefax (1874–1950) dismissed Kathleen as "a snob who tried to vamp [flirt dangerously or seduce] all distinguished men."[30] Janice Cavell, taking Colefax's view as substantiated to a degree by Kathleen's autobiography, observes that prior to marriage, Kathleen stimulated masculine passions before frustrating them so as to, as Kathleen put it, keep "my determined, my masterful virginity" intact.[31] This confession supports Crowley's more colorfully expressed

---

*Kathleen would find artist-writer friend Wyndham Lewis (1882–1957) accommodation next door when Lewis came to Paris in 1904 (Coleman, Milligan, and O'Donnell, *BLAST at 100: A Modernist Magazine Reconsidered,* 104).

assessment, as does, even more pointedly—no pun intended—Cavell's view that so "intense was her [Kathleen's] need for male adoration that she appeared to enjoy witnessing the pain which demonstrated her hold over her various suitors."[32]

Such behavior may have come not only from perverse delight for its own sake. Isn't it possible Kathleen was observing jealously the many suitors for Eileen's affections, while taking interior comfort from seeing their advances rejected, as she held out for the *ideal*? If Jasmine Rault was right in thinking a rift grew between Kathleen and Eileen over Eileen's attachment to Jessie Gavin, then such emotional disquiet was surely exacerbated by Eileen's amazing magnetism over *men,* and Kathleen may have unconsciously internalized *to herself* this strange, even supreme power of attraction, while tenaciously remaining prepared to sacrifice her virginity only in exchange for maternity: physical confirmation of an ideal femininity and the subjection of a man. Wouldn't Eileen making an exception of Crowley raise him in Kathleen's estimation, marking him as someone to subdue, while experiencing identity with Eileen's mysterious passion? In 1908 she sculpted Crowley as *Enchanted* Prince.

Such subterranean tremors make sense of Crowley's hindsight-laden, extended diatribe on the Englishwomen of the Quarter.

Studying closely the labyrinthine chapters of *Confessions* for this period shows how reflections appear like dream-memories rationalized and woven into haphazard anecdotes and mini-sermons. He didn't have much to say about the women themselves, or what he did with them, but evoking their images to the mind's eye clearly impelled expression of past frustrations, quickly rationalized into anachronistic, thelemite nostra. Thus, a once burning issue of virginity is treated impersonally. He complains of women students' "affectation" in demanding equal treatment, as if men. When Kelly called an Englishwoman "old fellow," it went down well, but excusing himself for the lavatory with an expression no man would even notice, Kelly returned to find the lady had "bolted." Crowley then insisted the expected equality could come only when women accepted men's morality "lock, stock and barrel," by ceasing to "set an extravagant value on her animal functions." Intolerant of any female defense that talking or acting in such a way would entail immediate downgrading by *men,* as well as personal degradation suffered for transgressing her entire upbringing, Crowley remained critical and, I think, hypocritical. I doubt whether Crowley would have delighted in hearing an adored woman tell him that she was "going for a shit." He then gets to the nagging point (perhaps with Kathleen Bruce in mind), casting contempt at an unmarried woman's concern with virginity: "The most high-principled woman (alleged) insists on the supreme value of an asset which is notoriously of no value whatever in itself."[33] The fleshly hymen might indeed prove worthless at a pawnshop, but he knew perfectly well its symbolic value in practically every corner of the world.

Furthermore, a sour Crowley cannot resist denigrating the intelligence and integrity of most of the artist colony, even of his fiancée, to whom he lent *The Sword of Song* in manuscript, written mainly in India, wherein he recounted reading "Lévi and the Cryptic Copts." Sitting for Kelly, Eileen asked Kelly what "Coptic" was. He replied, "The language spoken by the ancient Copts," and returned to the canvas portrait. After a long pause, Eileen asked, "What does cryptic mean?" "The language spoken by the ancient Crypts," "roared the *rapin* and abandoned hope of humanity," as Crowley related the incident.[34]

Amusing no doubt, but note the use of the French *rapin* for Gerald Kelly, painter. It means "thief" and refers to Kelly's current interest in exploring and applying the darkest hues characteristic of Whistler and Velasquez. This phase of self-education had a page earlier been used to establish another amusing anecdote. Kelly had allegedly taken an old canvas to paint over. He'd worked on it some time before realizing he'd painted over "his favourite portrait of the Hon. Eileen Gray," quite possibly the one he was painting during the "Cryptic Copts" joke. This may or may not have occurred, but there's something about the idea of Kelly painting over a "favourite" portrait of Eileen that suggests to me, given the frequently cryptic character of Crowleyan anecdote, that he saw Kelly somehow "blotting out" his image of Eileen, *an image that had become darkened*. Or, inversely, was it Crowley's perverse imagination accomplishing this through alleged "thief," Kelly? In someone's mind, Eileen's image was darkened, perhaps sullied.

When we come to Kelly's anger at his sister's marrying Crowley in summer 1903, we shall see the issue of Eileen Gray rearing an unexpected head. For now, I trust readers see that Crowley's arrival on a scene Kelly had carved out for himself with other young artists, and with distinguished professionals such as Marcel Schwob and Auguste Rodin, was bound to bring disturbance, perhaps unanticipated by the younger Kelly. It is hard to imagine that sexual jealousy did not mar proceedings, especially if Kelly saw Eileen giving more attention to the older, more world-experienced Crowley than to himself; and Crowley was seldom content with *one*! Newly appointed president of the Royal Academy, Kelly's dismissive putdown of the late Kathleen Bruce in 1949, nearly fifty years later, may be significant in this regard. Is it not strange that Crowley and Kelly both got themselves engaged around the same time and that Crowley's fiancée was someone who'd rejected Kelly's amorous advances? Kelly let Crowley—no blushing violet—in. He'd been through the fleshpots of Mexico, San Francisco, Colombo, Calcutta, and Cairo and was still looking for action. Fifty years later, Kelly opined that Crowley's home should have been Hollywood. I suggest it occurred to Kelly at some point that he didn't really want him in Paris. Such would bear all the character of the classic love-hate for an admired older figure that inevitably comes down on hate.

According to Jennifer Goff and Eileen Gray biographer Peter Adam, Eileen's relations with Crowley were pacific. She remembered sitting in Kelly's studio with Crowley "waiting for something 'magic' to happen."[35] Sometimes she found her sessions with him amusing, sometimes boring and "full of nonsense."[36] Later in life, she kept the books he gave her; Goff mentions an inscribed copy of *Tannhäuser* and *The Mother's Tragedy* (a collection of two plays and many poems, 1901), possibly the copy Kelly was asked by Crowley to retrieve from London. Crowley, according to Goff, explained that Tannhäuser's love for Venus, when refined to pity, allows him to attain full knowledge of himself, insisting it was a psychological study for the adept. Gray, interested in the mind and other dimensions of consciousness, found Crowley intriguing, as he suggested the mind's capacity for creating new worlds and personas. Both Eileen and Crowley were introspective, dreamy natures, but while Crowley's wit could be quick, and cutting, Bruce noted Eileen's remoteness, a quality perhaps endearing to "Alastor, Wanderer of the Waste."

Goff maintains that Crowley's writings influenced Gray's early lacquer and carpet creations (she mentions a rug called *Magie Noire* = "Black Magic," 1930), as well as feeding her philosophical and metaphysical musings. Gray's lacquer screen "Hail the Jewel in the Lotus" (1913) may have been influenced by Crowley's בראשית [*Berashith*]: *An Essay in Ontology with Some Remarks on Ceremonial Magic, by Abhavananda* (Aleister Crowley), Privately Printed for the Sangha of the West (printed by Clarke & Bishop, 338 rue St-Honoré, Paris, 1903), whose main text ends with that mantra: *Aum mani padme houm,* which likewise greets the "jewel in the lotus."

While Goff writes that Crowley gave Eileen a diamond brooch, possibly as engagement gift, Crowley's very sudden marriage to Rose Kelly in late August 1903 apparently led her to return it to save Rose embarrassment.[37] Nevertheless, Crowley, even while honeymooning in Paris with Rose in December 1903, presented Gray with an inscribed copy of *Berashith:* "Abhavananda to Eileen Gray 9 December." *Abhavananda* means "bliss of nonexistence," in tune with "Summa Spes" and Crowley's card sent out for New Year 1903: "Wishing you a speedy termination of existence." Goff sees Crowley's concern with raja yoga as influential on Gray over a long period: "Crowley's ideas on yoga also influenced Gray later, as she developed her theories on meditation which culminated in the Meditation Grove project, in 1941, where she designed a meditation garden on a hypothetical site outside St. Tropez."[38]

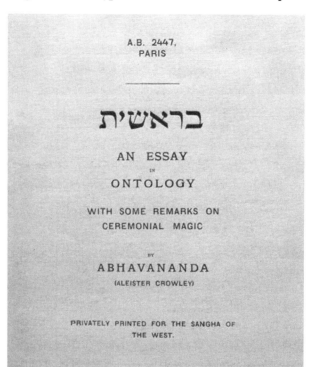

Fig. 6.9. Title-page: Berashith, An Essay on Ontology, with some remarks on Ceremonial Magic, by Abhavananda (Aleister Crowley), *printed by Clarke & Bishop, 338 rue St-Honoré, Paris, 1903.* Courtesy of 100th Monkey Press and Ordo Templi Orientis

THE STAR AND THE GARTER

Eileen Gray also received a copy of Crowley's poetry book *The Star and the Garter* (1903). Eileen inspired the spiritual meaning of the Star of the title: an ideal. Of the poem's background, Crowley gave a desultory explanation in *Confessions*:

> I gradually sickened of the atmosphere of Paris. It was all too easy. I flitted restlessly to London and back, and found no rest for the sole of my foot. I had even got engaged to be married, but returning after a week in London I was partly too shy to resume relations with my fiancée, and partly awake to the fact that we had drifted under the lee shore of matrimony out of sheer lack of moral energy. This lady claims notice principally as the model for several poems, notably (in *Rosa Mundi, and other Love Songs*) "The Kiss," "Eileen," and the poems numbered 14, 15, 16, 18, 21 to 28 [in 27, EILEEN GRAY appears as an acrostic]. She was also the "Star" in "The Star and the Garter," which I wrote at this time; and the three women connected with the "Garter" were an English lady with a passion for ether, an acrobat and model whom I called my boot-button girl because her face was "round and hard and small and pretty," and thirdly Nina Olivier. Nina is described in the poem itself and also in several lyrics, notably "The Rondel"—"You laughing little light of wickedness." My adoration of Nina made her the most famous girl in the quarter for a dozen years and more.[39]

Kelly's somewhat stingy memory concerning Nina differed from Crowley's: "A.C.'s adoration of Nina cut no ice in the Quarter. She was a model I painted. If she became famous, (and I never heard of it) it was after I left in 1906."[40] William Breeze regards this comment of Kelly's as clearly exhibiting either the latter's faulty memory or his ignorance of the modern art scene in Paris, for "Nina Olivier," Breeze discovered, was in fact Eugénie (Nina) Auzias (1882–1949). According to Breeze: "Such was her [Nina's] ability to move between and fully inhabit parallel worlds that the woman Crowley scholars have long known as Nina Olivier is even better known and studied as Eugénie (Nina) Auzias by biographers of Gertrude Stein and her brother Leo; readers in neither field realized that they were the same woman. She married Gertrude Stein's brother Leo Stein (1872–1947) in 1921 after a long and complex courtship dating back at least to 1909."*[41]

Leo and Gertrude Stein had moved from London to Paris in 1903, where, at their home at 27 rue de Fleurus, near the Luxembourg Gardens on the Left Bank, they assembled a notable collection of works by, among other artists, Cézanne, Gauguin, and Renoir, which in time, by judicious, farsighted selection, grew into a startlingly colorful haven for modern art, with the addition of works by Matisse and Picasso. Salons held at the Stein home on Saturdays famously attracted many of the now accepted leading lights of modern art and literature. Outstanding attendees would include Pablo Picasso, Henri Matisse, Francis Picabia, F. Scott Fitzgerald, and Ernest Hemingway. According to William Breeze, "Gertrude Stein usually gets the credit for 'breaking' artists [such as Picasso and Modigliani] but most of them came to her through Leo."[42]

I hope I shall be forgiven at this point for jumping ahead somewhat in the chronology of our narrative. The importance of Breeze's startling identification of Nina Olivier and Eugénie Auzias, and the longtime significance to Crowley of his relations with her, necessitate looking more closely at Nina's story, a story that, even by itself, would make a marvelous movie. Fortunately for our purposes, many of Leo Stein's letters have been preserved in *Journey Into the Self: Being the Letters, Papers & Journals of Leo Stein,* edited by Edmund Fuller and, we may note, "dedicated to Nina Stein."

According to Leo's friend Mabel Weeks's foreword to the book, "Leo was devoted to Nina and often told me she was the most remarkable personality he had ever met. He needed her warmth and expansiveness. . . . She presided beautifully in her own home in Paris, the apartment out near the university."[43] Van Wyck Brooks's introduction reveals Leo Stein's having discovered Cézanne "for himself" (without Gertrude), and being "the first" to recognize Matisse and Picasso as "the two most important men."[44]

---

*The material on Nina Olivier that follows is drawn mostly from William Breeze's research, given form in "Nina Auzias Stein" (lecture presentation), "Magick, Mysticism and Art" Conference, Academia Ordo Templi Orientis, Barcelona, June 24, 2018. Note also that Nina appears in the Yorke Collection OS EE2 "Lovers List" (Crowley's lovers) as "Nina Stein," which confirms the identification.

Notably, the collection of Stein's letters includes a manuscript written by Nina herself in which she describes being stunned at the sight of Leo in the Luxembourg Gardens in May 1905. On that occasion, Nina prophesied she would marry the man her artist friends Miko and Polo dubbed "the great American Maecenas." In the months that followed, a shy Nina encountered Stein again in Montparnasse with friend Miko. Overawed, she couldn't bring herself to speak to him. On one occasion in the Dôme café, he smiled at her, whereupon she put her tongue out at him, and hated herself for being so stupid. After some months, attending the Steins' salon, she couldn't take her eyes off Leo, who sat talking on the floor "like an Arab."[45]

"Years passed," wrote Nina, until she found herself sitting opposite a curious Leo Stein in a café, probably (if we compare her version with Leo's account) during winter 1908/09.[46] Nina had been trying to read *Also sprach Zarathustra,* "which," as she recorded, "a young Englishman had presented to me, dedicated 'To Nina, the soul of the Quarter.'" The gift of Nietzsche's book and the dedication suggest it may have been a present from Aleister Crowley. William Breeze, however, rather thinks the "young man" was more likely Isadora Duncan's pianist, James Henry "Hener" Skene, who, as Crowley himself recorded in *Confessions,* had an "affected" interest in Nietzsche. Writing disdainfully of Hener Skene, Crowley referred to meeting Nina and "latest conquest" Hener Skene at the Dôme in—note—1911 (see page 105), when, as Leo Stein recorded, Nina's affair with Hener Skene was in full swing. Crowley was also partial to Nietzsche's philosophy and undoubtedly held Nina to be "the soul of the Quarter" (the phrase could have been taken from Crowley by Hener Skene). Anyhow, Leo Stein, sitting opposite Nina, read the dedication to Montparnasse's "soul," then uttered mockingly: "Her figure is much better," to which Nina replied, "Disgusting!," and left. The next time they met, Leo said, "Come to pose in the nude for me tomorrow." She replied, "I am too badly built to pose for you." She eventually agreed, only to receive Leo Stein's insult: "Yes, you are right. You are badly built, and not at all inspiring." Eventually, after a series of mishandled ploys and misunderstandings, Leo Stein asked her to come and tell him stories about her life, for his psychoanalytical studies. He paid her 20 francs for her time, but by her own account she didn't tell her tales for much-needed cash, but for the chance to be near him.[47] By the end of 1909, Leo was, as he would be to the end of his days, completely smitten.

Fig. 6.10. Leo
Stein (1872–1947),
photograph by Alfred
Stieglitz, 1917;
Metropolitan Museum
of Art.

Fig. 6.11. Nina Olivier
(Eugénie Vittoria
Auzias), 1882–1949.

NINA OLIVIER

Born Eugénie Victorine Auzias on July 28, 1882, in Gap, in the French
Hautes-Alpes region, Crowley's sometime lover Nina was raised by

parents Marie Madeleine Adelaide Camille (née Brutinel) and mathematics teacher Joseph-Ville Auzias at Baumes Les Dames, near Besançon on the French-Swiss border. As Leo Stein put it, Eugénie "ran pretty wild at home" before leaving for Paris at eighteen in 1901 for a voice-trial and examination at the Conservatoire (Leo Stein to Mabel Weeks, February 15, 1910).[48] Instead of working for her admission, Eugénie formed a liaison with a socialist worker, neglected her voice, and failed her exams, at which her father refused to send her any more money. Undeterred, she sang in the streets below the windows of appreciative patrons until constant exposure to the elements and colds caused the loss of her singing voice. She left the socialist worker, posed as a model occasionally, and enjoyed light affairs with "some young Americans,"[49] supplementing her income by escorting expatriate artists to the heart of the Paris art scene. Adopting the surname Olivier, Nina's beauty and charm wove its own spell as she moved in artistic circles that overlapped directly with those of Crowley's later lover Jane Chéron, with whom he first appears to have enjoyed relations in Paris in late 1910 (Crowley's "Three Poems for Jane [Jeanne] Chéron" appeared in *The Equinox* (vol. 1, no. 6, September 1911, pages 41–52). Remarkably perhaps, exotic model Jane Chéron was *Leo Stein's* girlfriend before Stein fell for Nina. According to Brenda Whineapple's *Sister Brother: Gertrude and Leo Stein,* Leo Stein, when not facilitating the progress of new artists, was, in 1907, studying the nude model at the Académie Colarossi where friends like Max Weber and Hans Purrmann painted and with whom he'd take breaks at a café to talk about art or slope off to meet "real beauty," model Jane Chéron. Whineapple reports that Leo and Gertrude Stein's American friend Andrew Green, when looking over some photographs Leo sent him, wondered "with raised eyebrow" whether Leo had been "doing 'Rodin' sketches" of Mademoiselle Chéron.[50*]

Nina would in time attract celebrity as "Nina de Montparnasse," or as Crowley called her in his *Confessions:* "La Dame de Montparno, the Queen of the Quarter." Breeze refers to her "colorful gaiety" enlivening

---

*Crowley's first poem to Jane Chéron ("The Waif of Oceanus") opens as follows: *She is like a flower washed up / On the shore of life by the sea of luck; / A strange and venomous flower, intent / To prove an unguessed continent. / New worlds of love in the curve of its cup! / New fruits to crush, new flowers to pluck.*

the Café de Dôme, ensuring her center-stage in legends and stories that did the rounds in the last, fading decade of the Belle Époque.

An artist herself, Nina attended sketching lessons at the Académie de la Grande Chaumière near the Académie Colarossi, *in Montparnasse,* but singing had been her great love. Strangely, her singing voice returned in 1911 after her whirlwind romance with Hener Skene. Skene tried giving her singing lessons himself, but amid quarrels and reconciliations, he arranged instruction for her from an operatic singing coach. Encouraged by Leo Stein, who was convinced a singing career would solve her lack of stability and purpose in life, Nina maintained her practice for years.[51]

Intimate with Crowley after their first encounter in 1902, Nina found her way not only into Crowley's long poem *The Star and the Garter* (verses numbered xx and xxiii, particularly) but also into Crowley's short story "The Ordeal of Ida Pendragon" (attributed to "Martial Nay" in *The Equinox* vol. 1, no. 6, [1911], 113–48; see also page 230). In the story, leading man Edgar Rolles has a lunch appointment with Ida Pendragon, for which Ida has given him advance instructions: "Bring a girl." Thus Nina springs from page 136 as "Ninon":

> "Right," said he. "But I wonder what she means." And he strolled out to the Dôme to find good-hearted Ninon, "la grande hystérique" of the Quarter, half-mad and wholly amorous, half gamine and half great lady, satiated and unsatisfied indeed, but innocent withal. La Dame de Montparno they called her; she dominated her surroundings without effort. Yet none could analyse or explain the fascination to which all surrendered. She had more friends than lovers, and no one ever told a lie about her, or let her want for anything.
>
> She welcomed the invitation with joy. "Ida Pendragon!" she said, "oh! I know the type. Name of a tigress . . ." and she rattled off a story of a stag-hunt at Fontainebleau in which the Cornish girl had played the principal, an incredible part.
>
> The café pricked up its ears, and dissolved in laughter at the culminating impossibility.
>
> But Edgar Rolles only frowned. "I am sorry for Ida," he said slowly. "If your story were true I should be glad; but she is only the painter with his palette mixing paints: she never gives her soul up to the canvas. Tigress? yes: but not the Bodhi-sattva who let the

tigress eat him. She always wins; she cannot lose. As the proverb says: 'Lucky at play, unlucky in love—and 'God is love.' "

"Listen! he is saying the Black Mass again," cried Ninon, and springing on a table began the Dance of the Postman's Knock, just then the rage of Montparnasse before the infection spread to Paris and London. A Polish youth jumped on to the table opposite and joined her; in a minute the whole café was aflame with it.

Some months before posing nude for Leo Stein in 1908 (see page 102), Nina also appeared as a splash of delight in Crowley's remarkable diary of self-initiation "John St. John" (see pages 211, 223), usually manifesting amid the flurry of the Dôme, to which café Crowley regularly repaired when not focused on attaining samadhi with his "Holy Guardian Angel." Not long after Crowley achieved that communion, Stein, who was attempting to get more in touch with himself through Freudian psychoanalysis, became transfixed hearing Nina tell stories of her amorous escapades. One wonders how—or if—she spoke of the English poet and magician who had, and would, sing Nina's praises for years, until her long and episodic courtship with Stein led eventually, if unpredictably, to marriage in 1921: a dénouement displeasing to the Beast.

A diary entry for January 9, 1924, reveals Crowley making summary notes about events in 1904 and 1908. They end with a reference to Nina. While she was typified in Crowley's 1904 notes as "Queen," his concluding notes to 1908 presented Nina as butt to his perennial sangfroid when confronted with bourgeois marital convention: "Debacle—the spirit fled. Nina dethroned & exiled—married!" Nina's availing herself of social respectability—as Decadent Crowley viewed the marriage tie—doubtless knocked her off a long-cherished visionary pedestal. The dizzy heights of that vision he expressed volubly in a *Vanity Fair* article, "Jeremiah in the Quartier Montparnasse," which appeared on June 3, 1908. Crowley's story recounted meeting "Ninon" that year, after years of separation:

My old friend, the blossom of the Quartier, caught me and kissed me in the midst of the broad boulevard. (Ninon, I will call her, the name is as good as another.) . . . She who had been the blossom of the Quartier, was now its seed, its soul. Perfectly without the consciousness of sin, beautiful without knowing it, hating fine clothes because one cannot romp in them, there was the Child Eternal. . . . A woman she had been at twenty-one; today, at twenty-six, she had become the Avatar of the Quartier. . . . She is yet too young to know—yet she has grown grave, strong, profound; I think she suspects!—she has set herself the hopeless task of bringing one of our modern students to the light of her own wisdom, "all will be well as long as I do what I like." . . . But he is not even an artist; she will soon abandon the unequal contest.*52

To Crowley's delight, Nina had always been generous with her company, and after 1909 she counted as lovers—to Leo Stein's sporadic but tolerant discomfort—not only Hener Skene but also, to Stein's knowledge, a middle-aged Englishman who could hardly live without her and two American artists: sculptor Arthur Lee (1881–1961) and abstract painter Morgan Russell (1886–1953).

Leo Stein shared his and Gertrude's common household and remarkable collection of paintings until 1914 when, with some acrimony (partly over Nina and partly over Gertrude's partner, Alice B. Toklas, whom Leo considered vampiric), Leo relocated to Settignano, near Florence, dividing the art collection, concerning whose judgment in acquisition for the years 1905–1907, Alfred Barr Jr., founding director of New York's Museum of Modern Art, commented, "[Leo Stein was] possibly the most discerning connoisseur and collector of twentieth century painting in the world."53 Now that art historians are beginning to recognize the vital role played by relatively unlauded women in opening the male gaze to beauties other than themselves, we may wonder to what degree it was also the case that behind the acutely discerning eye of Leo Stein there also twinkled the penetrating intelligence of Nina Olivier.†

Crowley's poem *The Star and the Garter* gains in significance when we consider that unlike the somewhat remote, sometimes surgical and

---

*Nina also sparkles in Crowley's dedication to her of the rondel "La Casque d'Or" in *Rodin in Rime*. She also helped to inspire *Clouds without Water* and appeared again as "Ninon" in "Ezekiel in the Quartier Montparnasse," published in *Vanity Fair,* August 12, 1908, p. 211.
†Two years after Leo's death in 1947, Nina Stein committed suicide.

selective manner applied to those events in *Confessions,* the poem is
roughly contemporaneous with the events described. *The Star and the
Garter* reveals Crowley's view of the time that the problem, as he saw it,
with the female students he met in Paris was that they could not separate love and sex. Crowley, on the other hand, saw sex as a physiological
appetite to be sated by mutual agreement, no strings attached, freeing
the mind for loftier engagements. If it served to exalt love, so much
the better, but the demands of *love* were, he believed, essentially spiritual and had to do with ideal spiritual states and could be, and in certain cases should be, divorced from what he called "the caged animal,"
which had the tendency to subdue love for lust's satisfaction that ultimately could not satisfy, being parasitic on good relations. He symbolizes the two states, love and lust, as the Star and the Garter. Virginity,
he would say, has nothing to do with it, a view the "liberated" woman
of a then unseen tomorrow would generally share. One can see, apart
from her lauded honesty, frankness, spontaneous intelligence, sincerity,
and warmth, why Crowley adored Nina Olivier, for Nina, too, found
happiness in what she referred to Leo Stein as "disinterested loves,"[54] a
conception that Leo found extremely difficult but which came naturally
and logically to Aleister Crowley.

The cleverly composed, sometimes lyrical poem dramatizes the
"argument" Crowley expresses in its preface. It begins with an unpleasant silence dividing the poet and "his lady." Wondering as to its cause, he
notices a garter left in the room by another woman. He sees an opportunity for a frank argument that might lead to "better understanding."
The word *love* enters, and he becomes enthusiastic about the idea of
them going off somewhere together; all it takes is courage, rare, he says,
among the bourgeoisie. *She* still wants an explanation for the garter. He
then shows that mental states are not inseparable from a physical basis,
while doubting immortality and free will. She must accommodate the
facts instead of wasting life on an ideal. He says that everything he does
actually subserves his love for her:

> Accept me as I am! I give
> All you can take. If you dislike
> Some fragments of the life I live,
> They are not yours: I scorn to strike

One sword-swift pang against your peace.
See! I'm a mountaineer. Release
That spirit from your bonds: or come
With me upon the mountains, cease
This dull round, this addition sum
Of follies we call France: indeed
Cipher! And if at times I need
The golden dawn upon the Alps,
The gorges of Himalayan rock,
The grey and ancient hills, the scalps
Of hoary hills, the rattling shock
Of avalanche adown the hills—
Why, what but you, your image, fills
My heart in these? I want you there.
For whom but you do I ply pen,
Talk with unmentionable men
Of proofs and types—dull things!—for whom
But you am I the lover? Bloom,
O flower, immortal flower, love, love!
Linger about me and above,
Thou perfumed haze of incense-mist!
The air hath circled me and kissed
Here in this room, on mountains far,
Yonder to seaward, toward yon star,
With your own kisses. Yes! I see
The roseate embroidery
Yonder—I know: it seems to give
The lie to me in throat and teeth.
That is the surface: underneath
I live in you: in you I live.

This (eminently frustrated) assurance elicits approval. He's willing to reveal plainly who the garter's owner is since this person is no more her rival than dinner is her rival. She doesn't grasp the point so he describes the owner, as well as two other mistresses, a model and an acrobat. "Are these rivals in *Love*?" he asks. His lady shouldn't be distracted by physical resemblances; there is no "taint of passion" in his love for her. She feels this due to something *lacking in her* (Crowley's poem "Eileen" in *Rosa Mundi and Other Love Songs* begins "The frosty fingers of the wind"). She "offers her person." He refuses it for fear it will destroy Love, and tries to show her that sexual intimacy is "no truer than virginal intimacy." When he first realized his love for her, the stirrings of passion were "caught and smothered in a higher ecstasy." The "necessary duties of sex could be performed elsewhere." But should they become unnecessary, they could voyage to "solitude and peace." Still, they should, as it were, turn back from Nirvana and not despise others but instead retire and meditate as to how to redeem them. Here is heard the lesson from Buddhism that he's applied to himself: this altercation between poet and true love has real value; it is a "stepping-stone to the ultimate."

Well, that's a message to banjax some romantic women, fascinate others. Crowley was of course idealizing a kind of spiritual union practically remote from ordinary society, and for that reason, the preface to the poem is titled, when translated from Greek: "To the Unknown God" (Acts 17:23). The recurrence of the ideal as the Star we see in *The Book of the Law* a year later, where we learn that "every man and every woman is a star," where the Star is the essential, divine being in Crowleyan metaphysics. Through Eileen, Crowley glimpsed it, and in print, she remains the Star evermore. The poem's last words:

> Be silent, O radiant martyr! Let the world fade slowly
> afar!
> But—had it not been for the Garter, I might never
> have seen
> the Star.

The printed poem of 1904 added a Greek codicil to the initial quotation from Acts where St. Paul pointed to the Athenian altar reserved for the "Unknown God." Paul is replaced by Crowley's new wife, Rose: "Whom therefore [i.e., because of the poem] thou dost ignorantly worship, him do I Rose declare unto thee." The point of this addition is found in a footnote to an appendix that appeared in the second printing of the poem: "A young lady in the Montparnasse Quarter chose to imagine that she was the 'Star' itself; not merely the model for that masterpiece, as was the case." We surely see here a distinction Crowley made to accommodate his love for Rose Kelly, perhaps to reassure his wife that Eileen was no rival. Rose must have known something of Crowley's adoration for Eileen, either from observation or through her brother and mutual friends in Paris. Rose Edith Kelly had every reason to be concerned when Crowley proposed to her in August 1903. Crowley set down in print here that Eileen was not the Star herself, but the "model" for that august being. This, I suspect, gainsays past history and suggests Crowley put the mantle of Star upon Rose, which rather implies a casuistic downgrading of Eileen to Garter: the means to perceive the Star in Rose Kelly. The irony here is that Crowley's love for Rose was passionate indeed; their honeymoon he would describe as an "uninterrupted debauch." The sexually experienced Rose, unlike Eileen and her friends, could both elicit Crowley's deepest love and perform with the skill of a professional when aroused. Her distinction was then, for a time at least, to fuse Crowley's fleshly and transcendent love ideals: perhaps the key characteristic of his nascent Thelema system—that is, identification of flesh and spirit—a religion centered on metaphysical orgasm.

Confusion over Eileen Gray's status in Crowley's life, and his treatment of women in general, also illuminates a detail in an important letter Crowley would write to Kelly the day he married Rose, August 12, 1903, reproduced in its entirety here for the first time:

[Caledonian Hotel notepaper] Bol[eskine] Foyers Aug 12, 03

My dear G

Your note touched me close. I will do what you desire, though I hope you may yet know me better.

If I must weary you, let it be my excuse that *I cannot let pass your statement that Miss Gray was my mistress. She was never anything of the sort, nor within a million miles of it. I never wished it, nor she* [my italics].

Likewise, you are utterly unjust to me in the motive you ascribe to my action of yesterday [eloping with Rose] and today [marrying her]. It is grotesquely untrue. I may have been a pig-fancier in my youth; but for that very reason I should not attempt to make a sow's ear out of a silk purse. It is the ignorant that make such mistakes. I have been trying since I joined G∴D∴ in '98 steadily and well to repress my nature in all ways. I have suffered much, but I have won, and you know it. Coffin-worms and their like are as much chips (as opposed to coins? [Cows?]) to me as to you. I wanted to seal my victory with a very mighty blow. If I failed, it is of over-generosity, over-trust in your *real* friendship for me which you have, after all. There *is* such a place as Inverness, and an early train thither: don't think me a Guido passportless;* and for you, don't let pleurisy get start of Providence.

Let me say one thing; even in so good a cause as yours there are liberties to the liberties one should take with another's property. You are fond of appealing to Back [Dr. Ivor Back, a good friend of Gerald's]: *in this*? Did your sister want to hear the true history of my past life, she should have it in detail; not from prejudiced persons, but the cold drawn stuff of lawyers. And English doesn't *always* fail me.

If your worst wish came true, and we never met again, my remembrances of you, with or without a beard would, as you say, be good enough to go on. But I am ambitious (like the ornithoryness [*ornithorhyncus* = sharp-nosed bird] of Mrs Malaprop) I hope one day to convince you that I am not only a clever (the 4^{tos} [quartos = uncut printed sheets] have "mentally deformed") man but a decent one and a good one. Why must 9/10ths of my life, i.e., the march to Buddhism, go for nothing; the atrophied 1/1,000,000th always spring up & choke me, and that in the house of my friends? For my method I ought to apologise; I had my reasons; but I told you precisely, and you might have seen the Ring, even if you distrusted the Book.†

---

*A reference to character Count Guido Franceschini, impoverished nobleman accused of murdering his adulterous wife, in Robert Browning's verse-novel *The Ring and the Book,* 1869.

†Another reference to Browning's *The Ring and the Book,* itself based on a "yellow book," discovered by Browning, containing witness and legal depositions from the actual case on which Browning based his poem; the "ring" is significant in the story, being at once a ring Browning had made for his great love, Elizabeth Barrett Browning, and a symbol of the making of the story from the "ingot" of raw legal depositions, and the necessary "alloy" of the poet's imagination, for it is his fiction that makes fact alive (the ring symbolizes a corpse raised), just as the jeweler needed to add an alloy to make the gold workable into a ring signifying true love. Crowley wrote a short witty pastiche of Browning's story in an undated letter to Kelly, probably sent from Mexico in 1900 / 01, under the name "Algernon Robert Charles Brinburning" (YC NS4).

All luck, and the greatest place in the new generation of artists be yours.

So sayeth Aleister Crowley, always your friend whatever you may do or say. Vale! Till your Ave!

What, presumably, Crowley meant when he said Eileen wasn't his mistress was that he was content basking in love but did not regard her as a regular route to sexual satiety, reserving the word *mistress* for those identified with the Garter. Other than Nina Olivier, I should say the identities of the English lady fond of ether and the "boot-button girl" cannot be identified with any certainty. I don't think the English lady was Kathleen Bruce (as has been frequently repeated), who in any case was Scottish, with no evidence for ether interest, and Kathleen certainly didn't resemble the tiny tight visage of the girl whose face reminded Crowley of a boot button.

One thing is certain, Crowley's idealized, Buddhistic, and rather formulaic, distinction of Star and Garter took quite a blow when he and Rose crashed into love, an occurrence that very naturally astonished and confused Rose's brother Gerald.

Whether Eileen remained in Crowley's memory years after as Star or Garter, or whether his love for her somehow merged into unexpected happiness with Rose, his feelings do not seem to have made any great difference to Eileen; it was Crowley's mind that interested her. Where Crowley, according to common analysis, made a catastrophe of his own life, Eileen went on to make a great success of hers, winning recognition, after the Great War, for her designs in fabric, furniture, innovative interiors, and architecture, a reputation revived since rediscovery in the seventies. This distinguished daughter of Erin is now reckoned among the greats in her field. It is significant that she kept all the books Crowley gave her, and perhaps treasured memories of him, the depth or otherwise of which we shall probably never know.

SEVEN

Where Soul and Spirit Slip 1903

Crowley worked on his poetic version of the biblical Ahab story in India and Burma in 1901. Completed in Paris on December 9, 1902, and published the following summer as *Ahab and Other Poems,* its dedication to George Cecil Jones suggested Crowley was still, after a month in Montparnasse, "at sea" in himself:

> DEDICACE
> TO G. C. J.
> Pilgrim of the sun, be this thy scrip!
> The severing lightnings of the mind
> Avail where soul and spirit slip,
> And the Eye is blind.

A curious collection, *Ahab* included "Balzac, Hommage à Auguste Rodin," which introduces us to what soon became a preoccupation: cultivation of a creative relationship with the great man whose shockingly innovative sculpture of French writer Honoré de Balzac had, since its first display in 1898, aroused such furious opposition that Rodin withdrew the plaster original to his atelier at Meudon. The fervor Crowley demonstrated as a youth in liberating love from parental interference by forced marriage or prohibition was now directed specifically in the cause of Art: Crowley's "Child" was rising Horus-like, even as he saw in Rodin's sculpture inner being emerging titan-like, from the folds of the repressive world to violate the domination of restricted form. In *Balzac,*

114

Crowley saw a solid reflection of his inner struggle with the "comédie humaine."

A letter of January 14, 1903, from Crowley's rooms at 8 bis rue Campagne Première to Gerald at Camberwell, south London, indicates Kelly's temporary return to his father's rectory, perhaps for a bereavement or Mrs. Blanche Kelly's operation referred to on page 83.

> My dear Gerald,
>
> I was very sorry to hear last night from Simpson* your bad news, though how bad is not very clear. I should like you to remember at such times that sorrow is not less so because unapparent and in my intense happiness of last night (while you were going an unpleasant journey on a bitter errand)—for E[ileen] was with me—there was sorrow implicit therein. I don't know if this sort of thing seems cold comfort: it is all I have to give and is sufficient for myself at all times. And if my comfort is poor my sympathy is large and warm not only for you, for whom I should always cherish the deepest admiration and affection, but for the others of your family, less fortified mentally (for Christian consolation is a poor thing, as far as I have observed its operation) than yourself to oppose a fortress to the battalions of calamity, and to build an island in the seas of sorrow.
>
> Ever yours ever. Aleister Crowley[1]

It may be that Gerald, while in London, became ill, as suggested by a notecard of January 27:

---

*While this might be Alice Isabel Simpson, it's more likely, given later references (see footnotes on pages 117 and 119) to be American Art Association of Paris member, Theodore Spicer Simson (sometimes spelled "Simpson,") medalist, sculptor, painter, illustrator (born Le Havre, 1871–died Florida, 1959), who studied at the École des Beaux Arts 1892–1895, marrying in America and moving back to France in 1896 to live in Montparnasse, where in 1903 he began making portrait medallions on which his reputation rests. The A.A.A.P. exhibited at the church of Notre-Dame des Champs on the Boulevard du Montparnasse. See Theodore Spicer-Simson, *A Collection of Characters: Reminiscences of Theodore Spicer-Simson,* Coral Gables, Fla.: University of Miami Press, 1962. On the A.A.A.P., see Emily C. Burns, "'Of a Kind Hitherto Unknown': The American Art Association of Paris in 1908," *Nineteenth Century Art Worldwide* 14, no. 1 (Spring 2015).

Dear G

On (your concierge) dit [*On dit* = "one says"] that you are ill. Let there be a writing to Crowley by your hand or another to say how things are.[2]

A fascinating letter from the same period indicates Kelly was still in London, for Crowley asks him to "call at Tooks Court," home to the old Chiswick Press. In 1810, Charles Whittingham (1767–1840) of 21 Tooks Court established a printing works at High House in riverside Chiswick Mall. Nephew Charles Whittingham (1797–1876) transferred business from Chiswick to Tooks Court, Chancery Lane. Crowley appreciated the Chiswick Press's having pioneered a market for reasonably priced, finely printed books, often pocket-size. Crowley had ordered a heavy Gothic typeface, but found they'd retained modern type for exclamation and question marks, dashes, and brackets:

Dear G.

Thanks for your two letters. There are one or two waiting you here [at rue Campagne Première]—one from Kite*—what shall I do with them?

---

*Born in Taunton, Devon, Joseph Milner Kite (1862–1945), having enrolled at the Académie Julian in 1883, specialized in Impressionist-style landscapes and portraits. In 1886, inspired by Normandy and Brittany, Kite associated with Roderic O'Conor and the Pont-Aven school favored by Gauguin and the Nabis. Kite returned to the Académie Julian in 1891 and exhibited thereafter. Kite's reception at the informal salon upstairs at Le Chat Blanc, 93 rue d'Odessa, Montparnasse, is described thus in Crowley's satirical *Snowdrops from a Curate's Garden* (1904): "Needless to say, so brilliant a galaxy attracted all the false lights of the time. T— [identified as "one Kite" in *Confessions,* 348] the braggart, the mediocre painter, the lusty soi-disant maquereau of marchionesses, would seek admission (which was in theory denied to none). But the cutting wit of C— [Paul Wayland Bartlett, American sculptor (1865–1925)] drove him headlong, as if by the cherubin, from the gates of the garden of Eden." It appears from an undated card to Kelly, probably from summer 1903 when Crowley was at Boleskine, that *Kelly* was friendly with Kite, for Crowley answers a presumed suggestion of Kite visiting Boleskine: "Kite would be *miserable* here. Abest cauda ["no tail"] *utterly*! I have my own periods of depression. If you can. Avoid fate Bo-peep's sheep A macG [= Aleister MacGregor]." (Letter, YC D6.)

12pp Ahab have arrived. The ? !,—, ( ), are absurdly modern. Shall I get you to design, and have cast, proper types, or shall I use full stops only (to the prejudice of the reader)—and replace the dash & brackets by the hyphen mark—spaced? You might call at Tooks Court & see the proof I am sending back by this post. Thanks for your bibliogr[aphy]. & note. I think you should bring back all M.S.S. of these with you—*especially* Unto us a child is born.

Mater [Latin for "mother"; possibly Mrs. Simpson, or a close female artist (Eileen?), or, most improbably, Crowley's own mother] is breaking down my nerves. Cadell* saved me[x] [top of page: [x] *Me*!!!] from a "crise" last night but to-day I am worn out & v[ery]. ragged. Haweis's party was a great success. S.[†] arrived as Bambinella[‡] & Pollitted[§] C. [?] all night—*un peu trop fort* ["a bit too strongly"]. Miss L.[**] was delicious—I know what you will say, but I would not that you said it.

I can of course do *no* work. Mater gets in about 8 hrs a day hysterics &c &c & I'm going on strike. Carrière[††] is better: so Mrs. B & John [?]. I bid you an a.f[arewell]. My love to all. I have nobody to

---

*Edinburgh-born "Scottish Colourist" Francis Campbell Boileau Cadell (1883–1937) moved to Paris in 1899, enrolling at the Académie Julian; inspired by French Impressionists and Fauvists.

†Possibly Gerald Kelly's mistress and fiancée of 1903, Sibyl Meugens. It is also possible that *S* here refers to Alice Simpson, mother of Crowley's friend Elaine née Simpson, or to American sculptor Theodore Spicer Simson (see page 115).

‡"Bambinella" usually refers to Mary Bambinella: the Virgin Mary as a baby.

§*Pollitted* is obviously a fanciful verb understood by Crowley and Kelly: something to do with behavior typical of Crowley's ex-lover Herbert Pollitt, perhaps referring to impersonation, dancing, cross-dressing, or homosexual advances. If we knew who *C* was, it might help; possibly "Crowley."

**"Miss L" is probably artist Mina Loy (then called "Lowy"), whose beauty obsessed Haweis; four months after having seduced her and got her pregnant, he had to marry her in December 1903.

††Symbolist painter Eugène Anatole Carrière (1849–1906), president of the second Salon d'Automne in 1904, at which Haweis exhibited. Close friend of Rodin who contributed works to the independent salon, Carrière's monochromatic palette influenced Picasso. Crowley met him shortly after the party referred to above, recovering from an operation for throat cancer. Crowley recalled his remark "casual to the point of indifference, 'If it comes back, I shall kill myself'" (Crowley, *Confessions,* 341).

love me and it's rot doing it all in the Chitakesa.* Isn't it? *A.C. very limp*—half-alf!³

It appears from the following (undated) letter from 8 bis rue Campagne Première that Gerald was still away, as Crowley responds to events in London, probably communicated by letter from his friend. The letter suggests Crowley knew something of Rodin's thinking, having perhaps now met Rodin personally or else having been informed via an intermediary such as Haweis or Kathleen Bruce. "Tweed" was Scottish sculptor John Tweed (1869–1933), based in London, who'd gone to Paris in 1893 hoping to study under Rodin, but for which Rodin insisted on four years' commitment. Tweed and family met Rodin in Paris in 1902, sculpting Rodin's profile in a plaster relief (Victoria & Albert Museum). Tweed's reputation grew through friendship with Rodin, which became widely known when that year Tweed organized a banquet in Rodin's honor to celebrate a subscribers' presentation to the South Kensington Museum of a cast of Rodin's *John the Baptist*. So excited were Slade School students that they unharnessed Rodin's carriage from its horses and pulled it triumphantly through the streets. Such appreciation was bound to encourage Anglophilia in a Rodin criticized in France and susceptible to English attention.

Dear G,

Rodin cannot say definitely "Tweed is competent" since Tweed is a young man.† R[odin]. considers, as far as I can judge, that he is the man, *but* should be given time. And for Tweed's sake he will not risk Tweed's reputation by becoming sponsor.

The whole affair is rather Greek to me. Probably the Bishop & Dean & Chapter have put their heads together by now, and the

---

*"Chitakesa," or Sanskrit *chidakasha:* unconditioned, pure consciousness in which duality ceases to exist, or the space of consciousness behind the forehead, accessing higher consciousness or consciousness of senses; the ultimate "Self" shines in the chidakasha.

†On Sunday, October 13, 1907, Crowley had lunch with Tweed in London (see *Aleister Crowley in India,* 399–400). Tweed was perhaps present at Crowley's last raucous encounter with self-styled guru Mahatma Agamya Paramahamsa. The meeting with Tweed was probably occasioned by publication of Crowley's *Rodin in Rime* (1907); Tweed was known as the English Rodin (though Scottish).

statue will not be equestrian. Even Dean Milner (after Palm Sunday) cannot object to anyone riding in on an ass.*

Having spewed forth my venom, I will now turn to the fact that you are still away and that everything is going to hell without you. I am looking after your property as well as I can; am even keeping it in my rooms more than work dictates but it is getting worn out for all that. Come and water it with your tears and wipe it with the hairs of your head. Gavine† is now at St George's Hospital. She is quite well and in good spirits, having preached a sermon to her people on the text "And he arose and smote him." But this is all very sad: the Salon [Salon d'Automne] must have a Kelly in it: Must. Commissions and cash and therefore independence hang thereon: and I have the selfish reason that I am personally very keen on your future. So come quickly. The Spirit and the Bride say: Come! And whosoever will, let him take the water of St Gaulinier [an eau de cologne?] freely.‡ Even "*so,*"!!! come, Lord Jesus. I am "*the same*" yesterday today and for ever." *Exactly*! That is why Bambinella S.P.P.ed. [*sic*] He took his trousers off and played Blind Man's Buff for Buggers: so he tried to do it on the staircase. We wrote to White Hat§ (not White Head) explaining—he, being a very cautious man, must be pleased that he gave it away to us so completely in a few hours. Your ever Aleister Crowley.⁴

---

*There was no "Dean Milner" of St. Paul's in 1903 at the time of the sculpture controversy. Crowley possibly refers to someone he and Kelly probably knew as legendary Cambridge intellect, mathematician, inventor, and evangelical, Isaac Milner, Dean of Carlisle (1750–1820), President of Queen's College, Cambridge, Lucasian professor of mathematics, who converted William Wilberforce to the antislavery movement on Christian grounds. Dean Milner followed and articulated the evangelism of "Cambridge prophet," Charles Simeon. It was, of course, Jesus who entered Jerusalem "on an ass" on Palm Sunday.

†"Gavine" refers to Jessie Gavin, lover of Eileen Gray. By adding the *e* to her name, Crowley almost certainly puns *Gavin* with *gamine*—a gamine being a slim young woman, attractively boyish, and mischievous (Crowley had earlier recommended that Kelly take a gamine as a model, see page 55).

‡Crowley is parodying Revelation 22:17: "let him take the water of life freely."

§In a card from "8bis" to Kelly dated January 27, 1903: "Simpson [probably U.S. sculptor Theodore Spicer Simson; see page 115] went as d'Artagnan into the S.P.P. [Sucker's Piss Pot?] & has not been seen since. We now know why Miller wears a white hat. They are both N.B.U. [No Bloody Use?] & L.B.O. [?]" (YC D6). "Miller" is likely American Impressionist painter Richard Edward Miller (1875–1943), then studying at the Académie Julian.

Crowley's reference to "Bishop, Dean and Chapter" refers to a controversy that erupted in 1903 when John Tweed's name was mooted to complete his late friend Alfred Stevens's memorial to the Duke of Wellington in St. Paul's Cathedral. Principal objection was Wellington's image being *mounted* in a sacred building (note Crowley's joke about the "ass" on page 119, explained in the footnote) in addition to reservations over Tweed's competence to complete Stevens's memorial; hence, the argument involved Rodin.

TO NICE

There seems no particular reason why Crowley left Paris for a holiday in Nice and Monte Carlo in February 1903, though mention of attending a masked ball suggests an invitation. Encounters with former Boleskine houseguest Humphrys from Cambridge may also have decided it. Frustration probably stimulated recourse to "garter" treatment after a period of relative restraint.

Girded by steep hills, the brand-new, six-story palatial Hotel Impérial in the Piol district's Parc Impérial provided as grandly expansive a location as could be imagined in the Belle Époque, an era the like of which will never occur again, though Crowley was not overly impressed.

He wrote on a Saturday to Gerald, now back in Paris:

Dear G,

Nothing in this leprous hole so amusing as to write to you. I enjoyed the masked ball on ♂ [Tuesday] since then I bask and sleep all day and night. Hope to go to Monte tomorrow. I shall break the bank— my bank. O it's deadly dull.

With Humphreys [*sic*] for one's only acquaintance—figure to yourself! Yes, Humphreys.* He has forgiven our "little French

---

*William Evans Hugh Humphrys, twenty-six-year-old Cambridge contemporary, motor enthusiast, and journalist whom Crowley hadn't seen since, presumably, 1900 (see page 40, including footnote). He'd motored all the way to Nice—remarkable in 1903. Nice had a large Automobile Club, which in April launched delayed tour-races to Monte Carlo; such might have stimulated Humphrys's tour.

Fig. 7.1. The Hôtel Impérial, Nice.

milliner" joke. I would even now to a Great Anticlimax but all the lydies [cockney accent for "ladies"] are of the sort so masterly described in Alice Intro.* You pays your money—and you does not take your choice. So knowing these, I forbear. Luckily last night a w.d. [wet dream?] came to my relief: But I am gorgeously dull today. Sun makes up for a lot, though. You may expect me back confidently before long, I think. My laziness alone prevents my coming this week. I hope you're working well. How's the G[rea]t. Illusion [Sibyl?]? My own [Eileen?] is pretty sick—it could never be. How sad & mad & bad it was. But then how it was sweet. But I see nothing in the world of Gods nor of Demons nor of men nor of material things nor of immaterial things which abideth not Impermanence. Anicca [Impermanence in Buddhism], Dukkha [Sorrow], Anatta [no permanent soul]! Aum [ultimate reality]! So long. I feel well, as a hog is well. Yrs ever as ever AC[5]

"I am beginning to doubt whether Nice is dull after all"—so Crowley wrote in jocular fashion to Gerald on a day that began badly,

---

*Introduction to *Alice: An Adultery* (1903), for whose introduction Kelly wrote a tongue-in-cheek "Brief Critical Essay."

playing billiards "in despair." His cue cut the cloth for the first time in his life—something, curiously, dreamed during his Far Eastern travels. Sneaking away undetected, he took refuge in the reading room and tore a newspaper: "In disgust, I went out, met a charming girl and had a real good old-fashioned face fuck in the grounds." This did not, I suspect, refer to french-kissing. Returning to tea, "fearful of the fatal third tearing," he ripped the tablecloth with his penknife—but the day was not entirely lost. He "made a successful evening of it" by preaching the "Good Law" to Humphrys—the "Law" being the *dhamma* (Pali for the Buddhist universal law). Things improved markedly: Crowley won five francs at the "Little Horses," most likely at nearby Cagnes-sur-Mer hippodrome where the *petit chevaux* pulled drivers in two-wheeled sulkies. Flush with success, Crowley met "the girl I'd been hunting ever since the Masked Ball," before meeting a third girl, and "getting another v[ery].g.o-f .f.f."—doubtless among the characteristic "vulgarisms" referred to by Kelly some sixty years later to Jean Overton Fuller (see page 51).

Gerald was also informed:

As for Monte [Carlo]: I hope to go to-morrow: but Humphreys [*sic*] has promised to motor me over in a day or two: so I may wait. Needless to say, I don't play a system [at the casino]: in vain you reproach me with "It is the Pyrrhonism of a Pilate." I shall lump the lump I mean to lump and then loop the loop I mean to loop. But I have a system which cannot lose. I play a louis [gold coin]—anywhere—if I win, I win: if I lose, I Léonce de Miranda* for that time—expecting no miracle, as I do not accept MacGregor's [probably Mathers's] idea of a female Holy Ghost. That is all my system, and it never fails. If the genito-urinary system fails, that is not my fault and there is always Dr Paterson and the Injection Payrat.

---

*Léonce de Miranda is principal character in Browning's blank verse poem *Red Cotton Night-Cap Country* (1873) in which guilt-laden Miranda, torn between religion and earthiness, throws himself off a priory as an act of faith, believing he'll be caught by angels and carried to his church.

Crowley's letter about Monte also contains a rare reference to contemporary music. Readers will recall it was precisely at this time (late winter 1903) that critical attention turned favorably toward Debussy's opera *Pélleas and Mélisande,* something Crowley might have gleaned from the newspaper he tore; perhaps it explains the tearing! "Away with this new-fangled Melisande Friggery!" he ejaculated, "(and you can tell E[ileen] (& S[ibyl]) I said so)." Perhaps he was annoyed by the somewhat nihilistic psychology in Maeterlinck's story, where, having lost her lover at her husband's hand, Mélisande approaches death with no recognition of what's occurred, reflecting the author's suspicion that human beings understand neither the world they're living in, nor each other, nor themselves; not simply because of human weakness but because there *is* no definite reality to be known. While such might have resonated with Crowley's Buddhism (impermanence and anatta), he nonetheless needed ideas with a definite shape, looking to science for clarity and reality. His mind was in conflict with itself— an abiding frustration:

> I resume Saturday, after the best girl game. By an artifice I shall have secured another v.g. o-f. f.f. with the accent on each word separately accentuated. But, fine as the weather is, a place may be *too* hot for one, and the moral of that is, I am off to Monte Carlo to win or— lose (die is absurd) & then p.d.q. [pretty damn quick] back to Paris where obscurity may help me and blot the hole where I squat. Of course if I won very largely, I might liquidate the Hotel & hold high my head amongst honest men again.[6]

In a Monte Carlo casino, he wrote a "Rondel," published in his 1905 collection, *Oracles: Biography of an Art,* from which these lines are taken:

> There is no hell but earth: O coil of fate
> Binding us surely in the Halls of Birth,
> The unsubstantial, the dissolving state!
> There is no hell but earth.

Vain are the falsehoods that subserve to mirth.
Dust is to dust, create or uncreate.
The wheel is bounded by the world's great girth.
By prayer and penance unregenerate,
Redeemed by no man's sacrifice or worth,
We swing: no mortal knows his ultimate.
There is no hell but earth.

One can see the roulette wheels spinning like the dharmachakra amid hot cigar smoke and pungent perfumes.

Crowley returned to Paris to pick up the pieces.

EIGHT

✡

Rodin

Probably back in Paris by February 25, he was in good time to receive word from Auguste Rodin penned that day:

> Dear Monsieur Crowley,
>
> By the same post I'm sending Marcel Schwob—11 rue Saint-Louis-en-l'Isle—the two sonnets that you had the kindness to compose for me.
>
> > Yours very sincerely,
> > A. Rodin[1]

Fig. 8.1. Auguste Rodin in middle age, Tucker Collection, New York Public Library Archives.

125

Here is Crowley's homage to Rodin, before Schwob translated it:

RODIN

Here is a man! For all the world to see
His work stands, shaming Nature. Clutched,
    combined
In the sole still centre of a master-mind,
The Egyptian force, the Greek simplicity,
The Celtic subtlety. Through suffering free,
The calm great courage of new art, refined
In nervous majesty, indwells behind
The beauty of each radiant harmony.

Titan! the little centuries drop back,
Back from the contemplation. Stand and span
With one great grip his cup, the Zodiac!
Distil from all time's art his wine, the truth!
Drink, drink the mighty health—an age's youth—
Salut, Auguste Rodin! Here is a man.

Forty-six years later, Sir Gerald Kelly didn't miss a trick in demolishing the poet, his former friend, commenting on passages in *Confessions* concerning Marcel Schwob and the great sculptor, both of whom Crowley humbly praised without reserve:

Another illusion—Rodin accepted money for some of his statuettes, but had little use for the poems, except as possible advertisements. Marcel Schwob hated having to translate the sonnets. A.C. is credulous enough to attach any meaning to Marcel Schwob's polite statement that *Alice* was a "little masterpiece." Poor A.C. He evidently doesn't know about Paris and literary life there.

Rodin invited A.C. to Meudon? Surely not—or, maybe, for a day. I know that I had to bargain with R[odin]. for the bronzes A.C. bought.

    Marcel Schwob told me he thought A.C. ridiculous and a bad poet—but that he had *had* to translate the sonnets.[2]

With respect to the view ascribed by Kelly to Schwob in 1949, Crowley wasn't a "bad" poet, though he knew, and expressed realistically and humbly to Kelly by letter in 1905, that he only very rarely created lines worthy of the poets he most admired: Shelley, Browning, Swinburne; time, he believed, would judge the rest (see page 197). Furthermore, contemporary evidence does not support Kelly's dismissal of Crowley's judgment. Whether Rodin was just "being polite" or not, here follow two letters Rodin wrote to Crowley on reading Schwob's translations (Rodin had no English). The first, Crowley included in his deluxe edition of *Rodin in Rime* (Chiswick Press, 1907), which included the two sonnets translated by Schwob (the other was "Balzac"), eighteen "Divers Measures" (including one, "The Golden Casket," dedicated to Nina Olivier), and twenty "Sonnets and Quatorzains," including nine poetic representations of Rodin's sculptures, the which Crowley translated himself into French at Rodin's request in 1907. Pride of billing was accorded seven watercolor nudes from ten Rodin presented to Crowley in 1903, crafted into luminous lithographs by Auguste Clot in Paris.

182, rue de l'Université

My dear Crowley,

Your poetry has this violent flower, this good sense, and this irony, which is unexpected.

It's of a powerful charm and resembles a beneficent attack.

Your poetry is therefore violent, and this side pleases me too.

I am honoured that you took my drawings and am also honoured in your book.

Yours, AUG. RODIN

Having read Schwob's translations—arguably undertaken because Rodin sent him the manuscript (though presumably Crowley requested Rodin convey the sonnets to Schwob, who'd doubtless been asked)—Rodin wrote the following to Crowley on March 14, 1903:

182, rue de l'Université, March 14, 1903

Dear Monsieur A. Crowley,

I've read two sonnets translated and copied with care on luxury paper, sent by Monsieur Marcel Schwob who seems to me to have interpreted the poet magnificently.

You have composed two sonnets which are two corollary works to mine, they really express that we breathe the same air. I haven't found a comparable eloquence for mystery and energy veiled with poetry, which makes the impression moving and indefinite.

Of the rest, dear sir and friend, I make praise for your *sonnets,* of your *poetry,* even better in my plaster.

> Accept my feelings of recognition
> from sculptor to poet,
> Aug. Rodin[3]

This is one of ten letters that Rodin sent Crowley and preserved in the Yorke Collection, Warburg Institute: two from 1903, one from 1904, the remainder from 1907, in which Rodin writes of Crowley as "dear Poet," "dear and great poet," "my dear friend," "my dear artist and friend, with warm memories," "my dear monsieur Crowley, friend, with all warmth and sympathy," "my dear friend, in cordiality and artistic sympathy," among other friendly and respectful phrases. Such mutual recognition does not encourage us to accept Kelly's arguably denigrating and cynical comments as altogether true. Furthermore, as we shall see, in April 1903, Schwob took Crowley into his inner sanctum and assisted him gracefully with publicity.

We've heard from Crowley of his attending one of Stephen Haweis's fancy-dress parties with Sibyl Meugens and Eileen Gray (and possibly Theodore Spicer Simson). Written by Haweis for July 1918's *Vanity Fair,* "Reminiscences of Auguste Rodin" told of Haweis's visits to Rodin's Villa des Brillants at Meudon to photograph his work, later treated for artistic effect with sometime photographic partner Henry Coles, whom Crowley nicknamed "Mrs. Coles" for some reason (see page 174). This was the same period when an awe-filled Crowley likewise observed the master at work. Haweis described Rodin as "a Nature worshipper," loving equally the beauty of *La Pensée* and the ugliness of *The Man with a Broken Nose.* He knew body and soul were one, that "they were one with all that has life, and if that One were not God, he knew no other." Crowley would similarly root his philosophical system in the idea of a universal continuum in nature, where occult knowledge was inseparable from the observable universe. Crowley, however, found Rodin's statements about his art amusingly simplistic. He held Rodin's art to be intuitive, not intellectual: works of genius synthesized by the energies of his subconscious from data absorbed. Thus, Crowley privately dismissed as "puerile platitudes" Rodin's stammered statements such as "nature is the great teacher."[4] Crowley jested never having met anyone so intellectually ignorant of art as Rodin; he was *better than that.* He'd left the prigs behind. Crowley maintained that what Rodin did with *Balzac,* for example, was to suggest "through the medium of form" the "spiritual abstraction" of the *real man* behind the *Comédie Humaine.*[5] Balzac's *actual* features were a *veil,* insisted Crowley, both getting the point and defining the point of magic. Shakespeare would still be Shakespeare if he had no face, Crowley insisted. The theory here of abstracted essence expressed in form—or the symbol recovered—is that of Symbolism, and if one fails to grasp that, one will never grasp Crowley, lover of Baudelaire. The Egyptian gods, for example, were to Crowley expressions in art of abstracted cosmic formula, or as Newton maintained: the original religion and the original science were *one.* As Wittgenstein would maintain two decades later, "the world is everything that is the case," indeed, but Crowley would add, there's more to "everything" than meets the eye. Gold exists where nothing appears to glisten.

Haweis remarks on Rodin's happiness in having his work, and himself, photographed, so long as it was done well, recalling: "The best portrait I made of him was from a peculiarly bad negative taken in his dressing gown against the rising sun, as he stood in the field behind the Villa des Brillants at Meudon. He wore, I remember, a huge pair of sabots [wooden peasant clogs] to protect him from the dew."[6] Rodin's cottage next to the studio was unfurnished, but for myriad artworks given him or which he'd bought from the officially despised Salon des Indépendants. One can see why Crowley liked him. Crowley would harangue an ambitious Gerald Kelly with Browning's poem about "what we have lost" for a "riband"; that is, what an artist surrenders of him or herself and the truth for public recognition. If officialdom "passed" a work of art, it probably meant it was, whether well or poorly painted, conformist to acceptable fashion, but, of course, and very naturally, both Crowley and Rodin relished recognition, though neither would change their ways to achieve it. Crowley *would* be recognized, but as a caricature; the veil has seldom been rent, and publicly, never. The image sells the man out. Rodin saw further.

According to Haweis, Rodin "loved flattery, as all human beings do, and would listen attentively to rhapsodies from almost anybody, though they do say a pretty lady got more attention from him than a half-starved journalist." Undoubtedly flattered by Crowley's attention, did he not also see peculiar genius in the "violent" poetry of his atypical visitor, one among so many to pour through his studio on Saturday? When Haweis met him, Rodin had only recently returned from being fêted by admirers in London. Surely Rodin could tell the difference between the Lord Mayor of London who introduced him to the pleasure of turtle soup, and Aleister Crowley.

Where Crowley found it remarkable to see Rodin respond to a piece of music with a hand gesture, as though music immediately registered to him as sculpted form—that is to say, Rodin perceived *universality* in all arts—Kelly dismissed Crowley's observation as an embarrassing commonplace . . . at least he did years later, after achieving numerous ribands.

Haweis mentions the domestic devotions of Rodin's longtime loving housekeeper, Rose Beuret, whom Haweis calls Madame Rosa, mother of Rodin's son (Rodin only married Rose two weeks before her death in 1917; he died shortly after). No one seems to have noticed a possible link here with Crowley's using three of the ten Rodin lithographs to adorn three anonymously published poems inspired by *his* wife Rose: "Rosa Mundi," "Rosa Coeli," and "Rosa Inferni." Crowley's *Rodin in Rime* also included the poem "Madame Rodin," which observes that "behind the great, is the good." One wonders: When Crowley first found love with Rose Kelly in August 1903, did he also see the woman at Meudon who'd been Rodin's passionate lover when young, who'd since accommodated his loves for other women, particularly beautiful assistant and fellow sculptor Camille Claudel, who, anguished with jealousy, left Rodin in 1893 to later lose her mind through failing to possess the man? Is this not the Star and the Garter as perennial dilemma?

Fig. 8.2. Camille Claudel (1864–1943), sculptor, aged twenty-one, by César.

Depth of commonality linking Crowley and Rodin has not passed entirely unvalued in the nearly 120 years of Sodom that separate us from their present. Crowley—prophet without honor in his own country, certainly, but a recent essay by poet, editor, writer, and self-described "sophist" André Murcie, born in Ariège in 1951, hears a different drum: "49 toasts pour un siècle qui s'éloigne" ("49 toasts for a century that drifts away: Rodin/Crowley: an exemplary encounter") introduces *Le Dit de Rodin* (2018), the only French version of *Rodin in Rime*, empathetically translated by Philippe Pissier.

Murcie first notices Crowley's "congenial immodesty" but considers it saved him from mediocre contemporaries: "unfading is the pride of poets," Murcie reminds us, and asks whether one could imagine two more dissimilar characters than Crowley and Rodin side by side. The idea of a sulfurous mage or apocalyptic beast in his atelier would, one would think, make Rodin hasten to eject him, but "decidedly, Crowley will always surprise us."[7]

A few weeks before Rodin met Crowley, Rodin had another visitor, one of the century's great poets (which Crowley would never be), Rainer Maria Rilke, born the same year as Crowley. Whereas today those who are desperate to give meaning to our epoch find more help in Rilke than Rodin, in 1902, Rilke, Rodin, and Crowley were, as Murcie observes, on the same shore, with Rilke and Crowley both attracted by the "Baudelairean pharos of Rodin," as Murcie puts it. But

Symbolism was fading even before romanticism fell in Flanders fields, torching a vast epoch of artistic drama amid mud, rubble, and grave.

Crowley had the perception to see the end of an epoch, but was he, like Rodin, at its end, or sign of a new beginning? He would in the future take *himself* as sign or "logos" of a new "aeon," but he carried the old one in his poetry, until eventually loosing grip on the unequal struggle with changing times and declining fortune before the first *aeon-war* (as he saw it) began. But in 1902, there was still some futuristic shine left on the Wagnerian dream of "total art," even though the Mallarmé who'd sojourned in Manet's studio was now dead, and Villiers de l'Isle-Adam, who'd been received by Wagner, was long gone. And here we have at Meudon, again, notes Murcie (with the Renaissance in mind) the poet and the sculptor, the latter describing their works as mutual "corollaries." What more in tune with total art could it be for Crowley to create *Rodin in Rime* (with Crowley dismissing the modern spelling of *rhyme* as pretentious), unapologetic, rough, direct: *Rodin in Rime* was what you got, and Rodin responded, and asked for more, despite the artists' very different sensibilities.

"Health and sickness," notes Murcie, are two sides of the same coin; that is, while Nietzsche was philosopher of decadence and nihilism, he also upheld joy and life. The dejected writer of "Summa Spes" needed a shot in the arm. A balance twixt nothingness and joy, precarious as it may be to bear emotionally, is the tightrope Crowley trod, essential to his doctrine, 0=2, the incompatible compatible, the magical reversal of exiting orders, the alogical positive nothing: "delicious languor, force and fire, are of us" (*AL* II:20).* How can langor lie with force? Look at Rodin's work! No, you need not; it bears down on you: energy, "in your face," like being brought up short by the inhuman stones of Avebury on a dark night.

Murcie recognizes that a current passed between the two men, a "poetic idyll" not born of accident.[8] Alphonse Legros, Slade professor of art, invited Rodin to London in 1881, introducing him to poet William Ernest Henley and novelist Robert Louis Stevenson, who departed for Polynesia taking a mental image of Henley that became *Treasure Island*'s Long John Silver. Marcel Schwob gave Crowley the prized introduction to Henley, whom Crowley visited near Woking on returning to England;

The Book of the Law is abbreviated in citations as *AL*.

humbled in his presence, Crowley could hardly speak. When the old man advised Crowley to ditch the sonnet form in favor of the quatorzain, and to desist from reproducing his Rodin poetry in French, Crowley complied.

Did Crowley see in Rodin's body-to-body working of tough material into "flesh" a parallel with his mountaineering, as well as with his poetry? All three quests aimed at a summit, requiring body-to-rock contact, intense states, and will to live and overcome obstacles, to reach for what ordinary men thought impossible.

For Crowley, poetry was largely a technical accomplishment, and once climbed, one descended quickly. Murcie suggests that Crowley's facility of execution delighted Rodin; Crowley seldom resisted excessive verbosity when reaching for or experiencing inspiration. Was this comparable to Rodin's superabundant energy applied to several statues simultaneously? For Rodin, however, a work was never finished; public exhibition was, Murcie writes, "a regrettable interruption." Crowley, conversely, disliked editing and in the early years was mostly content with Gerald Kelly's comments, while Kelly's friend Ivor Back (1879–1951) made cuts in the oeuvre in summer 1904 for the "collected works" (1905–1906). Being an obstetrician and surgeon, editing was a fitting pastime for Back— and Crowley needed the help, for he was never really sure which bits were good, and which required time's perspective to reveal their value, if any. He didn't like to interfere with these extensions of his subconscious, hoping discerning readers might see into the material, beyond the veil of words to the active consciousness struggling for the stars beneath them. Few realize the excesses of his *Confessions* exist largely because he never found anyone willing to fashion them into the great work he knew lay within the colossal empire of material he'd spewed forth amid the extremities of 1922–1924. Murcie believes a "community of artistic references" united Crowley and Rodin *unconsciously:* a hidden life within the material both beautiful and true.[9]

There was more: when Rodin adopted perhaps the biggest work of his life, *La Porte de l'Enfer,* he consciously chose the gate of hell over paradise—a "promethean sign of revolt" after the death of his elder sister when he was twenty-two. Rodin had thought of taking the novitiate; a superior advised the profane world of sculpture. "Thank God!" cries Murcie, who notes that Crowley, after a puritanical upbringing, likewise took the "infernal choice,"[10] identifying with the apocalyptic beast: better hell than the heaven of Plymouth Brethren! But Rodin was not anti-Christian; the "metaphysics of sex" did not preoccupy him as it did the young Beast whose mother insisted that her son understand *ladies had no legs*.

Force and fire . . . Murcie, writing about "Balzac," is reminded of Victor Hugo's words: "I am a force which goes." For Crowley, the true will does not ask, it goes. After taking up painting in 1917, he said the artist's task was to paint the "will" and give it form; it helped if the form were recognizable; the abstract deserved form the natural mind could enter. Murcie says that, unlike Rodin, Crowley never confounded will and desire; rather, as he puts it, "the will of the desire was superior to the desire of the will."[11] Crowley recognized in Rodin's *Balzac* the triumph, and posterity has judged that after it, Rodin progressed no more, except in technique, sensitivity. Crowley would say he'd seen the Star, and the Star had seen him.

Such occurred to Crowley in April 1904, in Cairo. As Murcie puts it succinctly: "It's there, on the 8, 9, 10 April 1904, that Crowley becomes Crowley." The Mage supplants the poet, Murcie notes, and his preoccupations are more prophetic than poetic. However, in contrast to Victor Hugo's new religion in *La Fin de Satan* and *Dieu: Solitudines Coeli*, Crowley's revelation does not seek to convert; his writings contain less catechism than Nietzsche's "fifth gospel," *Thus Spake Zarathustra*.[12]

Launched in 1903, Crowley never surrendered the *Rodin in Rime* lithograph series, corresponding with the sculptor until after completion four years later. He didn't let the old man down: Rodin would see his statues become literature. And today, Murcie notes, we're invited "to listen to the clear laughter of these two titans, we, orphans of our own past," assailed with problems seemingly intractable, "we only have as weapon and inheritance, the reminiscence of their legendary stature."[13]

NINE

Le Chat Blanc

Close to the Louvre, across the rue de Rivoli from the Jardin des Tuileries, Léonard Tauber's Grand Hotel Régina hadn't been open three years when on Tuesday, March 24, 1903, Crowley, sheltering from an unseasonal heat wave, was recognized in its handsome restaurant by Major General Sir Hector Archibald Macdonald, K.C.B., D.S.O. (1853–1903). A popular hero in Scotland for being the only British general to have risen through the ranks, he'd been raised at a croft not far from Crowley's Boleskine estate. They'd have had plenty to discuss; Macdonald was the army's commander in chief in Ceylon, where Crowley had spent summer 1901 with Allan Bennett.

On March 27, *L'Écho de Paris* reported:

SUICIDE OF GENERAL MACDONALD

Put in a coffin—The body at the Gare du Nord

The body of English General Macdonald rested all day yesterday at the hotel Regina. At three o'clock, permission to inter was delivered and the body was soon placed in a coffin in the presence of Monsieur Egarteler, commissioner of police, his secretary Monsieur Baillet, and a representative of England's ambassador.

During the night, the body was transported to a mortuary depot, General Macdonald having expressed the desire that his remains be interred in Paris.

No seals were affixed to the room; no important documents were

135

found in the suitcase that constituted the general's entire baggage. Only two little notes in English have been seized by the police commissioner. It's been said a photograph of a particular nature was found in the general's pocket. This detail has been recognized as inaccurate. It must have come from the imagination of an overly inventive reporter.

Some persons recently arrived from Ceylon recount that in the colony where Macdonald commanded, the rumor was that he was accused not only of bad morals, but also of having squandered quite considerable funds of which he was custodian.

Retiring to his room after speaking with Crowley, Macdonald shot himself there next day. Crowley was likely the last person with whom he conversed. Page 3 of the previous day's paper (March 26) reported that the general had left Ceylon for London seeking justification from his peers against accusations of homosexual acts. From London he'd come alone to the Regina. "Yesterday morning, around ten o'clock, he received a telegram. A little after, a domestic entered his room and found the general stretched out on a sofa, shot in his right temple. The revolver had fallen to the floor." There seemed little doubt that the telegram precipitated the act.

L'Écho de Paris believed it knew the general had been informed that the accusations were taken seriously, exposing him to "the pains which hit English poet Oscar Wilde, whose trial was so controversial eight years ago."

The hotel kept his death hidden while the corpse remained. The paper learned it was the general's first stay at the hotel, to which he'd given his real name and rank. Not saying how long he intended to stay, he took a room by the mezzanine on the rue des Pyramides.

Macdonald was described as one of the bravest and most popular generals in the British army. Joining the Gordon Highlanders at eighteen, he'd become a sergeant during the Afghan War, later distinguishing himself for courage at Majuba Hill in the first Boer War. Rising to colonel, he commanded the Egyptian brigade during the 1898 Khartoum expedition. Covered with decorations, including the Victoria Cross and the Order of the Bath, he wasn't yet fifty when appointed general after thirty years battle service for England. Consulting with Lord Roberts about the accusations, Roberts had advised he return to Ceylon by the shortest route. Macdonald requested a court-martial composed of officers from India. "The general left London on Friday morning and arrived the same evening in Paris. One knows the rest."

Crowley believed the immediate cause was "an outrageously outspoken" article against Macdonald published in the *New York Herald*'s French edition the morning after they met. The paper's front page showed his picture, stated he'd decided to return to Ceylon to face a court-martial, and made public the charges:

> The purport of the charges cannot be entered into here, but it may be stated that; while they do not constitute an offense under the laws of Ceylon, they are criminally punishable at home.

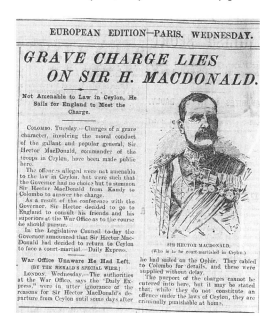

Fig. 9.1. *The* New York Herald*'s announcement of charges against Sir Hector Macdonald.*

Crowley may have been right about the immediate cause. The day after the suicide the *New York Herald,* under the headline HE BLOWS OUT HIS BRAINS IN HIS BEDROOM IN THE HOTEL REGINA, stated: "With a copy of the HERALD lying near him, containing the news from Colombo that charges of a grave character had been made in public against him . . . &c." The paper implied the act had to do with subheadline *Reading Colombo Telegram.* The two notes had nothing to do with the affair, the paper said, but mentioned "fancy" pictures found in the general's pocket. The description of the shooting was different: shot himself standing before a mirror with his jacket and vest off, said the *Herald*. According to the *Herald:* "He was, however, seen in one of the corridors yesterday morning, and again about noon. On the latter occasion he had in his hand the open paper [*Herald*], on the first page of which the Ceylon dispatch was printed alongside his photograph. A few moments after this the shot was heard."

Crowley himself returned to Ceylon at the year's end, where at Colombo's Galle Face Hotel he encountered a deputation of elders from Macdonald's Highland home, greatly perturbed by the number of witnesses testifying against him, after his death, at the tribunal. Crowley consoled his Scottish neighbors, observing that in Ceylon, the more witnesses the more likely it was they'd been bribed.

Nine days before Macdonald's suicide, *L'Écho de Paris* (*Journal Littéraire et Politique du Matin;* Monday, March 16, 1903), devoted a couple of columns to its society gossip column, "Lettres à Valmont," attributed to Marquise de Merteuil, a character from epistolary novel *Les Liaisons dangereuses.* Following an account of Robert, Comte de Montesquiou-Fézensac's poetic talk on "Mystery" and the beauties of France at Louis Sherry's restaurant, 5th Avenue, New York, attended by Prince Sapieha of Lithuania, sculptor Prince Paul Troubetzkoï, the Madames Astor, Whitelaw Reid (former U.S. ambassador to France), Cornelius Vanderbilt III, Lady Bache Cunard (mother of Nancy), Symbolist painter Edmond Aman-Jean, American novelist Francis-Marion Crawford, and British novelist Richard Le Gallienne, the "Marquise" addressed Paris's artistic scene:

> Our dear Paris remains always, you see, Valmont [the Marquise's imaginary correspondent], despite her caprices for negro dances, the eternal home of Beauty. In the end, it is to her all these errant children come, as an indulgent mother to the worst excesses of art. Sometimes it is the "enfants terribles" she adopts, terrible and charming, like Miss Barney [Natalie Clifford Barney, 1876–1972] who simultaneously adores both the gods of Greece and the unknown god of Anarchy, or Miss Hannah Lynch [Irish born writer, 1859–1904], who strongly disconcerted Monsieur Bergeret,* last month, when speaking of his books with somewhat Irish license.

---

*Probably a reference to novelist Anatole France (1844–1924), whose 1901 novel *Monsieur Bergeret à Paris* dealt partly autobiographically with the notorious Dreyfus Affair.

It is to Paris that the seekers of the infinite find their refuge. Is this not why Aleister Crowley comes to us, this English poet of Celtic blood, who has sung the glory of Rodin having descended from an audacious 7,000-meter ascent on K2 of the Himalayas? Aleister Crowley seems a fair brother to Maurice Maeterlinck, pale, thin, and firm as an arrow-shaft; his poems of a sensual metaphysic which exalt themselves to the peaks of the Earth and of Art; and, after having thought amongst us about some new drama, he departs again for India, to conquer Gaurishankar.*

Thanks to prolific journalist and short-story writer Marcel Schwob, Aleister Crowley's next appearance in a Parisian newspaper occurred ten days after meeting the general. Regarded as precursor to the surrealists, influential on writers Jorge Luis Borges and Roberto Bolaño, Mayer André Marcel Schwob (1867–1905), despite anti-Semitic prejudice, remained familiar with every literary and artistic luminary in Paris, as well as outstanding visitors to Paris. Indeed, it was at one of what Crowley calls Schwob's "afternoons" (either at home or visiting Kelly's studio) that Crowley met Staffordshire-born writer Arnold Bennett (1868–1931), then riding on the success of novels *Anna of the Five Towns* (about real life in Stoke-on-Trent) and a novel Crowley liked, *The Grand Babylon Hotel* (1902). Crowley seems to have liked Bennett, though was snooty about Bennett's north-Staffordshire accent, commenting two decades later in *Confessions* that Bennett was

> very ill at ease to find himself in Paris in polite society. He must have had a perfectly lovely time; everything was alike a source of innocent wonder. He was very much pleased by the generous measure of respect which he received on all hands simply for being a novelist. His speech and his appearance attracted no insult from literary circles in Paris.[1]

That Crowley suggests he felt himself perfectly at ease in Parisian literary circles owed much to the kindness of Schwob, who, at his home on the Île St. Louis, hosted an interview so journalist and poet Fernand

---

*Gaurishankar is the second-highest peak of the Rolwaling Himal.

Hauser (1869–1941) could meet Himalayan-explorer Crowley. This encouraging act and its outcome hardly suggests that Kelly's revisionist account of Schwob's attitude to Crowley was entirely fair.*

Beneath the headline RETURN FROM THE HIMALAYAS / A POET TRAVELER / *At the home of Monsieur Marcel Schwob / The Irish poet Crowley / On the mountains / At a height of 8000 meters / Buddhist?* Hauser's long article appeared on pages 1 and 3 of *La Presse* (Friday, April 3, 1903):

> An old mansion in the rue Saint-Louis-en-l'Île, one of those survivors from yesterday that once sheltered princes; today, it's a poet who survives under this roof, Monsieur Marcel Schwob, author of that beautiful translation of *Hamlet, Prince of Denmark,* which was performed at Sarah's house.†
>
> A Hindu, bearing a lantern of red glass, opens the door and introduces me in the drawing room where the master of the house, entirely clean shaven, making his brilliant, ascetic eyes shine all the more, receives me; Monsieur Marcel Schwob interrupts a conversation with Monsieur Aleister Crowley to introduce us to one another.
>
> Monsieur Aleister Crowley, with whom I was thus acquainted, thanks to Monsieur Marcel Schwob, is a being somewhat apart in the world; an Irishman, glabrous, skinny, and tall, who regards you with dreamy eyes and who speaks in the soft voice of his race, when they are poets; and Monsieur Crowley is a poet; he is also Buddhist; he is, finally, a traveler; but what a traveler! Monsieur Crowley had returned, quite simply, from seeing the Himalayas.
>
> My conversation with Monsieur Crowley was fairly strained; my interlocutor expressing himself in rudimentary French; but Monsieur Marcel Schwob speaks admirable English, and he served as interpreter.

---

*I am grateful to William Breeze for pointing to the original articles in *L'Écho de Paris* and *La Presse;* translations are the author's.

†Sarah Bernhardt played Hamlet to Schwob and Paul Morand's translation in 1899. Rapturously received in Paris, the performance at London's Adelphi on June 12, 1899, was criticized on account of its female Hamlet.

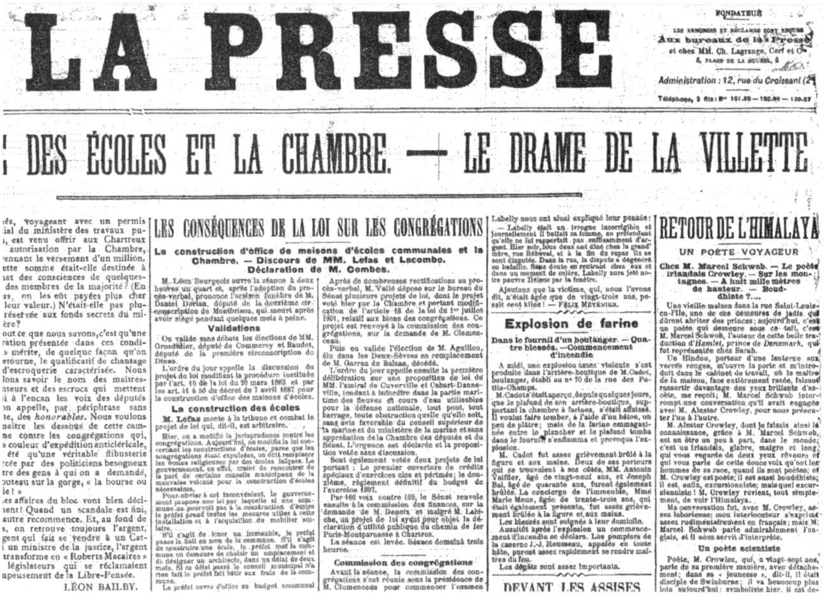
LA PRESSE

FONDATEUR

LES ANNONCES ET RÉCLAMES SONT REÇUES
Aux bureaux de la Presse
et chez MM. Ch. Lagrange, Cerf et Cie
8, PLACE DE LA BOURSE, 8

Administration : 12, rue du Croissant

DES ÉCOLES ET LA CHAMBRE. — LE DRAME DE LA VILLETTE

LES CONSÉQUENCES DE LA LOI SUR LES CONGRÉGATIONS

La construction d'office de maisons d'écoles communales et la Chambre. — Discours de MM. Lefas et Lacombe. Déclaration de M. Combes.

Validations

La construction des écoles

Explosion de farine

Commission des congrégations

DEVANT LES ASSISES

RETOUR DE L'HIMALAYA

UN POÈTE VOYAGEUR

Chez M. Marcel Schwob. — Le poète irlandais Crowley. — Sur les montagnes. — A huit mille mètres de hauteur. — Bouddhiste ?....

Une vieille maison dans la rue Saint-Louis-en-l'Ile, une de ces demeures de jadis qui durent abriter des princes; aujourd'hui, c'est un poète qui demeure sous ce toit, c'est M. Marcel Schwob, l'auteur de cette belle traduction d'*Hamlet, prince de Danemark*, qui fut représentée chez Sarah.

Un Hindou, porteur d'une lanterne aux verres rouges, m'ouvre la porte et m'introduit dans le cabinet de travail, où le maître de la maison, face entièrement rasée, faisant ressortir davantage des yeux brillants d'ascète, me reçoit; M. Marcel Schwob interrompt une conversation qu'il avait engagée avec M. Alester Crowley, pour nous présenter l'un à l'autre.

M. Alester Crowley, dont je faisais ainsi la connaissance, grâce à M. Marcel Schwob, est un être un peu à part, dans le monde; c'est un Irlandais, glabre, maigre et long, qui vous regarde de deux yeux rêveurs et qui vous parle de cette douce voix qu'ont les hommes de sa race, quand ils sont poètes; et M. Crowley est poète; il est aussi bouddhiste; il est, enfin, excursionniste; mais quel excursionniste ! M. Crowley revient, tout simplement, de voir l'Himalaya.

Ma conversation fut, avec M. Crowley, assez laborieuse; mon interlocuteur s'exprime assez rudimentairement en français; mais M. Marcel Schwob parle admirablement l'anglais, et il nous servit d'interprète.

Un poète scientiste

Poète, M. Crowlez, qui, a vingt-sept ans, parle de sa première manière, avec détachement; dans sa « jeunesse », dit-il, il était disciple de Swinburne; il va beaucoup plus loin aujourd'hui: symboliste hier, il est de-

Fig. 9.2. La Presse, *Paris, April 3, 1903; far-right column: the Crowley interview.*

A Poet Scientist

A poet, Monsieur Crowley, aged twenty-seven, first speaks with detachment about his "youth," when, he said, he was a disciple of Swinburne; he goes a lot further today; yesterday a Symbolist, he became a scientist; I mean to say that he dreams of works where his poetry would be purged by scientific doctrines. He has already given us a *Tannhaüser,* whose legendary hero he imagined very differently to Wagner; that was a nebulous work, among others.

Currently, Monsieur Crowley is preparing a work in which he'll try hard to project thoughts that evoke the works of Rodin; thus he has written verses on the celebrated *Balzac,* and here is Marcel Schwob's translation. [Omitted here.]

How had this poet, who, in these several verses appears to us, such as he is, a visionary, had the idea of climbing the very highest mountains? Is it love of the heights? The bird sings only when perched on high. . . . Must the poet wish to see the sky at its closest? Has he had the desire for altitudes, the obsession with summits; is this the "bitter science" which drives him toward the snowy peaks, where there is the "sad wisdom," or again, has he wished to feel "the air in a stupor shuddering on his flesh"?

"My father adored mountains," Monsieur Crowley told me. "I owe my love of peaks to him; as a child I climbed the summits of Ireland, then I went to the mountains of Scotland and Wales, of Switzerland and Austria and of Hungary; later I went to Mexico; I wanted, on the heights to see extraordinary things; the Mexican mountains are high; I climbed them very fast, I broke all the world's speed records. I wanted to do even more, that's why I left for the Himalayas."

—You are a sportsman, then?

In the Himalayas

—"Perhaps, I don't know. I desire to do the things everybody doesn't do; with five men and 200 coolies, I climbed the massif of Mustach in the Himalayas, a group situated on the borders of Turkestan and Baltistan; the highest peak is K2, known to locals as Chogori; more than 8,000 meters high. I climbed there, the highest ascent possible in the world; in the Himalayas there's Gaurishankar, which is 250 meters higher than Chogori, but it's inaccessible.

"To get to Chogori, you must get to Srinagar, the last town inhabited by Europeans; and to get to Srinagar you have seven days march; after that, you march twenty-seven days until you get to the last village, Askole. After that you march fourteen days and reach the foot of the mountain; then you make your way by paths you carve out yourself, in the midst of deserts strewn with stones, among rare plants, you come to the glacier; nothing to eat; to drink only snow-water; the only living beast, the ibex, a kind of goat the color of stone, ravens and birds that resemble the partridge; it was summer when I was there: we had 20° below zero during the night, and 40° above in the sunshine.

"We had to eat wretched tinned food and sleep in sleeping bags.

"To get to the summit required climbing a further fifteen days; a raven and a butterfly had followed us to a peak in Mexico, already, I had seen a butterfly at 5,000 meters, fluttering on the snows."

—Did you suffer altitude sickness?

—"No, when one climbs slowly one doesn't suffer from the rarefaction of the air."

—Were you a long time on the mountain?

—"Sixty-eight days, between 5,000 and 8,000 meters, and amid snowstorms; the vistas were terrible; it was fine; it was grandiose; you couldn't help but admire it all hugely; in life's miseries, in the midst of savage and uncultivated Nature, one loses the aesthetic sense; the absolute concentration of the brain is on the question of life and health; think about our expedition, so close to the Equator, was almost an Arctic expedition. We were fifteen days from life; one finds at the Pole the same physical conditions as the Himalayas."

—You had studied your itinerary?

—"I had no guide, but with our friends, we had organized the expedition methodically and scentifically."

—No one before you had seen Chogori?

—"Six years ago, an Englishman, Conway; but one had no idea how far he had climbed."

Buddhist

Now Monsieur Crowley talked to me of his determinism. He is persuaded that "life is decided in advance"; that's why he's become a fervent Buddhist; he went on pilgrimage to Anuradhapura in Ceylon; one of his friends, Allan Bennett, has done more, having entered as a monk in a monastery; Monsieur Crowley would like to introduce the Buddhist religion into the West in its real and pure form, as practiced in Burma and Ceylon, reliant on the Pali canon.

Monsieur Crowley's conversion is not only philosophical, it is religious and mystical. Perhaps even, one day, Monsieur Crowley might cease writing and become an apostle of the Buddha's doctrines. And that Monsieur Crowley told me, with shuddering lips, and fevered eyes.

Whilst Monsieur Crowley expressed his fervor for the Buddhist cult, I heard Monsieur Marcel Schwob insist on the sincerity of his conversion.

Has Monsieur Marcel Schwob, who returned to Ceylon, and who also went to Anuradhapura, returned to us, like Monsieur Crowley, a Buddhist?

I did not dare ask him, and I left, with curiosity unsatisfied, directed again to the street by the Hindu bearing a lantern, this time, with greenish hints.

Fernand Hauser

Let's suppose Crowley left the interview around dusk for his favorite café, Le Chat Blanc at 93 rue d'Odessa, Montparnasse, about a mile and a half southwest of the Île St. Louis, set anciently in the Seine opposite Notre Dame's splayed, blackened buttresses on the Île de la Cité. The most direct route across the river was the old Pont de la Tournelle—not the single span bridge of 1928 but the now vanished six-arched, stone bridge of 1654, to which industrial science gracefully added curved steel girders and tracery, supporting pavement and handrails. Now standing on the Left Bank before high Second Empire residential tenements, Crowley would have headed west on the boulevard St. Germain—which then ran to the river—toward St-Nicolas-de-Chardonnet church with its curiously juxtaposed Romanesque clock tower and seventeenth- and eighteenth-century neoclassical porticos and Roman arches. The church had meaning for Crowley. St. Nicolas was the site of the seminary into which hero Éliphas Lévi entered in 1825, where Abbé Frère Colonna directed the ordinand's thoughts toward exploring magic. Believing Lévi his former incarnation, Crowley later confessed déjà vu in parts of Paris familiar to Lévi. Was his mind passing that way now?

Girding the lush Jardin des Plantes to his left, he entered the Latin

320. PARIS — La Seine et le Pont de la Tournelle   C. M.

Fig. 9.3. The old Pont de la Tournelle across the Seine; Notre Dame in the distance.

Quarter, taking the rue des Écoles, soon approaching, to his right, the magnificent fifteenth-century Musée de Cluny (a museum of the Middle Ages)—in those days lent additional character by ivy and greenery cascading over its high, old, unwashed walls, beneath quaint turrets, like a discreet Oxford college in days of aquatint. He'd have passed many young men of the Sorbonne, who perhaps were struck by his unwieldy rings and astounding green satin waistcoat, spotted with yellow.

Turning left at the end of the street he entered the busy boulevard St. Michel and turned south, with the Palace and Gardens of Luxembourg to his right and the no less palatial Sorbonne university buildings to his left. Dodging his way amid knife sharpeners and street sellers, hawking umbrellas and vegetables and bread and sweets, the darkening boulevard began to glow in blurry smudges as incandescent gas lamps cast charcoal shadows over the cobbles and sets, echoing to the tick-tock hooves of hauliers, donkeys, cabs, and coaches.

Taking a shortcut southwest through the Luxembourg Gardens below looming marble monuments to past greatness, Crowley could hear the chug and steely rattle of a Purrey steam tram chuntering its way east up the wide boulevard de Montparnasse, bells ring-a-dinging.

Quickening his step, Crowley caught a glimpse of himself in a stately shop window, splashed with passing lamplight, punctuated by cyclists darting past like shifting images on a carousel. He sniffed and sought a place to cross the mighty boulevard. It occurred to him it needed a footbridge or a balloon to traverse it. He'd less chance of hurting himself on the Eiger or Burma's Mindon Chong than on the boulevard Montparnasse as night fell.

Desisting until the junction with the boulevard Raspail, he approached the swelling Rotonde café and gazed opposite to the great awning of the no less fabled Dôme, surrounded by tables and seats and artists, and models, and poets and hopefuls earnest and enervated. Spotting a gap in the traffic, Crowley marched across, studiously ignoring the voluble throng, then struck out west up the boulevard, through pools of dark shadow cast by the plane tree branches above, past the church of Saint Denis des Champs to the right, and on toward the Gare de Montparnasse, a marvel of 1852 whose now vanished magnificence wouldn't have seemed awkward in Florence. Just before the boulevard intersected with the rue de Rennes, Crowley, eschewing the station's wide, Paladian embrace, turned sharply left into a narrow street that cut back southeastward. Halfway down, on the left, at 93 rue d'Odessa (now number 13), he found the sanctum he sought, Le Chat Blanc.

THE UPPER ROOM

I cannot tell whether the "White Cat" was named in conscious opposition to the famous Chat Noir ("Black Cat") café-cabaret north across the Seine at Montmartre, long since established by Rodolphe Sallis. The infamous Hydropathes, sometimes rowdy and sometimes brilliant, artistic and literary club, had quit Montparnasse in the early 1880s and (in Sallis's view) made Montmartre the center of France's artistic world. Montparnasse refused to accept the insult, and the Anglo-American artistic contingent there was encouraged to see Montmartre as a place of risqué or lowbrow entertainment rather than high culture. The choice was black and white.

Crowley chose the white cat, or rather, it was chosen for him. According to Kelly: "It was I who introduced A.C. to the Chat Blanc."[2] Crowley glamorized his sessions at the Chat Blanc's furnished "upper room"—one notes his immediate allusion to the upper room arranged for Jesus's Last Supper, or attendance on the Holy Spirit at Pentecost. The glamour becomes a kind of élite halo, emanating not from apostolic heads but from Crowley and Kelly's lips, a kind of hyperintellectual double-act supported by associates praised to the skies by "master" Crowley, galvanizing tribunals on visitors like a Satanic magistrate or Socratic referee overseeing an Olympian test of wits.

Romanticized memories of times spent upstairs first appeared in 1904 when Crowley composed a collection of obscene stories and verses to entertain his wife, confined for the birth of daughter Lilith. The "Nameless Novel" section of *Snowdrops from a Curate's Garden* (printed in Paris by Philippe Renouard) hides the identities of interlocutors, but *Confessions* spilled the beans, giving identities in a footnote.

Crowley describes regulars of the club thus (we've already encountered habitué Joseph Kite, painter; see page 116): Paul Wayland Bartlett (1865–1925) is "the brilliant but debauched sculptor, caustic of wit, though genial to his friends"; Canadian landscape painter J. W. Morrice (1865–1924) is "the great painter, whose royal sense of light made his canvases into a harmonious dream: he [is] also the sweet friend of Bacchus, who filled him with a glow and melody of colour and thought." Crowley is "poet and philosopher," whose expression is "noble and commanding, yet sly," and Kelly, whose "eager face like a silver moon starting from a thundercloud, his hair, would pierce the very soul of the debate and kindle it with magick joy or freeze it with scorn implacable," was painter "and—I fear—pederast."* While Crowley looked on with "cold acumen," Kelly's "superb indignation, expressed in fiery swords of speech, would drive some luckless driveller from the room. Or at times they [Kelly and Crowley] would hold down their victim, a bird fascinated by a snake, while they pitilessly exposed his follies to the delighted crowd. Again, a third, pompous and self-confident, would be led on by them, seemingly in full sympathy, to make an exhibition of himself, visible and hideous to all eyes but his own." Sitting next to Kelly, and "ever ready to laugh at the intricacies of his own intellect," Crowley's "deep and wondrous eyes lit with strange light," he uttered "words like burning flames of steel," tearing "asunder the sophistries of one and the complacencies of another."

Another regular was "ethicist" Arthur Clive Heward Bell (1881–1964; better known as Clive Bell, who married Virginia Woolf's sister Vanessa). Like Crowley, Bell was a Trinity man who in 1902 gained a scholarship to study in Paris, where he took up art. To Crowley, Bell was "fair as a boy, with boy's gold locks curling about his Grecian head; the pure and subtle-minded student, whose lively humour and sparkling sarcasm were as froth upon the deep and terrible waters of his polished irony. It was a pity that he drank." Then there was Kelly's friend Ivor Back (1879–1951). "The great surgeon and true gentleman, in spite of his exaggerated respect for the memory of Queen Victoria, Back would join in with his ripe and generous wit. Handsome as a god, with yet a spice of devil's laughter lurking there, he would sit and enjoy the treasures of the conversation, adding at the proper interval his own rich quota of scholarly jest."

Anyone who showed a weakness, without the wit to defend themselves, could, Crowley asserted, expect short shrift, left to squirm

---

*As his identity when *Snowdrops* became available was not mentioned (he was "L"), Kelly needn't have objected to Crowley's silly joke, knowing it was a joke, and typical of his (at that time) friend.

their way out. There were survivors. Crowley mentioned cover artist Penrhyn Stanley Adamson, known as Penrhyn Stanlaws (1877–1957), who became a film director in the early twenties. He appeared thus to Crowley: "a popular painter, upon whom the whole Dog pounced as one man, to destroy him. But when they saw that his popular painting was not he, that he had a true heart and an honest ambition, how quickly were the swords beaten into absinthes and the spears into tournedos!" Another survivor was "one Root," possibly American Robert Kilburn Root (1877–1950), author of *The Classical Mythology of Shakespeare* (1903), who two years later became instructor in English literature at Princeton University, and afterward dean of faculty. "Root," with "a face like a portrait by Rembrandt," was judged "a man of no great intellect, but making no pretence thereto. How he was loved for his jolly humour, his broad smile, his inimitable stories!" But sincerity alone was not enough to save the "average man," no less than the charlatan, from a hurtful encounter, even though "among themselves no set of men could have been more genial, more fraternal. United by a bond of mutual respect, even where they differed—of mutual respect, I say, by no means of mutual admiration, for it was the sincere artistry that they adored, not the technical skill of achievement—they formed a noble and harmonious group, the like of which has perhaps never yet been seen."

Among this elusive club sat Roderic O'Conor, whom Crowley held in some esteem. Born in Roscommon, Ireland, in 1860, O'Conor came to Paris in 1886 to study under society portraitist Carolus-Duran, but the following year left to join the Pont-Aven school of Symbolist-inspired lovers of Brittany, whose number would include Pierre Bonnard, Paul Sérusier, Maurice Denis, and Paul Gauguin. O'Conor then moved with Frank O'Meara and John Lavery to an artist colony 44 miles south of Paris, at Grez. By 1902 he was back in Paris, having inherited a good income from the family estate. He began frequenting the Chat Blanc. Clive Bell described O'Conor as "gruff" and "misanthropic," while novelist William Somerset Maugham (1874–1965, introduced as a friend of Kelly) took against him and used him to model an artist character in *Of Human Bondage* (1915) and *The Magician* (1908).

However, according to *Confessions* (written with considerable hindsight), Maugham himself didn't escape serious ribbing. One needs to bear in mind, however, that Crowley's hindsight acquired its venom from the fact that Maugham, impressed by Crowley for both good and ill, used aspects of Crowley's self-projection to create the evil figure Oliver Haddo in his early novel, *The Magician*. Crowley was flattered to have inspired such a feat and on its publication would congratulate Maugham on preserving some of Haddo/Crowley's otherwise ephemeral repartee, while spilling the beans on Maugham's extensive plagiarism to U.K. *Vanity Fair* editor Frank Harris in an article titled "How to write a Novel! After W. S. Maugham" published under the pseudonym Oliver Haddo on December 30, 1908 (pp. 838–40). Crowley's article provided a hefty, detailed itinerary of Maugham's plagiarized accounts of occultism and other things. But that moment was still a few years ahead.

Having the chance in *Confessions* to put himself above the (now famous) Maugham, Crowley spared no wit in showing him in 1903–1904 as a figure sufficiently inferior to be patronized. First he introduces Maugham as the younger brother of an English solicitor connected with the British Embassy. The solicitor was married to a fascinating and beautiful woman who was best friends with Gerald Kelly's elder sister, Rose; that is, Crowley's first wife. Crowley then suggests any deficiencies in Maugham's presentation of either O'Conor or himself could be accounted for as sour grapes when winded by wanton wit at the Chat Blanc.

O'Conor, Crowley insists, didn't even find Kelly's friend "funny." To O'Conor, Maugham was "like a bed bug, on which a sensitive man refuses to stamp because of the smell and the squashiness."[3] This feeling was allegedly mutual, for according to Crowley, the man Maugham "most hated was Roderic O'Conor." This seems borne out by Maugham's picture of O'Conor as O'Brien in *The Magician* (chapter 3, "The Chien Noir"):

> That is Mr. O'Brien, who is an example of the fact that strength of will and an earnest purpose cannot make a painter. He's a failure, and he knows it, and the bitterness has warped his soul. If you listen to him, you'll hear every painter of eminence come under his lash. He can forgive nobody who's successful, and he never acknowledges merit in anyone till he's safely dead and buried.[4]

Crowley then assesses the artist himself without rancor: "This man [O'Conor] was intimate with Gauguin, Van Gogh, and Cézanne. In my opinion history will class him near them as a painter. I do not think he has many superiors in art alive today. But very few people have seen his pictures. His contempt for the world goes beyond that of Balzac and Baudelaire. He cannot be bothered to give a show. He will turn rudely from his door a friendly journalist bent on making him famous and rich. Also, he is a cad."[5]

Crowley's treatment of Maugham seems on the one hand a posy of friendly flowers, on the other a wreath of dog roses and thistles. "His literary method," Crowley says of Maugham, "when it transcends plain scissors and paste, is the shirt-cuff method of Arnold Bennett." Yet Maugham is also a "luckless victim," who is rendered the more so when Crowley states it was Canadian J. W. Morrice who located Maugham's weak spot. This apparently consisted of no less an infirmity than Maugham's having taken a medical degree. Tormented on the subject by Morrice, Crowley alleges, Maugham's "distress" was accentuated "by his being a confirmed stammerer." In *Morrice's* "defense," Crowley admits the painter was invariably "mellow drunk all day and all night. He would look up from his crème de menthe and *oeufs sur le plat,* clear his throat and tell Maugham with grave importance that he would like to consult him on a matter concerning the welfare of art and artists. 'What would you do if—' and after repeating himself in a hundred ways so as to prolong the rigmarole to the utmost, he would wind up by confessing to the premonitory symptoms of some comic and repulsive malady. It was really needlessly cruel, for, bar his pretensions to literature, there is not an ounce of harm in Maugham, any more than there is in a packet of sterilized cotton wool. Even the pretence is after all a perfectly harmless affectation." Somerset Maugham . . . *sterilized cotton wool.*

Crowley then comes to his point: Maugham's subsequent conduct shows he asked for it. "Maugham suffered terribly under the lash of universal contempt and did his best to revenge himself by drawing portraits, as unpleasant as petty spite could make them, of some of his tormentors."[6]

Ever, naturally, without malice in his own mind, or projection, Crowley allows that while it was "right" to chivy Maugham in 1903, he (Maugham) did subsequently go "around the world, and set to work with his powers of observation to help an imagination which had by now become original and vigorous. He turned out some first-class work; and, what is in some ways better, work on the right side."[7]

The conclusion of all this would seem to me to be that Crowley was saying, "Don't mess with *me!—whoever you are.*"

Gerald Kelly, with even greater hindsight, and his target being two years dead, found Crowley's attitude absurd:

I'm purposely ignoring the remarkably successful position W. S. Maugham has enjoyed during the last 40 years. In 1908 he was quite small beer and *The Magician* is quite the poorest of his books, but A.C. at his highest point was never in a position to patronise Maugham. It may have annoyed his vanity—but tis so. It's years since I read this silly book [*The Magician*].[8]

Not content with that, when reading later in *Confessions* the passage where Crowley meets Maugham in 1908 after having demonstrated plagiarism in Maugham's novel, Kelly reckons Crowley's one-liner putdown delivered to Maugham—"I almost wish," I said, "that you were an important writer"—was rather what the "French call *l'ésprit d'éscalier*,"[9] meaning a line coming to one "on the stairs" *after* the encounter, which one wishes dearly one had possessed wit to say at the time!

Nine years after Crowley's death, Maugham's publisher decided to reissue *The Magician,* even though Maugham had long excluded it from his oeuvre. It duly appeared in 1956 with "A Fragment of Autobiography." This gives us Maugham's view of Crowley, written with considerable hindsight, long after Crowley's reputation in Britain was obliterated, as far as the cultural mainstream was concerned. Maugham's introduction of Haddo at the Chien Rouge (Chat Blanc) in *The Magician* will serve as introduction to Maugham's recollections of Crowley himself.

Maugham describes the establishment as the Quarter's most charming, with a public room downstairs for the hoi polloi where cheap, but good, food was served, overseen by a retired horse dealer building up business for his son. The first floor was narrow with seats as a horseshoe, reserved for a small number of English or American painters, and a few Frenchmen with their mistresses. One of the Americans Maugham calls "Clayson"—clearly Paul Wayland Bartlett (1865–1925), American sculptor in heroic realist style. Crowley liked him, admiring his cutting wit, which, as we saw earlier, allegedly drove "one Kite" from the room. Kelly, in his "Comments" on *Confessions* thought Crowley deluded about Bartlett, noting on one of Crowley's effusions in that regard: "It's spoiled by the reference to 'my friend Bartlett.' I used to know Paul Bartlett well; it was I who introduced A.C. to the Chat Blanc. P[aul].B[artlett]. disliked and disapproved of A.C. for his bad manners, arrogance, pretentiousness etc."[10] Maugham doesn't seem to have liked Bartlett, describing Clayson as having "a vinous nose and a tedious habit of saying brilliant things. With his twinkling eyes, red cheeks, and fair, pointed beard, he looked exactly like a Franz Hals; but he was dressed like the caricature of a Frenchman in a comic paper. He spoke English with a Parisian accent."[11]

When Haddo enters, he is jibed for posing, and Clayson, laughing, says Haddo couldn't help posing if he tried. Haddo's well-turned response sounds like Crowley: "How often have I explained to you, O Clayson, that your deplorable lack of education precludes you from the brilliancy to which you aspire?"

It's odd how Haddo's appearance resembles the impression Crowley made a decade later when he put on weight. He's more than six feet tall (Crowley was less than six feet), has a huge paunch, and his face is fleshy. Crowley in 1903 was like a bean pole, well-knit and fit.

Haddo throws out more witty, wordy ripostes responding to O'Brien's rudeness, and in greeting everyone else, alienating sufficient people to secure himself elbow room at the table!

Haddo's eyes were modeled on Maugham's response to Crowley's: pale blue, but creating embarrassment; where other eyes converged when engaged, Haddo's stayed parallel as if looking through the head to the wall behind, disconcerting the interlocutor. A general uncanniness meant unsureness as to his seriousness, an effect increased by a sardonic smile and air of mockery. Was he having a joke to himself at everyone's expense?

Haddo proceeds to make various extraordinary claims about his big-game hunting skills, but the claims are not exaggerated. Accused of suffering from no false modesty, Haddo retorts that false modesty indicates ill breeding, from which *his* birth amply protects him. Class consciousness was a factor annoying (later at least) to Kelly, whose view was that "A.C. was not well born. His parents were of humble origin— his mother noticeably so. Why," Kelly wailed, "does he harp upon being 'a gentleman.'"[12] Knowledge of his upbringing and early life makes the answer obvious, but Kelly may never have enjoyed empathetic understanding of his older friend.

Haddo went to Eton and Oxford, quite unlike Crowley, and his estate—"Skene" (obviously Boleskine)—is somewhat ludicrously set in *Staffordshire,* a county Crowley seems to have deprecated for its association with industrial pottery-making (thus a mark against Arnold Bennett!): a pure and rather sad case of transference since he was himself accused of having acquired wealth through his family name's association with *trade,* and the "low" business of *brewing* to boot. Crowley was a snob, but snobberies, endemic in England, as elsewhere, come in many forms, as Thackeray observed in detail. Crowley was determined not to be repressed by snobbery, so assumed his interior sense of aristocracy as external fact; in 1903, aristocracy meant power, allied to chivalry—that is, independent *virtus,* or strength. Crowley didn't trust the world enough to be humble. He could only affect indifference through elevation. His system would advocate "kingship" to all who found their "true wills."

One thing comes over from Maugham's dialogue for Haddo. Haddo knows his occult onions and can communicate cryptically or plainly as case requires. In attending to the ambiguities, Maugham creates a fascinating character, whose evil is not wholly dark, for there's a hint of some elusive enlightenment in what Haddo knows, regardless of attendant scientists' urge to ridicule and dismiss magic as outmoded belief. It is obvious from Maugham's autobiographical fragment that he has built into Haddo positive and negative aspects of his reflections on the strangeness of Aleister Crowley.

MAUGHAM ON CROWLEY

Maugham doesn't tell us exactly when he took a fifth-floor apartment near the Place Denfert-Rochereau, Montparnasse, at the intersection of boulevards Raspail, Arago, and Saint-Jacques, but that some months earlier he'd made friends with "highly talented, abundantly loquacious, and immensely enthusiastic" young painter Gerald Kelly, with a studio on the rue Campagne Première and who soon introduced him to the Chat Blanc, where certain artists met regularly and were joined by occasional visitors who, he says, were often made unwelcome. He met Clive Bell and Arnold Bennett there, and "casual visitor"

Aleister Crowley, who was wintering in Paris—which detail dates the encounter:

> I took an immediate dislike to him, but he interested and amused me. He was a great talker and he talked uncommonly well. In early youth, I was told, he was extremely handsome, but when I knew him he had put on weight, and his hair was thinning [Maugham's memory is at fault here]. He had fine eyes and a way, whether natural or acquired I do not know, of so focusing them that, when he looked at you, he seemed to look behind you. He was a fake, but not entirely a fake. At Cambridge he had won his chess blue and was esteemed the best whist player of his time. He was a liar and unbecomingly boastful, but the odd thing was that he had actually done some of the things he boasted of. As a mountaineer, he had made an ascent of K2 in the Hindu Kush, the second-highest mountain in India, and he made it without the elaborate equipment, the cylinders of oxygen and so forth, which render the endeavours of the mountaineers of the present day more likely to succeed. He did not reach the top, but got nearer to it than anyone had done before.[13]

Maugham addresses Crowley's poetry. His view seems in accord with Kelly's 1949 assessment, by which time at least, Kelly was loath to believe Crowley ever took himself seriously as a poet, finding his claims for successes in the art "bosh": "The overwhelming majority of those who had tried to read A.C.'s works were bored not frightened . . . at least one surgeon [Ivor Back?]—thought he was mad. Many thought that he was a nuisance. Men of letters—Yeats, W. S. Maugham, Bennett, etc. thought he was imitative, bad, verbose, tawdry, but not terrifying nor hate worthy."[14] Maugham says Crowley was a sumptuously self-publishing "voluminous writer of verse." Having a gift for rhyme, his verse had some merit, being greatly influenced by Swinburne and Browning (something Crowley was ready to admit). He was imitative, but not "unintelligently" so. He gives an example of a line by Crowley one would happily accept as the work of "the master," Browning, likewise a stanza here or there recognizable as up to Swinburne's standards but which in fact was Crowley's, even though it might be inserted into a Swinburne work unnoticed.

Both Kelly and Maugham seem not to have seen the numerous

favorable, if critical, reviews of Crowley's poetry published in magazines and newspapers for the decade up to circa 1910.

When Maugham knew him, Crowley, he says, was "dabbling" in "Satanism, magic, and the occult," there being a vogue in Paris at the time "for that sort of thing," occasioned, he surmised, by interest in Huysmans's *Là Bas*—well, Huysmans's tale of Satanically corrupt clergy was published in *1891* and the "vogue" for *mainstream* Parisian interest in occultism was practically exhausted by the end of that decade; *Là Bas* was a novel *Maugham* consulted for *The Magician*. And needless to say, Crowley did not *dabble* in "Magick."

Maugham refers to "fantastic stories" told by Crowley. Were they true or was he pulling someone's leg? After meeting Crowley "several times" that winter, Maugham wasn't sure. As for his role in *The Magician,* Maugham was at pains to state he didn't think much of it stylistically, though was amazed, reviewing it, to see how much research it contained but reckoned it was too influenced by the descriptive art favored in contemporary French novels. Though Crowley was a model, Haddo was not a portrait, he insisted. He gave Haddo a more striking appearance and made him "more sinister and more ruthless than Crowley ever was." Haddo's magical powers might have been claimed by Crowley, but Crowley "certainly" didn't possess them. Crowley, he knew, recognized himself in Maugham's "invention," reviewing the book in *Vanity Fair,* signing it "Oliver Haddo." Maugham didn't read it but wished he had, though it was likely a "pretty piece of vituperation." Nevertheless, like his poems, Crowley's review was probably "intolerably verbose."[15] Nothing vituperative *there,* then!

Years later, Crowley wrote to Maugham, hoping to renew relations, but Maugham replied that while he liked to meet new people, he'd no taste for reviving old acquaintances. Maugham concludes his autobiographical fragment by reporting that Crowley, having hit rock-bottom poverty, wrote to him years later, but Maugham didn't give him any money, and Crowley proceeded to live "for many disgraceful years."[16] By 1956, of course, most readers would have heard about Crowley's "disgrace," but very few indeed knew the truth behind it.

TEN

I Piped When You Danced

In June 1903, Crowley decided Scotland had warmed up sufficiently for him to resume a sporting life as laird of Boleskine (a courtesy title going with the property). *Confessions* attributes leaving Paris to ennui with pretentiousness amid tedious, tangled relationships in the artistic quarter, but the account is warped. Besides, he'd return to Montparnasse at every opportunity until its pleasures were denied him.

Paternally and fraternally jealous of others' influence over Kelly, Crowley was temperamentally an outsider, with limited tolerance for social milieux. Shelley's "Alastor," wanderer of the waste, was Crowley's self-image. Wary of closeness and addicted to solitude, he yet needed one close friend. Favoring an ideal life, Crowley persisted in trying to "wild-up" Kelly, to *teach* and render him a fit companion—in 1902 he'd pleaded Kelly to gird his loins and become K2's expedition artist. Kelly tolerated Crowley's chiding his attachment to social and artistic comfort zones for the sake of his libertarian wit.

Predictably, it took little time before the laird found boredom at Boleskine and in July teased Kelly with prospects of golf at Strathpeffer, whose club, founded in 1888, lay in Ulladale, above Strathpeffer Spa. As Kelly's mother needed a health cure it suited everyone that Gerald and sister Rose accompany Mrs. Blanche Kelly to the spa, leaving Gerald opportunity to play with Crowley at Boleskine and on the Strathpeffer course while Blanche pressured her widowed daughter (having already advanced money for an abortion) to choose one of two suitors from whom Rose had kindly accepted marriage proposals. One was an American, Howell, the other an elderly solicitor named Hill, who'd join Kelly on the links. What Blanche didn't know was that Rose was committed to a third man, one Frank Summers . . .

Rose was in a quandary.

Arriving in Strathpeffer, mother enjoyed the spa's sulfurous springs, pump room, hospital, and hotel, as well as entertainments and lectures presented in the grand pavilion. Crowley had met Rose before, in Paris if not also in Camberwell, and cannot have been blind to her charms, but he was shy and conscious she lacked cultivated intellect. Hating small talk, Crowley didn't know what to say to her. Rose would have heard much about the rich, clever poet and explorer, who had much experience and drew his own bounds.

Filling the conversational gap with her dilemma, Crowley at last recognized a subject that aroused his passion. It had long been his sincere conviction that no girl should be denied true love to suffer unwanted marriage: a crime Crowley believed cursed the generations.

Confessions insists Crowley felt his engagement to Eileen Gray lapse when he (and/or she?) realized they'd slipped into the marrying groove from "moral failure" to resist conformity. Having decided marriage was, for the free spirit, mere convention, Crowleyan logic demanded Rose be relieved of obligation to marry someone she didn't love—by marrying *him*! Shackles broken, she'd be free to enjoy love with her latest fancy, or anybody else. If the vicar of Camberwell wanted a marriage to end family frustration with her flightiness, a marriage he would get!

While Crowley's notion of wide-open marriage might seem prescient of *Bob and Carol and Ted and Alice* (1970; for those who remember), its dénouement proved worthy of a Mills & Boon fairy tale of love conquering all, crowned with wedlock.

Rose and Aleister jocularly announced their engagement on August 11, then caught the train early next morning to Dingwall to see the sheriff. According to Crowley, this wasn't the first time he'd scotched the designs of Camberwell vicarage (no pun intended). The family had done its utmost to prevent Gerald marrying Sibyl Meugens in Paris, with Rose as envoy. Crowley claimed he'd forestalled a threatened withdrawal of funds for Kelly's education by offering to subvent his friend himself! Crazy Crowley had done it again, assuming Gerald, at least, might perceive spiritual nobility in his liberating gesture.

We can tell from Crowley's letter of August 12 (see page 111) that Gerald—who arrived too late that morning to prevent the marriage registration—echoed his family's insistence on immediate annulment. He may also have implied Crowley was still obligated to Eileen Gray, or that engagement to Eileen had served sexual purposes, with Crowley now repeating excesses upon Gerald's own sister. Crowley had often enough boasted to Gerald of his amorous adventures; Kelly had even abetted the efforts, contributing mock censure to *Alice: An Adultery,* for example.

The haze around these issues is dimly illuminated by some curious, previously unpublished cards, and a letter, sent by Crowley at this time that survive in the J.F.C. Fuller Collection in the Harry Ransom Center, University of Texas, Austin. It is possible that two of them were enclosed in a single envelope addressed to "Mdlle Meugens, 17 rue Campagne 1ère, Montparnasse, Paris, France." Dated August 14, 1903— two days after Crowley's marriage—one hurriedly written card begins:

Dear Sibyl,

The *most* impossible thing has happened (not the 2nd most, the very most) That ought to tell you. No one – went [event?] guess fulfils conditions. a. [*sic*]

P.S. Has Earle* lost his sense of humour?

An identical card (with hieroglyphic cartouche printed top left), addressed to "My dear chela [Sanskrit for pupil of a guru]," and signed (in Sanskrit) "Abhavananda," was perhaps intended to be passed on by Sibyl to Eileen Gray, for as we have seen, Crowley, as "Abhavananda," would inscribe Eileen's copy of *Berashith* in December 1903 (see page 99). The card continues:

---

*William Breeze, who kindly sent me copies of the cards, noted that Edward Earle Meugens (1875–1929) was Sibyl Meugens's brother, a chartered accountant. He was educated at Malvern College, as was Crowley for three terms. Since their dates overlap, they may have known each other from that time. Crowley entered Malvern's lower 5th for summer term 1891, leaving Easter 1892; Meugens left Malvern at Christmas, 1891.

Will you allow me to pull yet another fibre from your heart in the shape of a copy of Tannhäuser? I have promised my editor one. When you are running short, tell me. There is a large supply (worse luck!) in London.

Yrs ever

Abhavananda [in Sanskrit script]

William Breeze suggested this second card was possibly addressed to Gerald Kelly since Kelly may have had access to author's copies of *Tannhäuser* in Paris. If so, it would be the sole known correspondence wherein Crowley addressed Kelly as his "chela." Unfortunately, the card carries no date. Not having its own envelope (the card is written on both sides), it *might* have been in the envelope sent to Sibyl Meugens (August 1903). The reference to an "editor" may possibly refer to Ivor Back, who we know visited Boleskine to edit Crowley's "Works" in autumn 1904 (but may conceivably have been a visitor to Boleskine in early September 1903).

Now, it is just possible that the card is contemporaneous with that sent to Sibyl apparently referring to the sudden marriage, being intended as a somewhat cryptic note to Eileen Gray, who better fits the jocular description of "chela" than does Kelly at this point. The request to return a copy of *Tannhäuser* may have come because Crowley's presentation copy to Eileen perhaps bore an inscription from him whose wording could embarrass him now that he had married Rose—that is, were it to come to the attention of either Rose or her brother Gerald. This is, admittedly, speculation on the evidence available, but it is perhaps less unlikely if we consider some ambiguous evidence for Rose being interested in Crowley's prior relations with Eileen Gray. Such might be discerned from a joint, undated letter that Rose and Crowley sent to Sibyl Meugens (also in the J.F.C. Fuller Collection), a letter that, incidentally, suggests Rose had known Crowley in Paris before their meeting in Scotland—when she was in Paris as envoy for her parents' refusal to entertain Gerald's intended marriage to Sibyl. The reference in Rose's letter to Sibyl concerning Ivor Back's planned visit to Boleskine in September might suggest it was sent in summer 1904 rather than at the time of her whirlwind marriage in August 1903, though it is possible, as we noted above, that Ivor Back intended to, or did, visit Boleskine in early September 1903. Crowley wrote to Sibyl on the letter-headed side, while Rose wrote to her on the reverse. Crowley's message was apparently in reply to one Sibyl had posted to Crowley from Paris, after having visited Gerald Kelly's parents' vicarage at Camberwell, south London:

Dear Sibyl,

I hope you like the Vicarage [at Camberwell]: it must be rather dull for you, though,: and the Camberwell people are not as chic as the ¼ [Montparnasse Quarter], of course. You have got back to Paris? A French stamp implies this.

It is easy unravelling riddles when you have [Henry] Coles to tell you in English.

What official notice can you take anyway?

Sorry you have not seen Earle [Sibyl's brother]. Where is Nelly?

Yes: the Vicarage must be (have been?) *very* dull.

Y^ts <u>Ye Bard</u>
"anyway, what is it all about?" A.C.

On the other side, in Rose Crowley's flowery hand:

Dear Sibyl

Neither the Poet or I can make out what on earth you want to know!!

Why so puzzled?

Put your question plainly!

G[erald] was up here the other day in great form. Unfortunately he could not stay. I believe he's now in Norfolk. We hope he and Ivor Back are coming here in Sept.

Great [Grease?] haste

I'll write again soon

Yrs. "Rebecca"* [Rose]

---

*"Rebecca" comes from a Hebrew verb meaning "to bind," or "to snare." As a noun it means "noose." Perhaps Rose was alluding to the idea that while one [Eileen?] had—she may have thought—wanted her husband, *she* (Rose) had snared, or tied, him. Alternatively, Rebecca may have been a familiar name between herself and Sibyl from earlier times in Paris.

P.S. What is the silly rumour about a "marriage"! Can you trace it?*

Anyhow, in August 1903, Crowley was convinced that by "emancipating" Rose, he'd done right, and on August 17, sheriff substitute Alexander Dewar of Ross, Cromarty, and Sutherland, issued the required certificate, and—*Abrahadabra!*—the kiss of legality tipped the couple into a swoon of genuine love. Crowley's dark world changed its pallor at once. Yes, Rose *was* an empty-headed woman of society—but now . . . how intelligent she was, how beautiful, how sexy and right for him she was!

The will to write (or suffer) departed; the long existential abjection vanished. Crowley was hopelessly in love with the most beautiful woman in the world!

Or, put another way, the lonely man had found a *companion:* one nearly as barmy as himself.

The world being what it is, arguments rumbled on with Rose's family into late September, when Crowley wrote to Gerald from Boleskine (September 24, 1903), indicating intentions to honeymoon in Paris for a fortnight beginning October 8:

My dear G.,

Your letter is the most cryptic I have ever had from you. It is kind to say that I am clever (I take your whole letter as kindness albeit I understand it ill) but on my word, to this hour I see no jab in the juxtaposition. I have plied in vain an imagination whetted by persistent and successful efforts to discover indecent illusions in the Binomial Theorem:† I have turned and twisted the names about: all is in vain. If you will devote a week of your valuable time to explaining verbally when we get to Paris, I shall discover a new point of

---

*Was there a rumor that Crowley had already secretly married Eileen Gray in Paris, or did some persons believe Sibyl had secretly married, or was going to marry, Rose's brother Gerald?

†The binomial theorem shows how to expand mathematical expressions like $(a+b)^n$, regardless of the size of the power (in this case: "n").

Coptic and if Rose and I get as far as Cairo this winter, my name will go down with Bruce & Harris.* For I will be avenged upon you by not putting you in The Papyrus:† Herewith the end o' th' Sword— *Benedictus esse* ["to be blessed" = inscription on a medieval sword]. I cannot even find from your letter whether you have written to your mother to smooth things over or no. "The allusion to Rev. F. F. Kelly is beneath contempt and meaningless"‡—I felt inclined to echo your effervescence! till I saw it was merely a classical example of the trans-ferred epithet. I have not twisted or doubled to anybody. I maintain, as always, that no insult was offered to B[lanche].K[elly]. in my con-sciousness or R[ose]'s and therefore no apology was possible. I am very sorry but I did no wrong. You are mistaken. At present the new method of conducting the controversy is exclusively employed: that hurts R[ose] and B. K. [Blanche Kelly] but neither you nor me, save mediately. I have had great benefits of you & you of me: we are art-ists and should quarrel with buttons on—Touch me, & I'll call the guardian angel, let us calm the indignant ones. Your letters will (I suppose) be received at the Vicarage: I suggest you write. We come south on the 8th—till 23rd about: do not let R[ose]. leave England, perhaps for months, without seeing her mother. I am deadly busy so write no more; but paint hard; send news of the Quarter and believe me "God's poet'"A.C.[1]

Judging from an undated letter on Paris's Hotel Langham notepaper, Crowley and Rose probably booked into the Langham, 24 rue Boccador,

---

*Explorer James Bruce (1730–1794), who returned from Egypt with the Gnostic "Bruce Codex," and British collector Anthony Charles Harris (1790–1869), who discovered the "Harris Homer" papyrus.

†In Crowley's surreal, allusive manner, the references to papyri brought from Egypt in context of visiting Cairo will strike readers as curiously related to what he expected he might achieve there; recall the shared joke at Eileen Gray's expense regarding Coptic (Egyptian) being the language of Copts and cryptic being that of Crypts (see page 97); somewhere in his mind lay the idea of a cryptic text from Cairo related to fame, blended with his brother-in-law's previous letter being largely unfathomable to him.

‡According to *Confessions*, Rev. Kelly had asked for a £10,000 settlement on Rose, add-ing that the daughters of his family never married without a settlement; considering this pompous, Crowley replied as he saw fit, holding Kelly's father's assertion a lie: Rose had no settlement on her first marriage.

PARIS — Langham Hôtel

24. Rue Boccador,
just a view
where I am now

O. Bourgeade. - Paris

Fig. 10.1. The Langham Hotel, 24 rue du Boccador, just north of
the Pont de l'Alma (now the Hartwood clothing shop).

a quarter mile south of the Champs Elysées.* Long gone, only the hotel
dining room's exquisite Art Nouveau glass (installed 1896–1998) survives, still evoking delight at La Fermette Marbeuf restaurant today.

My dear G,

Thanks for your amusing note and enclosure. I felt at the time you
were only bitter because you felt yourself wrong. May not the "red
herring" consist only in one's own inability to see the actual import
of the discussion? I am the only living man who can equal you in
argument, and I give you my word of honour that I am always serious, sincere, and as lucid as I can be. But since you describe [Ivor]
Back as a surgical sleepwalker—for which I think you ought to beg
his pardon—I can hardly complain if I am a mental cardsharper in
your eyes. It *was* a bad lunch [hunch?]; I admit it.

---

*As this letter to Kelly is undated, it's possible, though unlikely, it was sent some six
months later (April–June 1904). The Crowleys stayed at the Langham on returning from
Cairo, April 22, 1904.

Letters intended for me find me more easily if addressed "Lord Boleskine" without further circumlocution or ambiguity. I am entitled to this address and I intend to assert it. "Aleister Crowley" is of course a "nom de plume" now, and a name for literary use only. Is not courtesy "old fashioned"? You write charmingly even when you think you want to quarrel: but all that is no odds, you can only make me angry by attacking my wife—and that I hope you will be too much of a gentleman to do, in the future. Also it only annoys *her* if you try to influence my conduct through her. Don't write hurried letters; sit & smoke.

Yours ever as ever Aleister

P.S. This letter is to be read with a pipe in good order. If an agreeable response is not forthcoming, try a grain of calomel [purgative] & read it again.[2]

Of the trip to Paris in October 1903, Crowley had little to say; Gerald Kelly was not mentioned; perhaps he was not there (which would explain the letter). *Confessions* states only that the couple "dazzled" the city, but, that is, for a chance meeting with Moina Mathers when approaching the Pont d'Alexandre III. Engrossed in conversation, Crowley forgot to introduce her to Rose. Apologizing afterward, he was staggered by Rose's assumption that the strange woman was one of his old "models." Long respected and admired as Vestigia, Moina had, Crowley realized, been caked in cosmetics, neck unwashed, clad in threadbare garments. He later claimed penury had compelled Mathers to force Moina to pose naked in a Montmartre show: a story uncorroborated.[3]

The Crowleys' stay in Paris must have been longer than anticipated as their next appearance in the historical record occurs at Les Verrières in the Swiss Jura during an overnight stay chez Dr. Jules-Jacot Guillarmod, from November 7 to 8. Expedition doctor and scientific observer on the 1902 K2 (Chogo Ri) expedition, Guillarmod was completing a remarkable photographic account: *Six Mois dans l'Himalaya,* published in nearby Neuchâtel in 1904. Living on family land of distinctly Alpine character near the French border, Guillarmod's diary records finding Crowley "rather greedy"; love certainly builds an appetite.

Thin Crowley and stocky doctor doubtless discussed intentions for another expedition: an assault on Kangchenjunga between Sikkim and Nepal, third-highest mountain in the world. Guillarmod invited several friends to join Crowley's next mountaineering venture in 1905 (see *Aleister Crowley in India*).

Love's light wings then whisked "Lord and Lady Boleskine" to Marseille, Naples, and Cairo (where they spent a magical night in the Great Pyramid); thence to Ceylon, expecting to proceed to Rangoon (it's just possible he, or they did; see page 167). Finding Rose pregnant, it was decided to return early. They left Colombo for Port Said to spend February, March, and most of April 1904 in and around Cairo, where, as most readers know, extraordinary events occurred, detailed in *Aleister Crowley: The Biography*.

A most surprising aspect, easily overlooked, about how Crowley came to experience what he was convinced was angelic dictation of "this threefold book of Law" (*AL* I:35) on April 8–10, 1904, was that Crowley's contemporary diaries and subsequent accounts show *Rose* as initiator and controller of his path in the matter—a process he maintained he resisted on rational grounds. Even after *The Book of the Law* was in the bag, he long wavered over it, struggling, he claimed, with aspects of its contents. It took years before he rued his slack response to a voice Rose told him belonged to "Aiwass," whom Crowley eventually understood as "angel" or messenger of the sovereignty of the universe: a Secret Chief.

It began in March. "They," Rose said, were "waiting." It was "all about Osiris" and "the child." Crowley naturally thought she'd had too much sun or was affected by pregnancy. Asked to clarify *who* was waiting, she pointed to a stele from the old Bulaq Museum collection on the Cairo Museum's top floor, declaring, "There he is!" Crowley observed the label "Stele 666" but dismissed it as an "obvious coincidence." Before leaving Cairo, he had the stele translated by museum staff, and a copy made.

Taking a ground-floor apartment in the new Standard Life Insurance Building (according to Danish Thelemite Sigurd Bune's extensive research), Rose outlined a ritual, a curiously woven invocation of Horus, one Crowley thought "broke all the rules" he'd acquired in the Golden Dawn. The setting was certainly remarkable in the annals of magic.

The Standard Life Insurance Building stood on the southwestern corner of Midan Soliman Pasha Square. Sublet by Congdon & Co., probably (according to Sigurd Bune) from Col. George Mackworth

Fig. 10.2. The Standard Life Insurance Building, Soliman Pasha Square,
Cairo, in the 1920s. Crowley's apartment was apparently on the ground floor,
just left of the big windows of the entrance, on the side street. That's where,
according to Sigurd Bune's investigations, it is most likely he invoked Horus
and later received The Book of the Law.
Courtesy of Sigurd Bune (Perdurabo ST); see Forthethelemites.website

Bullock C.B. (1851–1926), Bullock vacated his apartment when
appointed colonel at Alexandria's garrison. Rose bade Crowley enter
the apartment's "temple" for one hour precisely at noon, Friday,
April 8; Saturday, April 9; and Sunday, April 10. Crowley sat with
pen and paper at two windows in a room to the left of the entrance
hall. The windows looked onto the side street, just before the square
that the entrance faced. From over Crowley's left shoulder, as though
from a corner of the room, Crowley heard a voice of "pure" English.
Over three lunchtimes, the voice dictated three chapters.

In Paris, twenty years later, Crowley remembered something that escaped all official accounts of the Cairo Revelation. He'd suffered a tongue lesion contracted in Ceylon. It affected his "sensorium," and he wondered not whether it engendered hallucinations but rather whether sensory abnormality had made preternatural communication *audible*.

Curiously perhaps, in no extant letters to Gerald Kelly was the subject of the communication ever raised; nobody ever interviewed Rose about it—she left no corroborating testimony. Although Crowley would subsequently base his raison d'être and life message on three chapters he believed to have been dictated in Cairo, his behavior and attitude back in Paris in April 1904 appeared unchanged.

Shortly before the Cairo events, he'd met pioneering psychiatrist Henry Maudsley (1835–1918) aboard ship from Colombo. They'd discussed whether trances such as Crowley's "dhyana" of 1901 could damage the brain or inhibit the mind's healthy state. Maudsley opined that the phenomenon was likely due to overstimulation of one part of the brain, counseling extreme care in such matters, not to overdo things. Well, Crowley arrived in Egypt in a somewhat fantastic mode, dressing himself as Persian dignitary Chioa ("Beast" in Hebrew) Khan, with jeweled jacket, sash, and fez, with his lady wife Ouarda (Arabic for "rose"), all, he claimed, just for the hell of it. He also took some kind of instruction in Arabic and Arabic Kabbalah, as well, he claimed, as learning "tricks" familiar to the Sidi Aissawa Sufi tariqa; that is, when he wasn't shooting birds, golfing at Helwan, or hobnobbing with English ex-pats at the Turf Club. In the circumstances, ambivalence about what occurred was justified.

One realization, however, Crowley deemed inescapable. As far as the Secret Chiefs were concerned, Mathers was a busted flush; the Golden Dawn required dissolution and recasting. This Crowley made conditional upon achieving supreme absorption in Godhead, known to Hindus as *samadhi*, or as Crowley called it, "knowledge and conversation of the Holy Guardian Angel."

Future workings would be based upon what Crowley understood as ancient Egyptian conceptions of a cosmic relation between infinite space (typified as goddess Nuit) and that which occupies space, illustrated on stele 666 as a form of sun god Horus, whom Brugsch Bey's Cairo Museum team transliterated as "Hadit" (Hor-Behedite); that is, *light*. Given infinity, relation of star to star, or sun to sun, was necessarily relative. Crowley deduced from this that within a synthesis of infinite relativity, individuality was absolute. Crowley came to see this metaphysical universe as the Cairo experience's central revelation: a magical, ethical system expressed as "Every man and every woman is a star"; with its corollary, "thou hast no right but to do thy will." While philosophy and abstract physics breathed behind the idea, it would be presented to the modern world as *prophecy* in the context of occultism, and fared accordingly.

Arguably, the system Crowley would call Thelema puts human being at the center of Einstein's famous formula published seventeen months later: energy equals mass multiplied by the speed of light, squared. The speed of light is the absolute of motion. If energy can be transformed into, or expressed as, moving mass, and vice versa, what Crowley understood by "magick" was scientific fact, for *will* was essence-of-movement in infinite space. The name of God in the Bible is usually translated: "I am that I am." Being and will presuppose movement; noun and verb are identified; of this dynamic, Crowley intuited sex as the symbol, and stele 666 as its illustration.

A KHAN IN THE CITY OF LIGHT

Crowley announced his return to Paris by medium of surreal telegram, sent to Gerald Kelly at 17 rue Campagne Première on April 22, 1904:

> PARIS LAROCHE GARE—FANGOW OUTRAGE ARCHANGEL ALLEGES ALIBI HUSBAND WRINGS PIGEONS NECK SHERLOCK HOLMES SUSPECTS POET YOM PRESENCE DESIRABLE ARREST GARE DE LYON TO NIGHT TEN FORTY

Another "message," equally cryptic, followed:

> PARIS DE MODANE PEA SHOOTING AFFRAY IN RANGOON RUMOURED ARREST OF GABRIEL VICTIM LYRING LANGHAM HOTEL PARIS TOMORROW—BOLESKINE=[4]

Kelly wasn't the only person to receive a telegram on April 22. According to writer Arnold Bennett's journal for that day, written in the rue de Calais (Pigalle), Paris, and having spent the previous evening watching a "stupendous" performance of Gluck's *Iphigenie en Tauride* at a "crowded and brilliant" Opéra Comique, with Rose Caron performing beautifully as Iphegenie . . .

> In response to a telegram I went to lunch with Aleister Crowley and his wife (Kelly's sister) today at Paillard's.* He had been made a "Khan" in the East, and was wearing a heavily jewelled red waist-coat, and the largest ring I ever saw on a human hand. I rather liked him. He said some brain specialist [Maudsley] had told him that what made a great brain was not the number of facts or ideas known, but the number of facts or ideas co-ordinated or co-related. I said: "Of course."[5]

Fig. 10.3. Restaurant Paillard, 2 rue de la Chaussée d'Antin and Boulevard des Italiens (closed in 1930 due to shift in social center).

Transposed to 1910, this encounter was used in chapter 3 of Bennett's *Paris Nights and other Impressions of Places and People* (1913) to describe the Mahatma, a character frequenting the unnamed Chat Blanc, Montparnasse:

---

*Established 1880, named after the famous Escoffier-trained chef who gave his name to the *paillard,* or veal cut and pounded translucently thin before momentary frying or grilling, Paillard's stood on the corner of the rue de la Chaussée d'Antin and the boulevard des Capucines, close to Edmond Bailly's Librairie de l'Art Indépendant (hub of Paris's Hermetic movement in the late 1880s). Favorite dishes included chicken archduke, Georgette potatoes, calves' sweetbreads with asparagus tips, fillets of sole Chauchat, and the pièce de résistance, stuffed duck.

"By Jove!" said the violoncellist. "There's the Mahatma back again! Oh! He's seen us!"

The peering face preceded a sloping body into the café, and I was introduced to a man whose excellent poems I had read in a limited edition. He was wearing a heavily jewelled red waistcoat, and the largest ring I ever saw on a human hand. He sat down. The waiter took his order and intoned it in front of the service-bar, proving that another fellow-creature was hidden there awaiting our pleasure. When the Mahatma's glass was brought, the Scotchman suddenly demanded from the waiter the total of our modest consumption, and paid it. The Mahatma said that he had arrived that evening direct from the Himalayas, and that he had been made or ordained a "khan" in the East. Without any preface he began to talk supernaturally. As he had known Aubrey Beardsley, I referred to the rumour that Beardsley had several times been seen abroad in London after his alleged death.

"That's nothing," he said quickly. "I know a man who saw and spoke to Oscar Wilde in the Pyrenees at the very time when Oscar was in prison in England."

"Who was the man?" I inquired.

He paused. "Myself," he said, in a low tone.

"Shall we go?" The Scotchman, faintly smiling, embraced his friend and me in the question. We went, leaving the Mahatma bent in solitude over his glass.[6]

Fresh—well, perhaps not exactly *fresh*—from Cairo, it's intriguing to see Crowley still in Chioa Khan guise on his first night back in Paris. The occasion was referred to dryly, and patronizingly, in *Confessions,* without reference to his dress:

My wife and I passed a short time in Paris and renewed old ties. One incident stands out in my memory as peculiarly amusing. We asked Arnold Bennett to lunch at Paillard's. He was completely overpowered by the deference of the maitre d'hôtel, who knew me very well, and his embarrassment at being introduced to such splendours was childishly charming. He was, of course, enormously pleased, and very kindly offered to give me an introduction to H. G. Wells. As Arnold Bennett had gratified the public with a highly spiced description of me in *Paris Nights,* I hope that he will take it as a compliment if I imitate his frankness in the matter of personalities. His accent and dialect made his English delightfully difficult. As we were leaving the restaurant, he told me that there was one thing about Wells that I mustn't mind: he spoke English with an accent.

Alas, I lack the skill to construct composite portraits. My own poor effort is the most crude photography. Also, I beg him to excuse my personalities. He is too great a man at heart to resent jests at the expense of his perishable vehicle; he is himself a Star bright-blazing, the more glorious for the thickness of the terrestrial vapours which it has had to pierce.[7]

"Composite portraits" refers to a 1911 note from Bennett to Crowley about a recent article in the *English Review.* Its Crowley-inspired description reappeared in *Paris Nights* two years later.

59 rue de Grenelle, Paris,
14 Feb[ruar]y 1911.

Dear Aleister Crowley,

Many thanks. I am very glad to have the volume. I will mention it in *The New Age* [journal], but I no longer write for *T.P.'s Weekly.* Not a portrait of you—my dear Crowley—in the *English Review!* For all you sat for was the waistcoat, the title, and the poetry. All these portraits are composite.

Yours sincerely,
Arnold Bennett[8]

It's possible that "Lord Boleskine" at least was still in Paris on June 29, when Anglo-Saxon Lodge No. 343 was petitioned to initiate "Aleister St. Edward Crowley, poet." The Grande Loge de France, which chartered the lodge in 1899, was then unrecognized by the United Grand Lodge of England. One wonders if Lodge Secretary James Lyon Bowley, chaplain to the British Embassy, Paris, who signed the petition, informed Crowley of this. Like Oscar Wilde, Bowley had been initiated in Apollo University Lodge No. 357, Oxford, October 1889, resigning in 1899.[9]

The Crowleys were back in Boleskine in July, employing Dr. Percival Bott as live-in obstetrician and Crowley's much loved Aunt Annie as housekeeper. It's unclear whether Legitimist L. C. R. Duncombe-Jewell a.k.a. Ludovic Cameron was still operating as factor. Ivor Back, surgeon at St. George's Hospital, arrived to edit Crowley's collected works and to enjoy himself with Bott and his host at billiards, paddling in a Canadian canoe in the trout pond he'd built, and rock scrambling locally and across the loch in more perilous climbs.

Crowley maintained that before leaving Paris, he'd informed Mathers by post that the Secret Chiefs had appointed him visible Head of the Order, with a new Magical Formula for the Aeon. Incensed, Mathers attempted a "magical attack," which, over late July, if we believe Crowley's account, caused the deaths of most of his bloodhound pack, amid outbreaks of inexplicable violence and illness among people connected with construction and house services. Crowley employed talismans from *The Sacred Magic of Abra-Melin the Mage,* evoking Beelzebub and his "49 servitors" to offset further harm.

Around this time, possibly prior to Mathers's attack, Crowley wrote to Kelly on fresh stationery, its striking letterhead unique in 1904. On blue paper was embossed an orange crest *B* for Boleskine, with the embossed Gaelic motto (also in orange) *'S RIOGHAL MO DHREAM* ["Royal is my race"] / *E'EN DO AND SPARE NOT,* followed by the Buddhist salutation *Namo Tassa Bhagavato Arahato Sammasam buddhasa*—"Honor to the Blessed One, the Exalted (or Perfected) One, the fully Enlightened One." Orange and blue together created what the Golden Dawn called "flashing colors." Do bear the Buddhist salutation in mind as you read on.

My dear G,

When Saul gets among the prophets* to the extent of a revered and noble lady writing: "Gerald is gone back to Paris. He was vaccinated as there was bad chicken-pox about where he lives— which might have been the other pox—who knows?" (I quote

---

*From 1 Samuel 19:23–24; Saul was counted among the prophets because he was seen to be filled with divine spirit.

my m[other]-in-law verbatim) it is evident that the war in heaven should be over and that silence for more than half a year is not too much to listen to strains so ravishing.

En effet, my dear boy—have I caught the divine effluvium?*— especially as I have to thank you for the great and even intelligent care that you have taken of my children (teste [witness] Cameron)†—news of the inglorious fourth‡ from your pen would be esteemed. As for your canvas, I hear great things, but from fools, so can't judge. But I am sure the astral mud must be gone by now; what you said about the mouth was so clear to the point that all must be well.

> Through the love of God our Saviour
> All will be well
> Free and changeless in his favour
> All, all will be well
> Cheerful if in God confiding,
> Peaceful if in Christ abiding
> Holy through the Spirit's guiding
> All must be well . . .

But as for me, why, there's a hell of a lot doing. "Oracles" [published

---

*The "divine effluvium" refers to immersion in spirit, enabling oracular speech. See Conwell, *The Hymns of Homer,* 69: "The oracles were delivered by a priestess called Pythia, who received the prophetic influence in the following manner; A lofty tripod, decked with laurel, was placed over the aperture, whence the sacred vapour issued. The priestess, after washing her body, and especially her hair, in the cold water of Castalia, mounted on it, to receive the divine effluvium. She wore a crown of laurel, and shook a sacred tree, which grew by. Sometimes she ate the leaves; and the frenzy which followed, may, with probability, be attributed to the usage."

†"Cameron" is sometime friend Louis Charles Richard Duncombe-Jewell (1866– 1947), who came for a week, then lay low at Boleskine, summer 1903, serving as factor, possibly continuing while Crowley and Rose honeymooned. He called himself Ludovic Cameron, after a Jacobite army hero who fought at Culloden. Legitimist Duncombe-Jewell wanted to restore Don Carlos VII of Spain and Charles XI of France and make separatist Celtic states, designing a flag for Cornwall.

‡Possibly referring to American ex-pats in Montparnasse celebrating Independence Day in Paris (July 4).

1905] a hotch-potch of dejecta membra* is uniform with the M[other]'s T[ragedy]. It contains "The Balloon," "In the Great Pyramid of Ghizeh," "Anima Lunae," "Hymn to Apollo," and other beastlinesses too foul to cumber up my M.S. case any more. "Why Jesus Wept" uniform with Sword. 'Tis good: wouldst thou see proofs? There is another; but there grim silence reigns. There is also "the Bromo book"—has O[scar].E[ckenstein]. sent you "Micturating Mary"?†

Bar an essay on "Time"‡ a dialogue between a learned Indian and a British sceptic, this leaves clear the road for the accursed Orphy [*Orpheus*]. We'll be at death-grips in a day or two, and this time someone *shall* succumb.

Do you still see gold tarnished and the Gray above Gavine? [my italics] How, in short are the [illegible] stools generally? And "Mrs Coles"? I suppose a subtle blind, for he runs at the nose too much for anyone.§ Or is the Norfolk Jacket the Parisian for the Bruxellois regulation tight trousers? Has anyone conceived any cynical ideas lately? Or is invention dead? But I want news; also guns for buffaloes pall. The beasts don't charge and toss me it's a lie. Like concealed crevasses—just to make shikaris [hunting expeditions] expensive.

Excuse my concealing or appearing to conceal my address. It is only that letters miscarry and that without £40 for the job. The moral of which is don't do it again! Excuse me still more if I wander; but I'm not a Jew at it, but—ah! If I told you that I should tell you more than (perhaps) I know myself For [*sic*]—is there an "I"? This is no doubt the central problem of all philosophy and how to attack it puzzles me. Yet I hope I suppose I may add that R[ose] [sends?]

---

*Probably a pun on *disjecta membra,* "scattered remnants."

†The "Bromo Book": part of *Snowdrops from a Curate's Garden* (1904), with "Micturating Mary" one of the obscene verses in that parodistic collection, some of which was allegedly written to entertain Rose during confinement.

‡Or "The Excluded Middle," included in the 1905 version of *The Sword of Song* for his collected works.

§Henry Coles, Stephen Haweis's photographic partner. Crowley had Coles and Haweis create a photographic portrait of himself, used as the frontispiece of his *Collected Works* (1905).

anything there is handy. (there's little handy here but one's .44 and the canoemen—but Lord!, you're welcome to *them*!)

Need I say more? Yours ever as ever. Aleister Crowley

Did you see a letter about you in the N.Y. Herald in Jan. or Feb? If Maugham asks you, go swear re that bugger Bles & my contract.* A.C.[10]

Please note Crowley's asking Kelly whether he'd seen a letter about himself in the *New York Herald* in "Jan." or "Feb." Had it not been for assiduous searching, one might conclude, on account of references to buffaloes, Crowley's .44 rifle, and canoemen that this letter derived from December–January 1903–1904, when the Crowleys were in Ceylon after big game, or late 1905, when they sailed up the Irrawaddy through Burma toward China. Which January or February was Crowley referring to? 1903, 1904, or 1905?

The *New York Herald*'s European edition, published in Paris during this period, included "Letters from *Herald* Readers" on many, but not all days. After long scouring old papers, an almost familiar name leaped from the Letters column, page 6, January 17, 1904:

LETTERS FROM HERALD READERS

*Chamberlain's Fiscal Policy Calls
Forth Pertinent Reflections
From Dinnis McCarty*

FIGURES OF GREAT PROMISE

*Edward A. Crawley in Far Off Rangoon Appreciates the Herald
as an Art Medium*

Edward A. Crawley? A likely story! The aroma of our man is unmistakeable. Like any camp follower, I followed the column:

---

*"Bles" is Arthur Bles, editor of Parisian anglophone *Weekly Critical Review,* devoted to the arts. Contributors included Havelock Ellis, H. G. Wells, W. B. Yeats—and Aleister Crowley, publishing fourteen of Crowley's Rodin poems between May 1903–January 1904. The two Schwob translations appeared in *Les Maîtres Artistes* (dedicated to Rodin; October 15, 1903).

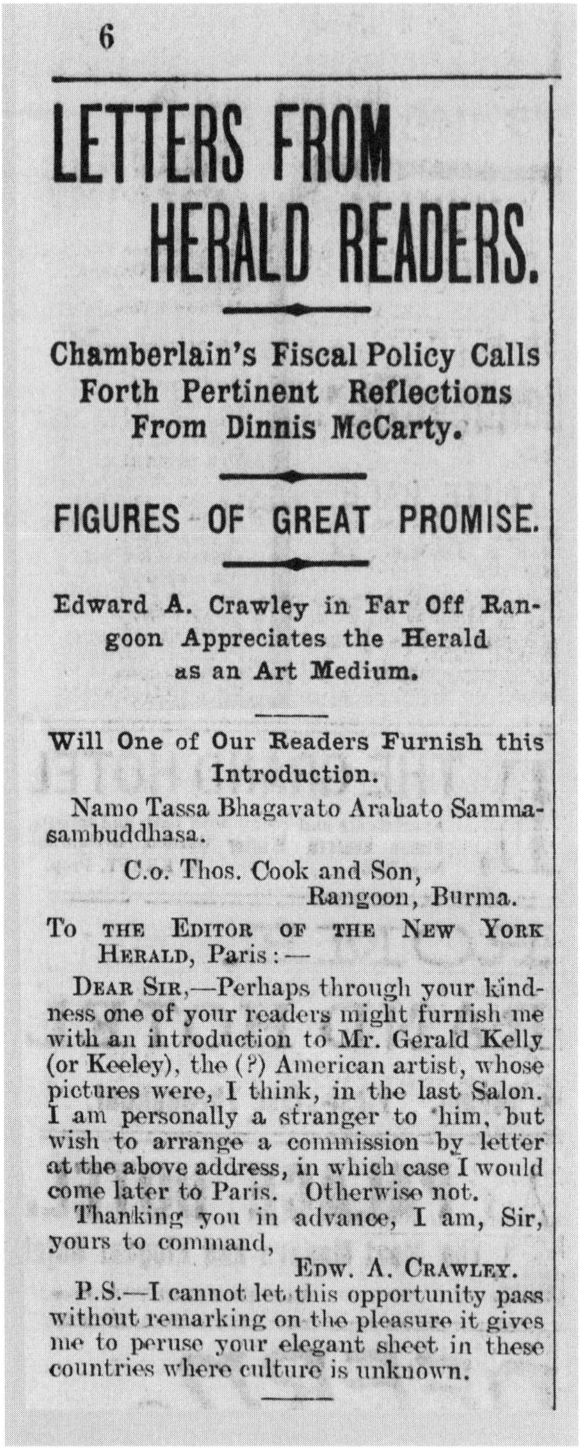

6

LETTERS FROM HERALD READERS.

Chamberlain's Fiscal Policy Calls Forth Pertinent Reflections From Dinnis McCarty.

FIGURES OF GREAT PROMISE.

Edward A. Crawley in Far Off Rangoon Appreciates the Herald as an Art Medium.

Will One of Our Readers Furnish this Introduction.

Namo Tassa Bhagavato Arahato Sammasambuddhasa.

C.o. Thos. Cook and Son,
Rangoon, Burma.

To THE EDITOR OF THE NEW YORK HERALD, Paris:—

DEAR SIR,—Perhaps through your kindness one of your readers might furnish me with an introduction to Mr. Gerald Kelly (or Keeley), the (?) American artist, whose pictures were, I think, in the last Salon. I am personally a stranger to 'him, but wish to arrange a commission by letter at the above address, in which case I would come later to Paris. Otherwise not.

Thanking you in advance, I am, Sir, yours to command,

EDW. A. CRAWLEY.

P.S.—I cannot let this opportunity pass without remarking on the pleasure it gives me to peruse your elegant sheet in these countries where culture is unknown.

Fig. 10.4. New York Herald *(European edition), January 17, 1904:* "Edward A. Crawley" *strikes!*

Will One of Our Readers Furnish this Introduction.

Namo Tassa Bhagavato Arahato Sammasambuddhasa

C.o. Thos. Cook and Son,
Rangoon, Burma

To the Editor of the New York Herald, Paris:—

Dear Sir,— Perhaps through your kindness one of your readers might furnish me
with an introduction to Mr. Gerald Kelly
(or Keeley), the (?) American artist, whose
pictures were, I think, in the last Salon.
I am personally a stranger to him, but
wish to arrange a commission by letter
at the above address, in which case I would
come later to Paris. Otherwise not.

Thanking you in advance, I am, Sir,
yours to command,
EDW. A. CRAWLEY

P.S.—I cannot let this opportunity pass
without remarking on the pleasure it gives
me to peruse your elegant sheet in these
countries where culture is unknown.

So there it is. I doubt if anyone had read Crowley's encouraging joke letter to his friend from Rangoon (?), or Ceylon, since its first and (nearly)
last appearance in Paris that Sunday 128 years ago! It proves Crowley's
"buffalo" letter must have been written in 1904, after leaving Paris, and
if the unsavory (!) *canoemen* weren't Orkney canoemen paddling about
Loch Ness (Orkney supplied canoemen to Canada at that time), then
perhaps he was envisioning Bott and Back in his trout pool. The buffalo could have been Scottish, too.

The second remarkable thing in the "buffalo" letter is Crowley's

Fig. 10.5. Cover of catalogue for the Paris 1903 Salon d'Automne *(Autumn Salon).*

Fig. 10.6. Boleskine House, from Crowley's "autohagiography" The Spirit of Solitude, *vol. 1.*
Courtesy of 100th Monkey Press and Ordo Templi Orientis.

cryptic question: *Do you still see gold tarnished and the Gray above Gavine?*

Here's a nice little adventure into Crowleyan allusiveness. Astute readers will have noticed "Gray" and "Gavine." Yes, that's Eileen Gray and Jessie Gavin the gamine, as Crowley saw her.

The line is from Swinburne's *Poems and Ballads* (1873), fifth verse of the ten of "Ballad of Burdens":

> The burden of bright colours. Thou shalt see
> Gold tarnished, and the grey above the green;
> And as the thing thou seest thy face shall be,
> And no more as the thing beforetime seen.
> And thou shalt say of mercy "It hath been,"
> And living, watch the old lips and loves expire,
> And talking, tears shall take thy breath between;
> This is the end of every man's desire.

This is the end of every man's desire . . . Crowley is sad about a love that's "expired," no doubt, but there's a double meaning, with a joke sting. This he will lay bare in the collection *Oracles: The Biography of an Art* (1905) with this brief prelude to a caustic poem:

SONNET FOR A PICTURE

ποικιλοθρον, ἀθανατ ' Αφροδιτα.
Σαπφω.

"—We have seen
Gold tarnished, and the gray above—"
—Swinburne.

The Greek above Swinburne's line introduces a poem by Sappho, ancient Greek lesbian poet, who at the time was lauded in Paris by Natalie Clifford Barney and friends. The first line begins Sappho's plea for Aphrodite's help: "Iridescent-throned, deathless Aphrodite," Aphrodite answers:

> Who is now abusing you, Sappho? Who is
> Treating you cruelly?
> Now she runs away, but she'll soon pursue you;
> Gifts she now rejects—soon enough she'll give them;

Now she doesn't love you, but soon her heart will
Burn, though unwilling.

Crowley's message seems directed most at Jessie Gavin but could
apply to both her and her love, Eileen Gray. Crowley cannot resist making Gavin the butt of his pretension-busting "Sonnet for a Picture," and
one might just suspect Miss Gavin had *something* to do with the previous
year's broken engagement to Eileen. *This is the end of every man's desire . . .*

As some lone mountebank of the stage may tweak
The noses of his fellows, so Gavin
Tweaks with her brush-work the absurd obscene
Academicians. How her pictures speak!
Chiaroscuro Rembrandtesque, form Greek!
What values! What a composition clean!
Breadth shaming broadness! Manner epicene!
Texture superb! Magnificent technique!
Raphael, Velasquez, Michael Angelo,
Stare, gape, and splutter when they see thy colour,
Reds killing roses, greens blaspheming grass.
O thou art simply perfect, don't you know?
Than thee all masters of old time are duller,
O artiste of the Quartier Montparnasse!

[This parody on the style of my own poems on the Art of Rodin
was written to furnish the subject of it with a critical eulogium
for domestic use. May she forgive one who has not less a sincere admiration for her work because he is capable of a jest at its
expense!—A. C.]

He takes away with one hand, gives with the other; Crowley could
never resist a joke.

Throughout the summer, conscious of what Kelly might be doing
in Paris, Crowley was keen to involve him with his own art. He wrote
from Boleskine on August 15: "Now be good and do the sketch for Rosa
Mundi. Have you a copy? O dear! I wish I could see you. I am perhaps
coming to Paris in October, solus [alone]. If so, much will become clear

to you."[11] Eckenstein considered *Rosa Mundi* (1905)—Crowley's tribute to wife and "miracle lover" Rose—too personal to publish, so Crowley had Renouard of 19 rue des Saints-Pères print it under pseudonym the H. D. Carr. Kelly didn't warm to Crowley's call for a sketch for a love poem to his sister, so one of Rodin's ten ink-and-wash designs for *Rodin in Rime* (still unpublished as a book) was used instead—but only after first surreptitiously inserting Kelly's sketch *The Blood Lotus*. Inspired by a long poem from *White Stains* (1898), *The Blood Lotus* was included in *Oracles,* where it appropriately prefaced Crowley's Baudelaire translations, "The Litany of Satan," with its refrain "O Satan, have pity of my long misery," among them.*

Disappointed by publisher Kegan Paul's desultory distribution and sales effort, and strongly desirous of realizing himself artistically, Crowley started publishing under the cheeky acronym S.P.R.T.: *Society for the Propagation of Religious Truth,* parodying long-established fount of global evangelism, the S.P.C.K. (Crowley's father had also self-published and distributed religious works, though without pleading for Satan's pity).

While the program involved Ivor Back writing footnotes for "Aleister Crowley, Hys Workes" (collected works) as Duncombe-Jewell compiled an early bibliography, Crowley pined for contact with Gerald:

> I would a word winged from your civilized place to my savage lair. I have not written a line for months, but have corrected much etc. Yet O[rpheus] is near its dismal end. It should make 200–250pp. Jephthah format. I appropriated your blue-lotus for my pome to the Kid [*Rosa Mundi*]—I think you saw it. That too should be out soon. In short I am busy in the beastly way; like you stretching canvas I suppose.
>
> The Kid and the small thing [baby Lilith] are well, unexpectedly well. But let me hear of Art. Have you a new studio? There is talk of my hurtling Quarterwards across the sunkissed abyss of the Channel about October days. They live on old brandy, caviar, and truffles in *Hell.* Nuff Said!
>
> Write,
>
> yrs ever B [Boleskine][12]

---

*The Blood Lotus emerged during Crowley's 1897 Amsterdam trip, where, violently rejecting the image of the crucified savior, the lover-poet passionately embraced death.

Unhappy with Crowley's using his *Blood Lotus* sketch, Kelly either considered it unsuitable for a poem addressed to Rose, or—perhaps sensing his work had advanced—didn't want attention for that image in this context. It's been suggested that Kelly feared a reputation tarnished by association, but there's no reason to think so at the time; besides, it was him *or Rodin*— fear of comparison might have stimulated the objection. Reluctantly, Crowley succumbed to withdrawing Kelly's work, while asking for more:

Your last received with mingled pain and pleasure. I disagree about the B[lood].Lotus. I think it very fine; and your name is not compromised.

But the vignette is I imagine not yet printed; I am writing to Renouard to hold it back, and to wait. I send you a size to draw a better design to, since you are so good, and it is to your sister that the book is. I long ago accepted Stanlaws's price for the heads (or drawings). Please tell him. What I want is illustrations for the L[over]'s A.B.C.* *I rely on you for 12.* Rodin 9 or 10 Stanlaws 6 Maurice Greiffenhagen† some. 12 and 10 and 6 and 6 equal 34.

Maurice – you promised me some. 12+10+6+6=34 52 wanted. (I think 26 to begin—vol I as it were.)

"Is The God Eater out?"‡ Do you live in a ditch, d.d. [dead duck?] or l.a p. [lick a prick?] or in b with a b? [bed with a bitch?] It was out last October. Prices have gone up since Argonauts came out. In "Collected" there is much careful revision—a fair amount cut out. I

---

*A set of simple love poems begun in Cairo in 1902, shortly before arriving in Paris. "The Lover's ABC" idea was transposed into *Rosa Mundi and Other Love-Songs* (1905), including numerous Eileen Gray–inspired poems.

†Penrhyn Stanley Adamson, known as Penrhyn Stanlaws (1877–1957), cover artist and film director (early 1920s)—a Chat Blanc regular (see page 148).—and Maurice Greiffenhagen (1862–1931), British landscape painter, illustrator, and poster designer. He exhibited at the Royal Academy of Arts from 1884 and was made Royal Academician in 1922; a friend of H. Rider Haggard, he illustrated Haggard's *She: A History of Adventure* (1889)—a favorite of Crowley's—and the serialized *Ayesha: The Return of She* (1904–1905). His 1891 painting *An Idyll* inspired D. H. Lawrence's *The White Peacock*.

‡*The God Eater: A Tragedy of Satire* was a play written in mid-July 1903, shortly before the Kellys visited Strathpeffer. Published by Charles Watts & Co. in October 1903, it reflects the thought that while Jesus's admirable personality engendered the misery of Christianity, so vile and irrational acts may engender human happiness.

gave Back a free hand with the blue pencil. The fact is neither you nor I can tell which is the indifferent work. They may know in A.D. 2904.

But I am moral. For the Nameless Novel (a bloody good title [first part of *Snowdrops from a Curate's Garden,* Paris "Cosmopoli,"* 1904]) Book of the Rules (7/6 net)

1. Let no sentence stand without reference by name to something usually nameless.
2. Never use the same name twice.
3. Never voluptuous.
4. Indicate personal friends (Arnot [possibly New York art collector, Matthias Hallenback Arnot, 1833–1910], Haweis, and sich [*sic*] like) with close accuracy.
5. Never mind anything else.

Back [Ivor] will give you an idea of the present scope of the contents—D[uncombe].J[ewell].F[actor]'s disjecta literae [bibliography]—if you have it not. It is on the cards that I may have to run south in a week or so. I hope not, for literally I grow to Boleskine. We shall see.

Give me your I of W [Isle of Wight] address. I suppose you'll fix yourselves somewhere. What may you do to amuse yourself? If you may read I could lend you a Tale of Archais.

Yours ever Boleskine[13]

Kelly requested that Crowley return *The Blood Lotus.* Doing so, Crowley doubted the judgment of "the Master," Kelly:

> I think you have underrated the enclosed fine example of the Master's early work. As a finished still life in the Louvre it would look ill by the 13 men [Salon Jury?]; but as a vignette to fill up letter press I think it good: very good like the 6 [days] of creation [Genesis 1]. But you are the master. Only I must have some vignette. [for *Rosa Mundi*]

---

*"Cosmopoli" was the imprint of Johann Valentin Andreae's anonymously published satire *Menippus* (1618). Andreae was founder of the Rose-Cross fraternity mythology; the imprint might also be an allusion to Paris's cosmopolitan status.

P.S. <u>Thoughts on Karma</u>

If I gave way to the Camberwell theory of life, how would my wife look in Inverness?* I care little for people—you know!—but I don't want her the laughing-stock of the county, now just beginning to be nice. B [Boleskine][14]

Clearly, Crowley hankered for involvement with Montparnasse, as in this leg-pulling (?) letter of August 29, with its likely reference to Theodore Spicer Simson and the hint that Kelly had suggested a *Rodin* lithograph didn't match a Kelly vignette:

I'm afraid you have been in much pain [left testicle], and I am an unsympathetic aesthete (the polite word for Simpson [*sic*]). I send you a R.M. [*Rosa Mundi*] I don't think it's any odds having a non-Rodin vignette—I wanted you to have a hand in a thing entirely your sister's (What's called nice feeling this is) I agree to, but loftily ignore, your oil-and-water argument [that Kelly and Rodin didn't belong together].

What is your left testicle doing—just occulting [?] or more? Tell me in simple language what you know about the juggins that broke up your liaison with the charming Sally Muggins[†] [Sibyl Meugens]. Where do nerves come in? I thought bollocks varied inversely as brains—one down t'other come on. But I am a brute—it is ill jesting with a sore bollock—never give a bollock sulphur! If you do you'll repent it. There's nought like pea-coddling—you let the bollock alone and he'll let you alone—(You read The Londoners [?]). I'm really frightfully sorry and wish you would rest here instead of the I of W [Isle of Wight].

Yes: you, Back (and I in less degree) should collaborate the intro-

---

*Rose's family objected to addressing letters "Lord and Lady Boleskine." Crowley exerted himself in the county to establish that "laird" went with the estate, a courtesy like that extended to Scottish judges; *laird* was Scottish for "lord." Accepted socially as Lady Boleskine, withdrawing the title could embarrass Rose.

†Samuel R. Wells's 1889 treatise, *The New Physiognomy, or signs of character manifested* (New York, Fowler & Wells), put an upper-class, white English face captioned "Princess Alexandria" next to a stereotyped Irish immigrant face captioned "Sally Muggins." Crowley's joke on her name might indicate he thought her common, or of uncertain origin.

duction to the Bromo Book [a section of *Snowdrops from a Curate's Garden*], to rag the one of whom Browning mellifluously chanted.

Just for a socket and surplice he left us.*

Just for a riband to stick in his coat.[15]

RETURN TO PARIS—ALONE

Crowley was due for Masonic initiation in Paris on October 8, but before departure, a near tragedy occurred. Vacationing at Bournemouth's Imperial Hotel on the south coast, Rose, whose menstrual cycle hadn't resumed after Lilith's birth, became convinced she was pregnant. Begging help from the nurse Crowley employed for the baby, the nurse dosed Rose up with ergot, to force an abortion. Rose finally confided in her husband that she thought the nurse was poisoning her with a noxious draft. He rushed her up to London, to the Savoy, where Dr. Bott and Ivor Back were astonished to witness rare ergot poisoning. Crowley alerted Gerald, who was to use guile, force, or the police if necessary to keep the nurse where she was, lest she discover her crime was detected.

Assured the doctors had saved Rose's life in the nick of time, Crowley crossed to Paris for initiation into Anglo-Saxon Lodge

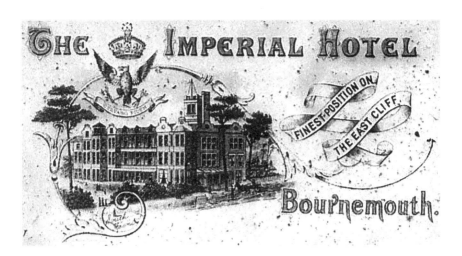

Fig. 10.7. Bournemouth's Imperial Hotel, 1904.

---

*Crowley here parodies Browning's poem about corrupt social climbing, "The Lost Leader"; original first line: "just for a handful of silver he left us."

No. 343, under the aegis of Worshipful Master, Edward Philip Denny. Crowley then wrote to Gerald from the luxurious Hotel d'Iéna, across the Seine from the Eiffel Tower:

Dear Gerald,

R[ose] like an ass forgot to give you my long explanatory letter. The point is not R[ose]'s entreaties (no doubt true) e.g. if X in pain asks Ivor for morphia, no blame attaches to X (a mere fool) but to Ivor who knows in case of harm coming. The details are utterly immaterial. Everyone is lying, anyway, probably even the chemist is pestling a poisoned potion behind his crimson lights [drawing of crown, four leaves; under: "A.T." = 4-2]

But G. Chesterton—a dumb fellow so far.* Thanks for your trouble, which I'm sorry to have caused. But Ivor will have told you that the danger [to Rose] was serious.

I had to go to Paris. All went well. I am not wroth with you for telling Ivor and the Guv, they having balls. It's cunts I'm skeery of.

Trot out your Brit. P [British Public? Or, possibly, "Prick"?], and I will find the loggerheads [blockheads?]! As to the cash it's cunts again making trouble. R[ose] is wrong not to pay B. K. [Blanche Kelly] but on the other hand B.K. promised to pay R[ose]'s expenses for the trip [to Bournemouth, presumably]. If this happened between men they would strike a balance. R[ose] owes £10 about, B.K. about £20 or £30. So it is absurd to fuss. (I—personally myself Ego Aleister Crowley) shall refuse to be made a cat's paw any longer for these feminine frays. It's only a try-on to get a ballster to take an interest in them. They're like spoilt pet dogs—all of them. So let us keep aloof—I don't think we should have quarrelled before, save for false representations on the part of womb-artists. Ann [Aunt

---

*On September 24, famous British writer G. K. Chesterton reviewed Crowley's *The Sword of Song* for the *Daily News* under the headline Mr. Crowley and the Creeds. Chesterton observed that its contents exhibited more than love for Buddhism; they demonstrated hatred for Christianity, which Chesterton challenged. Calling Crowley a "good poet," his *The Soul of Osiris,* written in "an Egyptian mood," merited praise, whereas *The Sword of Song* was "Browningesque in a Buddhist mood." Chesterton promised a follow-up, but it never appeared; hence, Crowley refers to Chesterton as being "dumb"; that is, unable or unwilling to speak, or respond to Crowley's written response.

Annie?] lied, you remember, but I don't believe she knew it. Their idea is to arouse sympathy: they suppress or subtly alter to suit; they rarely fabricate—"more rarely" because they lack the imagination in common with other high mental faculties; being fools, they usually fail even to attract the sympathy. R[ose] has written any number of exquisite letters to stir me up against F.F.K. [Frederick Festus Kelly, Rose's father], B.K. and yourself. This time I had the wit to see through it. I know they bully her—and so do you, don't deny it!—but that is no reason for embroiling an already strained situation. I propose that R[ose] shall Vaugirard* me for a bit here and return with but a cursory call or none at the Vicarage. There is no doubt that your charming family are much nicer to outsiders; you do bicker dreadfully between yourselves; and I think the painter G.K. [Gerald Kelly] like the poet A.C. [Aleister Crowley] had best follow Christ's advice about leaving father mother†—etc.—all the prohibited degrees in fact—and follow Art.

The above is really my doctrine of Non-interference—call it the Primrose doctrine, an you will.‡ But I'm sure you will subscribe to it.

Yours more than ever. Aleister Crowley

P.S. A.C. as soon as I can settle in a flat.[16]

Gerald replied from London, updating Crowley about the nurse's "crime," while repeating his mother's desire for repayment:

Hotel d'Iéna, Paris 16me.

Dear Gerald,

Yes! It is humiliating to think that after sneering for years at the man who

> Wound up the clock
> With the head of his cock
> and rogered his wife with the key

---

*A reference to joining him at the rue Vaugirard; that is, Montparnasse.
†Luke 14:26.
‡"an": archaic form of "if."

I should myself mistake a Sandow Home Exerciser* for a telephone. I should thank you for details of crime. The purport of my instructions was—you guess, of course, to have a handle against Nurse if she turned to bay (like the Old Guard of God) for "wrongful dismissal" or something. B.K. [Gerald's mother] is evidently right about money. The proposal and acceptance of £3 aid to a £30 job needs no witnesses—its idiocy is its guarantee. Vide enclosed. "Silurian" paper† seems atavistic to a fabulous extent.

Have in cortex [mind] a fine defence of the "smart set" with a whack at E. F. Benson.‡

? [sic]—Yrs ever, Aleister Crowley[17]

Irked by G. K. Chesterton's not making good his challenge, Crowley sought Gerald's assistance:

Dear Gerald,

Chesterton is dumb. Will you be kind enough to do what you suggested as to finding out what is the cause thereof? If it is mere dumbness I shall compare myself to a fishing boat from Hull fired at by Admiral Chestertenskyovitch, who retreats when he finds there is a Channel Fleet ready to biff him in the Channel of the Daily News or anywhere else.

Bell,§ with whom I talk much, thinks G.K.C[hesterton]. too journalistic.

But bid me smight the fellow or abstain. I will take your word for it. But haste.

---

*Eugen Sandow (1867–1925): Prussian bodybuilder who popularized bodybuilding; the "Exerciser" was a chest expander.
†"Silurian": paper made at the Silurian paper mills, Knighton, Radnorshire; also a distant geologic period, hence "atavistic."
‡Edward Frederic Benson (1867–1940): popular social-satirical novelist, homosexual (fell in love with Gerald Yorke's father, Vincent Yorke, when at Cambridge). His 1897 novel *The Babe, B.A.* based on Herbert "Jerome" Pollitt (see page 28). The *Smart Set:* American popular literary magazine (founded 1900; edited by H. L. Mencken) aimed at a market based on Ward McAllister's claim that only 400 upper-class New Yorkers were really fashionable; *smart* meaning "sophisticated."
§Clive Bell (see page 147).

The only question is whether I shall add a short Postscript to my reply twitting him with his pusillanimity.

Y[ts] (care Bowley* 25 rue de Longchamps) or at Hotel St. James, Aleister[18]

Possibly a guest of British Embassy chaplain Rev. Bowley in the rue de Longchamp—round the corner from the avenue d'Iéna in the swish Quartier Chaillot—Crowley was conscious the prestigious Salon d'Automne was imminent. Held for a month at the Grand Palais des Champs-Élysées from October 15, the salon jury admitted Haweis's work, but not Kelly's. Crowley deflected any disappointment by acclaiming an unalloyed triumph:

Dear Gerald,

I hope you will allow me to congratulate you on having advanced so far in painting that even the jury shit can see something new and therefore to be suppressed in your work. You are better than I thought you were: I have been loathing you of late for your puerile delight in the measure of toleration contemptuously accorded you by the *hoi polloi* [written in Greek]. You may now sit in the same box as I—it is the best for a true view of the stage.

For the rest, I hope you will not as reported make Cyprus your farthest point.[†] It is too much like St. Pauls 3rd journey. What you want is open sea or open sand—no damned objects to catch the eye. And 8 weeks is pure folly: 8 months more to the point. I have been doing silence here—you have no idea till you do it how perfect a recreation it is to feel alone in the dark with not a thought astir.

I can already think—I shall be able to work soon. For you, go where you can sleep in the open air for weeks together, without even a tent. That is another great secret of moral & mental & physical health. There is always a great struggle to get such conditions—so I find; but—"once in, How the delighted spirit pants for joy!"

Y[ts] ever, more than ever, Aleister[19]

I have given it up, and got a secretary to do my hard work. Sounds like biz, eh?

---

*Rev. Bowley, who proposed Crowley to Anglo-Saxon Lodge, Paris.
†Kelly was thinking of going abroad.

Crowley followed up with an encouraging letter in self-deprecating style, mollifying Kelly's disappointment by exposing conventional paths to fame as mediocre. To have work noticed at a salon could indeed lead to purchase "for the nation," even . . . knighthood. Posterity, however, would find the truth . . . at the Louvre! Kelly was on the way to *real* greatness, if, that is, he stayed true.

Die ♄ [Saturday]

My dear Gerald,

I cannot pass this opportunity of congratulating you on the great success. Bought by the Nation is that sad fingerpost to the Sword*: "Attention drawn to Kelly's work. Alas! Not here. Look in the Louvre, posterity!"
already halfway true.
Great! Remember I have always bid you go high, piped when you danced, but refused to weep when you mourned unto me.
My reward is your success.
Browning in some first edition ends a line "old nuns' twats." They told him and he said "twat" means "coif" or "hood" but withdrew the edition.
Can you place this? I am hearing from New Zealand about it but that's a long time yet.
I have just done—yesterday—my great Dialogue between an Indian Mystic and British Sceptic.† A most wearisome job! i.e. to write. Nobody can ever read it.
You will like why Jesus wept.‡ Plagiarists will follow with "When

---

*"Sword" refers to a knighthood. Compare with what Decadents in the 1880s and 1890s called "the way of the Cross."
†"The Excluded Middle: or, The Sceptic Refuted," in *Collected Works* 2:262; in logic, the law of *excluded middle* states that for every proposition, either this proposition or its negation is true.
‡*Why Jesus Wept: A Study of Society and the Grace of God* (first edition printed by Renouard, Paris, 1904, included "Mr. Crowley and The Creeds and The Creed of Mr. Chesterton with a postscript entitled A Child of Ephraim Chesterton's Colossal Collapse"). The poetic play was inspired when, during the Colombo honeymoon, Crowley encountered British mediocrity and snobbery combined.

Ghosty Fucked." "What happened to God." "The left Mr Right" (in Him i.e. Arich Anfim [?*Aesch Ayim* = "dual fire," in Hebrew Kabbalah] all is right) and "The Galilee Buggery" with J-F as John the Beloved Disciple. If you are not yet a Mason it is worth your while to become one in a *French* Lodge. Ask Bowley, who likes Tannhäuser, or says he does, and all sorts of sweet things. You should all get hot and cold in a week.

Ever yours ever   A.C.[20]

Booking into the grand Hotel Regina, 2 place Rivoli, Crowley wrote to Gerald on October 18, soon after the Salon d'Automne opened under Président d'Honneur Eugène Carrière:

Dear Gerald,

Sandow Home Exerciser—exercises (e.g. patience)
Hence any woman.
Telephone transmits messages faithfully.
Hence applicable to any woman.

Fig. 10.8. Hotel Regina,
2 place Rivoli, Paris, 1904.

Silurian. A geologic period of early date.

Hence its paper is "atavistic."

Chesterton is still dumb. Has [Penrhyn] Stanlaws gone to America? I believe I have found a use for American men. This is admittedly cryptic; I will explain it ere Monday. I hope this letter will allay the exacerbation caused by my last. Why should I, for all my brave words, follow after feminine trouble? I have had my lesson. God do so to me and more also if—

Y^{rs} ever A.C.

P.S.

Why the devil shouldn't I go to the "low Latin ¼" I met Howard [?] last Sunday; he seems a good man. I went to Autumn Salon. Haweis* represented by the most awful daubs I have ever seen; Patterson† by a unique Duke of York's entry into Melbourne which God may forgive him for I never will! A firework "14 Juillet" not quite so bad and a very muddled "impression" of a café bar.

---

*Entry for "Haweis, Stéphen, né a Londres—Rue Campagne-Première, 17," *Catalogue de peinture, dessin, sculpture, gravure, architecture et arts décoratifs: exposés au Grand Palais des Champs-Élysées. . . . Du 15 Octobre au 15 Novembre* (Evreux, 1904): Nos. 599–604—*Ombre* (*portrait de Mme M . . .*); *Le coiffeur* (*nuit rouge*); *Nu au crépuscule*; *Au jardinet* (*le chêne*); *Verrière le Buisson*; *les Lutteurs* (604). ["Haweis, Stephen, born in London—Rue Campagne-Première, 17," *Catalogue of painting, drawing, sculpture, engraving, architecture and decorative arts: exhibited at the Grand Palais des Champs-Élysées. . . . From October 15 to November 15* (Evreux, 1904): Nos. 599–604—*Shadow* (*portrait of Mrs. M.*); *Hairdresser* (*red night*); *Nude at dusk*; *To the garden* (*the oak*); *Verrière-le-Buisson*; *Wrestlers* (604).]

†Australian painter and printmaker Ambrose McCarthy Patterson (1877–1966) studied art in Melbourne and afterward at Académie Colarossi and Académie Julian, Paris; friends with soprano Nellie Melba; studied with John Singer Sargent. Exhibited five paintings at 1905 Paris Salon where Matissse and the Fauves made a splash. Patterson's 1904 Salon d'Automne catalogue entry: "Patterson (Ambrose-M.-Carthy), né a Baylesford-Victoria (Australie)—Boulevard Saint-Jacques, 51. 963.—*Le mastroquet du coin.* 964.—*14 Juillet.* 965.—*Voyage du Duc d'York à Melbourne.*" [Patterson (Ambrose-M.-Carthy), born in Baylesford-Victoria (Australia)—Boulevard Saint-Jacques, 51. 963.—The Corner Mastroquet. 964.—14 July. 965.—The Duke of York's visit to Melbourne.]

Lavery* had a nice "Mary in Green" and the most appalling full-length of a German officer that imagination could picture. Well-painted, they say; but never you fire off your "subject-matter" cant on me again! I shall reply "Lavery" or "Count Schnitzel von Scheishund" or whoever he is & you will squash like a moon-man in Wells.

Honestly, there is hardly a decent picture in the show, bar Toulouse-Lautrec who fascinates and Rodin the draughtsman who has some dozen drawings, new in method & more purposeful.

Y^{ts} A.C.[21]

Shortly after Crowley's visit to the Salon d'Automne, he went south, to Switzerland, to the resort of St. Moritz, booking into the Hotel Kulm, where Rose joined him in November, having left the baby at

Fig. 10.9. Catalogue for the Salon d'Automne, Paris, 1904.

---

*Friendly with Haweis and Eileen Gray, Irishman John Lavery (1856–1941), later knighted, painted portraits and wartime paintings. The 1904 catalogue lists two works: *Lieutenant Frecheron von Reumano* (no. 749); 750: *Mary in Grein* (*sic*)—described by Crowley.

Camberwell with her parents. Crowley did not care much for skiing, unless it was fast downhill, with a jump, but loved tobogganing on the Cresta Run.

While at St. Moritz, Crowley received a letter from Rodin at 182 rue de l'Université:

> My dear Crowley,
>
> Are you well in St Moritz?
>
> I envy you to be so close to the sky, skating and exploring.
>
> I'm so preoccupied that I can only speak to you about the bust in a month or less.
>
> My respects to madame Crowley, and to you my lively sympathy dear and great poet.
>
> A. Rodin. December 9, 1904.[22]

Whether the business about the "bust" involved purchase or commission is lost to history.

Returning to Paris, Crowley was raised Master Mason at Anglo-Saxon Lodge, December 17, 1904—more than eight months since *The Book of the Law* declared, "Abrogate are all rituals, all ordeals, all words and signs" (I.49).*

As winter 1904/05 ended, Crowley returned to Boleskine in what *Confessions* recalls as a kind of blissful or at least blank state, happy enough to shock and annoy people with his S.P.R.T. publications, or to play practical jokes on people, while taking only magic seriously, which studies were in abeyance anyway, though he made disappointing efforts to resume raja yoga (see *Aleister Crowley in India*).

Crowley's last extant, and with hindsight, sad letters to Gerald Kelly in Paris come from late 1905, after a brave but disastrous attempt on Kangchenjunga that began when he sailed from England on May 12 that year, arriving in Bombay in the hot season on June 9, whither he traveled by train to Calcutta before heading to Darjeeling where the expedition proper began.

By October's end, Crowley was back in Calcutta, where Rose and

---

Abrogate as an adjective, incidentally, had long been obsolete in 1904; as a verb, *abrogate* appears in the sixteenth century, meaning "to repeal" or "do away with."

baby Lilith's arrival from England coincided with advice from senior Calcutta lawyers that he quit India lest his shooting of hostile muggers in the red-light district detain him in court appearances indefinitely.

By the time Crowley wrote the following from Calcutta on October 31, 1905, two other events had occurred: first, October 12 marked Crowley's thirtieth birthday; second, the Salon d'Automne jury admitted four Kelly paintings for exhibition (October 18– November 25). Here is Kelly's catalogue entry (note the reference to Somerset Maugham's brother, Charles Ormond Maugham [1865–1958; misspelled as "Maughan"] who pre-bought one of them):

> Gérald KELLY né a Londres (Irlandais) ["born in London (Irish)"]
> 238, boulevard Raspail
> 832.—*Sandown*: *Sundown*, p[ainting].
> 833.—*Gaby*, p.
> 834.—*Le Corsage écarlate* ["The Scarlet Corsage"]: portrait, p.
>   (Appartient a ["belonging to"] M[onsieur]. C.O. Maughan.)
> 835.—*La cravate noire* ["The black tie"], p.

Kelly had changed studios, leaving Mademoiselle Sibyl "Mengens" (misspelled)—who exhibited two drawings at the Salon—at 17 rue Campagne Première: same address as "Mlle Mina Loy (b[orn] Hampstead)," who exhibited four drawings amid great unhappiness with Stephen Haweis—and the same address as Haweis, who exhibited three engravings and three paintings. Mademoiselle Kathleen Bruce ("Irlandais"), of 22 rue Delambre, exhibited "Portrait de Charles Hoffbauer (statuette patinée verte)," ["green patinated statuette"] sculpture no. 247.

The group Crowley first met in late 1902 had "done good," sharing salon space with "Basile" Kandinsky, Renoir, Sickert, and other artists then or now famous.

I think Crowley's letter, while recognizing Kelly's achievement, bears an underlying sourness, and soreness. Its implications would likely have driven further a wedge between two friends. A distant Crowley was watching his closest friend drift away toward established success, something denied him, or something he might claim denied by himself. That Crowley includes himself in the designation "intellectual prig" takes nothing from the force with which the phrase would almost certainly have hit Kelly, someone Crowley in happier days dubbed a "geniass." How much more of Crowley's sometimes condescending advice would Gerald Kelly be prepared to take?

My dear Gerald,

You are certainly magnificent and have scored all round. At last (from what Rose tells me) you seem to have taken another step on the path which leads to glory and the grave. It is well that you should act in this masterly fashion; what you have done I can't say I know, but it seems to have made people angry.

For all that you are wrong in sticking to Paris: You ought to be spending your nervous energies on savagery, rather than on the purely false culture of the "intellectual" prigs. What we have both failed to see hitherto is that *we* are prigs, worse—because more knowledged—than the crowd that bumsucked Schwob, and that still bumsucks Rodin.

You are, I think, worse than I, ostensibly at least; for I have pretended to despise my art, while you have always worshipped it. Though our speech has reversed these roles, this was the truth.

Now Shaw is quite right: people who have achieved a true style are people who have had something to say and were mad to say it. But the something has been assimilated and become instinctive therefore uninteresting or rejected therefore absurd. Hence the style is the permanent truth, as you have always said.

Your mistake was in not seeing the cause. And thus the ridiculous Milton & Bunyan are masters as well as the admirable Huxley [Thomas Henry Huxley (1825–1895)]; and the filthy minded Baudelaire as the virginal Crowley. *Poems & Ballads* [Swinburne] is an orgasm; the later work a wet dream. You can't paint a picture without muscular exertion, though nothing is so calm as a picture. If you try to obtain the calm by going to sleep, you don't get it. Lust after a woman and her imperfections are beautiful; admire her, & she becomes at once a dowdy. A lily achieves beauty by trying to grow. . . .

I suppose you have heard nothing of my Kangchen[junga] trip. It was good fun, made me fit, and I got through some hard reading. Tell Miss Bruce I am back on her track—for I read Kant's *Prolegomena* recently and am about to start the *Critique of Pure Reason*.

My views are changing in many ways—it is in a very limited sense that I can call myself a Buddhist. [Sidenote: "Rangoon, Nov 6. Allan, however, has much widened his own views, so that if I am no Buddhist, he is none."] If you have not read Burton's *Kasidah*,* do—even if it costs you an effort. It seems to me pretty well the ultimate of human wisdom, as distinguished from my own advance upon the possible.

I wish Eckenstein would wire whether he is coming out or not. In the meanwhile, I hope to go to Burma and Persia: the former for Allan, the latter for the book of verses &c with Rose & Lilith to sing in the bloody wilderness.

I seem to myself much more settled & solid; the actual keeping up my end in the fight here has done me good† in that way. But I have written damned little, bar a very fine pome on Kali (114 ll [lines])

Rangoon Nov 6. Too hot to worry to write more: so I send this.

Love & luck Y^{rs} A.C²³

In similar mode comes the following undated fragment of a letter sent around the same time (Crowley reflects on reaching thirty), while repeating his warning about the price of repetition to please judges:

I have thought too of turning to serious writing again, the Jephthah-Waikiki Beach style. But I am 30 and a proud papa. Shelley and Keats never touched 30. That day is over for me. I think some small bits of my work are classable with theirs; I must perforce leave it at that. But I may yet do good on more solid lines—perhaps the tragic. Anyway, I hope I shan't simply go bad like A.C.S[winburne]. At least I am certain to avoid the blunder of making a good thing and copying it for ever. Hence I am Shelley reincarnate; for he alone has avoided this. Versatility is the mediocrity's curse, the artist's salvation. Kelly

*Sir Richard Burton's poem "The Kasidah" (1880) should be read to understand Crowley's fundamental viewpoint.
†He may refer to the press-hounding, and his asserting innocence for his part in an expedition in which two climbers and a bearer were killed, or his response to being mugged by dacoits (other attacks on non-Indians had resulted in deaths).

on [or?] Velasquez, the brilliant experimenter in all sorts. And—go thou and do likewise. Unless you have gone back, you are technically good enough to paint anything you see. If so, you should be dashing off masterpieces. I have always been afraid of your doing the Patterson trick [see page 192]: perfecting touch and paying for it with sight. R[ose]. said you destroyed the "Portrait of Lord B."* An error. T'was the best thing you ever did—thanks to W. S. Maugham's idiotic chatter that P.M [afternoon]. Proof: the verdict of the Salon judges. They are v[ery]. like the public; will pass any amount of "good painting" and "bad painting"; but are alarmed and angry at "new painting." Lycidas,† vile as it was, was yet rejected for its one excellence—its originality. I admit *I* couldn't see even that; but the suspicious bourgeoisie of an R[oyal].A[cademy]. detected it or made him think he did.

I rather thirst for news of you all: I hear vague rumours of interesting things, and want more. I hear Haweis has returned to the vile dust from‡ [rest missing].[24]

The following year, 1906, after completing a family trek across a region of southern China, daily invoking "Adonai"; after the sudden, shocking death of daughter Lilith in Rangoon; after a voyage across the Pacific, a journey across Canada to New York City, a return across the Atlantic to Britain; after psychological shock, illness, and convalescence in a nursing home, Crowley experienced samadhi, and for the next eleven years, the artist died to the prophet, mystic, and magician; and the friendship of poet Aleister Crowley and painter Gerald Festus Kelly died, too.

---

*Crowley sat for a portrait as "Lord Boleskine" in a green satin waistcoat, splashed with yellow (see page 50). Kelly destroyed it; why?

†Sculptor Harvard Thomas's unconventional approach to sculpture made him an outsider to Victorian taste. In 1905 the Royal Academy rejected his *Lycidas* as its nonheroic or nonidealist realism was felt too shocking.

‡Haweis separated from Mina Loy briefly in 1906; they went to Florence in 1907.

ELEVEN

Adonai 1907–1908

January 1907 opened with fresh correspondence from Rodin, writing from 182 rue de l'Université, running parallel to the Quai d'Orsay on Paris's Left Bank. Crowley, in London, took fourth-floor rooms at 60 Jermyn Street, Piccadilly, where he dieted, practiced hatha yoga, bhakti yoga, meditated, and experimented with hashish obtained from Whinerays apothecary a short walk away. Things were going badly with Rose; alcohol had become her secret mainstay. It's unclear whether Crowley's numerous affairs constituted cause or reaction; both probably. Crowley had his "True Will," but while *Liber Legis* (*The Book of the Law*) had a role for a Scarlet Woman who'd killed her heart and was "shameless before all men" (III.44), it held naught for Rose's comfort.

On January 6, Rodin replied to Crowley's inquiry about an appropriate publisher for *Rodin in Rime,* suggesting Fischer Unwin, 1 Adelphi Terrace, London (publisher of Frederick Lawton's Rodin biography); Grant Richards (who published an edited version of Lawton's book); and Scribner & Son, 115 5th Ave., New York:

> It would be a genuine shame, my dear friend, if your book, which is a work of art, couldn't be disseminated, although this is unfortunately the fate of all that is good.
>
> But personally I don't know English publishers or their genres of publication. My information can therefore be of only feeble assistance.

Best wishes to you, my dear artist and friend, with my cordial memories.

Aug. Rodin[1]

The day Rodin wrote, Crowley was in Bournemouth, experimenting with hashish, in a state of *atmadarshana,* which is probably meaningless to describe without the experience. Crowley tried: the universe freed of its conditions—or, each part of the world contains the whole, or . . . shall we say "matter and spirit no longer opposed"? Or, absolutely clear perception of spirit inseparable from everything else. "All as one . . ." Words fail.

Ten days later, Rodin requested more details about Crowley's intentions with the poems and lithographs, as Rodin was speaking to a publisher about another book featuring his work. Rodin needed assurance the books' materials wouldn't overlap.

Writing a week later, having received lithograph copies from M. Auguste Clot (1858–1936), an impressed Rodin agreed to the seven chosen for a volume for which Rodin promised to offer better thanks when he could read it in French.

Rodin dispatched his last extant letter to Crowley on January 29, 1907, by which time printers Chiswick Press had delivered a version of the book, modestly titled *RODIN IN RIME: Seven Lithographs by Clot, from the Water-Colours of AUGUSTE RODIN, with a Chaplet of Verse by Aleister Crowley:*

My dear Crowley,

Thank you for all the information about your book.

I've kindly received your volume from Miss [Kathleen] Bruce, and it's very good, and I voluntarily give you the frontispiece letter for this volume consecrated to my art, and by which you honour me.

Only, I unfortunately don't hear English, and can't read your works in the text. Could I most sincerely oblige you to translate several poems for me, four or five for example, so I can get an idea?

You're more able than anyone to do so given your perfect knowledge of French, and if you could devote some hours to your own translation, you'll be more certain not to be betrayed.

Aug. Rodin

P.S.: I've read two of them on another occasion, those Marcel Schwob translated, which were very fine and delicate in feeling, and vigorous in expression, but it was a long time ago. I'll be able to read them again. But also I'll be delighted to get to know the new ones from the new collection.[2]

Miss Bruce was now a feature of Crowley's life. She sculpted him as an "Enchanted Prince" on February 23. Sitting again for her three days later, Crowley realized an analogy existed between sexual attraction and union with the Holy Guardian Angel, though joy with Kathleen was somewhat frustrated. Rose, meanwhile, was proving herself unable to care properly for new baby daughter Lola Zaza. Lola was poorly that month, and when Blanche Kelly also demonstrated incompetence by ignoring doctor's instructions, an anxious Crowley kicked her out, literally.

The prophet was in Cambridge on February 28 for an exploratory "missionary journey," meeting talented undergraduate poet Victor Benjamin Neuburg, recommended by Crowley admirer Captain Fuller. Neuburg would become a devotee. However unlikely he looked for the role, Crowley now saw himself as aeon-teacher, working with old G.D. member George Cecil Jones to reconstitute an order linked to the Secret Chiefs for the further initiation of the planet. Crowley's enthusiasm was not shared by Cambridge University's intercollegiate Christian Union, which worked surreptitiously to damn this Pan-oriented paganism sprouting among undergraduates shamefully dissatisfied with Christ crucified.

At February's end, dinner with George Montagu Bennet, 7th Earl of Tankerville kick-started fresh adventure—but, as Crowley began to realize, Tankerville was stark, staring mad, imagining all kinds of hostile occult influences emanating from his mother's alleged sexual deviance amid other baleful powers. Recognizing the downside of evangelical hysteria, confident his Thelemic understanding could free the genius from constraining neurosis, Crowley convinced himself, Tankerville, and Tankerville's beautiful American wife, Leonora Sophia, that he could strengthen Tankerville's spiritual resources, rendering him invulnerable to spiritual attack. Crowley was under no illusion that the aristocrat's problems were imaginary, so worked on the imagination to convince Tankerville he was safe. Straightened out, Tankerville, Crowley thought, would be cured of irrational paranoia.

Pursuing distance from "Tanky's" fears, Crowley proposed a North African and Spanish tour. Exercise, fresh air, and Crowley's watchful company would give Tankerville's inner life opportunity to right itself. Working on a similar principle to what would become known years later as Jung's self-regulating psyche, Crowley's magick was, he believed, science of the subconscious, whose "spirits" could be evoked by will of superconsciousness, a process of clearing illusions and concentrating energy.

Thursday, June 27, 1907, saw Crowley and Tankerville leave for Paris, where they took a train to Marseille. Enjoying respite in Morocco, Tankerville began speaking quite sanely about his marriage and sex life, but the lull in the storm was brief, and the remainder of the trip proved an endurance test for Crowley. By the end of July, relations ended; the Countess of Tankerville terminated Crowley's services by letter.

While Crowley returned to his yoga, and experimented with mescaline, the dark clouds of Rose's condition congealed. By September's end he discovered she'd consumed 120 bottles of whiskey in 150 days. By contrast, A.C. found himself "scribe" of the higher mind. That higher mind or identity called Adonai, or "Holy Guardian Angel," was in *his* samadhi, writing by "A.C.'s" pen the "Holy Books" of Thelema. Crowley believed himself on track to becoming a Master of the Temple, beyond ego: the universal Self. He felt almost continually inspired, at least, that is, when cozy in his Jermyn Street flat. It was another story when with Rose at 21 Warwick Road, Earl's Court (Boleskine was rented out). Crowley, Eckenstein, and the Kelly family finally agreed that he and Rose should live apart until Rose recovered from alcoholism; the Kellys would care for Lola Zaza.

PARIS, 1908

Crowley began *The World's Tragedy* in February 1908 while visiting his mother at Eastbourne. Eventually printed in 1910 by Renouard in Paris, and dedicated to Pan, its title page declared it "privately printed for circulation in free countries. Copies must not be imported into

England or America." Crowley wished to free up love through a collection of scathing reminiscences, essays, poems, and short poetic plays. Open advocacy of male homosexuality, opposition to Christianity ("the religious expression of the slave-spirit in man"), and ability to expose vice in British government determined its place of printing, and tiny circulation.

First draft finished, restlessness drove Crowley to the kindly Bourciers's Hotel Blois, 50 rue Vavin—people, he said, in whom the spirit of d'Artagnan persisted, who welcomed the footloose *gentilhomme*. Drifting back to England, he played golf at Deal on the Kent coast, then faced the music about Rose's condition. They decided to separate after two months at a Leicester clinic for inebriate ladies proved a failure.

Returning to Paris, he took up short stories, writing a horror story about a malevolent surgeon who dissects a stolen brain to find the soul: "a nice Christmassy idea," as he called it. Finding Paris "disgusting" (he doesn't say why), he sought peace at Morêt (Moret-sur-Loing) in the Île de France, where artists Sisley and Renoir found inspiration; Crowley didn't. He went to Venice with a sore throat, inspiring another "Christmassy idea" about a painter who imagines he's suffering from throat cancer (suggested by Eugène Carrière's death in 1906), realizes he's insane on the question, is advised to go motoring by his doctor (modeled on Crowley's Paris doctor Edmund L. Gros), reaches the Pyrenees, and cuts his throat.

He was, he said, "incurably sad about Rose."[3]

Back in Paris, Nina Olivier brought him out of the doldrums, and he wrote a better story, "The Dream Circean," full of romance, about a man who saves a girl from her evil mother but, wishing to return, cannot find the house. He meets Éliphas Lévi, who tells him he can be cured of monomania so long as he never enters the street where he thought she lived. After Lévi's death, he enters the street to prove it no longer obsesses him, whereupon the obsession returns and he spends the rest of his days searching Paris for the girl with the golden hair, knowing she must now be an old woman.

Rose's father contacted Crowley in Paris, urgently; he must return: Rose was better. She wasn't. Back at Warwick Road, she'd be so drunk by breakfast she could hardly speak.

♦ ♦ ♦

On July 8, he returned to Paris, working on various pieces, including the autobiographical section of *The World's Tragedy* and the strangely compelling, somewhat perverse poem of obsessive love, dedicated (secretly) to Kathleen Bruce, *Clouds without Water*, which took Crowley's ironically objective cynicism to new heights, or depths.

Crowley also wrote "After Judgement," a powerfully natural, direct, rebellious, passionate poem about his love for Augustus John's sometime lover and model, Euphemia Lamb (1887–1957), who was in Paris (Dorothy in the poem). It appeared with many other poems, including "Telepathy" (another warmly impressive paean to Euphemia) in his entertainingly rich collection *The Winged Beetle* (1910):

> Farewell! O God, in endless bliss
> Crowned, with Thine angels singing by:
> I go to hell, with her last kiss
> Yet tingling in my memory.

Fig. 11.1. Euphemia *by Ambrose McEvoy (1878–1927); Euphemia Lamb in 1909.*

Lancashire-born Bohemian, Euphemia married painter Henry Lamb in 1906. Moving to London, they attended Vanessa Stephen's Friday Club before Vanessa married Clive Bell (lately returned from Paris) in early 1907. Fair skinned, fair haired, and boyishly lithe, lovely Euphemia journeyed to Montparnasse with Henry in March that year. While Henry studied under Augustus John (who became Crowley's lifelong friend), Euphemia modeled for him. Fascinating John, the sexually extravagant, realist, and fantasist Euphemia could pass for a man in men's clothing so effectively that she and John were once arrested as homosexuals, with Euphemia forced to strip at a police station. John encouraged Henry's relationship with partner Dorelia McNeil (1881–1969), and by summer 1907, Euphemia was practically independent, able to shower her charms on an appreciative Crowley, among others. Initially resentful that she could satisfy herself sexually without personalizing the attraction with the idea of love, Crowley grew to admire her "keeping the planes apart."[4] She remained a good friend, well read, an interesting talker, funny, gay, alluring.

Victor Neuburg, shy and inexperienced, visited Crowley in Paris in summer 1908. Crowley masked his longing for direct contact with nature by larks with Nina and Euphemia. They all took Neuburg to the Bal Bullier ballroom-bar and got him plastered on absinthe and Pernod. He fancied both ladies but was inept at wooing. The two girls had their fun, teasing and putting him down, pretending his clumsy, over-lush approaches hurt their honor. Out of his mind, he offered Nina money and the next day couldn't rise from bed so heavy was the hangover.

Euphemia and Crowley both enjoyed inducing people to make fools of themselves and cooked up a little scheme at Neuburg's expense. Crowley told Neuburg that Euphemia was hurt by his approach because she'd fallen in love with him. Neuburg should make amends. Euphemia at first pretended to hide her "true feeling" but gradually yielded, and Neuburg considered himself engaged. Crowley advised him against neurotic obsession; he should understand the difference between love and sex. His cure should consist of some physiological realism, so Crowley took him down the rue des Quatre Vents near the Odéon to meet an accommodating professional, "Marcelle." Crowley then affected shock to discover Neuburg had proposed to Euphemia (that she was married to a man around the corner, Crowley said, mattered little in Montparnasse!)

and Neuburg must confess his "infidelity." This he did at an arranged dinner party, where Euphemia extracted the details from Neuburg, bit by embarrassing (to him) bit. Euphemia then berated Crowley for mismanaging his responsibilities: "What *would* his parents say?" Crowley pretended to beg her forgiveness as she took Neuburg down the boulevard with her, Crowley entreating her from behind. She rebuffed him coldly; he wouldn't be forgiven, nor would Neuburg!

Poor Neuburg took it all to heart. He'd brought suffering to the fairest maiden who ever walked, and Crowley let him wallow in remorse a few days until he called on Neuburg's hotel to announce it time to understand some other facts of life. Neuburg didn't believe Crowley, doubting neither Euphemia's virtue nor Crowley's infamy. Neuburg had to be practically dragged back across the road to Crowley's room, where Neuburg found Euphemia, naked, smoking a cigarette on his bed. Crowley lay the cause of Neuburg's suffering at "romantic idealism," and felt he'd done the fellow a service; without shock therapy, he'd have been prey to every vampire who fastened on to him for the rest of a disappointed life. Crowley took pride in the change in Neuburg, who, he said, dropped all food fads, got healthy, overcame nervousness and inhibitions and developed his magical powers accordingly. He was cured of insisting nature is what one thinks it ought to be and entered reasonable relations with humanity. Romantic delusions about nature are still a global problem, or so Crowley would argue. I wonder if he had the cure.

Crowley dedicated further tutorials for Neuburg. He needed to understand how things actually come about in the world, what providing something as common as bread actually requires. So on July 31, with five pounds between them, they left Paris for Bayonne, then walked across the Pyrenees, heading for Madrid on foot. After being entranced by Velasquez's *Las Meninas* in the Prado, Crowley took Neuburg via Gibraltar to Tangiers for further enlightenment.

> The conclusion of my meditations was that I ought to make a Magical Retirement as soon as the walk was over. I owed it to myself and to mankind to prove formally that the formulae of initiation would work at will. I could not ask people to experiment with my methods until I had assured myself that they were sufficient. When I

looked back on my career, I found it hard to estimate the importance of the part played by such circumstances as solitude and constant communication with nature. I resolved to see whether by application of my methods, purged from all inessentials and understood in the light of common-sense physiology, psychology, and anthropology, I could achieve in a place like Paris, within the period of the average man's annual holiday, what had come as the climax of so many years of adventure.[5]

In the autumn of 1908, Neuburg returned to Cambridge, doubtless making quite an impression with his stories, while Crowley experienced samadhi in Paris.

Samadhi in *Paris*?

Yes, just like that.

TWELVE

John St. John, or Aleister Crowley's Great Magical Retirement, 1908

Crowley prefaced his record of magical retirement with a corrective to myths of a romantic East: "Paris is as wonderful as Lhassa, and there are just as many miracles in London as in Luang Prabang. . . . The Universe of Magic is in the mind of a man: the setting is but Illusion even to the thinker."[1] The important thing, he writes, is to tread the unexplored regions of the mind. In the midst of Paris, beset with appetites, Crowley set out to control his thoughts by will, for happiness depends on state of mind.

He began shortly before midnight on September 30 by taking the violet robe and ring of an Exempt Adept, the almond wand of Abra-Melin, a Tibetan bell of electrum magicum (the striker of human bone), magical knife and anointing oil of Abra-Melin, and performed the Lesser Banishing Ritual of the Pentagram, imagining and projecting pentagrams at the four points of the compass, uttering sacred words of invocation. He cut a tonsure on his head to let in light of infinity and cut a cross of blood on his chest to symbolize slaying of the body. He then made ten oaths of obligation, the last being to interpret every phenomenon as a dealing of God with his soul.

He then assumed an asana, performed pranayama, concentrated on the Third Eye and the will to knowledge and conversation of the Holy Guardian Angel. The bell was struck twelve times, and the thirteen-day operation properly began.*

THE THIRTEEN DAYS

Day One

He awoke, meditated, forced himself up, walked to the Café du Dôme on the boulevard de Montparnasse, had coffee and brioche. It was about 8:45, and a Thursday. In beautiful sunshine he took a gasoline taxicab to the Turkish bath and massage, meditated on the operation, determined to avoid aimless chatter, and willed the "Presence of Adonai." At midday he ordered a dozen oysters and beefsteak, noticing distaste for food had begun. Soon, impressions failed to connect; in Buddhist mode, he thought objectively about individual acts and thoughts—for example, "There is a tendency to perceive a being who is aware that

Fig. 12.1. Café du Dôme, Montparnasse (1920s).

---

*For exhaustive detail, readers may consult the supplement to *Equinox* 1, no.1 (1909).

something is swallowed; there is a swallowing &c." He performed pranayama: ten seconds breathing in, twenty seconds out. At about one, he took an hour's nap.

While he's napping, let me confess my thoughts wandered, and I asked myself: I wonder what happened while Crowley was napping? *This:* around Piquette Ave., Milwaukie Junction, Detroit, the early shift was arriving for the first day's official production of the Model T Ford, an object of sense, assembled in a day, that, reflected upon later, would appear to have revolutionized the world.

Crowley awoke refreshed, oblivious to either any alleged revolution or the morning's headlines about conflict between King Ferdinand of Bulgaria and the government of "Young Turks" who'd recently ousted Sultan Abdul Hamid in Constantinople. He got home, assumed his asana, and managed seven pranayama cycles, but the asana hurt a lot. He tried an Islamic mantra, hoping Adonai would reveal the best mantra "to invoke Him." He tried meditating in the easier hanged-man posture.

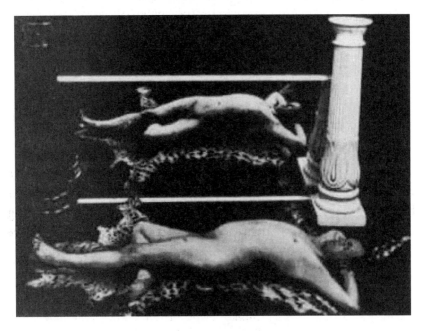

Fig. 12.2. Crowley demonstrating the hanged-man meditation posture,
Equinox *1, no. 7 (March 1912).*
Courtesy of Ordo Templi Orientis

At 4:15 he read *Liber 671,* a new initiation ritual "of the Pyramid."* In his state of concentration he found shopping especially dignified. He drank a citron pressé at the Dôme before returning "home" (Hotel Blois, 50 rue Vavin) with two pears, half a pound of Garibaldi biscuits, and a packet of gaufrettes (waffles).

Intending to collect some milk from the Dôme and retire for the evening (it was 10:50), he met Nina Olivier, accompanied by "that red-headed bundle of mischief, Maryt Waska." Maryt was duly taken to dinner (Crowley only had an omelette, some bread and camembert, milk, and a coffee), followed by two hours of Vajroli mudra "badly performed"—this being a hatha yoga posture for retaining semen (see the *Shiva Samhita,* a Sanskrit text). He wrote of reluctance, but saw it an act of "self-denial," lest, that is, "my desire to concentrate on the mystic path should run away with me," which strikes one as arch, ironic humor.

A "more straightforward type of meditation" involved this reflection:

> Naked, Maryt looks like Correggio's *Antiope* [ca. 1528]. Her eyes are a strange grey, and her hair a very wonderful reddish gold—a colour I have never seen before and cannot properly describe. She has Jewish blood in her, I fancy; this, and her method of illustrating the axiom "Post coitum animal triste" made me think of Baudelaire's "Une nuit que j'étais près d'une affreuse Juive" [Baudelaire, *Les Fleurs du Mal,* 1861]: and the last line "Obscurir la splendeur des tres froides prunelles" ["To obscure the splendor of the very cold plums"].

Additional comparison with Barbey d'Aurevilly's *Rideau cramoisi* ("The Crimson Curtain," first short story of d'Aurevilly's *Les Diaboliques* in which an old vicomte recounts his first sexual experience to a young friend) inspired a poem. It appeared as "The Two Secrets" in *The Winged Beetle* (1910), dedicated to "Mary Waska":

---

*According to William Breeze, Crowley was in the process of writing this A.·.A.·. Neophyte ritual. It was later modified for the use of one or two officers and as a useful opening, as well as closing, to other kinds of work, when the central initiation section would be omitted.

She used to lie, superbly bare
Wrapped in her harvest flame of hair,
And shooting from her steel-grey eyes
Inexorable destinies:
Mute oracles—mysterious—
A soul in a sarcophagus!
For I, through all my life astrain,
Through all the pulsing of my brain,
Through all the wisdom I had won
From this one and the other one
Saw nothing. Nothing. Had I known
And loved some Sphinx of steel or stone
While countless chiliads rolled, may be
I had not guessed her mystery.

So there she lay, regarding me.
And I?—I gave the riddle up.
I drank the wine, admired the cup;
As I suppose a wise man does
Unless he be the Man of Uz
To scrape with shards a sore that grows
The more he irks it. I suppose
All men are fools who seek the truth
At such a price as joy and youth.

. . . So there she used to lie.
Maybe Correggio's Antiope
Best paints you how she lay.
And I Loved her, and passed the matter by;
Ending at last, one may dare say,
In thinking that those eyes of grey
Meant naught, suspected naught, were blind,
Expressed the vacancy behind.

So life went on. One winter day
So silent and so still she lay
That I took cold, regarding her.

I rose, I wrapped myself in fur;
Then came to her, my thought untold
Being that she, too, might be cold.
I laid my hand upon her breast.
Cold! Icy cold! Ah you have guessed.
Right. She was dead, quite dead.
    And so
You see, friend, I shall never know.
She kept her secret.
      —Leave me alone!
Or—I shall hardly keep my own!

He retired before midnight after crossing himself with his knife to indicate mastery of body and doing ten pranayamas, which made him perspire. After midnight, he persisted with meditation, mantra, and the Bornless One invocation. It was all hopeless. His mind wandered freely, hallucinating visions of either his father or Lévi!

Day Two
Awaking at 7:44 for thirteen cycles of "mediocre" pranayama, he ate a pear and two waffles for breakfast before meditating in hanged-man position. Thought wandered but for a conception of glowing fire, like Mars, that interrupted concentration, then "went out, dammit!" He wrote letters, drank a citron pressé, performed a Bornless One ritual in asana, which was excruciating, and at 11:13 did thirteen pranayamas. He reflected on his yoga successes at Kandy in 1902 and assured himself he was a "Dhamma-Buddha" who renounces the supreme reward, returning to "hell" to teach the Way.

At midday he entered a pure thought of curious type, simultaneously wide awake and another part, "perfectly asleep." He slept and awoke, after horrifying dreams, for lunch of Garibaldis and waffles. He adopted a mantra and went for a walk. The brain took it up well, and he felt a distaste for "everything but Adonai." Having found "all sorts of people" at the Dôme and drank a fruit juice, Maryt showed up at 6:30. She was with him in his room after 8:00 p.m., and he tried to meditate: "Charming as she is, I don't want to make love to her." At 8:40 he mixed mantra and caresses, calling it a success. She asked for some narcotic; he gave her a "minimum dose." Meditating, blackness dispersed and he saw the "sushumna," or prana energy in the spine, as a galaxy of stars, suggesting the stars are the ganglia of the universe.

Finding asana painful, the "New Monster" amused him, but getting rid of her for a while, he managed fourteen cycles of pranayama and got a headache. Reflecting on his walking mantra he found it related to the Visuddhi chakra (throat chakra, or Hindu nerve center opposite the larynx), so he meditated on that. The idea of interpreting everything as a dealing of God with the soul meant a state of indifference to everything, while being interested in it, attending on its spiritual meaning to come through. He realized the headache came from hunger and ate a waffle, which cured it. When he concentrated on the Visuddhi chakra he kept seeing where the boulevard Edgar Quinet opened to the Montparnasse cemetery. He'd been impressed by the gate before (it's gone now); was it recorded, he wondered, in a brain cell close to that recording the chakra idea? At 11:17 he tried meditating on the mantra but entered a reverie about a castle and soldiers. He tried to maintain the high aspiration but slept.

Day Three

The day was beautiful when he woke at 6:55, but he felt unclean. He'd denied urges in the night to rise and meditate, so did fifteen cycles of pranayama, which cleared his mind. By 8:05 he was in hanged-man position doing a mantra on the throat chakra. He felt "the Spirit move," or consciousness really flowing. He found the Muslim mantras rippled, where Hindu mantras boomed. He was up properly at 9:00 a.m. reading letters, still persisting with the mantra semiconsciously.

He reached the Café de la Paix at 10:38, still mantra-ing, and sending it up and down his spine "with good effect." He had a coffee, then off to the "Turker." He was still in prelims, detaching thoughts from impressions: "One looks at everything without seeing it." The aim—to get thought in one direction only: Adonai. He blessed the coffee, that it, too, serve. At the Hannam, he found the mantra alleviated pains of massage. He consecrated his oysters and bread and butter to the Great Work, chewing slowly, "giving praise to Priapus the Lord of the oyster, to Demeter the Lady of corn, and to Isis the Queen of the Cow." He believed Romans 7:19 summed up his problem: "For the good that I would I do not: but the evil which I would not, that I do."

At 3:00 p.m. he was sitting by the great fountain in the Luxembourg Gardens, wondering how meditation practices affected the "sexual process," speculating on violently exciting the muladhara chakra associated with the genitals at the risk of a clergyman thinking him a "Black Magician." He felt very peaceful, but like a corpse! He looked into the glorious reflection of October sunlight in the waters of the fountain, yet found not Adonai there, nor in the caverns of his mind. He must press on, for "He only is God, and there is none other God than He!"

Crowley begins to refer to himself, the man, as "John St. John" without explanation. Perhaps the idea is that *John* is a common name, but St. John was joined to Revelation, and the name associated with the Beloved Disciple, close to the Lord, Adonai: "God with us." He sat at the Dôme with the mantra going well, thirty times a minute. He found that the smell of food made him nauseous; this would suggest something shadowing the aspiration, for all things should work to the glory of God.

At 4:25, Maryt appeared. She'd reacted to the narcotic, fainted, and been to a hospital; a coffee started the reaction.

At 5:30, awake and energized after a nap, the mantra continuing, yet "so far from the Path" he felt like blaspheming every divinity but the dark ones: "I want to say Indra's mantram till his throne gets red-hot and burns his lotus-buttocks." He felt he might be going through the "Apophis" part of the Isis Apophis Osiris IAO formula—Apophis being the evil serpent opposed to Ra in Egyptian mythology, representing death in a birth-death-resurrection formula. "7:35. The Sandwich duly chewed, and two Coffees drunk, I resume the mystic Mantra. Why? Because I damn well choose to."

By 11:00 p.m. he'd got rid of Maryt, "who, by the way, is Quite Mad," and hopefully the Apophis-Typhon (Set, killer of Osiris) aspect. He performed the Pyramid ritual and got a glimpse of Adonai, but felt he'd done it in the spirit of rehearsal rather than in earnest.

Day Four
Having performed the opening of *Liber 671,* he invoked the Angel in the hanged-man posture.

At 8:00 a.m. he reflected on a conversation he'd had the previous evening with a Dr. R who suggested Crowley write for magazines between serious work. Crowley thought such writing "rubbish" and a real danger, having cleared his mind all these years "to think cleanly and express beautifully." (Dean Inge called novel writing "prostitution of the intellect.") Crowley swore to write only in praise and glorification of Adonai. He would perfect the ritual 671, make it more lucid and more effective.

He reflected on the previous day. Those under "fads," of eating or whatnot, are under Apophis, he mused. This day he would eat neither gluttonously, nor ascetically, but what he fancied, great or small.

At 10:50 he'd spent an hour wandering about the Musée de Luxembourg in the rue de Vaugirard and summarized the new ritual, which began with Death summoning Life and, after ordeals, climaxed in the "descent of Adonai" and perfecting of the "pyramid" of aspiration.

At 1:15, lunch: twelve oysters, Cepes Bordelaise, Tarte aux Cerises, Café Noir. "Now more mantra, though by the Lord I'm getting sick of it."

Spending the afternoon on the new ritual, at 6:15 he entered Chez Lavenue to read over the record and have dinner: Bisque d'Ecrevisses, Tournedos Rossini, a Coupe Jack, half a bottle of Meursault, and coffee. Resuming his mantra an hour later, he noticed the wine had much less effect than usual; intense magical work changed the system around, he concluded.

At 8:10 he noticed mantra-yoga independent of reverie; he could wander in thought, but try to write a sentence and the thing stopped.

He adopted a strict asana and found himself jumping like a frog. He read the *Shiva Samhita* and noticed the Hindus identified the Ganges with the Ida-Nadi (prana channel) and Benares with the space between the nadis; he saw a connection with his identification of his throat and the gate of the Montparnasse cemetery (behind the gate is a long path to the cemetery proper, which might subconsciously suggest a nadi heading for the lowest chakra, or the gate with the mouth, and the path as throat; mourners gathered at the gate, suggesting duality of death and resurrection).

Day Five

Intense pranayama work after midnight was followed by sleep, but he awoke at 2:18 after a surreal dream and got on with the mantra, followed by pranayama. He fell asleep and woke up several times before finally getting dressed at 8:45, having spent ten minutes on the Bornless One invocation.

Having suffered diarrhea the previous evening, and the morning chilly and damp, he went to the Dôme for coffee and a sandwich, while the mantra carried on the moment he stopped thinking, but think he did: about the differences between Eastern practices, Muslim mantras and Hindu, and the Western magical tradition, which he found closer to "harmony." The important thing was to train the Will into a formidable engine so the point of magical climax sent the being straight into receptivity to the higher. He also observed how patterns of sleep were breaking up. He went to arrange photographs of the various asanas for aids for devotees (he was formulating the A∴A∴). He worked on the new ritual in the morning, took lunch of a dozen marennes vertes and an andouillette aux pommes, and met Zelina Visconti, "more ugly than ever in her wild way. She says that she is favourably disposed towards me, on the recommendation of her concierge!!!"*

At 5:15 he went to the Dôme for a sandwich and citron pressé and to correct *Liber 963,* "The Treasure-House of Images" given him to correct by Captain Fuller, who wrote it. Visconti, arrived for twenty minutes around 8:00 p.m. and he found her kiss "half given, half taken" revived him. A sandwich and two coffees at the Versailles was chased by a citron pressé at the Dôme and chatter with a lady before midnight.

Day Six
After midnight he bemoaned his laxness: "Somebody once remarked that it had taken a hundred million years to produce me [Capt. Fuller]; I may add that I hope it will be another hundred million before God makes such another cur."

After an equilibrating ritual, his thoughts wandered: "What is the Astral Plane? Is there such a thing? How do its phantoms differ from those of absinthe, reverie, and love, and so on? We may admit their unsubstantiality without denying their power; the phantoms of absinthe and love are potent enough to drive a man to death or marriage; while

---

*Zelina Visconti is the name of a courtesan in Crowley's play *Mortadello* (1912), written July–August 1911, Café Riche, Paris.

reverie may end in anti-vivisectionism or nut-food-madness."

The next day was wayward and doubting, he went to the Louvre to investigate something about Egyptian alchemy, ate well, but with little enjoyment or sense he was on the right path at all. He castigated himself for not sticking to a disciplined, tougher regimen. He watched poker played at the Dôme but found he couldn't distinguish between one thing or thought and another. He saw both sides of every question with no power of discrimination.

Around 11:30 p.m. he invoked Adonai earnestly but stumbled on the fact that Adonai is formless, and while one could form an image and Adonai inform it, it would still fall short of communion. He wondered if this was the origin of the commandment about forbidding graven images and having "no Gods but me." There was no escaping Truth, but truth required formless wordlessness, which was somewhat difficult given magic's use of imagination. The Hindu yoga method was to kill all thoughts as they arise in the mind. This might fend off arrows, so to speak, but "St. John" was aiming at a target. He wanted to define the "knowledge and conversation with the Holy Guardian Angel" as being equal to Neroda-Samapatti, the trance of Nibbana.

At 11:55 he realized he'd reproached Adonai, that for six days he'd invoked in vain, and got the reply: "The Seventh Day shall be the Sabbath of the Lord thy God."

Day Seven

After midnight he managed eight breath cycles only to find constipation a problem, for which he took cascara sagrada, which led to diarrhea. He waxed lyrical as being like the darwesh whose turban was stolen and was told the thief had taken the road to Damascus, and the holy man said as he walked to the cemetery: "I will await him here!" "So, therefore, there is one place, O thou thief of my heart's love, Adonai, to which thou must come at last; and that place is the tomb in which lie buried all my thoughts and emotions, all that which is 'I, and Me, and Mine.'" Behind the self-deprecating humor and irony and cynicism, the aspiration was genuine.

He went to sleep, composed, like a child knowing its mother was there, and had many strange dreams, yet comforted by a sense of the love of the lord Adonai.

He broke his fast at 11:35 with coffee and a sandwich, then sat for young Lithuanian sculptor Michael Brenner (1885–1969), "who will one day be heard of." Crowley was right; only very recently has his name been pulled from relative obscurity. He'd been in Paris since 1901 and studied at the Académie Julian. Eventually admired by Braque, Picasso, and Gertrude Stein, who commissioned a bust, Brenner disliked the hollowness of artistic competition and did not sculpt for money or fame, like Crowley.

Crowley noted why he recorded food and drink. Food is an intoxicant and one should be able to point out that a result was due to drink or starvation; it's too easy to mistake these induced states for the real "Kether," or divine crown.

Create the conditions; establish the will. It's hard to set the process going, but eventually, the gravity switches, and what seemed distant begins to come. Crowley had taken all the obvious sense of ethics and morality from the process. What was right was what worked. This is what he meant by his motto when he became Master of the Temple in 1909: "By the force of truth I have overcome the Universe." "So now the whole destiny of the Universe is by me overcome; I am impelled, with ever-gathering and irresistible force, toward Adonai."

In late afternoon he realized the mantra had slowed; its noise signified conflict. Now there was a peace, a flow:

> The Concourse of the Forces has become the Harmony of the Forces; the word Tetragrammaton is spoken and ended; the holy letter Shin is descended into it. For the roaring God of Sinai we have the sleeping Babe of Bethlehem. A fulfilment, not a destroying, of the Law.

For dinner, at 6:15, hors d'oeuvre, tripes à la mode de Caen, filet de porc, glace, one-half bottle Graves (Bordeaux).

He pondered the exactitudes of expected spiritual experience. Need it be catastrophic? Surely, it will be on a higher plane, for it is. To see a football on the pavement is agony; it is not Adonai. His hearing is sharpened. He's only 30 yards from the electric trams on the boulevard Montparnasse, and it's rush hour; yet he did his early invocations on Chancery Lane by Fleet Street! "And the Visconti may turn up! Lord.

Lord! Why hast thou forsaken me!" To avoid the Visconti, he goes to the Dôme for citron pressé. It's 8:45.

He went home and tried to sleep, and was struck by this thought:

> And then—as by a flash of lightning—the Abyss of the Pit opened, and my whole position was turned. I saw my life from the dawn of consciousness till now as a gigantic "pose"; my very love of truth assumed for the benefit of my biographer! All these strange things suffered and enjoyed for no better purpose than to seem a great man.

Stabbing at the soul of his integrity, there was no answer to it, and he could but destroy it as a "last temptation." For if it were so, there would be no path, no attainment, and all in vain, and the "Dweller on the Threshold" would have scored the victory as he turned back, without a path to turn to.

He started trying to awaken the kundalini, the magical serpent that sleeps at the base of the spine, coiled about the sushumna, but instead of pumping the prana up and down the sushumna until Shiva and Shakti were united in the Sahasrara chakra, he tried—"God knows why"—to work the whole thing in muladhara (between perineum and coccyx). The result, he self-scorns, was "obvious." Presumably: nothing. Nevertheless, "the longest way round is the shortest way home." Error leads to knowledge. "This is a strange country, and I am very lonely."

He decided to clean himself out of devils of discouragement with a banishing ritual, the Bornless One invocation, Calls I–VI of John Dee and Edward Kelley, to summon angels to his aid, an invocation of Thoth, and an impromptu invocation of Adonai. The ritual felt good; visualization of powers cleared the mind; but the mind was still there, and only Adonai should remain.

Around midnight he knew he was never so far, and never so near, affirming Unity with "my lord Adonai."

Day Eight

At 9:10, after fitful sleep, he took coffee and a brioche and went to Michael Brenner's studio and spent the morning modeling Siddhasana ("Accomplished Pose" asana). After midday, he thought he'd been in a spiritual desert for three and half years (the time since seriously practicing pranayama and meditation at Boleskine before Kangchenjunga).

In late afternoon, he examined his record, trying to see where he'd gone wrong. He'd got to the Dweller of the Threshold and had been turned back. He found error. He'd written that he'd "hugged" himself before sleep. Too pleased with the "heralds" of the Lord's coming, he should have risen like a bridegroom meeting the bride. He must mortify self-satisfaction. He would perfect the ritual and memorize it.

At sixish, he met Dr. R, who said he'd teach him (Crowley!) how to have astral visions. Crowley sat listening, hoping for a secret word. He then went to a "Secret Restaurant" at 7:15 for six oysters, rable de lièvre poivrade purée de marrons, glace "casserole" with a small bottle of Perrier water. At 8:30 he had café cognac and a cigar. To meet the Dweller is not to have the path blocked but already to have strayed.

And he kept straying. In near hopelessness he did twenty-five cycles of pranayama at 11:30, but "it nearly killed me."

Day Nine

He was up in the wee small hours—now as John St. John—awaiting illumination. Surely Nature's reaction against the Magical Will must be wearing down! More pranayama until nearly bursting. He didn't want to oversleep and miss an appointment with Brenner. He found he'd written "I," indicating a smug contentment using the John St. John name was meant to dispel. He'd now got 70 percent of the ritual by heart. Café-croissant at the Dôme at 8:35. It took about half an hour to walk to Brenner's studio, reciting the ritual; he then took his pose and felt interior trembling as the studio filled with "subtle light." The Violet Lotus of Ajna appeared "flashing like some marvellous comet." He tried to slay every thought that hindered concentration, including the Ajna vision, but an overwhelming fear of annihilation came upon him. Unable to shake it, he dared not enter.

Then Brenner said, "Let us take a little rest!" Such irony! John St. John was too tired at 11:30 to resume the pose (the sign of Exempt Adept). He tried again to storm "the Walls of the City of God," but failed.

Reciting the ritual, he went for lunch with Dr. R and "H." but they'd forgotten, so he went to Lavenue's for epinards, tarte aux fraises, glace au café, and half a bottle of Evian water. His distaste for food was great; meat was repulsive. It was very hot. He retired to invoke Adonai in hanged-man position, then napped.

Awaking, he pondered the destiny of so many he'd known, thinking of his perilous raft voyage down the Red (Hong) River in Yunnan, China, where he'd seen great wreckage in the waters as he held on for dear life to his raft, with his family, and then remembered all those he'd known who'd succumbed to "alcoholism, insanity, disease, faddism, death, knavery, prison—every earthly hell, reflection of some spiritual blunder," and he, still going, for all his manifold error, knowing he would endure to the end. Would Adonai provide harbor for his will to attain?

After 6:00 p.m. he burned incense of Abra-Melin, and felt a calm, soon interrupted by reflection on the morning's failure, impossible to deny since it was recorded. He trimmed his beard and went out for dinner, all the time his thoughts racing, his ego rising, and eating bread, radish, beef, and potato as if all at once—and that after hors d'oeuvres, bouillabaisse, contrefilet rôti, glace.

Overexcited he returns home, and at 9:48, ritual learned by heart, he is robed, clean with temple ordered. As a ritual of renunciation of all that he was proceeded, keeping only the ring, he feels assailed by every opposition. The room is filled with "ultra-violet" or "astral" light, seeming like daylight, greater even than that scene in the pyramid of Giza in 1903 when he showed Rose the sylphs on their honeymoon.

> 11:34. splendour. The infinite abyss of space, a rayless orb of liquid and colourless brilliance fading beyond the edges into a flame of white and gold. . . . The Rosy Cross flashing with lustre ineffable. . . . and more, much more which ten scribes could hardly catalogue in a century.

The Exempt Adept is not content with this, not even with a vision of the Holy Guardian Angel from afar; the temple is closed (11:49 p.m.).

Day Ten

He fell asleep before 2:00 and awoke at 6:23 to a Paris cold and damp after rain. Following pranayama, doubt assails him: is there any path of attainment at all? The streets are now sodden with rain, like his hopes.

After breakfast, back at Brenner's studio, he was finding it difficult to concentrate. He took a light lunch and strolled down the boulevard St. Michel, calling in at "M's" studio. He had a café crème in the afternoon and forty minutes at the Académie Marcelle (presumably a prostitute or bordello) and then to the Musée Luxembourg to look at pictures. At 4:10 he walked back through the gardens, strewn with fallen leaves, making it look sad, and on to the Dôme for fruit juice, wondering what psychiatrist Henry Maudsley would have made of the devotion to Adonai. "Like other bad habits, mysticism grows by what it feeds on," but surely Adonai, he countered, by definition, "is that thought which informs and strengthens and purifies, supreme sanity in supreme genius. Anything that is not that is not Adonai." Anything less is not IT. Besides, since the experience transcends reason, it's useless to argue about it.

At 7:10, bored by a poker game at the Dôme, he walked down to the Versailles for hors d'oeuvre, escargots, cassoulet de Castelnaudary, glace, half a bottle of Evian, and felt a failure. The snails repelled him. He went home, wrote a letter to Fuller and signed it with a broken pentagram.

Just after 8:00 he began the old Hindu mantra "Aum Tat Sat Aum." He then "wasted" another hour chatting to Nina Olivier and "H." He did more pranayama, consulted his treatise on mysticism *Konx Om Pax* (1907), then thought of sleep. He conquered it.

Day Eleven

Powers of asana and pranayama returned and engendered egoistic pride hard to suppress. He wrote it was like being asked to judge a band contest and able to do anything but listen! More fitful sleep or fitful waking. He was awake and out just before 9:00, in perfect weather. Taking breakfast he practiced a new pranayama-on-the-march method and walked for a couple of hours.

Lunch at the Panthéon: rumpsteak aux pommes soufflées, poire, and half of an Evian.

> Was meditating on asceticism. John Tweed once told me that Swami Vivekananda, towards the end of his life, wrote a most pathetic letter deploring that his sanctity forbade his "going on the bust."

What a farce is such sanctity! How much wiser for the man to behave as a man, the God as a God! This is my real bedrock objection to the Eastern systems. They decry all manly virtue as dangerous and wicked; and they look upon Nature as evil. True enough, everything is evil relatively to Adonai; for all stain is impurity. A bee's swarm is evil—inside one's clothes.

"Dirt is matter in the wrong place." It is dirt to connect sex with statuary, morals with art.

Only Adonai, who is in a sense the True Meaning of everything, cannot defile any idea. This is a hard saying, though true, for nothing of course is dirtier than to try and use Adonai as a fig-leaf for one's shame.

To seduce women under pretence of religion is unutterable foulness; though both adultery and religion are themselves clean.

To mix jam and mustard is a messy mistake.

Crowley wanted to prove that attainment was reward for Work, and failure meant errors were made. His "atheism" consisted in confidence that all phenomena were as explicable as hoarfrost or glaciers. Attainment was as beyond the understanding of the disparaged rationalist as it was the superstitionist.

Arriving at Brenner's at three, he left at 4:20, walking to the Dôme with the mantra. He thought about how even great artists' conceptions of God were inferior to the idea of "Utmost God hid in the middle of matter." Feeling awe at "the inscrutable mystery of the nature of common things," he wrote profoundly of the quest for the divine through all things and experiences, then at 8:22 sat down at the Versailles, and at 9:10 dined on half a dozen marennes, rable de lièvre, and citron pressé. As he crossed the boulevard to the Dôme just after 10:00, he gazed at the bright moon high and stately in the east, and the message came from the sacred Magic of Abra-Melin: "And thou wilt begin to inflame thyself in praying," which he proceeded to do shortly after midnight.

Day Twelve

A lamp on the altar provided the sole light in the room as Crowley prayed for Adonai, burning a pantacle he'd made of Him by way of renouncing all images, "that Himself might rise in me." The room had the glow of ultraviolet with no source as he recited the "Book Ararita" (received the previous winter).

> Then subtly, easily, simply, imperceptibly gliding, I passed away into nothing. And I was wrapped in the black brilliance of my Lord, that interpenetrated me in every part, fusing its light with my darkness, and leaving there no darkness, but pure light.
>
> Also I beheld my Lord in a figure and I felt the interior trembling kindle itself into a Kiss—and I perceived the true Sacraments—and I beheld in one moment all the mystic visions in one; and the Holy Graal appeared unto me, and many other inexpressible things were know [sic] of me.
>
> Also I was given to enjoy the subtle Presence of my Lord interiorly during the whole of this twelfth day.
>
> Then I besought the Lord that He would take me into His presence eternally even now. But He withdrew Himself, for that I must do that which I was sent hither to do; namely, to rule the earth.

The light and a divine perfume remained, according to the record, and "a comfort not to be told," and he knew his "Redeemer liveth." Absorbed in the "light," he slept, waking at 7:55 like, he writes, a young eagle ready to soar. Walking through the Luxembourg Gardens on his thirty-third birthday at 9:20, past his "favorite fountain," he found the beauty of dew and flowers in October sunlight indescribably wondrous; the brilliance too great for his eyes, weakened by the vision. The very striking of the Senate clock "ravished" his ears "with its mysterious melody." He understands all psalms of benediction, for spontaneous praise sings from his heart as a fountain: "The authors of the Psalms must have known something of this Illumination when they wrote them." What had looked disharmonious, incoherent in the operation now seemed a straight line. His consciousness was of "Neschamah," highly illuminated mind above the abyss where reason ends its dominion. To write any more would be to descend into mind of "ruach," or rational sense, and he desired to stay where he was. At 10:00 he was at Brenner's studio. Taking the pose, the trembling began again, and the "subtle brilliance" flowed through him. "Consciousness again died and was reborn as the divine, always without shock or stress. How easy is magic, once the way is found!"

He was conscious of many visions offered to him in the hour but rejected all "for being in my Lord and He in me, there is no need of these toys."

At Chez Lavenue at 12:40 he pondered what could have helped: a magical cabinet, a disciple to care for things, a private garden, proper magical food ceremonially prepared, but it was enough to know it could be achieved in a great city and a small room. He enjoyed his lunch, "the Burgundy came straight from the Vat of Bacchus"; the Havana cigar, the best he'd ever smoked. He found his record hilarious, then the "beauty of the women in the restaurant!" John St. John would have dismissed them as old hags. "My soul is singing! My soul is singing!" Enraptured, it mattered not what he would do: "The Lord Adonai is about me as a Thunderbolt and as a Pylon and as a Serpent and as a Phallus."

He carried on, beautific, doing what he normally did. At 10:30 he felt the rapture beginning to carry him away but turned back to his billiards for politeness sake. Even in the busy Dôme "was the glory within me, and I therein." He was as a lover swooning with pleasure at the first kiss of the Beloved. Failure at a billiards stroke counted nothing; looking up he inhaled ambrosial air, then returned to his room. Setting the altar, he enflamed himself in praying once more.

Day Thirteen

At 8:00 in the morning, he entered into the Silence, as he put it: "let me abide in the Silence!" And so, batteries thoroughly recharged, he returned to London to organize the new order A∴A∴ and start his new biannual journal, the *Equinox,* to secure the wisdom should civilization fall.

THIRTEEN

Ragged and Wilde 1909–1913

Crowley worked hard on the *Equinox* until March 1909, when this lavish, 255-page "Review of Scientific Illuminism" appeared with a "Special Supplement" detailing, hour by hour, his magical retirement in Paris. The supplement alone ran to 139 pages—some "Review"!

He then focused on launching the new order with George Cecil Jones and Captain John Frederick Charles Fuller (1878–1966), with whom he'd corresponded regularly in Paris.

Meanwhile, problems with Rose reached crisis point. *Confessions* insists Rose's doctor recommended her signing herself into an alcohol-free institution for two years. Rose refused. Exasperated and unable, or unwilling, to take further responsibility for her, he began divorce proceedings. Crowley's *Confessions* indicates both parties had committed adultery but that Crowley agreed to being defendant, with evidence manufactured "in the usual way": a detective hired, assignations arranged. They continued to live together, sometimes amicably, at 21 Warwick Road.

There was, however, more to the divorce than Crowley's account. *The Aberdeen Daily Journal,* for example (Thursday, November 25, 1909), reported the divorce proceedings heard before Scottish lawyer Lord Salvesen. According to the court hearing, Crowley had asked Rose to temporarily take care of the baby of an intimate friend. Rose inadvertently opened private correspondence that revealed that the mother of the baby was one Jennie Zwee (printed as "Swee" in the newspaper) and that the father was apparently Crowley. Crowley was defendant, and the court recognized the adultery that warranted divorce was his alone. Granting a decree of divorce, Rose obtained custody of their daughter Lola, with the "aliment" fixed at the rate of £1 weekly.*

In *Confessions,* Crowley recalls Gerald Kelly "at twenty-one" saying he (Kelly) wondered why Crowley "hadn't put his foot down sooner."[1] Crowley wrote that it was love for Rose's sweetness that prevented it. Forty years after the events, Kelly commented: "'Gerald at twenty-one'—presumably this means that I went to 21 Warwick Rd. (or Square—whichever it was). I'm vague about the past, but to the best of my present knowledge I never went to this house. I knew that A.C. and R[ose] were getting on badly."[2]

Explaining Crowley's decision to play defendant, *Confessions* states that to have done otherwise would have breached "the pledge to protect one's wife, which is the first point of a husband's honour."[3] Kelly's comment: "*Says you.* I remember the negotiations; A.C. was very guilty—there wasn't, as I recall it, any defence possible."[4]

According to *Confessions,* Crowley was in England until autumn 1909, "apart from short trips to Paris."[5] About these short trips, we know nothing, though I think the John St. John record gives us some idea of what he was about.

---

*According to the British Census of 1911, in April of that year Rose Edith Crowley (divorced) was living comfortably with her daughter "Lola Zazza" (Rose's hand), aged four, at 32 Albany Mansions, Battersea (six rooms), with servant Mary Anne Thompson and nurse Alice Knowles. She was not institutionalized as an incurable alcoholic as the biographical myth goes. As to her status, Rose entered "Widow," which may indicate she was still angry with Crowley. The nurse (likely a governess for Lola) crossed out "Widow" and penciled in "divorced her husband." A son was born to eighteen-year-old Jennie Zwee in October 1909, a month before the divorce trial, registered with no indication of the father. William Breeze found a marginal note to the "Crowley-Windram [copy of] *Thelema*" concerning the Prophet's (Crowley's) then three children, indicating a 1909 birthdate and the name Maurice Cyril. Less than six months after Crowley's death, the birth was re-registered according to a 1926 law allowing illegitimate births to carry the name of the father retrospectively. The father was named as the man Jennie Zwee married a year after the child's birth. While Crowley and Rose believed the child to be his, it is equally possible Jennie already knew the man she would marry in 1910 and that he, or even someone else, was the father. I am grateful to William Breeze for sending me copies of the Census return, the Scottish newspaper, and for additional information regarding Crowley's divorce. See also *Ordo Templi Orientis News,* May 30, 2013, section 7, online at www.oto-uk.org/News.html.

*Fig. 13.1. Present-day
21 Warwick Road,
Earls Court.*

Before autumn 1909, Crowley had invited Neuburg, who'd recently completed his studies at Cambridge, to Boleskine for June and July, with another Cambridge man, Kenneth Martin Ward (1887–1927). Ward was son of James Ward, Cambridge Professor of Mental Philosophy (Psychology) and Logic, and Mary Jane Ward (née Martin), Irish suffragist, lecturer, writer, and the first woman to pass the moral sciences tripos examination with first class honors. Neuburg would voluntarily undergo the ordeals of the Neophyte in the A∴A∴, whereas Ward was more interested in some old skis Crowley had promised him. Seeking them in the attic, Crowley found the original manuscript of *The Book of the Law,* as it came to be known. Crowley took this as a sign from the Secret Chiefs and was pinched with the thought that past troubles were attributable to five years of insufficiently attending to its imperatives. From July 1909 onward, Crowley made greater efforts to apply the work to his life and integrate it with the Order and his magic in general.

In November 1909, Neuburg went to French Algeria with Crowley where they shared extraordinary adventures, details of which have appeared in numerous studies* and needn't be retold in a book about Crowley and Paris, but since Neuburg and Crowley did practice experimental magick in Paris (in 1914), it's pertinent to hear Neuburg's reflections more than twenty years later on what they accomplished, as related in Jean Overton Fuller's biography of Neuburg, whom she'd known and admired in the 1930s (*The Magical Dilemma of Victor Neuburg,* originally published in 1965).

Ms. Fuller recalled a Friday evening in March 1936 when Neuburg spoke "spontaneously" about his days with Crowley: "At any rate we did something which has never been done before! Well, not for hundreds of years anyway. We had no predecessors in the times in which we live."

Neuburg told Overton Fuller about the Calls for communicating with angels indicated to Queen Elizabeth's scientific adviser, Dr. John Dee, by Dee's scryer, or seer, Edward Kelley. "It's doubtful," continued Neuburg, "whether even Dee himself ever called them. We didn't know what would happen. We went to sea in a sieve. And some things we did were quite original. At any rate in the form we gave to them, they could never have been done before. We made up our own rituals and thought out everything we would do." Neuburg looked deeply into her eyes: "We didn't know. We had no one to tell us. We were simply groping. We had the courage of our convictions. We got right off the beaten track."[6]

In December 1910, a now divorced Crowley returned to Algeria with Victor. Leaving Victor at distant Biskra, Crowley returned to France alone. In Paris, at the Taverne Panthéon, he wrote "The Ordeal of Ida Pendragon," a short story about one Edgar Rolles who takes a girl to a fight between a white boxer and black heavyweight—based on Joe Jeanette (1878–1959), whom Crowley admired, having just seen him

---

*But see especially Crowley's *The Vision and the Voice,* edited by Hymenaeus Beta [William Breeze].

fight in Paris. Edgar takes Ida to his studio and, seeing her as a member of "the Order," proposes she pass the ordeal of the Abyss, which she flunks. Ida meets the black boxer, who loves her; they lunch with Edgar and a character based on Nina Olivier. Ida cruelly teases the boxer, and when the boxer reacts and sinks his teeth in her throat, Edgar kills him. A Secret Chief tells Edgar to take Ida away; she has in fact passed the Abyss. Edgar marries her on the formula that "perfect love is perfect understanding," but she dies in childbirth as price for earlier failure in wanting everything and giving nothing. "Ordeal" appeared in the *Equinox* (1, no. 5) in 1911.

Having completed that issue, he returned to France, alternating his time during 1911's gloriously fine summer between Paris and Montigny-sur-Loing on the Forest of Fontainebleau's southern edge, whither he returned many times. He kept fit by walking from Fontainebleau station to the Loing and back.

The summer inspired numerous short stories and some handsome lyric poetry, such as "The Sevenfold Sacrament," published in the *English Review,* written at an "adorable inn," the Vanne Rouge, where he languished happily by the banks of the Loing overlooking a weir. On August 10, he wrote "A Birthday" for the twenty-sixth birthday of his new love, "Mother of Heaven," Australian violinist Leila Waddell, who'd just gone to England as ladies' orchestra leader for Oscar Straus's operetta *The Waltz Dream,* revived at Daly's Theatre with Lily Elsie and Amy Evans. Crowley's poem charts his and Leila's relationship. It was published in the *Equinox* (1, no. 7):

> It was the forest and the river that knew
> The fact that one and one do not make two.
> We worked, we walked, we slept, we were at ease,
> We cried, we quarrelled; all the rocks and trees
> For twenty miles could tell how lovers played,
> And we could count a kiss for every glade.
> Worry, starvation, illness and distress?
> Each moment was a mine of happiness.
>
> Then we grew tired of being country mice,
> Came up to Paris, lived our sacrifice

> There, giving holy berries to the moon,
> July's thanksgiving for the joys of June.

That same month, Crowley wrote two plays in a single, extended session, which must be a record of sorts. Staying at 50 rue Vavin as usual, the idea of *Adonis* came to him, so he went to the Dôme for a citron pressé as a preliminary. Sitting there were old flame Nina Olivier and "latest conquest" Hener Skene,* whom Crowley remembered as "an unpleasant and cadaverous hypocrite" from 1902 (soon to be Isadora Duncan's pianist). They were accompanied by a "charming girl" introduced as Fenella Lovell, "a consumptive creature in gaudy and fantastic rags of brilliant colours,"[7] who worked as both model and "gypsy" fiddler-dancer, while living at 203 boulevard Raspail. According to Richard Kaczynski, she was of Romany descent and a member of the Gypsy Lore Society.[8] British Symbolist poet Arthur Symons (1865–1945) found Lovell's language-teaching skills impressive when she gave him Romany lessons in summer 1908.[9] Fenella also modeled for Augustus John's elder sister Gwen. Gwen John painted at least two portraits of Fenella, one from the nude, with a nonerotic candor unusual at the time. Appreciating her "pretty little face," Gwen nonetheless found her "dreadful" and doubted she'd sell the paintings.[10]

Fig. 13.2. James Henry Skene (1877–1916).

---

*Second Lieutenant James Henry Skene; born Hammersmith, 1878; killed during attack on Fromelles with Forty-Eighth (South Midland) Division, July 13, 1916.

It transpired that Nina and Skene were getting their jollies whipping and otherwise mistreating Fenella; for Hener Skene, Crowley declared, this pose was no more sincere than Skene's former affected discipleship of Nietzsche. Crowley immediately pictured put-upon Fenella as doomed heroine "Fenella Lovell, the gypsy" in new horror-story playlet, *The Ghouls,* set in Foyers and Boleskine, and published in *The Equinox* in March 1912 (vol. 1, no. 7, 161). Clearly finding Lovell's excesses enticing, Crowley painted a literary portrait of his fantasy figure in red, yellow, and blue costume, hair adorned with flowers, short skirts revealing "spider legs" under pale blue stockings and high-heeled golden shoes. Fenella's pale face is rouged and powdered, her lips painted, with round black eyes ablaze as shoulder-bones "stare" from her low necked dress, while a diamond dog collar clasps "her shining throat." That *The Ghouls* was really a barmy comedy did not stop it from finding favor in poet Harold Monro's review in the September 1912 issue of *The Poetry Review.** Describing Crowley as "extraordinarily entertaining," *Poetry Review* editor Monro recognized that *The Equinox* was almost wholly "a creation of the amazing Mr. Crowley. His antics are as wild as the devil's," he continued, for Crowley "dances through its pages like a mad magician." As for *The Equinox*'s place in literature, Monro considered this was not "to be decided by contemporary criticism at all. I, at any rate, will not commit myself to attempting a decision." Monro lamented that

> unfortunately, only four of his contributions to the present issue (of *The Equinox*) are in verse; I must not fail, however, to draw attention to one of the two fine plays that happen to be written in prose. "The Ghouls" is possibly the most ghastly death-dance in English literature. If Oscar Wilde had written it (but he could not have) every one would know it. It is the very pith and marrow of terror. Cynical it may be, indecent it may be, but I defy the lord of dreams to send any more plutonian nightmare to haunt our mortal sleep.
>
> Mr. Crowley plies the knack of writing as if he would have us believe he can make poetry, but, for some reason, does not wish to make it. It is hard to tell whether he thinks all his readers

---

*Harold Monro (1879–1932) owned London's Poetry Bookshop, which he established in Bloomsbury, encouraging all poetry, and especially new writers.

inevitably such fools that it cannot be worth while to give them true sense; or whether he is but praising the old ruse of covering an inability to be serious by the pretence of preferring to be flippant.[11]

Crowley completed *The Ghouls* that night, then picked up *Adonis* from the back of his mind. Published as "An Allegory," Crowley's verse-play *Adonis* was set amid antiquity's wonder of the world, the Hanging Gardens of Babylon, with characters such as King Esarhaddon, the "lady Astarte," Hermes, Psyche, and Adonis himself. *Adonis* concludes with a rousing chorus, sung by "All":

> The Crown of our life is our love,
> The crown of our love is the light
> That rules all the region above
> The night and the stars of the night;
> That rules all the region aright,
> The abyss to abysses above;
> For the crown of our love is the light,
> And the crown of our light is our love.

Wildly different, the first play was prose, the second lyric poetry, mystic and sensuous. Harold Monro described them as "a sort of enchanted variety entertainment," praising highly *Adonis*'s more "serious" passages. Crowley attributed his energies in this period to his samadhi of October 1908.

Later in the summer he launched his talents into a bigger project, one he'd try to sell for stage or cinema for nearly thirty years: a five-act play, in Alexandrine meter with tortuous internal rhymes, *Mortadello,* which gained numerous admirers but no committed investors. Written at the luxurious Café Riche (1785–1916; corner of boulevard des Italiens and rue Le Peletier), it concerns bygone Venice in the heyday of the Doge, where twenty-year-old Monica, with her black lover's assistance, aims to be the city's autocrat, and succeeds—rather like a Netflix take on Catherine Cookson.

Crowley also wrote no less than nineteen books of magical instruction, all with built-in nondogmatic, skeptical attitude (published in *Equinox* 1, nos. 6 and 7).

♦ ♦ ♦

Back in London, relations with Rose had ended altogether. In April 1911 she was living with their daughter in a pleasant flat in Battersea. The following year she married Dr. Joseph Andrew Gormley (1849–1925), who had pursued her affections for years (much to Crowley's past amusement). Rose died on February 11, 1932, aged fifty-seven.

Isadora Duncan's pianist, Hener Skene (who was enamored of Nina Olivier), turned up again on October 11 when Crowley was invited to a party given by the divine Isadora at London's Savoy. He found himself squatting on the floor "exchanging electricity," as Crowley put it, with Isadora's close friend Marie d'Este. Mary d'Este Sturges (1871–1931)—born Mary Dempsey in Quebec—was soon swept into a romance that at October's end was passionately consummated at Zurich's National Hotel, followed by fun in St. Moritz. A magic quest through Italy followed her joining Crowley in "astral plane" operations that generated recorded encounters with supposed Secret Chief Ab-ul-Diz. Communications stimulated the writing of *Book Four,* the first version of Crowley's masterwork on magical theory and practice. Mary's son joined them for Christmas. Thirteen-year-old "brat," Preston Sturges would eventually write and direct the movies *Sullivan's Travels* and *Unfaithfully Yours.* He was dismissive of Crowley (an untypical response toward Crowley from a child), but his mother was enamored, and in 1912 and 1913 she worked as editor of the *Equinox,* with Neuburg subbing for her.

Come spring 1912, Crowley was dictating part 3 of *Book Four* to Leila Waddell (Laylah, as he called her) at Fontainebleau, during a period described by Crowley a decade later as one spent "hovering" twixt London and Paris,[12] in which he wrote the witty, paradoxical *Book of Lies* (1913), full of enticing, kabbalistic slices of Parisian life, such as "tea at Rumpelmayer's"—Austrian confectioner Anton Rumpelmayer established his first Parisian shop at 226 rue de Rivoli in 1903—or "dinner at Lapérouse," 51 Quai des Grands Augustins on the Left Bank, opposite the Île de la Cité; or "breakfast at the Smoking Dog," a restaurant Au Chien qui Fume, founded 1740 in Halles, 33 rue du Pont Neuf; or a "walk in the forest" at Fontainebleau.

It seems it was June 1912 when German Freemason and Theosophist Theodor Reuss called on Crowley in London to point out Crowley's familiarity with the central secret of Ordo Templi Orientis (O.T.O.), a still-unfinished para-Masonic edifice or "Academia Masonica" first proposed to Reuss and former Blavatsky acolyte Franz Hartmann by Austrian industrialist Carl Kellner (who died prematurely in 1905) as an umbrella body for all Masonic degrees, with a central interest in yoga and a notion of sexual magic, the clue to whose existence was discerned in patristic heresiologies. The recipe blended a little knowledge of kundalini yoga with myths that such knowledge was precious to Knights Templar in Syria, whose possession of it ensured their suppression: an easy equation—that is, sexual repression = suppression of heterodoxy—therefore, liberating gnosis = true secret of Masonry.*

Reuss learned of Crowley through Manchester Mason John Yarker, who'd chartered Reuss to establish the Antient and Primitive Rite of Memphis-Misraim in Germany, while in England Yarker bestowed the 90th and 96th degrees of the Rite on Crowley after an appreciative review of Yarker's *The Arcane Schools* in the *Equinox*. The upshot: Reuss offered Crowley leadership of a British O.T.O., based at 33 Avenue Studios, South Kensington, S.W., and advertised in September's *Equinox*.

A little more than a fortnight after girl-band manager Crowley launched Leila and six other raggedly dressed fiddler-dancers onto the stage of the Old Tivoli Theatre in the Strand as the Ragged Ragtime Girls—*now* we know where that idea came from!—John Yarker died. It was March 20, 1913, and Yarker's death left the Antient and Primitive Rite vulnerable. Sensing an opportunity, Theosophist leaders Annie Besant and Charles Webster Leadbeater—who'd already woven mixed-sex French Co-Masonry into their version of the Theosophical Society—saw not only a chance for additional Masonic integration for their members, and a path to Masonic recognition, but also channels whereby to gain credentials for their Order of the Star in the East, founded in 1911 to establish Leadbeater's Indian protégé Krishnamurti

---

*That he met Reuss in June 1912 would seem implied in a letter to O.T.O. treasurer G. M. Cowie (September 7, 1914; YC NS4): "I did not know until June 1912 the tremendous importance of the knowledge held by the O.T.O., and even when I knew I did not realize it. It has taken me practically two years hard work to assimilate the instruction then received in three short words."

Fig. 13.3. The Old Tivoli Theatre, the Strand, London, 1908.

as coming "World Teacher." Since Crowley saw himself as Secret Chief–sanctioned prophet of the Aeon, Krishnamurti constituted an obstacle.

In May 1913, Crowley took a short holiday in Paris and the Channel Islands. Climbing about the massive boulders of the Rocher d'Avon in Fontainebleau's forest one morning, a snake crossed Crowley's path. It happened again, higher up; Crowley killed it, taking the serpents as danger signs from the Masters. Returning to London he found O.T.O. member Vittoria Cremers, who was handling business affairs for the Order, sowing dissent with Leila Waddell and Victor Neuburg.

Known simply as Cremers, with short hair in a bob, of obscured and disputed parentage, she'd been married in America and inspired to join Theosophy through a mystical work by Mabel Collins (1851–1927).

According to Crowley, Cremers suffered the "vision of the demon Crowley." If so, it was something she clung to. Jean Overton Fuller related Cremers bragging of having "destroyed" Crowley as late as the 1930s.[13] Employment on Blavatsky's journal *Lucifer* commended her to Crowley's effort to organize the O.T.O. Ms. Fuller believed an involuted whirlpool of obsessions and jealousies swirled around the *Equinox* at this time, impossible now to unravel altogether convincingly.

Alerted to Leadbeater and Besant's secretive "Alcyone" project to secure global recognition of Krishnamurti, Crowley wrote to Edward Philip Denny of Anglo-Saxon Lodge No. 343 at 55 boulevard Suchet on June 27, asking whether the lodge could secede from the Grande Loge de France on account of its tolerance of Krishnamurti-supporting Co-Masonry: "When I joined Lodge No. 343 I did so," he wrote, "on the understanding that the Lodge was in fraternal communication with the Lodge of England." It wasn't, while amity with the United Grand Lodge of England was required of members of the Antient and Primitive Rite. Referring Denny to the "blasphemous cult of Alcyone," Crowley suggested Anglo-Saxon Lodge brethren could go over to the U.G.L.E. When Denny appeared reticent, Crowley resigned—prematurely. His ex-lodge joined the Grande Loge Nationale Indépendante et Régulière pour la France et les Colonies Françaises, established November 5, 1913, and recognized by the U.G.L.E. December 3. Crowley ejected himself.

Despite being unrecognized by the U.G.L.E., Crowley's position in Memphis & Misraim was settled by special convocation of the Supreme Sanctuary of the Antient and Primitive Rite of Masonry held at 33 Avenue Studios, 76 Fulham Road, South Kensington, at 5:00 p.m., Monday, June 30, 1913, when Henry Meyer 33°, 90°, 96° was elected Sovereign Grand Master General (for Britain) in accordance with Yarker's wishes, with Crowley Grand Inspector General. As for Yarker's office: "the Honourable degree of 97 of Grand Hierophant made vacant . . . be conferred upon the most illustrious S.G.M.G. of France Dr Gérard Encausse (Papus [1865–1916]) 33°, 90°, 96°, on account of his world wide eminence and his successful labours on behalf of the Rite."[14] Papus, however, by 1913, had scant interest in para-Masonic activities, being devoted to a spiritually purified understanding of Christianity known as Martinism.

Henry Meyer soon disappeared from the Rite, and Crowley's immediate interest in them lay only in reducing them to a ten-degree

O.T.O. system he believed transcended regular Masonry. Papus's death from illness contracted while serving as medic on the Western Front in 1916 left the rite without a Hierophant, while Martinists were decimated and divided by the 1920s when Crowley returned to Paris after the war.

COVERING EMBARRASSMENT

After an extraordinary July and August 1913 in Moscow, where his Ragged Ragtime Girls performed amid wild scenes at the Aquarium fun palace (see *Aleister Crowley: The Biography*), Crowley returned to London, but not for long. Back in Paris on December 1 with Victor Neuburg, a long-running controversy suddenly piqued his interest.

In August 1912, Jacob Epstein's funerary monument to Oscar Wilde arrived in east Paris's celebrated necropolis Père Lachaise. Its erection overseen by Wilde's executor Robert Ross—familiar to Crowley through sometime lover Ada Leverson (friend of Wilde)—official unveiling was delayed when Epstein refused to alter the flying figure's enormous testicles of Derbyshire limestone, as official propriety demanded. Attaching clay to the offending member only exaggerated attention, so, with fabulous historic irony, Wilde's monument was smothered with a tarpaulin.

Crowley possibly heard about it from twenty-two-year-old artist Nina Hamnett (1890–1956).* She'd visited Crowley's Fulham Road studio sometime after February 1912. There she'd met "a beautiful man" to whom she surrendered her virginity. He eventually took her to Paris for five days: another first for Nina. She met Epstein, his wife, and sculptor Brancusi. Offended by the indecency charge, "every afternoon Epstein, his wife and I [Nina], would go to Père Lachaise and snatch the tarpaulin off. Eventually the French police were told about it, and, when we next arrived, hiding behind the tombstones were policemen who rushed at us and covered the statue up again."[15]

Crowley didn't claim to be first to challenge the tarpaulin; for him

---

*That Crowley's concern with Wilde's monument probably predated his Paris trip is supported by a letter of November 29, 1913, to O.T.O. treasurer G. M. Cowie (YC NS4): "My only hope of spending winter abroad is that they will put me in prison in Paris." Immediately after this, Crowley disputes with Cowie about the value of Wilde's later work, such as *De Profundis,* dismissed as cowardly efforts to curry sympathy.

Fig. 13.4. Jacob Epstein's tomb of Oscar Wilde, Père Lachaise, Paris, nearly a century later. However, since 2011, the lower part of the tomb has been protected with a transparent screen on account of cleaning off lipstick applied by devotees kissing the stone having damaged its surface: a repeat irony Crowley would have appreciated.

it was simply demonstrative of the sex scotoma that made otherwise sane people behave ridiculously. Parisian newspapers duly received copies of Crowley's manifesto:

IN THE NAME OF THE LIBERTY OF ART

The Artist has the right to create what he wants!

The fine monument of Oscar Wilde in Père Lachaise, masterpiece of sculptor Jacob Epstein, already mutilated and degraded by order of the Prefect of the Seine, remains veiled.

At midday, next Wednesday November 5, Monsieur Aleister Crowley, the Irish poet, will unveil it.

Come to him and offer your aid and sympathy, come to protest against the prudish and pornophile tyranny of the bourgeois, come to affirm the Artist's right to create what he wants.

Meet at the Cemetery of Père Lachaise, before the monument to Oscar Wilde, at midday, Wednesday, November 5.

There has long been error about dating Crowley's first intervention over the monument. Biographer Martin Booth misdated it to 1912; a Wikipedia entry puts it in August 1914. The fault lay in *Confessions,* where the event was placed undated and out of sequence. Researching the newspaper record, I was delighted finally to find this notice in the "Arts" section, page 4 of *Gil Blas,* November 5, 1913: "A Demonstration—We receive the following notice. We shall tell tomorrow what this demonstration was." They didn't; perhaps the Préfet de la Seine intervened.

According to *Confessions,* the day before the promised "manifestation" Crowley spoke to Monsieur Bourcier at 50 rue Vavin about his intentions. Bourcier reckoned he'd invite a line of bayonets, so Crowley contacted an "enthusiastic young American" (possibly Michael Brenner, who'd migrated to New York before coming to Paris) for assistance. Having waited for the cemetery gates to close, they attached fine wire to the tarpaulin, and Crowley cut existing cords until held by only a fiber. The plan was not to rush authority's stooges but for Crowley to make a speech at a distance and, at a hand signal, the "American," secreted in a tree 200 yards away, would pull the wires and lo! Once set up, they told the gatekeeper they'd got lost, and retired until next day, when Crowley returned to find a "distinguished concourse of enthusiasts" for the cause.[16] Crowley led them in solemn procession, while patrols scattered on seeing them. Thinking they sought reinforcements, Crowley anticipated a spectacular arrest. Arriving at the tomb, however, no one was there. Crowley surmised police had received orders that on no account should the "mad Irish poet" suffer interference; it would only add clay to genitalia. "I made my speech and unveiled Epstein's effort in the dull drizzling weather," Crowley sighed. "It was a disheartening success." Still, it made a splash in newspapers in France, Britain, and Chicago.

Poor sport, Jacob Epstein contacted the London *Times* (November 8, 1913):

> I have read with some surprise in your issue of November 6th a discussion of an unveiling of my monument by Mr. Aleister Crowley. In order that there may be no misunderstanding on the subject of my own views, I should be obliged if you would give me the opportunity of stating in your columns that I should have much preferred the monument to remain veiled until such time as the alleged improvements made against my desires have been removed. I do not consider any unofficial unveiling a compliment to me, though no doubt a jolly occasion for Mr. Crowley and his companions.
>
> Jacob Epstein

Crowley was obviously disappointed by Epstein's reaction and assessed Epstein's psychological weaknesses in a long digression in *Confessions;* his main point being that Epstein's genius was unconscious and intuitive, and when he applied other people's thoughts to it, he muddied his vision, conscious of competing with the latest modernist fad.

Nevertheless, Crowley did Epstein's monument one last service. Some time later, Ross, desperate for an official unveiling (he'd raised considerable funds for the monument), tried to persuade Epstein to accept a bronze butterfly being attached over the disputed detail. Despite Epstein's refusal to attend, Ross proceeded. A "cache-sexe," fashioned by another artist, was duly attached. Visiting to check if the tarpaulin had returned, Crowley found the new addition hilarious, especially— the butterfly being Whistler's emblem—its positioning constituting grave insult to Wilde, whose savagely witty disputes with Whistler were famous. Oblivious to Crowley's now portly dimensions, the gatekeeper let him out and, when next in London, Crowley donned evening dress, attaching the butterfly where modesty dictated, and entered the Café Royal "to the delight of the assembled multitude." Epstein himself was present, "and it was a glorious evening. By this time he had understood my motives; that I was honestly indignant at the outrage to him and determined to uphold the privileges of the artist."[17]

The story seems emblematic of the real Aleister Crowley, serious joker.

FOURTEEN

Fiery Arrows 1914

I have not even yet done a tithe of what is to be done [in researching the IX° O.T.O.]. The occurrence of the war has forced me to redouble my efforts; to conclude a thoroughly scientific investigation. We had a great attempt at this in Paris for six weeks, beginning with Jan[uary] 1st this year, but I was proceeding at somewhat unorthodox lines, anyhow, the record although a highly important document, is only one brick in the Temple. I have been criminally careless about my record of late, but I am now making amends; but I know already a good deal of the importance of this Secret.

CROWLEY TO GEORGE MACNIE
COWIE (1861–1948), SEPTEMBER 7, 1914[1]

Vouchsafed the O.T.O.'s primary, if rudimentary, secret by Theodor Reuss in June 1912, Crowley made his first "sex magick" experiment on December 2 that year. The next definite record of practical research began at 11:40 p.m., Wednesday, December 31, 1913, very likely at 50 rue Vavin, whose owners, the Bourciers, were now inured to strangeness in Monsieur Crowley's room, with incense and invocations and visitors. To get a sense of atmosphere, reflect that Wednesday's *New York Herald* (Paris edition) reported that all Europe's capitals were under heavy snowfalls; a picture showed stylish Parisiennes negotiating thick snow in the Bois de Boulogne, hands in fur mufflers with thick woollen scarves enveloping chilly cheeks; St. Petersburg's streets were jammed with sleighs; and London's parks were filled with children enjoying winter sports.

In a room one suspects not overly warm, Zelator of the A∴A∴Victor Neuburg would perform functions as "priest," with Crowley as priest and "virgin" (if I understand the record correctly) for no less than twenty-four strenuous operations of homosexual sex magick that closed with a forty-five-minute operation at 7:00 p.m. on Thursday, February 7, 1914.*

The temple consisted of the bed, in the east; a record of the god's words, in the west; the priest, in the north; in the south, a fire and thurible (a censer containing incense). In the center a foursquare stone held an image of the "Supreme, Vast, Forbidden, Ineffable, Most Holy God" (whatever that may have been), next to the book *Thelema* (containing the Holy Books), and the magical dagger, bell, and oil. The words employed came from *Liber 671;* the *Tu Qui Es* (You Who Are, based on the Bornless One invocation, beginning "Thou who art I, beyond all I am") and the *Quia Patris* (For of the Father)—both from Crowley's Gnostic Mass composed in Russia in 1913; *Liber 813* or *Ararita* (one of the Holy Books of Thelema); the Ceremony of the Thurible; and *Liber Israfel 64* (invocation of Thoth). In addition, Walter Duranty† translated into Latin from Crowley's English eight short Holy Hymns addressed to Juppiter (alternative Latin spelling), Mercury, Venus, Juppiter Ammon, Vesta (the Virgin), Iacchus, Priapus, and Mars—each one highly sexual, yet curiously chaste.

The operational intention was to invoke (separately) the gods Jupiter and Hermes, or Mercury; that is, to internalize the god-form of the deity through intense concentration on the qualities and associations of the god reflected in an image, to the point where the mind of the god indwelled the magi. To assist in identifying with the god, invocations

---

*For details of the Paris Working, consult *The Vision and the Voice,* edited by Hymenaeus Beta.

†Emmanuel College, Cambridge graduate Walter Duranty (1884–1957), Crowley's sometime lover, was in Paris working as *New York Times* correspondent, seeing his Parisian girlfriend (and later wife), model Jane Chéron, with whom he and Crowley took opium.

were voiced, while sexual intercourse (Crowley was usually passive partner) was employed to intensify further a magical, highly energized sense
of concentrated envisioning (one presumes both men were on their
knees, with the "sacrificing" priest behind and the "virgin" bent over).
At the moment of orgasm, it was vital a concentrated current of will
embodying the object of the operation was energized, maintained, and
projected into the ether, while a "hymn" ecstatically expressed the accu-
mulated energy. The drug mescaline was sometimes employed in moderate doses to assist mystical visualization. Thus, in the first working, for
example, Crowley noted that "Astrally the Temple was full of thousands
of flashing caducei of gold and yellow, the serpents alive and moving,
Hermes bearing them." Such a vision may have been a case of directed
imagination without chemical stimulants, or enhanced substantially by
mescaline. In this case, despite promising mercurial visions, seen with
the mind's eye, and identified with the mind invoking, Crowley noted
that "so young and so mischievous was He [Mercury/Neuburg] that the
sacrifice was impossible." The "sacrifice" of the priest was the rendering
holy the semen through sacramental orgasm.

At the second operation on New Year's Day, despite a "new-made
Image of the God in the East, a terminal phallic figure in yellow wax,
very beautiful" (made by Crowley that afternoon), Neuburg again "lost
control." After invocation, the practice was to write down what the god
communicated and for Crowley and Neuburg to ask one another questions, on the basis that one or the other was addressing the mind of the
god, who could prophesy. In this instance, Crowley accused Neuburg of
defacing the record with gibberish, having been overwhelmed in the rite.

It was further held that successful rites would affect happenings
in their world, according to the nature of the god. Thus, Jupiter was
associated with great wealth, abundance, banquets, and big happenings;
Mercury with communication, wisdom, trickery, and business. A bun-
gled invocation of Mercury, Crowley believed, left them without receiving mail for an otherwise inexplicable period. Crowley was certainly
hoping for money, as he was driven to the expedient of trying to get
Cowie to use his publishing contacts (he was art editor for religion and
education publishers Thomas Nelson of Edinburgh) to obtain translation work—labor Cowie felt was beneath the majesty of his guru.

Crowley and Neuburg gave Jupiter credit for an advantageous

bank rate in England that increased the value of Crowley's securities, an unexpected gift of £500 to the Order from a formerly poor Brother who'd received an inheritance. Neuburg seems to have come into some money but shared benefits with others, not Crowley.

Waking from a good night's sleep after the Ninth Working's invocation of Juppiter Ammon, Crowley remembered the details of a dream, which transcribed, became his story "The Stratagem," published in the *English Review* in June 1914, drawing high praise from Joseph Conrad, to Crowley's delight. The dream was preceded by a timely visit from Walter Duranty and Jane Chéron. Crowley was suffering badly with bronchitis. They prescribed opium, leaving him quietly when he entered the sleep that brought him "The Stratagem."

After the Twenty-Third Working, at 3:18 a.m., Crowley made a divination for Aimée Gouraud, having put his finger randomly into *Liber LXV* (IV.13): "Without pity, act. Guests dally on the couches of mother of pearl in the garden. Go to the Holy House of Hathor and offer the five jewels of the cow on her altar. Then go under the night-stars in the desert and invoke Nuit." Two days earlier, another divination to answer the question whether he should go to Tunis for Aimée had yielded from *Liber LXV* (V.49): "Is not the Nile a beautiful water?" In fact Crowley would be in Tunis in April 1914, though how it connected with wealthy, and very daring, heiress Aimée Gouraud (IX° O.T.O.) is unknown.*

Working XIII on January 27, 1914, yielded two accounts of previous incarnations in ancient Mediterranean history involving Crowley and Neuburg, who, if you believe it, "knew one another" in previous lives, with a sense of mutual bad luck attending those lives.

Crowley speculated one result of the Paris Working might have been World War I. This thought apparently arose (with hindsight) from the Eleventh Working (January 21–January 22) when, after the "Versicle," Neuburg obtained a message in Enochian "to the effect that the gods wish to regain Their dominion upon earth, these Initiated Brethren being as Fiery Arrows shot by Them in Their war against the slave-gods. A Four-fold sacrifice was demanded; and that a sacrifice of cruelty." After

---

*For Crowley's longstanding relationship with Aimée Gouraud, see *Aleister Crowley in America*. He dedicated his poem "The Disciples" to her, among others, in *Equinox* 1, no. 10. (Crowley, *The Vision and the Voice*, 395.)

war broke out, Crowley informed G. M. Cowie on August 19, 1914, that Neuburg interpreted hostilities in terms of *The Book of the Law:* "I have not made up my mind about the war at all. Neuburg suggests that it is the Overture of the Aeon of Horus. I am hoping it will be over in two or three months."[2] Crowley thought it might not last as he foresaw great practical failures (such as moving German troops on an unprecedented scale). He was partly right, because the deadly attrition that character-ized the conflict resulted from critical miscalculations that prevented the Germans reaching Paris quickly enough to secure a victory. On the other hand, just over a week later, Crowley also looked to *Liber Legis:* "so called civilisation is at an end, I hope for a couple of thousand years at least."[3] He urged preservation of the O.T.O.'s secrets in a kind of bombproof vault (following the Rosenkreutz legend), with the secrets engraved in steel by Bro. Benjamin Charles Hammond,[4] engraver respon-sible for Order seals. Bro. Hammond (VI° O.T.O.) joined Crowley and Neuburg for lunch in honor of Juppiter on Tuesday, February 3, before the Eighteenth Working.[5]

Nevertheless, the result this author found most interesting was insight occurring to Crowley during the Second Working, January 1 to January 2, 1914, that rather "pre-confirms" one aspect of the Nag Hammadi Gnostic library discovery thirty-one years later; that is, during the fourth century CE (at least), Gnostic Christians in Upper Egypt placed the revelation of Thrice Greatest Hermes (Mercury) next to Christ's, making play with parallel noetic ideas of uniting "above" and "below." Despite admitting to having read *The Vision of the Universal Mercury* (attributed to Samuel Mathers), Crowley found the identification astonishing, having formerly considered Christ a solar symbol akin to Mithras and Osiris, expressing J. G. Frazer's conception of *The Dying God* (1911). Invocation impelled understanding Christ as Hermetic or mercurial symbol, transcribed in Opus Two's "Esoteric Record":

> In the beginning was the Word, the *logos,* who is Mercury, and is therefore to be identified with Christ. Both are messengers; their birth mysteries are similar; the pranks of their childhood are similar. In the Vision of the Universal Mercury, Hermes is seen descending upon the sea, which refers to Maria. The Crucifixion represents the Caduceus; the two thieves, the two serpents; the cliff in the Vision

of the Universal Mercury is Golgotha [where Mathers sees the vision of Mercury between sky and sea from a dark and rocky cliff[6]]; Maria is simply Maia with the Solar R [Hebrew *Resh* = Head] in her womb.

The controversy about Christ between the Synoptics and John was really a contention between the priests of Bacchus, Sol and Osiris; also, perhaps, of Adonis and Attis on the one hand, and those of Hermes on the other, at that period when initiates all over the world found it necessary, owing to the growth of the Roman Empire, and the opening up of the means of communication, to replace conflicting polytheisms by a synthetic faith. (This is absolutely new to me this conception of Christ as Mercury.) . . .

To continue the identification, compare Christ's descent into Hell with the function of Hermes as guide of the Dead. Also Hermes leading up Eurydice, and Christ raising up Jairus's daughter. Christ is said to have risen on the third day, because it takes three days for the Planet Mercury to become visible after separating from the orb of the Sun. (It may be noted here that Mercury and Venus are the planets between us and the Sun, as if the Mother and the Son were mediators between us and the Father.)

Note Christ as the Healer, and also his own expression: "The Son of Man cometh as a thief in the night" [1 Thess. 5:2, Rev. 3:3, 16:15; Hermes is associated with trickery and theft as well as revelation]; and also this scripture: "For as the lightning cometh out of the East and shineth even unto the West, so shall the coming of the Son of Man be" [Matt. 24:27].

Note also Christ's relations with the money changers, his frequent parables, and the fact that his first disciple was a publican [Mercury is the god of finance].

Note also Mercury as the deliverer of Prometheus [who gave fire to humankind].

One half of the fish symbol is also common to Christ and Mercury; fish are sacred to Mercury (owing presumably to their qualities of movement and cold-bloodedness). [Crowley adds a note: "This I did not know before."] Many of Christ's disciples were fishermen, and he was always doing miracles in connection with fish.

Note also Christ as the mediator: "No man cometh unto the Father but by Me" [John 14:6], and Mercury as Chokmah [Wisdom], through whom alone we can approach Kether [the Crown].

The Caduceus contains a complete symbol of the Gnosis; the winged Sun or phallus represents the joy of life on all planes from the lowest to the highest. The Serpents (besides being Active and Passive, Horus and Osiris, and all their other well-known attributions) are those qualities of Eagle and Lion respectively, of which we know, but do not speak [Crowley is referring to the IX° alchemical secret of dissolving male and female sexual secretions as an "elixir of life" where the Lion is the spermatozoa and the Eagle is that which seizes upon it]. It is the symbol which unites the Microcosm and the Macrocosm, the symbol of the Magical Operation which accomplishes this. The Caduceus is Life itself, and is of universal application. It is the universal solvent. It is quite easy to turn quicksilver into gold on the physical plane, and this will soon be done. New life will flow through the world in consequence.[7]

In one sense, Crowley's surprise is itself surprising, as Hermetic identification of divine *mercurius* (protean; all-penetrating) with Logos-Christ permeates "Rosicrucian" literature from the early seventeenth century onward, finding contemporary voice in Anna Kingsford's idea of "Esoteric Christianity." Before the Rose-Cross movement, alchemist Heinrich Khunrath's famous *Amphitheatrum sapientiae aeternae* (Hamburg, 1595) explicitly identified Christ with the mercurial Stone. Indeed the tradition is vast, finding dramatic human expression in the figure of Mercurio (Giovanni) da Correggio, who entered Rome on an ass in 1484 wearing a crown of thorns, identifying himself with Christ, Poimandres, Hermes, and Enoch, as recorded by Lodovico Lazzarelli.*

Well, reading and *seeing* are two different things, and one can only suppose it was Crowley's reaction to Plymouthite indoctrination that somehow filtered out what ought to have been obvious when he was symbolically cross-bound in the Golden Dawn: the crucified mercurius is a common alchemical symbol. Prejudice against Christianity clearly created a scotoma on the issue. He could even have beefed up his Thelema message by examining carefully the Hermetic *Asklēpios,* which in its Nag Hammadi Coptic version (Codex VI, page 74, line 5)

*See my book *The Golden Builders,* which surveys the tradition's history.

declares: "for the nature of god is will. And his will is the good." Did not Crowley try to accomplish what Blavatsky also attempted (when she used words from John 4:34): to do "the will of him that sent me" (Greek: *to thelema tou pempsantos me*).

Crowley's interest in esoteric implications of Jesus's association with fish (apart from the well-known Greek word *ichthus* [or fish] providing an acrostic for *iesous christos theou huios soter* = "Jesus Christ, Son of God, Savior") would have benefited from Kabbalist writer Tuvia Fogel's recent, intriguing deciphering of a combined example of Hebrew and Greek gematria in John 21:11's miraculous draft of 153 fishes—Jesus's last miracle. Write the value 153 in the smallest number of Hebrew letters (each Hebrew letter is also a number); there are eighteen possible combinations of letters, but how many make words? None. All learned Jews knew Greek, the common language of the Eastern empire. Try (right to left): Ain (70), Gimel (3), Pe (80). Pronounced, it makes: *A-gà-pe,* the Greek word for . . . *LOVE. This* is the message the gospel leaves for humankind. When 153 fishes are caught, the net does not break, and readers will note that in the following verses, Jesus asks Peter *three times* if he *loves* him, using the Greek word for love.[8] And Crowley would hardly need reminding that according to the Greek "Qabalah" (isopsephy) he favored, agapē (αγαπη, meaning "Love") is 1+3+1+80+8, which equals 93, the exact value of *Theléma,* (θελημα, meaning "will") (9+5+30+8+40+1). As Hermes says: "God is will," and St. John, "God is love" (1 John 4:16).

DENNIS WHEATLEY AND THE LEGEND OF RAISING PAN IN PARIS

One of the many legends connected with Aleister Crowley is that drawn from the enormously popular, ubiquitous writings of Dennis Wheatley, who confessed to having dined with Crowley "several times" while researching the occult novel *The Devil Rides Out* (1934). Crowley's inscription to Wheatley of a copy of his *Magick in Theory and Practice* (1929) gives some idea of the context: Crowley presented the book to Wheatley "in memory of that sublime Hungarian banquet," dating it to May 1934. Crowley added pencil-written notes on the plain sheets at the front of the book. Wheatley noted in ink beneath that these were written at the time of presentation. Crowley drew an upright pentagram with explanation that the five points indicated the four classical elements with the symbol of the spirit at the "head" (making five), next to a corresponding drawing of a standing man, head up and arms and legs outstretched, opposite the words "= Jesus" (to the right of the pentagram), and "4 elements = limitation[s?] of matter." A sketched cross also indicates the four elements. A drawing of the hexagram of interlocking triangles "unites above and below," Crowley noted. Opposite the drawings Crowley inscribed "Recommendations to the intelligent reader humbly offered." These include, significantly "Read 'Hymn to Pan' aloud at midnight, when alone, with INTENTION to get HIM." Crowley then added:

> Read Introduction very thoroughly indeed.
>
> Skate lightly (at first reading) over Chapters (e.g., like Cap V) which go off the deep end over the Holy Qabalah. But go back to them studiously after getting Appendix V by heart.
>
> Study—early in the process—Appendix II, to get our Aim and Method.
>
> Study *Liber XV* pp 345 sqq [the Gnostic Mass] with a view to putting on this ritual in London as it is done in Hollywood. Amen.

One wonders if Wheatley ever followed the recommendations or truly absorbed the white magic Crowley was writing about. Anyhow, there's no evidence of it in the tale repeated by Wheatley (though attributed to an informant, not to Crowley!) of ghastly events in Paris that allegedly left Crowley mentally damaged. Intended as a warning against dabbling in black magic, Wheatley's account has been remarkably effective, certainly in keeping the curious from closer inspection of those facts that must never get in the way of a good story, as *Hammer, House of Horror* has tirelessly demonstrated. Wheatley repeated his yarn with slight modifications in his nonfiction *The Devil and All His Works* (1971), in his introduction to an edition of Crowley's novel *Moonchild* (1974), and in his memoirs, *The Time Has Come* (1979). The influence of Wheatley's few paragraphs has been great and lasting.[9]

The version of the story in *The Devil and All His Works* has probably been most influential. There we're told that several dinners with Crowley revealed him as "intensely interesting," though friend "Z" was told that Crowley couldn't harm a rabbit, to which "Z" countered: "Not now, perhaps. But he was very different before that affair in Paris," where Crowley apparently wanted to "raise Pan." A disciple owned a small Left Bank hotel, so Crowley and twelve (!) disciples took it over for a weekend, the servants given a holiday. A big room was emptied on a Saturday night for Crowley and "MacAleister" (main disciple: "son of Aleister") to perform the ceremony while eleven stayed downstairs. Warning was given not to enter the room until morning.

A cold collation was prepared in the little restaurant downstairs, and much was drunk, but the eleven only got "stale-tight." By midnight, the hotel was immensely cold, and from the upper room was heard banging and shouting. They approached the room in the morning, but it was locked and, their calls ignored, the door was broken. "Crowley had raised Pan all right." MacAleister dead, Crowley, robes gone, was "a naked gibbering idiot crouching in a corner."

Four months in a lunatic asylum followed before Crowley was able to venture forth again. We're then told that "Z" had been a disciple and had witnessed all this.

The version in Wheatley's memoir, *The Time Has Come,* has differences and embellishments. It says Crowley had been expelled from Italy because there was "little doubt" cats were sacrificed at his Abbey of Thelema to Satanic powers amid rumors of small children disappearing for the same purpose. "Little doubt" and "rumors" . . . Wheatley repeats the nonfact that a disciple owned a Paris hotel and refers to a "coven" of disciples arriving (that's witchcraft, not a para-Masonic Order). The rest is more or less the same. He adds that Crowley might have raised Pan, but Pan objected. "Anyhow, Crowley spent four months in a loony-bin outside Paris before he was allowed about again."

I'm pretty sure most readers will have seen this tale for what it is: an apocryphal nonsense linked to the Paris Working, misdated and rendered totally fictional (Crowley had no abbey until some six years after the Working).

Wheatley's biographer, Phil Baker, concluded likewise: "very vulgar," it wasn't even an exaggeration.[10] Baker thinks the tale owed its basics to Tom Driberg, columnist, M.P., later Labour Party chairman, longtime Crowley friend, and like Wheatley, friend of MI5. Wheatley named "Z" as an M.P. in the 1974 *Moonchild* introduction, which narrows the field. Baker concludes Wheatley's dropping the M.P. in was to weave intrigue into a fiction of the *Là Bas* type and that the source was probably a fantastically garbled account of the Paris Working dribbled by Driberg, who, incidentally, was *eight* at the time! Perhaps Neuburg's later consultations with Freudian doctor E. T. Jensen got injected into the mix. As for Pan, well, Crowley and Neuburg participated in an invocation of Bartzabel in 1910 at Rempstone, home of naval Commander Guy Marston (1878–1921), whose sole remarkable highlight was when the spirit of Mars, through Neuburg, correctly foretold that a coming war would ruin Germany and Turkey.

If one were looking for a villain in this piece, Vittoria Cremers might be considered. At the time Wheatley was researching the occult, she was boasting she'd destroyed Crowley, or his power. Cremers had embezzled O.T.O. funds and held a serious grudge; she may also have suspected close friend Mabel Collins was unusually interested in Victor Neuburg. *Neuburg* was the one with the powerful Pan interest, having written *The Triumph of Pan* (1910); Pan "triumphing" over Crowley is an obvious piece of the garbled fiction. Cremers's contretemps with Crowley, involving her turning Neuburg against his former guru, occurred during, before, and after the Paris Working.

It's also likely that Wheatley's urge to moralize through stories, his will to tell tales, tall if needs be, got the upper hand over any interest in fact. Wheatley had gratefully received an inscribed copy of *Magick* from Crowley, which he kept, and which he told Crowley he valued. He could easily have checked the ridiculous Pan story if he'd wanted to.*

The Paris Working's intense pressure seems to have crystallized old sores between Crowley and Neuburg. The latter quit his guru after a tiff, lending ear to embezzler Cremers's jibes, and as Crowley saw it, her

---

*One other possible tie-in for the story might be U.S. journalist Arthur Burton Rascoe (1892–1957), *Chicago Tribune* editor in 1924, who was familiar with Crowley's work. Crowley wanted to approach Rascoe that year over autobiographical serial rights and other article ideas (see page 275). In the late 1920s, Rascoe edited *Morrow's Almanac and Every-Day Book*. His replacement editor in 1930 published numerous Rascoe stories, including "Anecdote for a Winter Night," in which Rascoe told how "demonologist" Aleister Crowley failed to raise the devil.[11]

projection: the "demon Crowley." By siding with Neuburg she helped separate the magicians. According to Jean Overton Fuller, Crowley cursed Neuburg, and Pan's devotee never fully recovered.

Crowley left 50 rue Vavin for Tunis in late March or early April 1914. Whether he returned to Paris afterward, we know not. He was climbing, apparently alone, in Switzerland in July and August. While there, England declared war on Germany on August 4. Returning from Switzerland to London, he wrote to Cowie on August 19:

> Glad to get yours of today. I came down from the mountains to find the Swiss had mobilized and all the railways held up, but on the first day possible I went to Berne where the British minister informed me it was impossible to get back, that the line had been torn up for 15 miles beyond the frontier, and that he could not get his own men through. Reduced to desperation I consequently took the train and came home without any difficulty.[12]

As detailed in *Aleister Crowley in America,* Crowley left England for America in December 1914, not returning for five years. Having failed to find a government propaganda post, as other writers had, *Confessions* indicates his main motive for going was participation in a deal related to securing American bank loans so Britain could pursue the war. The background to this was Crowley's friend Raymond Radclyffe (of the *English Review*), financial expert and author of *The War and Finance* (1914), who explained the urgency. Interestingly, he wrote to Cowie on September 7, 1914:

> The Foreign Office write that they are considering very seriously, my proposition of sending a special embassy to the U.S.A. You might mention this in confidence to the editor of any paper whom you saw, or any publisher whom you might interview; to indicate that publication would be decidedly pleasing to the Government.[13]

Overcoming American neutrality intrigued Crowley. As for the idea of volunteering for active service, he wouldn't be passed as fit (even if he tried), as he told Cowie on September 14: "I shall be stuck on this board for at least another fortnight, and the quack [doctor] says it may be three months. The disease is alleged to be Phlebitis: its cause is unknown. I am not sure that it was not a magical imprudence." He added it was something that necessitated getting his written work completed, as well as tying up his finances (believing Consols, or consolidated annuities, would soon be valueless), and especially securing the secret wisdom of the O.T.O. While phlebitis was not immediately life threatening, "it is one of those things which may suddenly become mortal without any particular excuse."[14]

Anxious over Crowley's health, Cowie asked him his view of the war—the O.T.O.'s Outer Head was *German*. Crowley's response (September 17) gives an interesting slant on his position as British Head of the Order:

> With regard to the War, from the Masonic point of view, we have, of course, nothing to do with it. Every man fights for his own country if he wants to. Our business is to see that the knowledge is preserved, and if all the people that possess it get killed or die in some way, it will be a nuisance.[15]

The war and his American adventures ensured that Crowley would not return to Paris until 1920.

Fig. 14.1. Aleister Crowley, ca. 1907.

FIFTEEN

The Fool Is a Card 1920

New Year's Day 1920. . . . Having partied at Desti's, Mary d'Este and fourth husband, ex-army officer Howard Perch's new club, Crowley spent his last night in London "dossing it" on a sofa on Brook Street with a blue Persian cat. Leaving Victoria for Paris at 10:00 a.m., he intended a "very short intense Magical Retirement" while seeking a "government job" through old friend, intelligence officer Hon. Everard Feilding. He quickly fell in with Walter Duranty and well-traveled pulp-fiction writer Charles Beadle (1881–1947), who'd written a short story set in Montparnasse for the *International* in New York, when Crowley edited it.* Crowley also saw Canadian painter J. W. Morrice from the Chat Blanc days of 1903.

Crowley's Scarlet Woman, Leah Hirsig, also left New York at the end of 1919. Residing with her sister in Switzerland on January 3, she informed Crowley that she intended to come to Paris to have her and Crowley's baby. I Ching consulted, Crowley chose Fontainebleau for the birth. Next day he dined with Jane Chéron (engaged to Walter Duranty) and an "American melancholic" chez Germaine Bayle at 9 rue du Paul Louis Courier (7ème arrondissement)—bumping into "Willy" (possibly traveler and journalist William Buehler Seabrook, (1884–1945) with whom Crowley had stayed in Georgia in 1919) with Beadle at Lapérouse on the eighth. Reconnoitering Fontainebleau's forest the next day, he found Moret-sur-Loing as disappointing as pre-

---

*"A Doctor of Men" (April 1918). Paris based in 1920, Beadle appears in Crowley's 1939 diary, dining five times at Crowley's, picking Crowley's brains about Montparnasse for a book.

THE LATEST SIDE OF NIGHT CLUB LIFE : MONTMARTRE IN LONDON.
Montmartre came to London last week for at least one evening, as our photograph of Desti's Club shows. Every dancer was "got up" as an Art Student, and the mise-en-scène of bare boards, wooden bowls, and candles stuck in bottles to light the scene of merriment was complete. Madame Desti, the organiser of the club, is on the extreme right of our photograph.—[*Photograph by C.N.*]

Fig. 15.1. Desti's Club, a basement dancing club at 70 New Bond Street, London, January 1920. Mary Desti (Soror Virakam of Crowley's A∴A∴) is seated far right. The photo appeared in the weekly journal The Sketch, *January 28, 1920. Thanks to Sigurd Bune for researching this.*

George Sylvester Viereck gives an intensely interesting account of the great Danish critic, George Brandes. Turning from grave to gay, Charles Beadle contributes a delightful sketch of life in the Latin Quarter of Paris with its curious mixture of religious fervor and debauchery. The famous Japanese poet, Shigetsu Sasaki, has written a delightfully colored article on Shinto, the most interesting of the religions of Japan.

Fig. 15.2. Editor Crowley announces Charles Beadle's story about pre-war Montparnasse in the April 1918 issue of the International.

war, but "the gods" guided him to "charming people" at the Hotel de Bourgogne.

Back in Paris January 10 to meet Leah and son, Hansi Hammond; in England, Horatio Bottomley's jingoistic *John Bull* salivated: "Another Traitor Trounced—Career and Condemnation of the notorious Aleister Crowley." Charging "dirty renegade" and "treacherous degenerate" Crowley with wartime treason, the paper demanded his exclusion from

Fig. 15.3. Moret-les-Sablons, Hôtel de Bourgogne.

England. Timing was atrocious: Crowley was to meet Everard Feilding the next day. While Feilding knew Crowley's preposterous anti-Allied stunts stateside were intended to convince German propagandists that his anti-Britishness was genuine, Feilding conflicted with Crowley over that his present usefulness; Crowley's initiatives to encourage America to oppose Germany had been excessive, his reputation, too hot.

The question of usefulness rankled; *was A.C. even any use to the gods?* Invoking Aiwass for a sign he plunged a finger into *Liber Legis,* finding: "the omnipresence of my body" (I.26). On January 30: the sign. Purchasing artist's materials in Paris (he'd started painting in 1917), he called on Jane "like a drug of wonder" Chéron to make love, locate "Willy," and to smoke opium. Jaja, as he called her, had a surprise. In February 1917, she and Walter Duranty undertook an opium cure in Provence. In three months she made a four-foot silk appliqué representation of stele 666. Crowley saw Nuit as night sky, omnipresent body arched over "Hadit": a sign unmistakeable! *They* wanted him.

Next day, Crowley met Jules Courtier, perhaps at Feilding's instigation, for Courtier, of the Institut général psychologique (IGP) in the rue de Condé, had photographed Eusapia Palladino levitating a table in 1907 with the Groupe d'Étude des Phénomenes Psychiques. Feilding investigated Palladino for the Psychical Research Society. Crowley believed telekinesis involved invisibles akin to Hertz rays and radium, whereas *Liber Legis* proved (to him) that extrahuman intelligence actually existed.

Crowley maintained strict records of sexual magick. At 3:00 p.m. February 4, Opus III with Italian prostitute Eliane Vacari was "to get the New Current going." To Crowley's surprise, Eliane intuited he was bisexual.

Renting a pleasant house at 11 bis rue de Neuville, Fontainebleau, he contemplated an Abbey of Thelema, walking four miles south to Marlotte, where Cézanne had lived, and Sisley and Renoir painted, to examine a property on February 7. "Willy" and Beadle came to lunch on the tenth, and the next day, Crowley recorded Opus VI with Eliane, to inspire a play from Beadle's novelette *The Tree of Life* (1919).

On the thirteenth he revisited Marlotte with Ninette Shumway (1894–1989), lately resident of 31 Sudbury Rd., Concord, Massachusetts (according to her passport), whom Leah had befriended on the transatlantic voyage. Crowley reckoned French-born widow "Shummy," with young son Howard, good help for Leah. During a blissful twenty-mile roundabout forest walk, Ninette fell in love with the Beast. Crowley's mind, however, was preoccupied with abstract art: "the only important thing is beauty of the shape"—so perhaps he *was* thinking of lithe Ninette. A warm February, the two enjoyed the forest's long grass, culminating in a magical "hand-job" on February 20. Having decided to delay action on the *John Bull* article, 666 put energy into finding a suitable abbey.

On February 24 he and Ninette strolled along the Loing canal, taking lunch at Coq, between Montargis and St. Mammes, where the canal joins the Seine. The next day a romantic picnic on the hill led to Opus XI to invoke Pan. At 4:00 a.m. the next morning, Ninette announced that Leah had given birth: Ann Lea, but Howard called her Poupée (Dolly). The I Ching gave her an "obscure" hexagram: 41, meaning diminution.

Money ran out at the month's end. Cowie, as the war went on, had grown paranoid about Germans. Finally convinced that Crowley (in America) was pro-German, he voided the British O.T.O. of its assets, including Crowley's Scottish house and library. On March 1, Crowley asked, "What shall I do about Scotland? . . . Rely on Ninette." Sex magick with Ninette for a baby on February 28 resulted in Astarte Lulu Panthea nine months later. Now Crowley had a community for a Thelemic abbey. That same day, divination revealed its location: Cefalù,

Sicily. The I Ching suggested refraining from challenging *John Bull*—appalling advice.

Having organized an account with the Banca Commerciale, Palermo, Lamb, Crowley's solicitor, sent money, received on March 7. Perhaps Crowley sought financial favors from old friends, as the day featured Opus XVIII with Ninette for "success with Aimée [Gouraud]." Three days later Crowley dined with Aimée in Paris, taking lunch with Jules Courtier next day, probably at the Hotel Foyot.

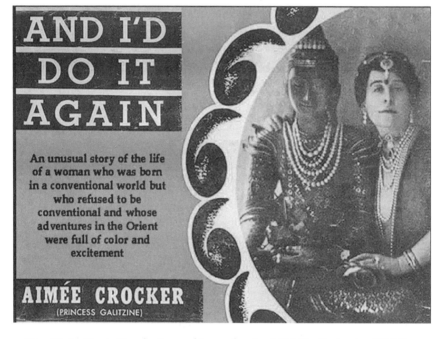

Fig. 15.4. Aimée Crocker's autobiography, And I'd Do It Again *(1936)—a sentiment with which Crowley doubtless concurred.*

Crowley's March 13 diary reveals the import of *John Bull* attacks was dawning on Crowley's Olympian indifference to public opinion:

> I lay awake meditating on my public statement about my work for England in the war. At 12:30 p.m. I started to write this, calling it "The Last Straw" [dictated without a break until 12:30 a.m. Sunday]. A feat of considerable endurance.

"The Last Straw" wouldn't be published for another decade (as an appendix to *Confessions*). Did Fielding advise against publication? Not responding was taken as a sign of guilt. Events proved Crowley too reliant on divination for his own good. As the I Ching also determined his abbey location, he might better have reflected on his diary entry for March 15: "I am ready to bolt to some country where children are unknown." From bachelor to family man with two mistresses, three children, and another on the way in a space of months, meant hard labor for any fool.

Attending Walter Duranty and Jaja's wedding party in Paris on March 21, the next day he saw Leah and Poupée off to London (on financial business), then joined "Beauty" (Ninette) "and the Brats" for a train to Marseille, thence Naples, where he noted on March 31 that "to call forth Spirits is to analyse the mind; to govern them means to recombine the elements of that mind according to one's will."

Still "cherishing hopes of the Honourable Everard Feilding," he was shown Cefalù's Villa Santa Barbara, site for his experimental community, on April 1. He might better have attended to the date.

SIXTEEN

Spiritual Poison 1921–1923

From January 1920, Americans wanting alcohol could either break the law or leave the country. Volstead's infamous Prohibition Act made Twenties Paris "roar" as dollars fueled a raucous nightlife fusing explosive black jazz music with easy sex and drugs amid a welter of artistic experiments. Cocteau transformed theater; Hemingway arrived for the *Toronto Star;* André Breton launched Dada; *Les Six,* venerating Satie, challenged Debussy and Ravel; Man Ray left New York for Paris in 1921; Picasso switched styles again—and Aleister Crowley, opening his soul to Gauguin's spirit, smothered his abbey interior with painted visions, before leaving for Paris at Christmas, to gather funds.

Crowley took a small room at the Bourciers's hotel, though attitudes had hardened with the war. A short walk away, Crowley found Nina Hamnett at the Café de la Rotonde. Nina introduced him to mathematician and science journalist John William Navin Sullivan (1886–1937). Happy to lend wife Sylvia to Crowley, the Sullivans declined invitations to Cefalù, unlike writers Mary Butts (1890–1937) and lover J. A. Cecil Maitland (1892–1926), who also met Crowley through Nina on arrival from London in March 1921; Mary joined the O.T.O. on March 11.

One of Nina's anecdotes in her autobiography, *Laughing Torso,* concerns an invitation for her, Cecil, and Mary to join the Beast for preprandial cocktails. Opening a cupboard in his room, Crowley withdrew bottles of gin, vermouth, and a small black bottle with an orange label marked "POISON." Containing laudanum, the mix created Kubla

Fig. 16.1. Fragments of Crowley's fresco are all that now remain of Crowley's painted "Abbey of Thelema," Villa Santa Barbara, Cefalù, Sicily. This word comes from what used to read "Stab your demoniac smile to my brain! Soak me in cognac Cunt and Cocaine!"

Fig. 16.2. Ruined frescoes, floor to ceiling, in a bedroom at the villa today.

Fig. 16.3. Photographic portrait of Mary Butts by Bertram Park (1919).

Khan No. 2, the stuff dreams are made on! Allegedly an aphrodisiac, only Maitland reacted to the delicious cocktail, darting deliriously into the street, in and out of cafés, accosting everyone he met.

On another occasion, Nina was at the Rotonde when confronted by an apparition of black frizzy hair sticking out wildly beneath a magnificent, expensive gray velour hat—the face heavily and badly painted. Normally completely shaved but for a twizzle of hair on top, it was Crowley: "I am going to Montmartre and I don't know of any suitable cafés to visit," he said, before heading to create a sensation somewhere. Later, out in a yellow kilt, Americans heckled him. Meanwhile, Nina had become intimate with a French countess who, hearing about Crowley, was fascinated. Nina, reluctant to arrange anything, was wary of Crowley's schoolboy perversity in pulling people's legs, often of influential people who'd otherwise have helped him. Appearing at the countess's luncheon party in black silk knee breeches, a tight-fitting black coat, black silk stockings, and shoes with buckles, with a high collar above a jeweled order, with a sword, Nina inquired of its origin. "The Order of the Holy Ghost, my dear," he replied before interpreting the guests' destinies, having accurately identified astrological characteristics. Crowley told the countess he'd known her in another life, the details of which could be found, Nina related, in a published story. Initially intrigued, reading the story horrified her: the character was monstrous. She refused future acquaintance. Nina also recalled giggling uncontrollably while sharing a pot of hashish-laced jam with Crowley.

A fine artist, Nina Hamnett observed Crowley's own burgeoning artistry:

> Crowley had taken to painting, and painted the most fantastic pictures in very bright colours. He painted a picture about a foot and a half wide, and nine inches high, of a man on a white horse chasing a lion. It was very interesting, a little like Douanier Rousseau; it had a great deal of life and action. I would have liked to have bought it, but I was very broke, and he wanted a high price for it. He gave me a painting, on a mahogany panel, of a purple negress, with a yellow and red spotted handkerchief round her head, and a purple rhinoceros surrounded by oriental vegetation. The rhinoceros had got rather mixed up with the vegetation, and it was rather difficult to distinguish between the trunks of the trees and the animal's anatomy; it was quite a beautiful colour however.[1]

Nina remembered Crowley was "greatly upset" about his daughter's death in October 1920—woe compounded when Leah suffered a miscarriage. Nina described Leah as tall, gaunt, a "Jewess" with wild eyes, strangely attractive.

When Crowley requested assistance from O.T.O. members, Norman Mudd offered a translation of Pierre Louÿs's collection of erotic, lesbian poetry, *The Songs of Bilitis*. Crowley replied on March 10:

> Your Valentine forwarded to Paris—joy!
> I did not get "Bilitis"—but I knew her long ago—thanks.[2]

Back in Cefalù on April 22, he thanked Mudd for the book, adding:

> Do you remember "Drunken James of Corpus"? He re-introduced himself to me in Paris where he is now. A highly placed official in the League of Nations—one more example of where drunkenness may lead to. Love is the law, love under will, Yrs. The Beast 666.[3]

Drunkenness wasn't Crowley's problem; drug addiction was. In 1919, Dr. Harold Batty Shaw of Harley Street prescribed heroin to relieve increasingly chronic bronchitis (associated by Crowley with the Kangchenjunga disaster). Cocaine sniffing began as inhibition loosener and became a psychological addiction. By December 1921, Crowley was a junkie in a vicious circle, and it wasn't magical: a descent closely observed by Ninette's sister Hélène Fraux. Though Hélène's stay ended on January 8, 1922, her spiteful disgust would return to haunt Crowley.

Determined to conquer addiction, he took Leah to Paris, hoping for assistance from Aimée Gouraud, Fuller, Neuburg, Sullivan, Walter Duranty, Lola Zaza (his daughter, now fifteen, with Rose), O.T.O. member Hammond, and Ella Burgin. In Paris he met "Princess Murat" and wondered how she might serve the Great Work. Margaret Stuyvesant Rutherfurd Murat (1891–1976), was an eccentric American heiress, dancer, actress, interested in what was then called "Oriental" philosophy or "Eastern wisdom." He asked the same question regarding Beadle's friend, English poet and critic, Beatrice Hastings (1879–1943), who had lived with Modigliani in Montparnasse and defended Blavatsky's legacy.

He moved into restaurant-hotel Au Cadran Bleu, Fontainebleau, on February 14, creating a special record as a psychological study to help other addicts. Confident willpower would prevail, he called it *Liber TzBA* (Hebrew for "Hosts," suggesting a battle).* The record shows him day by day, night by night trying bravely to abstain, with "open" and "closed" seasons, reduced doses, alternative stimulants (strychnine), long sleeps (when possible), long country walks—anything he could think of. The record shows the many tricks the addict's mind plays on the sufferer to get around, or pervert the self-rule. Efforts were frustrated by asthma attacks and painful bronchitis, for which heroin alone brought relief; cocaine cravings he overcame. Drugs obsessed, undermining a will already

---

*See Crowley, *Liber TzBA Vel NIKH, Sub Figura 28, The Fountain of Hyacinth*, edited by Steve Wilson.

lacerated by indigestion, rheumatic pains, vomiting, headaches, shivering, spasms, exhaustion, and a new tendency to paranoia. He noticed carelessness about personal hygiene and dress and indifference to sex.

On February 21 he was back on the Paris–Fontainebleau train, having concluded he must continue suppressing drug use altogether and establish Thelemic rules for taking drugs to express spiritual energies without destructive excess. He performed sex magick with "Madeleine K" from Les Halles, for health, and it worked, repeatedly.[4]

Woken with difficulty by Bourcier on March 6 at 2:00 p.m., Crowley found Leah's departure the night before for London brought relief. He saw her as "spiritual poison" because he couldn't resist drugs when she was around. Passing the following evening with Aimée Gouraud, Dr. Edmund Gros the next day recommended luminal (to calm anxiety), advising he attend Dr. Bornum's sanatorium at Divonne-les Bains, near Geneva, where Crowley vainly believed he could supervise his own cure. The thought relieved him; *Liber TzBA*'s last words: "I feel better already!"[*]

On March 13 he had a long talk with Arthur Augustin Booth-Clibborn. Born 1892, his mother, Kate Booth, was daughter of Salvation Army founder General William Booth. Crowley suggested Arthur borrow money from her, determining to repay it. Arthur sensed Thelema was a battle cry: "if he were self-slain and born to himself, how he could speak and write—lightnings and thunders of the old General [Booth] without his hounds of hell and death. He has vision, too."[5]

The next night he took cocaine to be "brilliant" at Aimée Gouraud's; he says he was, though dinner he considered a disgrace, recalling discussion "at a millionaire's table" as to whether there was enough tinned asparagus to go with the bad beefsteak, rice, potatoes, and cheap wine. He reckoned the servants were cheating her. "How can I save this woman [Gouraud], this splendid strong good-hearted woman, from the hell she is headed for?"[6]

On March 15, he performed sex magick with Jeanne Fernande for energy to propagate the Great Work and tried to initiate Arthur into the A∴A∴, though Arthur shied from signing the Probationer's Oath. Crowley believed treachery likely: "the usual state of mixed fascination

---

[*]First notebook only. Second *Liber TzBA* notebook begins March 10, 1922 (YC OSH3).

and fear,"[7] a judgment he applied to modernist pioneer poet Anna Wickham (1883–1947), who developed an unrequited passion for Natalie Clifford Barney. Anna received a "severe mauling" (figurative) from the Beast, who met her again on the seventeenth, recognizing talent but convinced she needed centering. On March 19 another opus with Jeanne Fernande and with Geogeo, "a gigantic market girl of 24."[8]

The next day Booth-Clibborn joined Crowley at the "Caveau" (vault), a bordello in rue Gregoire de Tours (Latin Quarter), asking the fat procuress for the negress. Crowley had now taken forty heroin doses in eleven days, just below the minimum dose of the "Cadran Bleu" battle.

On March 23 he was "cut" by poet Iris Tree (1897–1968), close friend of Nancy Cunard, out with Nina Hamnett. Crowley compared the "silly lydies'" airs to Doll Tearsheet snubbing Dante, but at 9:30 p.m. he finally got Aimée alone and "conquered." Opus IX with her at half past midnight: "I was very simple and masterful; I made a better impression than I had ever done yet."[9]

On March 27 he went to Boulogne, for a fortnight at Le Pré Catalan country hotel, Hardelot Plage with Leah and Booth-Clibborn. Aim: a new campaign for Thelema, involving plans for a fortnightly review to propose to Lord Northclyffe and Condé Nast, supported throughout April by sex magick with Leah and "Camille" (Booth-Clibborn).

Crowley crossed to London on May 2. A lucky meeting netted a novel contract from Collins, *Diary of a Drug Fiend,* whose hero and "heroin heroine" overcome addiction by Thelemic discipline, administered at "Telepylus" (Cefalù) by Crowley alter-ego King Lamus. Fiction indeed; and how curious is the relationship between idealism and fiction! Aiming at the impossible, Crowley had become a fictional character who on May 6 confronted another reality:

> I have just seen Gerald Kelly, annoyed and bewildered because Lion's daughters do not grow wool! Lola Zaza is unmanageable. She despises everybody, thinks she is a genius, is stupid, inaccurate, plain, ill-tempered &c &c. but it's good to be a Lion![10]

Crowley added: "But the sheep are many, & their pressure may suffocate Lion cubs." He made a divination to ascertain how he might "free her."

Novel completed on July 1 chez Betty (Elizabeth) Sheridan-Bickers,

Fig. 16.4. Gerald Festus Kelly at work in the 1920s.

who lived with her daughter at 21, Cleveland Gardens, Bayswater, he soon projected the fiction onto two living people. At a house lecture, Crowley met outstanding Oxford graduate Frederick Charles Loveday, who'd just married Jacob Epstein's favorite model, known as Betty May, aged about thirty, heavy drinker and drug taker.

Nina Hamnett knew her from pre-war days when Betty invested in Augustus John's Crab Tree Club for bohemian artists in Greek Street, Soho, in 1914. *Laughing Torso* informs us that Raoul (Loveday's romantic nickname) was Betty's fourth husband, and very different from her. "He was very good-looking, but looked half dead," recalled Nina.[11]

Late in 1922, Betty and Raoul joined Nina in Paris at the Dôme. In transit for Cefalù, Loveday was excited by Crowley's making him secretary and magical pupil. Nina saw warning signs. Having suffered surgery the previous year after a prank-climbing accident, Loveday was still unfit. Cefalù's mosquitoes, limited diet, and arduous magical training—and drugs—were, Nina insisted, potentially lethal. Loveday doubtless countered with Crowley's promised fresh air, bracing exercise, and conquest of Betty's addiction through Thelema. Nina begged them stay, delaying their journey by two days, telling Loveday if he went, he'd die.

On December 29, 1922, Loveday signed the Probationer's Oath at Cefalù.

On Friday, February 16, 1923, about 4:00 p.m., Loveday died from acute enteric fever after drinking stream water. Such hadn't happened to Peter Pendragon in Crowley's novel.

Quitting the abbey on April 30 after Mussolini expelled him in the fallout from Loveday's death, Crowley crossed to Tunis, soon joined by Leah and Norman Mudd. Ninette and Lulu Panthea Astarte were left in the care of landlord, Baron Carlo la Calce. Giving furniture to local traders in lieu of unpaid debts, they sold off all they could to survive.

Crowley believed "love under will" meant, precisely, gravitation, and though he spent eight months in Tunisia, suffering addiction, suspicion, poverty, and international condemnation, his personal center of gravity drew him back to Paris. First intimation of return was a letter of October 1 addressed to "My dear friends," the Bourciers: "I have not forgotten that I owe you 2000 Francs or whatever it is," promising to pay them "in full within a month of my reaching Paris at the latest."[12] Taking Leah, he left Tunis on October 9 for the Hotel de Djerid, Nefta: "Home again!"[13] He wrote a commentary on *Liber Legis* while performing magick with Leah and Arab friend Mohammad ben Brahim, who consoled him over what he called, ironically, "My 'failure in life,'" the words that head his following versified lines:

> By dint of divers pious courses
>   I might have gained immense esteem.
> I might have heard from valued sources:
>   "Your genius is quite supreme—
> By dint of divers pious courses."
>
> My friend Mohammed ben Brahim
>   Has his own method—it divorces
> My aspiration from the dream
>   Of fame—The cure for all remorse is
> My friend Mohammed ben Brahim.[14]

His ship from Tunis docked at Marseille on December 29. He went to Nice and lunched with journalistic bad-boy and notorious womanizer, Frank Harris (1855–1931). Despite noting Harris was "insane," Crowley accepted his promise of 500 francs, with which he bolted for Paris, feeling "rotten," early evening, Friday, January 4, 1924.[15]

✷

SEVENTEEN

I Died 1924

Crowley arrived in Paris Saturday lunchtime, meeting Walter Duranty and Berenice Abbott (1898–1991). Raised in Ohio, Berenice left New York with only six dollars to study sculpture at the Académie de la Grande Chaumière. Photographer Man Ray had just employed her as studio assistant in Montparnasse. There Berenice found her métier. Encountering this "extraordinary creature" at Café du Parnasse on Montparnasse Boulevard, Nina Hamnett remembered her "whitish green" face, with ginger hair cut boyishly with a fringe over big, beautiful blue eyes. Long in body with "rather short fat legs," she appeared very shy and "half conscious." Hamnett reckoned Berenice's embrace of photography produced some of the finest photographs she'd seen.[1]

Crowley began hawking serial rights for the "Hag" (autohagiography) and an article—"21 Years among the Artists"—to the Hearst Press, *New York Times,* the Associated Press syndicate, *Vogue* director Philippe Ortiz, and publisher Sylvia Beach (1887–1962). Sylvia's Shakespeare & Company published *Ulysses* in 1922, but she told Crowley she didn't want a reputation for "naughty books"; Crowley's comment: "—and it's all the reputation she *has* got!" Meanwhile, destitute Norman Mudd paid for Leah's ticket from Tunis to Cefalù.

Crowley lunched with Aimée at 20 rue Vineuse, Passy, meeting her adopted son Reginald's co-inventor, Louis Schroeder of the French

---

"I Died" was from a serialization of Crowley's life for a 1930s magazine, summing up his "destruction" by the gods in spring 1924, necessary for rebirth.

Fig. 17.1. Berenice Abbott (1898–1991), photographer unknown, perhaps self-portrait.

national broadcasting service (T.S.F.).* Things looked better, but 666 felt ill most of the time; heroin played havoc with his bowels. Reginald Gouraud and Crowley planned a ceremonial evocation of the 68th "Spirit" of Crowley's *Goetia* (1904), Belial, who requires "Offerings, Sacrifices and Gifts" from "the Exorcist" if he is to give true answers to demands, but nonetheless is described as a spirit "who tarrieth not one hour in the Truth, unless he be constrained by Divine Power" (according to page 29 of *Goetia*). Belial was to dwell in a brazen head like that attributed to fourteenth-century friar Roger Bacon; young Reggie would get a flat, advertise the "Head's" brief appearance in the city and take appointments for money! Crowley designed a temple for the purpose on paper: a circle bounded by the Hebrew letters for BLIAL, laid out with a nine-pointed star (three triangles with each point touching

---

*Inventor Reginald Gouraud was accustomed to invisible powers in the air. In his mid-twenties, Reginald lived with his adoptive mother while working at the Société française radio-électrique (radiotelegraphy company). *Wireless World and Radio Review* (May 7, 1924) reported Gouraud and partner Louis Schroeder planned to transmit across the Atlantic (32 m wavelength), using a 480-watt antenna, its aerial approximately 25 ft. of copper tubing, diagonal to the apparatus, optimistic signals would reach three valve receivers everywhere. In 1934, Gouraud invented a new television system.

The Co-optimists.
A plan to transmit telephony across the Atlantic on a wavelength of thirty-two metres is being evolved by Reginald Gouraud, a young American at present in Paris.
According to a Parisian correspondent, the set with which Gouraud and his partner, Louis Schroeder, are experimenting, will place 480 watts in the antenna. The aerial is composed of one piece of copper tubing, about 25 ft. long, led diagonally to the apparatus. The owners are confident that reception of their signals would be possible in any part of the world with a three-valve receiver !

Fig. 17.2. Wireless World and Radio Review, May 7, 1924, announces Reginald Gouraud and Louis Schroeder's plan to transmit telephony across the Atlantic.

the circle—a symbol of the fruits of the spirit and divine perfection); an altar behind a veil at the center (on which Crowley drew a four-pointed star or "cross,") before which, a flame rose from a censer opposite water in a cup; on the left a throne for the High Priestess (outside the circle, possibly Aimée), opposite the "Seat of the Boy Assistant" (possibly Reggie), between which was the "Place of the Postulant" before whom was envisioned a "Black Cloth for offerings (Gold Jewels &c.)."

Leon Engers appeared (see *Aleister Crowley in America*) and lent 500 francs, admiring Crowley's progress in painting while enabling a change of clothes—just in time for a visit from André Gide (1869–1951) on the fifteenth to arrange a lunch meeting. Perhaps they discussed homosexuality, which Gide defended in *Corydon,* published that year. Crowley preached Thelema that night on T.S.F. and began desultory efforts to buy the *Telegram* newspaper in Paris with Frank Harris, with guarantees, they hoped, from financier Otto Kahn.

Consultations started with a Dr. Jarvis over heroin, though Crowley still inhaled ether oxide, which, combined with chronic financial anxiety and pipe smoking, aggravated bronchitis and asthma. Jarvis sent someone with a needle; Crowley jibed Jarvis wanted him an "addict"; Crowley *sniffed*!

On February 9 he returned to the Rocher d'Avon in the Fontainebleau Forest, and next day visited Gurdjieff's Prieuré des Basses Loges,* where

---

*On January 4, 1924, Gurdjieff took most of his pupils to America for public demonstrations, leaving Frank Pindar (1882–1962) in charge of the Prieuré. My *Deconstructing Gurdjieff* devotes a chapter to Crowley and Gurdjieff.

Gurdjieff's aide, Major Pindar, offered "more sense and insight" than Crowley had heard "for years."[2]

Sense and insight did naught to allay descent into the hells. Crowley's diary records hours and hours through night and day of thoughts about heroin and everything else, all jumbled, mostly rational, often brilliant, and always, a craving for sleep. He took misery to his pen, making plan after plan as if the world was his. Mudd was around but merely annoyed him. Crowley shooed him off to England to "vindicate" 666. By February's end, Crowley's credit was exhausted, even with the Bourciers.

British Impressionist painter Bernard Harrison (1872–1956) visited on March 8. Harrison had been in the hospital, where a phonograph was played fifty or sixty times in a morning. He didn't like it, and the patient adjacent wept; Harrison called the nurse. She said, "The others like it; I can't help him." Crowley's comment: "That is war: that is democracy."

Four days later, Jane Chéron called and Leah's son Hansi wrote from Cefalù, begging his return. Crowley contemplated "woman's independence," concluding: "Nothing has been done so far. What she has gained is at the cost of giving up her right to bear children."

A week later, Nina Hamnett brought Lorimer Hammond of the *Chicago Daily Tribune* from 5 rue Lamartine to discuss serializing his memoirs: "The conversation excited and exhausted me." Hammond missed his appointment the following Wednesday: "I really feel utterly rotten. . . . There is a reason why the Fool must be the man to save the world; for were he not a Fool, he would be a Knave." Harrison showed up next day and "doled out" another £1.

By the nineteenth he no longer felt responsible for his actions regarding heroin. The scratching and pain from stubborn phlegm, which returned as soon as agonizingly coughed up, led to vomiting and back to that relief dubbed "aqua regia," the "kingly [self-deludedly heroic] water."

9:50 p.m. [Saturday March 21] Met Hope Johnstone at the Dôme. Since before the war I had not seen him: yet we fell at once into chat like old friends. I knew him only slightly at any time.

Formerly tutor to Augustus John's children, photographer and Bloomsbury Group associate Charles John Hope-Johnstone (1883–1970) edited the *Burlington Magazine* for a year until painter Roger Fry (1866–1934)* sacked him in 1920, whereafter he learned photography at writer Gerald Brenan's house in Granada.

Crowley retired to his room and prophesied to his diary concerning America's place in the future: its eventual susceptibility to dictatorship, which could end in "cold-blooded assassination of the human race." Aimée Gouraud showed up at 5:00 p.m., and he dined later with Hope-Johnstone, finding lots to agree about, including Gurdjieff, whose pupils unwilling to conform to Gurdjieff's "very artificial scheme" Crowley could take on. He later made notes for a promotional meeting with Lorrimer Hammond, suggesting Hammond co-opt enlightened *Tribune* editor, Arthur Burton Rascoe (1892–1957),† "who knows my work" (see page 253), to present him as "the man who won't fit in" to *Tribune* owner, Col. Robert R. McCormick (1880–1955).

Crowley saw more of Hope-Johnstone, suffering love problems, at the Dôme; Crowley advised from the I Ching not to be led by the nose by desire; *spiritual* compatibility provided sole basis for enduring love: "Twin souls are we, to one star bound in heaven." Crowley then considered the evils of modern war, predicting the suicide bomber: "not really courageous at all, but simply insane." He defined the modern politician: "cowardly, resourceful, smiling, and grim." Even in extremis, Crowley's mind bubbled with truth.

He discussed astrology and *Liber Legis* with Hope-Johnstone on March 25, aware he was speaking from inside a process of spiritual rebirth, his old self becoming white ash in the "urn," so he might identify with his Lord, Aiwass.

Austin Harrison, editor of the *English Review,* insisted Crowley sue the *Sunday Express* for their persecution campaign of 1923. Bernard Harrison (whose work Austin admired[3]) agreed to wire Austin Crowley's agreement to this—and could Austin send funds "to pay Bourcier something"‡ and for his and Leah's trip to London to motivate

---

*Fry coined the term *post-impressionism*. Nina Hamnett worked at Fry's Omega Workshops during the war.
†See Donald M. Hensley, *Burton Rascoe.*
‡Bourcier intended to "hoof" him out on March 30.

the action? He wrote to Mudd, suggesting renting a cottage in Seaford, on the Sussex coast, with its golf club, suitable for meetings,[4] while urging Mudd to get G. C. Jones to resign from Crowley's Trust Fund in favor of Benjamin Charles Hammond, Mudd, or Austin Harrison. He began constructing his defense for an imaginary trial; how he'd dropped sin, adopted pleasure, discovered literature; of his "real Puritanism," and how "The Decadents from Beardsley to Wilde to Yeats and Theodore Wratislaw seek to influence me. I am disgusted by their lack of virility, and write *Songs of the Spirit*"; of how sex is a magical sacrament and the natural expression of the True Will. Having laid it plain his enemies attacked a phantom, not the real man, he concluded "damages" were beneath him; he was not "versus" anybody. He wanted truth heard.

A kindly Hope-Johnstone appeared on April 1 to say goodbye before heading for Dinard to propose to a violinist half his age who supported a widowed mother—a bourgeois "more Gorgon than Medusa. . . . And he has no money! The Gods be with him and help him." He'd kindly been to 81 boulevard Malesherbes to collect Dr. Jarvis's potion: ammonium bicarbonate; Crowley was already taking the barbiturate Gardenal. "Hopeless!" he cried.

Crowley wrote on nature's wisdom in providing Spanish flu at the war's end to finish off those too weak to fight whose survival would impede recovery. Russia, ruthless, had recovered quickest from war. "Ra Hoor Khuit is Force and Fire—the impersonal impulse of Solar Energy which will purge the world of its dead winter leaves and vitalize the seeds of Spring. Love is the law, love under will."* A hard gospel for the "do-gooder."

"Wild Jaja" gave him an hour on Saturday afternoon, April 5, offering "marvellous Iris-like antimony of graphite," and giving Leah (back in Paris) 50 francs; Crowley gave Jane a sketch he'd made of her two years back, and thanked the Gods for keeping faith.

The following Tuesday, Nina Hamnett told him that painter and

---

*Crowley's view of COVID-19 may be deduced—Nature's view: cultivate strength, eliminate weakness. Sometime New York friend John Quinn would reply: civilization's virtue is to ameliorate Nature's indifference. (See *Aleister Crowley in America*, page 209). Crowley might conclude both arguments are true; there must be a balance, or the dilemma transcended.

Fig. 17.3. Mina Loy (center) in Paris with Jane Heap (publisher of modernist pioneer journal Little Review *and who became a follower of G. I. Gurdjieff in 1924) and poet Ezra Pound; early to mid-1920s.*

poet Mina Loy—who'd spent the war in New York's bohemian circuit with Man Ray, William Carlos Williams, Ezra Pound, Tristan Tzara, Jane Heap, and Marcel Duchamp—wanted to see Crowley but was afraid to: "She had suffered bereavement and poverty; and feared that meeting me again might bring her bad luck."

It was now twenty years since initial reception of Aiwass's word, and Crowley regarded subsequent fortunes reflected failure to act upon it, or acting weakly; this would cease. He reflected it was his "innocence" that betrayed him; he couldn't understand duplicity in human nature; he bore no malice and couldn't understand why everyone did not value what he valued. It worked the other way: he never mentioned that in May, June, and July, Paris hosted the Olympic Games (those featured, incidentally, in the movie *Chariots of Fire*).

Thursday April 24.

Give the highest wisdom only to the children for no one else is fit to hear it.

Kicked out on May Day by the Bourciers, Crowley took it as "birth" from the "womb." From a cheap room at an inn in Chelles sur Marne (east of Paris) he called for "kingly men" to attend his stable 'neath Thelema's star.

On May 9, using a "Poste Restante" address in rue Littré, Montparnasse (still there at no. 22!), a letter in Leah's hand was sent to "My beloved son." Mudd was informed:

> We have had no food for four and twenty hours and see no chance of any relief. . . . Jones sent £85 to pay Bourcier, arranging carefully that I should not have one penny of it, though supplied with two doctors' certificates that I was ill, unable to work, and in urgent need of rest in the country; also a wire from the Consul that my situation was desperate. . . . his action is dictated by deliberate malice . . . P.S. [Everard] Feilding* is a barrister and could presumably ask the Courts to remove Jones from the Trusteeship on the ground that he had maliciously allowed the beneficiary to starve.[5]

Kingly men appeared. On May 15, sun-inspired Argentinian artist Xul Solar (1887–1963) signed the Probationer's Oath. Two more "wise men" came: J. W. N. Sullivan and Leon Engers. They kept the Beast alive. Spiritually, he was radiating:

> Then what is this that I have thought of "all my life"—as "I"? A tree, whose immortality is in its seeds. And thus my thoughts of Wisdom, comprehension, kindness, energy, beauty—all these may take root and flourish in distant soil when my primal stem is withered and dead. So even the England that we loved and have lost survives— though unrecognisably—in her colonies. [May 21]

Meanwhile, Austin Harrison had told Mudd in London that Crowley was a "moral wreck" from heroin abuse, allegedly heard through Bernard Harrison as the view of Dr. Jarvis. Crowley, outraged, contacted Jarvis who replied on May 26:

---

*Feilding wrote to Mudd on May 3, insisting Crowley tried to serve England in the war, but an "admitted taste for farcical situations" made the authorities distrust him.

More especially do I absolutely deny having ever referred to you as "a moral wreck from the abuse of H." This is a very grave statement to make, even if justified. But in your case there could have been no justification for it, nor was it an expression of my opinion.

I resent very much this extraordinary misrepresentation of the true facts and I am very sorry that it should have caused you all this annoyance. Yours very truly, Charles G. Jarvis[6]

On June 27 a terrific storm occurred with raindrops like soap bubbles, flooding roads. When it stopped around dinnertime, Crowley and Leah walked to nearby Gournay for billiards. The storm returned shortly before 11:00 p.m. Crossing the Marne, they saw something like a comet with long a red tail and head of blue-greenish flame dropping vertically. It came as from nowhere, unlike a firework, with distinctly electric, natural character, reminding Crowley of the ball lightning experienced in New Hampshire in 1916, which Crowley had interpreted as a sign:

June 30

4:20 P.M. We mean by matter much what was meant by Ether 30 years ago. It is the medium by which phenomena take place or by which we become aware of them.

On September 16, at 8:00 p.m., having pawned his last jewelery, the whole sky over Chelles became blue violet (like copper cyanurate): "A most startling phenomenon. I have never observed anything remotely resembling it in France: or really close to it anywhere. (Q[uer]y. She decided to come to Europe on July 4 Q[uer]y date of meteor (?) at Chelles."

"*She*" was Dorothy Olsen, born in Chicago, September 6, 1892. *She* appeared at that moment to "change the death-magnetism to a new life." Dorothy sought a Wizard and brought a color of the rainbow.

By Saturday the twentieth, Crowley and "Soror Astrid" (beautiful goddess) were at the fine Hôtel du Grand Condé, Chantilly, north-northeast of Paris, witnessing, just after midnight, a moon with a filmy black bar across it, becoming thick "never before observed."

Returning to Paris on the Monday, Leah "collapsed." She had seen her replacement.

Fig. 17.4. Hôtel du Grand Condé, Chantilly.

◆ ◆ ◆

In late September, Xul Solar's studies with Crowley were coming to an end, freeing up the Beast to whisk his new Scarlet Woman to Tunis, and the desert.

Somehow enough money was potted to get them into the art nouveau–inspired Majestic Hotel on Tunis's avenue de Paris by early October. Gérard Aumont loaned them 200 francs for a trip out to Carthage on October 11 to see the excavations. Crowley wrote a manifesto: "TO MAN," responding directly to the Theosophical Society's claims for Krishnamurti as "World Teacher":

TO MAN

Do what thou wilt shall be the whole of the Law.

My term of Office upon the Earth being come in the year of the foundation of the Theosophical Society, I took upon myself, in my turn, the sin of the whole World, that the Prophecies might be fulfilled, so that Mankind may take the Next Step from the Magical Formula of Osiris to that of Horus.

And mine hour being now upon me, I proclaim the Law.

The Word of the Law is Θελημα [Thelema]

Fig. 17.5. Majestic Hotel, Tunis.

Given in the midst of the Mediterranean Sea
An XX Sol in 3° Libra die Jovis
By me ΤΟ ΜΕΓΑ ΘΗΡΙΟΝ
ΛΟΓΟΣ ΑΙΩΝΟΣ Θελημα

[To Mega Thērion Logos Aiōnos Thelēma = "The Great Wild Beast
Word of the Aeon Thelema (=Will)"]

It was issued as a flyer from coastal resort Sidi Bou Saïd (Dorothy paid).

On October 15, Dorothy and the Magus began motoring south along the coast to Sfax, then inland some 150 miles to Tozeur and Nefta on the Chott el Djerid lake. The plan was to march with camel and mule some 90 miles southwest to Touggourt. For this they purchased at Nefta coffee, cups, sugar, pepper, salt, sardines, sausage, flour, onions, green peppers, matches, cigarettes, rice, noodles, canned tomatoes/beans, hard-boiled eggs, kif, blankets, and bacon. In a tin box, rucksack, kitbag, yellow suitcase, and black suitcase, the camel carried ether, Dover's powder, quinine, toothbrushes, shaving soap, Gillette blades, cold cream, eau de Cologne, manicure scissors, strychnine, soap capsules of chlorodyne, maps, tea, brandy, burnous, perfume, stockings, a basket, tobacco. Bible, maps, mustard, oil, biscuits, Worcester sauce, books, pipes, envelopes, medicines, paints etc., sweaters, poncho, coat, drill breeches, gray shirt, cooking things, water bottle, thermos, .455 revolver, scarf, Book of Oaths, Magical Record, dark glasses, HAG (manuscript), Yi King + sticks, "grass," Arabic grammar, drawing block, spare clothes, Musigny (wine), Dorothy's vanity bag, toilet necessaries—and in a safe: valuables and "Magick."[7]

They left Nefta in extreme heat on October 21, on the first of five-to-ten-hour marches, with breaks for tea and lunch.

They'd seen three meteors: Dorothy's at Tunis; Crowley's between Sfax and Tozeur between himself and the mountains, just before dawn; and one seen by both at Nefta. "They are very brilliant green, move horizontally low down."[8] Meteors pointed the direction. Three rainbows had also been seen: one at Chantilly, on getting away from Paris; the second at Sfax, on getting away from Tunis; the third in the desert, on getting away from Nefta.

Leaving El Oued on November 5, having covered 62 miles, Crowley saw Dorothy thrown from a mule: "a wonderful sight." They proceeded into endless dunes. That night at Ourmas, a "charming village," they saw the moon occulted and "Mars a wonderful sight." The next day brought a long eight and a half mile journey to Moniet el-Kaid: a "vast sea of heaving swell."

They started again at 8:20: "A vast sea of average waves," arriving at 1:40 at "Bordj" (fort, or rest house). Dorothy's mule nearly threw her. The bordj was by a well, "very ornamental and comfortable—a spring mattress! Tables, chairs, cooking-place! XI° for D[orothy].O. 'good health and spirits'—Success."

Setting off on November 7 at 7:15 a.m. for Ferdjane, they arrived around 8:00 p.m. Crowley performed the IX° to invoke Djinn. They set off next day at 7:35 for M'Guitla: "Dunes (mixed) lots of green scrub then more dunes—a vast rolling sea. Bordj, big, empty, no bed. Guardian a thief. There was an epileptic in full blast. I had him dragged into shade: he recovered and went on to Touggourt next day. D.O. ill all night: I on bare floor, no blanket."

The next day (November 9) they marched to Touggourt. Crowley had a "marvellous ridge walk over the dunes" and witnessed the finest sunset he could remember. They checked into the hotel, but Dorothy

Fig. 17.6. The Hotel Royal, Biskra.

wasn't happy, as his consulting the I Ching on November 11 indicates: "How shall I act in present crisis? XV K/Earth. Khien. Humility (666. Be easy, gentle, yielding, but on a solid basis.) . . . If A[strid] wants to go to a pleasure resort, all right."

On November 14 they were 138 miles north at the Hotel Royal, Biskra, in Algeria, a journey presumably made by car. Able to recuperate amid Biskra's rich beauties, Dorothy nevertheless suffered badly from hemorrhoids, which cleared up on refraining from coffee and alcohol.

They left for El-Kantara to the north on November 27: "I did much Magick here with the Jinniyeh of the Springs." That must have been a sight, for the springs and gorge of El Kantara's copper shaded cliffs, deep green palms, pale rocks, and lustrous canopy of azure skies are, indeed, magical.

Back in Tunis on December 12. Crowley felt rejuvenated. His followers were not. In Cefalù, Ninette was spared starvation only by the arrival of her sister Hélène and Alma Bliss, Leah's sister. Alma concluded Crowley was brilliant but possessed by a wicked spirit. Scraping a few francs as scullion in a Paris restaurant, Leah had entered a mutually delusory relationship with poor Norman Mudd, whose vindication effort having failed, found himself on November 27 listed on London's Metropolitan Asylums Board for the Homeless Poor.

EIGHTEEN

✡

Man Is a Gambler 1925–1927

An hard penis turneth away wrath.
ALEISTER CROWLEY, MARSEILLE,
JUNE 26, 1928

Crowley's address book for 1925 offers insights into his priorities at the time. In alphabetical order, below Crowley's friend A∴A∴ initiate James Gilbert Bayley we find Col. Brown (Telephone: "17–83 Wagram").[1] Crowley would know retired Indian army colonel and fellow eccentric admirer of Sir Richard Burton's "Kasidah," Robert James Reid Brown (1863–1946), for at least five years after 1925. Distinguished service in Burma—Brown mastered three Burmese languages—led to regimental command (Seventy-Fourth Punjabis) and honorable retirement in 1920. At some point he moved to Houilles, northwest of Paris to create *Life's Echoes by 'Tis True!: A Possible Elucidation of the Mysteriously Cryptic Tessellations Made mostly by Byron, FitzGerald and Others from Omar Qayyam's Rubaiyat,* an erotic parody of Fitzgerald's *Rubaiyat* begun circa 1923 and published 1926 (I'm grateful to researcher Bob Forrest for this information).[2] Its numerous peculiarities (it begins in the middle where its covers are!) doubtless endeared it to Crowley, whose gay erotic parody *Bagh-i-Muattar* (1908) Brown quoted in his preface (p. 14), where Omar Khayyam is characterized as "a scientific astronomer by profession, a philosophic poet by inspiration, and a devil-may-care, worldly, man-of-pleasure by inclination." Sounds familiar.

Another remarkable name in Crowley's address book is François Marie Paul Georges Jollivet-Castelot (1874–1937). Founder of France's Alchemical Society and numerous alchemical reviews, including *New Horizons of Science and Thought,* he contributed to Papus's journals *l'Initiation* and *Le Voile d'Isis.* He'd known St. Yves d'Alveydre, Stanislas de Guaita, and Papus's Martinist circle. Influenced by Charles Fourier's Christian socialism (which also interested Crowley at this point), he had his own version of it. In 1920 he joined the French section of the Communist International (S.F.I.C.) while publishing esoteric novel *Destiny, or the Son of Hermes,* encapsulating his esoteric quest. His fascicle "Spiritualist Communism" (1925) earned expulsion from the S.F.I.C. for its spiritual and anarchistic ideas. A house fire (his alchemical lab was saved) motivated moving to Sin le Noble near Douai in 1924, the address Crowley noted (114 rue du Calvaire). December 1925 saw Jollivet-Castelot announce his transmutation of silver into gold. Seeking scientific authority to verify his work, requests were refused.

Other names include American "Rosicrucian" tarot aficionado, kabbalist founder of the Builders of the Adytum, Paul Foster Case (1884–1954); Frank Bennett, Frater Progradior of the A∴A∴ (Crowley's Australian representative); Martinist patriarch of the Universal Gnostic Church Jean Bricaud; Theosophical Society leader, Mrs. Annie Besant; writer Mabel Collins; James Branch Cabell of Dumbarton Grange, Virginia (Cabell paraphrased Crowley's Gnostic Mass in his pioneering comic fantasy novel, *Jurgen,* 1919); Sir Arthur Conan Doyle (Sherlock Holmes creator and Spiritualist); Madame Aimée and Reggie Gouraud; American journalist Henry Noble Hall (1872–1949); Austin Harrison; Bernard Harrison; Charles Stansfeld Jones (A∴A∴, Crowley's Chicago representative); art critic Paul George Konody (1872–1933); Augustus John (now in Mallard St., Chelsea); Hope-Johnstone (in London); and Edith Rockefeller McCormick (1872–1932), American socialite, daughter of John D. Rockefeller, philanthropist.* Crowley noted

---

*A believer in reincarnation (in 1923 she claimed Tutankhamen as former husband), Edith Rockefeller McCormick was treated by Carl Jung in Zurich in 1913 for depression, afterward patronizing Jung. A Jungian analyst, in April 1925 she and other wealthy Chicago women organized the world's first Woman's World's Fair to celebrate achievements of American women. Crowley was particularly interested in women's liberation in 1925–1926, recognizing his work's harmony with Jung.

addresses for specialist bookshops, including John Watkins in London and Émile Nourry's great Librairie Nourry, 67 rue des Écoles, near the Sorbonne. We also find pioneering Australian journalist Isabel Ramsay (30 rue Montpensier; died 1930); sometime Socialist editor of *The New Age*, A. R. Orage (at Gurdjieff's Prieuré, Fontainebleau); J. W. N. Sullivan (Paradise Farm, Chobham, Surrey) and wife, Sylvia (Hotel de la Chantelouve, Fontainebleau); Hearst journalist William Seabrook (1884–1945); Henri Say (Jockey Club, Brussels); Suzanne (Courturière, 2 rue Cherubim); Hon. Ralph Shirley (1865–1946), publisher of *The Occult Review* and author of *The Mystery of the Human Double: The Case for Astral Projection* (1938); Earl of Tankerville (Chillingham Castle, Northumberland); and Marius de Zayas, 22 rue Gustave Courbet.*

We also find three new German names, two of which will play significant roles in Crowley's life for many years—one of them, beyond it:

PARIS · Rue des Écoles (près le Boulevard Saint-Michel)

Fig. 18.1. Émile Nourry's Librairie Nourry, 67 rue des Écoles, near the boulevard Saint-Michel.

---

*Mexican antiquities dealer, de Zayas (1880–1961) brought modern art to America, hosting Picasso's first U.S. show in 1911 (at New York Gallery "291"), promoting Cubism (which Crowley saw as merely symptomatic reaction to "restriction" of style). Returning to Europe in 1921, on December 12, 1924, he paid 6,000 francs for Picasso's *Woman with a Book*.

Karl Germer (of Weida, Thuringia); Martha Küntzel (4 Tiefstr. Leipzig); and Heinrich Tränker (Hohenleuben).

In October 1923, Theodor Reuss, Outer Head of Ordo Templi Orientis, died. Crowley informed Charles Stansfeld Jones in December 1924 that before his death, Reuss appointed Crowley his successor. Thus, Crowley confirmed Jones as *Parzifal Tantalus Leucocephalus* (painted stork) X°, Grand Master for North America, recognizing Heinrich Tränker, *Recnartus* as X°, Grand Master for Germany, and they in turn recognized him as O.H.O. The O.T.O.'s future awaited "the Weida Conference," set for June 24, 1925.

Crowley spent much of 1925 in Tunis—cheaper than Paris—whence Leah was summoned from a Montparnasse restaurant kitchen to help Dorothy, Crowley being ill. Finding respite with French soldier Gérard Aumont—who translated *The Diary of a Drug Fiend* into French—Leah also had magical sex with William George Barron. Their son Alexander was born on December 4 when Leah was in Leipzig with Martha Küntzel, having served as Crowley's secretary for the Weida Conference, to which vicinity Crowley (in Paris) replied on May 25 to Karl Germer of Tränker's neo-Rosicrucian Pansophic Lodge: "I write in very great difficulties. I have no time—my wife [Dorothy] is ill, and needs much care. . . . As to how to get to Germany—well, I was always great on walking!"[3] Germer paid, and would go on paying. So impressed was Germer by Crowley at the conference at Hohenleuben (near Weida), he abandoned Tränker, who, jealous, turned against Crowley. Germer accepted Thelema, as did other Pansophia members (see my *Aleister Crowley: The Beast in Berlin*). Everyone recognized Crowley as O.H.O. of Ordo Templi Orientis but Crowley's intended primacy over other Orders was resisted.

Back in Paris, Crowley wrote to Germer on October 16: "I'm leaving all my other things here this morning and going down to Cassis—a painter's pet village, very cheap—till Monday, so as to prolong my existence as far as may be—and wander down to Hyères and look about me for a house or an island."[4] In Tunis by the end of the month, he was heading for Gabès and Djerba island: "from all indications it might suit us very well. I must do some real Magick down there—big Magick—strong medicine! I began eight days ago, in fact; but really I had so much leeway to make up that my effort has done not much more than bring me up to normal . . . it looks as if the future of my Work depended very largely on your [Germer's] collaboration. After all, my Summer in Germany was really a success; and this was (at bottom) entirely your work."[5]

At Houmt Souk on Djerba island (about 43 miles southeast of Gabès), around November 12, Crowley wrote these verses he numbered among his many "Oaths"[6] (his "Book of Oaths" survives in typescript):

HEAD OF THE SIXTH

In youth they urged me to be clever;
I've been as clever as I could,
And now I find that I am never
(or hardly ever) understood.

My fellow-men misunderstand me;
The simple fact that I insist
On love and friendship makes them brand me
As an immoral atheist!

My intellectual excesses
Have harmed as no vice could ever;
I pay with manifold distresses
The penalty of being clever!

AGAINST SUICIDE

Man is a gambler. Though we know
Our ruin absolutely sure,
We wait to see what each next throw
Will do for us. And we endure!

SUMMA SCIENTIA

One thing is certain here below:
The more you know, the less you know.

January 1926 found Crowley with Dorothy—their relationship cooling—at Tunis suburb La Marsa. Jane Wolfe arrived as secretary; Crowley recommended Leah return to America, Barron having failed her.

In spring, Crowley visited the French Riviera where MGM rented

Nice's Victorine Studios for Rex Ingram to direct Henry Wegener as Oliver Haddo in a big-budget movie of W. S. Maugham's *The Magician*. Director-to-be Michael Powell, who appeared in the film, reckoned Ingram should have made the Magician a "man you love to hate," a naughty boy the audience could root for, rather than accept Wegener's heavy style; the movie lost money—they should have cast Crowley.

Ninette and Lulu, meanwhile, languished at an empty Villa Santa Barbara, with little Howard laboring as shepherd boy from 6:00 a.m. to 8:00 p.m. Ninette complained how hurt she felt to hear him coughing every time he started out. Karl paid food bills. Ninette wrote to him on April 1:

Dear Karl,

I would like you and Beast to reconsider sending Howard to America. His aunt would take him while sister Helen defrayed expenses.

Howard will be 10 years old in July. . . . It might be best if I went to America too. . . . Could live in Florida, work for some money and have a big garden.

Contract for St Barbara ends in July. . . . I send my love to each and all. Let Beast hold no grudge—I put no ill will in this matter of Lulu.—Kiss him for me.

Ninette

[P.S.] Can't afford meat and charcoal all gone. . . . Please talk these questions over with Beast and Astrid.

The children are well. Lulu caught a light sore-throat from me but is all better again. The weather is rotten—rain and cold.[7]

On April 9, Crowley and Dorothy were at the Seniat el Kitou (Lion's Lair), rue Massicault, La Marsa, expecting to collect Lulu off the boat from Sicily. Ninette's letter of April 3 explains why it didn't happen:

Dear Astrid,

. . . Why this idea that I am delaying Lulu for personal reasons? Of course it is painful parting from her, but since she is going I am as anxious as you are to get her off. It does not depend on me. She needs a passport that the Commisario will not give me unless those Tunis papers arrive. . . . In no other way is it possible to send the child to Tunis.[8]

Germer made it to Tunis in May. Before leaving on the thirty-first he witnessed Dorothy's violent temper episodes, attributing them to Crowley's continued attachment to Leah—who Dorothy felt dragged Crowley down into "filth"—coupled with financial anxiety and Crowley's heroin use.

Fig. 18.2. Embroidered silk robes and dagger worn by Crowley in North Africa. In December 2014 the tunic, waistcoat, and knickerbocker were sold by auctioneers Dreweatts & Bloomsbury, London, for $17,288, while the dagger fetched $15,716. The sales catalogue indicated the outfit was originally gifted by Crowley to Deirdre Patricia Maureen Doherty, mother of his son Aleister Ataturk, to provide for future financial need. The costume can be seen worn by Crowley in several famous publicity photos from the 1930s.

Crowley sailed for France on July 19. Ejected from the capital's Vuillemont Hotel on August 7 for unpaid debt, he slept at Leon Engers's apartment for a couple of nights before taking a train to Pau in the Pyrenées-Atlantiques, staying at nearby village of Lagor for a week where Jane assisted Dorothy's rest cure and Crowley did his bit with sex magick.

Hopes of reunion with Lulu were dashed again. Ninette wrote on August 23, when Crowley was at the Hotel du Béarn, rue de Lille (Latin

Quarter), calling him an "utter damn fool": "Can you not get it into your thick head that the Consul will do every thing in his power never to get Lulu to you! That his is the power while you have no money and that he is personally interested in thwarting you in all your purposes?"[9]

On August 26, he switched from the Hotel des Ambassadeurs to the Atlantic, 12 rue Frochot, Pigalle, where he had sex magick with someone called Methnian. Within four days he'd met two likely ladies, K. Margaret Binetti and Kitty von Hausberger. Performing sex magick with Kitty on the thirtieth, he took Binetti to a Chinese restaurant on September 3—possibly with $30 just received from Karl in New York, and contemplated marriage. Sex magick with Kitty on October 4 was for success (cash) from Dorothea Walker's "World Teacher" mission in England.* The next day (and on the seventeenth and twentieth) he performed similarly with black girl Zaza Rachel Marguerite, though these desperate measures had to ease when Dorothy returned from Lagor for a "Big Lion night" on October 9.

Where Dorothy was on seventeenth we know not, for that day, Crowley performed for "Youth, Health, Energy" with Zaza and, unsatisfactorily, with one Gaston Bertrand. The next morning it was K. Margaret Binetti's turn.

The rejuvenation initiative continued into November when Louis Eugène de Cayenne, possibly a Creole from French Guiana, became Crowley's partner on the seventh. Crowley called him Polynesian and the month's serial magick delighted the mage: "I have had more pep than I have had for months." Sex magick further promoted fundraising for an Egyptian trip to "abstract" the stele; that is, to enact a ritual to release magically the "resistless" liberation of Woman. Extraordinary stuff!

On November 9, Aimée Gouraud requested divination on the possibility of divorce from much younger husband Prince Mstislav Galitzine. Crowley intuited freedom would result from death; it didn't. Galitzine lived until 1966; they divorced in 1927, Aimée claiming infidelity. The next day, sex magick "I[n] m[anu] D[omine]" (In the Lady-lord's hand) was performed with twenty-eight-year-old photographer Berenice Abbott. Object: health and energy, and the Egyptian trip.

---

*According to William Breeze, Scottish Theosophist turned Thelemite Mrs. Dorothea Walker (née Collins, 1870–1961), a.k.a. Soror Thea, wrote under pseudonym T.H.E.A.

Jane Wolfe was also in Paris, signing Crowley's letter of the eighteenth telling Germer not to trouble him, just pay $100 a month and cease ruminating on personal problems; Crowley had already recommended Germer contact past Scarlet Woman and chemist Roddie Minor in New York who could expand Germer's horizons.

Crowley still hoped K. Margaret Binetti might cough up for Egypt, confiding to his diary on November 25:

> Note that Margaret has been of late hinting secrecy as to our engagement. It is abjectly silly, as Princess Galitzin [Aimée], Reggie Gouraud, Lawrence Felkin, Jane Wolfe etc., etc.—to say nothing of the hotel people—constantly found her in my bedroom at the Atlantic! I had told my friends immediately of the engagement.

A rejuvenation opus on Friday the twenty-sixth with Zaza "worked very strangely. First exhaustion. Next a tremendous burst of energy. Last bad fatigue." Pressure mounted; Ninette informed Jane on December 5 that she'd sold and eaten her sheets; she couldn't stand the children's crying, and that they could only eat next day because she'd sold her clock.

> "Will Beast ever get me out of this terrible place? I will go *mad* if I must remain in Cefalu much longer. Write me and comfort me a bit Jane. I am desperate. I love you. 93 93/93   Ninette"[10]

Alerted by Jane, "Beast" sent her money straightaway. Ninette informed Dorothy on Christmas Day she'd notified "Beast" she'd received 1,100 francs, but the steamship agent couldn't get Lulu a passport due to a problem over her nationality. "Yes I am glad to have you take Lulu. She is an exceptional child. You will enjoy her."[11]

Crowley meanwhile persisted in motivating Germer to approach New York publishers with his plays, poems, and the "Hag" through Manuel Komroff (1890–1974), author, literary adviser, playwright, screenwriter, and translator, who'd recently enjoyed success with *Contemporaries of Marco Polo*.

January 1927's diary refers to "Eugéne and all his tribe" having disappeared, leaving Crowley with nine mistresses in Paris: Jane Chéron,

Berenice Abbott, Kitty, Binetti, Zaza, two Martiniquan women, plus Rachel V. and Marie Emakova. Attempting to economize and being particularly unhappy with Margaret Binetti's alleged "hypocritical falsity," she was dropped on February 6, 1927, by burning the talisman of Juppiter that protected her. Next month he'd found a new Assistant Magus, Mara Lita Gavriliokoff, with whom he magically greeted the equinox, having been for a long forest walk, seeing a dead snake while a lizard hopped onto his foot.

Having received the customary Word of the Equinox, Ninette wrote to Jane:

> Beast also sent me money—it means a breathing spell. But I don't dare use it as I should to get myself into shape. I am seriously ill with nervous breakdown and must have better food than we have been having and medicine. I have cut out meat, milk, eggs—all the expensive things, and we must get them back again. Also I must get out of this terribly noisy street and out into the country.
>
> . . . Of course I am keenly aware that my health is but a reflection of my spiritual state and that I have shattered my nervous system by giving in to my loose principles and disregarding my higher impulses.* But the kids are bound to my fate, and I must pull through somehow for their sake. It is an awful future that faces them if I give in. . . . Helen will only help if I separate myself from the children and seek work—my parents can't. They are old.
>
> . . . Only Beast, you will give me real help—I trust the Gods will enable you too. And I trust they will be kind to you and ease your way a bit. Alostrael sent me the Word of the Equinox. I send you and Beast my best Love
>
> 93 93/93   Ninette[12]

In mid April, Jane found a lump on her back and required an immediate operation at the American Hospital, while Ninette wrote to "Dear Beast, God bless you for seeing the best in me. Your letter and telegram this morning. Hearty thanks."[13]

---

*Ninette had borne a son, Richard, from one Arturo Sabatini; as well as a daughter, Jeannette (called Mimi after Ninette's twin sister), from landlord, Baron Carlo la Calce. I'm grateful to Lulu's son, Eric Muhler, for this information.

Before entering the hospital on April 28, Jane wrote to Karl how "Beast finds God in the ashes of his pipe," recommending the positive road of Magick: exalt yourself; know yourself as God, invoke the highest rather than mystic path of self abnegating resignation.[14]

Crowley informed Germer on May 23 that Jane was still in the hospital with a very doubtful prognosis. He, on the other hand, was distracted from other business by a great magical operation, though still managing to visit Jane and arrange her convalescence. He also reflected on vulgar ideas of respectability: "Some people are respectable, and some are respected: but you can't have it both ways."

Germer sent $500 on July 9, and Crowley took it as a signal for him to reenter public life by establishing himself in a flat where he could receive people. For this he needed $1,000 in two installments, adding mysteriously: "There is a certain snag about this plan. It would involve my entering upon certain ostensible activities to conceal real ones— all same [some? Germer unsure about handwriting of original] Secret Service." The purpose was to ensure France "officially" accepted the Law of Thelema, regarding which he wrote to Germer on October 1: "Have made connections with a Minister of State, and will get him to adopt Thelema as the New Principle of Government."[15] Meanwhile, poor Jane was still hospitalized: "The dear English have murdered her properly."[16] Three days later, Crowley duly moved into "the apartment occupied by Paterson at 6 rue de la Mission Marchand." This must have raised memories, for it was in Auteuil, only some 220 yards from the second entrance on the rue de la Source to the Mathers's temple.

A postcard survives dated August 27, addressed by Ninette to Sir Aleister Crowley, 6 rue de la Mission Marchaud, Paris, XVIième: "I hear from the French consul that he will give us all a 'laissez-passez' for France whenever we want to go! Now for the travelling money?"[17]

Crowley tried to raise money from his stock of first editions. One lot appeared to have been damaged in a July storm in London, the other lot had disappeared with Jones in Chicago, where, incidentally, Dorothy Olsen had recently begun working for a fashion magazine, while Crowley informed Germer that Leah's infringement of paragraph 4 of the "Comment on *AL*" put her outside any communication.

Money was the issue. He phoned Germer's well-off new lady friend, Cora Eaton, who was in Paris, and arranged lunch on August 21 while holding out for a $25,000 claim against transporters Pickfords over lost property sent from Cefalù. He expected progress when Sister Thea arrived for a conference and "London man" J. G. Bayley showed up. Germer never lacked for advice. Germer's Prussianism was, according to Crowley, his enemy:

> Aug 31. The Laws of Nature are curved. The Way of the Tao is infinite elasticity. In this lies all true strength. It is horrible to break things, for all things are good in themselves. To mould them into perfect shape is Art. It is precisely that rigid Prussian method which has brought her again and again to disaster, despite her admirable virtues. I hope that Einstein will prove the founder of a new moral philosophy for Germany—since even light is curved!

In late September, Crowley recommended Germer call on wealthy artist Robert Winthrop Chanler, of East 17th Street: "He knows me well, & might help *if you can strike a sympathetic note.* Anyhow a good pal, and worth knowing. A real Thelemite in practice, if he only knew it."[18] He also informed Germer he was "getting the Cefalu crowd up to a little house in Fontainebleau." Perhaps Jane Wolfe's sailing for New York on the *Lapland* on October 1 had something to do with Crowley's interest in a publicist who'd been in Hollywood struggling as an actor under the name Carl de Vidal Hundt when Crowley visited L.A. in 1916. Renamed Hunt, he was now a smart-talking "fixer" for the rich in Paris. Involving the worldly Hunt in his affairs was poor judgment. Crowley's head, however, was somewhat turned by the appearance of Polish lady Mrs. Kasimira Bass. The I Ching counseled against involvement, but that didn't stop his proposing to her.*

On October 4 he consulted the sticks over Reggie Gouraud's

---

*According to Richard Kaczynski (*Perdurabo*, 427), Kasimira was born February 10, 1887, in Lemburg (now Lviv, Ukraine), a Polish city that became part of Austria in 1772. She came to America in 1922 as Kasimira de Helleparth with daughter Marian from a first marriage in Vienna. She immediately married John F. Bass Jr. in Cleveland, Ohio, which, coupled with her living in Glendale, California, and husband in Chicago, suggests a marriage of convenience. She met W. T. Smith in California who told her about Crowley. Traveling in Europe, she aimed to meet him. He repeatedly proposed. She said she had to return to her birthplace (Polish again since 1918) but would return.

business with "Palmer and Sherwood." He concluded Reggie, at his mother's in rue Vineuse, lacked requisite qualities for the "dangerous job." "Violent action is needed, but don't lose your own head. . . . But get out quick when it's done," was his advice, wrapping it up with: "Even a practicing charlatan doesn't believe in Jesus outside of business hours."

He also asked Aiwass, through the I Ching sticks, about Kasimira's function, presuming she'd been sent by the gods to aid the Work he intended for Egypt.

By November 4, the "family" had been "extricated," and were in Fontainebleau "in a very nice little house with garden: they seem in A1 shape considering." Alas, not for long it seems. A defeated Ninette, living with Lulu at a house at Barbizon, a few miles northwest of Fontainebleau, was in trouble again:

Dear A.C.

. . . I have got myself into a worse state than I have ever dreamed by coming here without the proper credentials. I am being rejected as being a French woman and having no right in this house. They will want paying here, can you meet it? It is 440f.[19]

Jane meanwhile wrote to Germer, worried about the Beast's finances. He was in Fontainebleau with Ninette, Lulu, and Dorothy. After trying sex magick to pay for the Egyptian trip with one "Antine," and trying to borrow money from old follower Neville Foreman of Clacton on Sea on November 5, he had hopes in Sister Thea's arrival in Paris on December 1, believing Dorothea Walker would provide guarantee for a loan from Cora Eaton, or so he wrote to Germer on November 28. After urging his friend to encourage new Crowley aficionado young Israel Regardie in his studies of *The Equinox,* he talked turkey: "We need $2000 to put us on our feet. Ask her [Cora] to lend this sum at 1% more than she is getting for it now. Permanent or to be paid off in 3 years as she prefers."[20] He still thought he'd get to Egypt by the end of December for some potent magick.

By December 22 he was suggesting Germer's approach to Cora was inappropriate: "I think you may have failed to realise that the way to Cora's heart is cocktails and sprightly bandinage. She's starving for Life, and will jump at any adorable invitation! A woman's No always means 'I do love being asked. Go on a bit more; I'll come round when I'm tired of teasing myself.' If and when it becomes possible, I go to the 'Victorious City' [Cairo] for that 'abstruction.' A great Magical operation, and a sublime Act of Truth. I've been made ready—the Lord knows!—exactly as I was before, by being choked off all other Magick."[21]

The Egyptian journey was postponed. When he'd hoped to be in Egypt, a bold graduate of Cambridge University, twenty-five years old, first-class history graduate of Crowley's alma mater Trinity College, sportsman, and mysticism enthusiast, Gerald Joseph Yorke, received his first invitation to meet Crowley at the Hotel Foyot, VI[e], opposite Luxembourg Palace. Yorke arrived by plane at Le Bourget December 29. Yorke's significance?

Mon. 31.

55 Feng [I Ching hexagram] Make partnership, by means of Mystery; when aim attained, retire (Egypt). I think this refers to his attainment.

Crowley's wicked reputation again attracted, rather than repelled, an intelligent seeker. Yorke would be a feature of Crowley's life, to the end.

NINETEEN

✠

The Mortal Kiss 1928

You came a tale of peace to tell.
I cannot get a piece of tail.
Believe me, Jesus, it is Hell
When all the combinations fail.

ALEISTER CROWLEY, "THE MAGICAL DIARY OF
ANKH-AF-NA-KHONSU THE PRIEST OF PRINCES,"
JANUARY 20, 1928

Gerald Yorke returned to London in heavy snow January 2, 1928, leaving Crowley to spend until May flitting between Paris's Hotel Foyot and a pleasant two-story house at 3 rue de Fleury in Fontainebleau's center, a short walk from old haunt, the café Au Cadran Bleu, at 11 rue Grande, Fontainebleau's busy thoroughfare (the building survives, its old charm flayed away) where he read, wrote, and sent letters when the house crush overwhelmed him. On the verge of breakdown, Ninette festered there with daughters Lulu Astarte and Mimi (Jeanette).*

A big worry of Crowley's were three unpacked cases of notes and diaries from Cefalù (with ten or eleven more to come), containing magical writings, paintings, and scientific observations of psychology. Crowley feared a "demented" Ninette burning the house down or, if dispatched to Yorke, English customs destroying them, because a paint-

---

*Lulu's son Eric Muhler informs me (September 2021) that Lulu's *Aunt* Mimi would marry Crowley's onetime acolyte Cecil Frederick Russell (Frater Genesthai, 1897–1987).

Fig. 19.1. The present-day 3 rue de Fleury, Fontainebleau.

ing like *The Religion of New York* would be held blasphemous (as *The Origin of Species* was).[1] He hoped Dorothea Walker would housekeep and do secretarial work, but her arrival, when it came, was surreptitious, and set Ninette off. Dorothea hadn't expected children and recoiled. Crowley wanted Yorke to recognize that the Great Work meant facing his parents and getting *Book 4, Part III* published, with a better title, recommending publishers Rider, and the Hon. Ralph Shirley, which Yorke did. Crowley, who practiced degrees of "shock-tactics" on his pupils (ostensibly to whither dependency on the ego), was by ordinary standards almost perennially unfair and overcritical of Gerald Yorke's great personal efforts to serve the cause, despite his serious doubts about aspects of *The Book of the Law* and the very real opposition of his formidable father, who held the purse strings and knew when and how to tighten them. Many of Crowley's digs at his sometime pupil should be read today with a pinch of salt; Crowley had an unpleasant habit of blaming others for his own misjudgments. Gerald Yorke was a most remarkable friend and penetrating scholar of Crowley's work on many accounts.

Meanwhile Crowley had sex magick operations with Rughi, Juli

Victoriania, Andrea, Dédé, and Yvonne. Their objectives? Money
for the Egyptian "abstraction;" attracting Kasimira Bass; vigor and
strength. On January 10, he met one Michel, "a Dahomey negro, who
fucked me and sucked me off—in honour of Aiwass." The Great Work
with Aiwass was the intended object also of a March 4 operation with
swimming champion, Lili. Professional contacts in Paris included photographer Man Ray at 31 bis Campagne Première (a quarter century
now since Crowley lived there!) and Olympic fencer (1900 and 1908),
and writer on self-defense, Jean-Joseph Rénaud (1873–1953) of 232
boulevard Pereire, victor of at least fifteen duels.

Depressed in mid-January, we find his caustic humor stirring: "All
the nice people seem to be going: Thomas Hardy a day or so ago—and
now Ruth Snyder." Hardy died on January 11; Ruth Snyder faced the
electric chair for murdering her husband in New York.

On February 28, Rex Ingram's *The Magician* showed at Europe's
biggest cinema, the Gaumont Palace, 3 rue Caulaincourt, inviting
Crowley's lawyer to serve an injunction against Metro-Goldwyn-Mayer

*Fig. 19.2. The
Gaumont Palace
cinema, 3 rue
Caulaincourt.*

Fig. 19.3. A poster for Rex Ingram's The Magician *(1926) based on W. Somerset Maugham's 1908 novel: the closest Crowley came to screen incarnation in his lifetime.*

for publicity purposes (while recommending Yorke see it!). It moved to the Grand Boulevard at the end of March.

Kasimira's explosive arrival on March 5 generated scenes with Ninette and Dorothea Walker, who, Crowley informed Germer, was "obsessed."[2] Five day's later, Leah's red "abbai" arrived, which Crowley took as sign of Kasimira's new role, since the night before he'd explained to Kasimira the IX° secrets. Crowley's diary now became peppered with months of intense love-making episodes and operations with Kasimira for magical energy, and for promoting plans over *The Magician,* on the back of which he hoped to get *Drug Fiend* published in French, possibly with assistance from British publisher-genius of Paris-based Pegasus Press, John Holroyd-Reece (1897–1969). At the end of March, MGM offered compensation, which Crowley foolishly refused, holding out for publicity. The effort fizzled out as he persuaded Yorke to supervise his business and raise £500 to add to Germer's occasional subs from Baltimore, Philadelphia, and Brooklyn (where Germer worked for the Hamburg-American Line). Yorke and Montgomery Evans II visited Crowley in late April as the Fontainebleau lease ended, and he moved back to the Foyot.

Kasimira's visions, albeit vague, intrigued. Hearing Crowley mention "soul" on May 2, she said, "I have none, or else, two," chiming nicely with Crowley's "0=2" formula. The next day, they performed IX° magick, invoking Egyptian god mentu, of whom Crowley's alleged pre-carnation Ankh af-na-khonsu was ancient priest. Linked with Horus, this "strong-armed" solar deity fought enemies of cosmic order, truth. The couple moved to the Royal Condé on the rue de Condé on May 12.

When Yorke's £100 arrived May 19, Crowley dispatched Lulu to Madame Mathonat's little school at Mory-Montcrux, outside Ansauvillers, Oise, 50 miles north of Paris, afterward informing Yorke on May 25 he was "retiring" to Cassis, a "fishing village" where pensions charged only 25 francs a night. A jewel of the Riviera, beautiful Cassis was beloved of artists. Insisting his whereabouts be kept secret, he told Yorke that Paris now lacked the "prana" of the John St. John days, while little minds frustrated magical force.[3]

RETIREMENT—MAY 24–AUGUST 29, 1928

Kasimira and the Beast's three-month retirement to the Riviera and French Alps would make a charming illustrated volume, but being bound in space to Crowley and Paris, I will only summarize itinerary-fashion Crowley's colorful sojourn in the south.

The Riviera

> *May 24, Thursday.* Left Paris for Dijon. An "excellent dinner" at Le Pré aux Clercs restaurant (founded 1863) highlighted by views of Dijon's rainswept Place d'Armes (now Place de la Libération).
> *May 26.* Left Marseille for Cassis's Hotel Panorama, painted by Haweis's friend Francis Cadell (1863–1937) in 1924.
> *May 29.* Opus 54 to cure a nervously exhausted Kasimira calmed her temper, or was it the sunbathing?
> *May 31.* Crowley informed Germer—who'd dispatched $100—that Kasimira was teaching him German: "I feel that I have much to do there one day." This was true; in July he'd consider Hamburg as a favorable G.H.Q.[4]
> *June 5.* The couple joined New Jersey–born Langston Moffett and wife, Claudia, for a 10-mile excursion along the coast to Bandol.*
> *June 6.* Crowley requested Germer obtain $10,000 to establish proper headquarters. "I feel sure Cora [Eaton] is appointed

---

*Painting as a release from the machine age, useful contact Moffett (1903–1989) became *New York Herald* Paris correspondent in 1929.

to help you in this work." Cora needed to be freed from the "material outlook."[5]

June 7. Crowley introduced himself at the hotel to Lancelot de Giberne Sieveking D.S.C. (1896–1972). Sieveking's article "The Psychology of Flying" (*English Review,* 1922) was mentioned in *Drug Fiend,* a reference that embarrassed Sieveking in postwar Cambridge, according to his skeptical account of meeting Crowley in *The Eye of the Beholder* (1957, 245–60). Crowley asked his help in getting *Magick* published (Sieveking worked for the BBC). Sieveking suggested William Swan Stallybrass (1855–1931) at Kegan Paul. Crowley gave Sieveking Yorke's card. Visiting Yorke's London home with friend, Foreign Office official Arthur Vivian Burbury, Yorke passed them sensitive papers of Crowley's, despite Burbury's concealing his identity.* Crowley told Yorke Sieveking had "sent out an S.O.S. call to the Gods," coming to Cassis "for no reason."[6] Sieveking's account was that after his wife left him for another man, a friend suggested St. Tropez to recuperate.

June 14. In oppressive heat, the couple went up the coast to La Ciotat to investigate villas, then to Marseille and the Hôtel du Petit Nice, Corniche, maintaining publishing plans with Germer (*Mortadello*) and Yorke, who'd contacted Heinemann and Rider & Co. about *Magick.* Conditions suggested by Violet Evans, representing Rider (no ribaldries; no references to Crowley's "school"; no footnotes to books not published by Rider), proved unacceptable: "My ribaldries serve the excellent purpose of getting rid of prigs & prudes & people generally who want the Universe to conform with the standards of Bayswater."[7] Yorke was invited to join them on July 13. Meanwhile, sunbathing improved his health, though Sieveking recollected Crowley's skin looked green, moving like an elephant's— years of heroin poisoning, Himalayan extremes, anxieties, and North African sun took their toll.

---

*According to Richard Spence (*Secret Agent 666,* 195–97), suspected Soviet agent Sviatoslav Roerich's visa application for India landed on Burbury's desk in July. When Burbury suggested Crowley as an intelligence asset, Foreign Office colleagues H. L. Baggallay and C. M. Palairet insisted no contact be made, Crowley being, to them, undesirable. (See *Aleister Crowley: The Biography,* 298–306).

Fig. 19.4. Hôtel du Petit Nice, Corniche, in the late 1920s: "the most beautiful site on the Littoral [coastal path]."

Fig. 19.5. Contemporary view of the coast about the Petit Nice hotel, Marseille.

June 22. Crowley saw *Les Nuits de Chicago*, a French version of Josef von Sternberg's Oscar-winning *Underworld* (1927), calling it "a really good crook film"; it was a gangster classic: materialistic, barbaric, successful.

July 1. They investigated villas at the port of l'Estaque, painted by Braque in proto-Cubist style in 1908, a little north of Marseille.

July 2. To Carry-le-Rouet, 9 miles up the coast, and as far again to Martigues, looking for villas.

July 6. Crowley opted for the Hôtel du Chateau, Carry-le-Rouet, over a year before Salvador Dalì chose it for his analogous magic, the "paranoiac-critical" method.

July 13. Yorke arrived, arranging a regular allowance of £10 a week till the year's end while establishing a publishing syndicate to

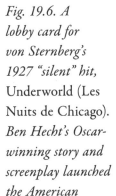

Fig. 19.6. A lobby card for von Sternberg's 1927 "silent" hit, Underworld (Les Nuits de Chicago). *Ben Hecht's Oscar-winning story and screenplay launched the American gangster genre.*

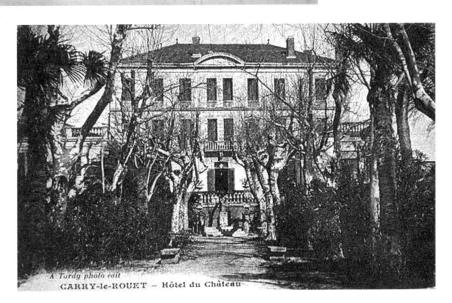

Fig. 19.7. Hôtel du Chateau, Carry-le-Rouet.

promote Crowley's works. Kasimira raved insanely in front of Yorke. Crowley thought her jealous of their talking.

July 18. Crowley sent 300 francs to Astarté (Lulu) and the next day was driven to Sausset-les-Pins, a little way east along the coast.

July 22. "Went to Martigues to dinner. A rotten hole."

July 26. Yorke left for London.

Fig. 19.8. Hôtel Splendide, Marseille.

Fig. 19.9. The Grand Hotel, Grenoble, in 1888.

5661·1. · Massif de la Meije (3982 m.) · À gauche, le Râteau, à droite, les arêtes de la Meije en avant le Pavé, vu du Pic Gaspard

Fig. 19.10. The Meije Massif (3,982 m).

July 30. From the Hotel Splendide, Marseille, he wrote to Yorke, suggesting P. G. Konody might help with publicity or even "rewrite the Memoirs" (Crowley was aware they were unwieldy). He then left for the Grand Hotel, Grenoble, arriving at 9:21 p.m.

The French Alps

August 1. Dinner in Sassenage, with its pretty chateau, just north of Grenoble in the Val d'Isère.

August 2. He wrote to Yorke: "I smelt the snows on the way here. I feel like a young colt. Nothing for it but to look once more on a great peak! Busing it to La Grave. I want to make K[asimira]. doss it in an alpine Hut! (She's a good kind.)"[8]

August 3. From the little ski resort of La Grave, some 21 miles south of Grenoble, they walked up to the ruined chalets below the striking Glacier de la Meije and performed Opus 88.

August 5. A tiring, five-hour walk to the glacier moraine. Receiving Martha Küntzel's letter from Leipzig telling him members of Hermann Rudolf's Theosophical Society (I.T.V.) expected the "World-teacher" (Crowley), he informed Yorke that Rudolf was a "Toshosophist" of the "namby-pamby school of yoga,"[9] adding he'd only go when requested by three important people—and (as Sieveking had suggested) with a proper suit!

August 6. He went up from La Grave more than half a mile to Les Terrasses to see glaciers and a Romanesque church. A letter from Sieveking made him wonder how to approach his initiation: "Spirit informing matter. Straight initiation. Be gradual. Be confident." Next day they checked into La Grave's Hotel de la Meije. He appealed to Germer: a German trip would require $1,000. He knew *he* was scruffy, but as for women, he noted on the tenth: "If women paid as much attention to the inside as to the outside, they might be beautiful."

August 11. They hiked to the Hut Evariste Chancel refuge (2,508 m), with a view of a lake: the first time in an Alpine hut, he noted, since August 1914.

August 13. "To Hotel de Glaciers, Col du Lauteret—a fine open position. Hotel bad—neither old style nor new. No service, vile food, and they steal one's wine. Poisoned by paté. Took K. up to snow. She was fine."

Fig. 19.11. The Evariste Chancel refuge.

August 15. They traveled two hours by car to Briançon's Terminus Hotel, some 40 miles southeast of Grenoble. Briançon is France's highest city with very steep, narrow streets and fortifications all about.

August 16. They took the train to Gap. Crowley liked the new, art deco Hotel Lombard. No longer a hotel, it's become one of the architectural gems of the city (architect: Georges Serbonnet).

Fig. 19.12. Hôtel Terminus, Briançon.

Fig. 19.13. Hôtel Lombard, Gap.

Édith Piaf, André Gide, and many other luminaries would visit. A thunderstorm broke the intense heat, and Crowley discussed Kasimira's offer of a $10,000 loan.

August 24. They drove to the Chateau de Charance, once the bishop's residence, with its botanical garden, where Crowley spoke to a Mr. Pelissier, possibly local politician Jean Michard-Pellisier (1909–1976).

On August 26, Kasimira Bass wrote to Yorke:

Dear Mr Yorke,

I have decided to work with Therion and will therefore invest $10,000 in the Publication Fund held by you on that behalf.[10]

Writing to Yorke from the Hôtel Lombard that day, Crowley added, with characteristic, misplaced optimism: "She cannot be absolutely sure that the money will be paid on time. There may be some delay, or she may get only a portion. But I see no reason why things should not go through without a hitch."[11] He wrote to Germer he was returning to Paris. They drove to Grenoble on the twenty-seventh and left on Wednesday, August 29, arriving in Paris at 10:04 p.m., heading for the Hotel Royal Condé, with Kasimira "practically her old sweet normal self, now we are in Paris again." They performed "Wundaschon" sex magick for "Gold" via the "unmentionable vessel."

On September 4, he saw Conrad Weidt in Richard Oswald's film *Le Baiser Mortel* (The Mortal Kiss) about a criminally irresponsible painter with syphilis who seduces his doctor's fiancée in Berlin and dies an addict. Its German title: "Should we be silent?"

A few days later Lulu wrote to her father in a beautiful hand, in purple ink:

8 September 1928

Cher papa,

j'attends une bonne lettre de toi en me donnant de vos nouvelles. Je
voudrai que tu vienne me voir bientot aussi que tu me ? forts espère
dans ta lettre . . . je vous embrace de tout mon Coeur.*

Votre petite. Loulou[12]

Yorke also wrote (September 5), unable to accept *The Book of the
Law*. Crowley replied: "Don't try to 'accept' anything. . . . *Liber Legis*
has bothered me from the beginning. The book is not written from
any human standpoint. It takes no account of man's ideas of what is
good for them, any more than a surgeon of his patient's pain." Crowley
continued modestly: "I do not think I am a great man, but I have been
chosen to do a Great Work."

His troubles were tests to purify the steel: "You have been tested
about the Demon Crowley &c and came through. Face the present
issue plainly and you will find that this Home Office bogey is just a
painted turnip on a sheeted pole in the graveyard of England's honour."[13] Crowley elucidated on the fifteenth: "*The Home Office*. There
is nothing against me. I know this for a positive fact. It is merely cowardly persecution. . . . Jix [Home Secretary William Joynson-Hicks†] is
a frenzied Evangelical, one can't expect him to like me. I am sure they
will not try to suppress the book [*Magick*] by any open action. A big
trial would be the dawn of Sun or Austerlitz for us! . . . I have a press
agent for one thing. You'll meet him today."[14] Yorke did, in London.
As things transpired, Carl de Vidal Hunt may have been agent for
the Devil. For publicizing Crowley's works, he received a hefty £20 a
month. Results: Jonathan Cape thought *Confessions* too libelous and
too long. Hunt offered World's Press News an exclusive interview in

---

*"Dear papa, I expect a good letter from you when I hear from you. I would like you to
come and see me soon as well? strongly hope in your letter [i.e., strongly hope you write
a letter] . . . I embrace you with all my Heart."
†December 25, Crowley advised Yorke: "I don't think you will hear much more of Jix
a few months from now" (YC OSD2, 130). In June 1929, the Conservatives unexpect-
edly lost the election; their leader Stanley Baldwin was, anyway, removing men older
than himself.

London for serialized memoirs: no result. Crowley's novel *Moonchild*, Hunt informed him, was "great but unpublishable" due to libels.[15]

And Lulu wrote to Kasimira:

Dear Kasimira

I thank you very much for the little cloths the Lady is going to mak me 2 apornes [*sic.* aprons]. I made a little cloth hat for the sunshine and 2 pears of pants.[16]

Crowley was better publicizing in person. On October 4, Montgomery Evans II took Crowley for dinner with gifted eccentric C. K. Ogden (1889–1957), sympathetic Kegan Paul editor versed in occultism and founder of Cambridge's Heretics Society (he was a Magdalen man) and psychic research journal *Psyche*. Crowley learned Sieveking's job at the BBC was quite minor: to persuade personalities to give interviews. Crowley informed Yorke: "I fear we were badly bluffed."[17]

More trouble: on October 11, Kasimira "bolted" with the "Grand Reserve" (5,000 francs), just in time for the arrival next day (Friday) of young Jewish American, Francis Israel Regardie (1907–1985), who'd written on August 4 from 3547 Hertford Place, Washington D.C., accepting Crowley's offer of board and lodging in exchange for secretarial duties in Paris. Regardie was met at the Gare St. Lazare on Friday, October 12, his impressive host's birthday, and taken to plush rented rooms at 55 avenue de Suffren. He would remain with Crowley for three years. A conference was held the next day with Yorke, American lawyer Clifford V. Church, Kasimira (who agreed to invest $10,000), and Hunt. Yorke remained pessimistic, Crowley the reverse.

On the twenty-third, Montgomery Evans introduced Crowley to Académie française writer, former naval officer Claude Farrère (1876–1957; real name, Frédéric-Charles Bargone), who wrote novels set in exotic places. They discussed China over supper, and perhaps Pierre Louÿs, Farrère's mentor. Impressed by a ghost story Crowley told, Farrère asked to use it as basis for a new short story, giving Crowley a warm letter of introduction to fellow Académie française novelist Pierre Benoit (1886–1962), author of *L'Atlantide,* filmed several times.

Kasimira returned on October 23 after Crowley handed her a

Fig. 19.14. Israel Regardie (1907–1985); contemporary photograph.

Fig. 19.15. Claude Farrère (1876–1957).

memorandum suggesting her promised money offer was frustrated by an unreliable Mrs. Reynolds in Los Angeles while lawyer Church could help get the money. Kasimira's moods swung more wildly than usual; perhaps she'd heard Hunt's doubts about Crowley. Crowley was getting irritated with Hunt, writing to Yorke on October 29: "He has got too many irons in the fire. We want him to be on the job all day and every day."[18] Hunt was suggesting Crowley use journalistic subterfuges to put himself over, including straight invention. Crowley was in two minds about Kasimira, valuing past fortitude but exasperated by illogical conduct. Yorke gave her credit for his health improvement;

Crowley insisted he'd've been healthier tramping the desert alone! Finding Yorke's pessimism over Cape's alleged "refusal" painful, he insisted they'd not refused anything he proposed: "I have maintained all along that the Memoirs, as written, are merely compilations of material for the production of a book."[19] (He still thought they merited publication at some point as permanent records—like *Hansard's*, which no one read for pleasure!) Crowley also had good advice about Germer's "German problem": A person who is "happy when a German plane crashes and happy when theirs doesn't is 'a schoolboy.' He has no idea of any cosmic point of view. That is, again the result of egoism. In order to seek protection from his personal inferiority to the rest of the universe, he attaches himself to a body of which he forms part; and he becomes a patriot. . . . You've got to destroy this 'I,' this moan of a hurt beast. The only refuge is to live *in* all and *for* all. . . . What you really need is some money and a Latin mistress!!"[20] Crowley, too; for on November 3, "Kasimira bolted. (PS I suppose finally). The Lord hath given and the Lord hath taken away: Blessed be the name of the Lord!" Two days later, he learned Hunt had told Kegan Paul to delay considering the manuscript, for some strategy of his own. Crowley wrote to Ogden direct.

The Latin mistress duly arrived on November 8: Maria Teresa Ferrari de Miramar, supposed Creole Cuban born in Nicaragua on May Day 1894, divorced from one Sánchez. By November 19 he was ecstatic: "She is marvellous beyond words, but excites me too much, so that I cannot prolong." That day, he wrote to Yorke: "Relieved from the strain of Kasimira I have been able to start serious magick with ritual precautions. The climax of the first ceremony was marred, as it should be, by the sudden arising of a violent wind, and subsequent ceremonies have been equally notable. I think the results are already beginning to appear; and bar accidents something important should break in the course of a week."[21]

On Monday, November 12, he dined at Paris's oldest restaurant, La Petite Chaise, 36 rue de Grenelle (seventeenth century), famed as a rendezvous for many great minds. At 10:45 p.m. Crowley kissed "P.R.S.," probably Australian communist editor P. R. Stephensen, introduced perhaps by Montgomery Evans. Stephensen joined Yorke's publishing syndicate, Mandrake Press, in 1929. The next night: sex magick with Annette de Ligon for "the Great Work." Back at the cinema on Wednesday for *Le Roi de Cirque* (*King of the Circus,* 1924) with French actor-director-comedian Max Linder, whom Crowley thought better than Charlot, as Chaplin was known. He also saw F. W. Murnau's *Le dernier des hommes* (*Der Letzte Mann,* 1924) with Emil Jannings. Crowley found its epilogue where the belittled doorman's luck suddenly turns, pleasing; it was magic, not realism.

Astarté "blew in from the country" on November 20 and studied *The Hunting of the Snark* with "High Priestess of Voodoo" Marie, though Lulu wouldn't speak English! A friend was motoring Crowley to Mory to see what it looked like. Meanwhile, Kasimira had told Crowley the money might take months, requiring a trip to L.A. to get it.

While Yorke fretted, Crowley performed a complex operation with Marie on November 26 for Gold "of quite a unique kind—ritual performance—many strange ideas—astral occurrence very remarkably

Fig. 19.16. Berlin poster for Murnau's movie, Der Letzte Mann *("The Last Man"), 1924.*

good—10:05 p.m." He noted "the Magical Phenomena in this apartment are now acute. Lights and shadows, dancing sparks, noises as
of people walking about, a large dark ghost in the bedroom lobby,
short attacks of rheumatism (to three of us) and a Nameless ear which
seized Regardie." Two days later, he wrote to Yorke about his magical requirements: "I want incense by the truckload, but I already have
enough oil for at least a year. Oil is wanted but rarely—A drop to
consecrate a given object—whereas incense can be burnt at the rate
of something like a quarter of a pound per day if one is getting mate-
rializations. This in fact is just what we *are* getting! The phenomena
that have taken place in this apartment, since the High Priestess of
Voodoo replaced the woman from Samaria, would be quite interesting to the Psychical Research Society, if any of them are not in a state
of coma."[22] He complained that Hunt was doing nothing, neither
introducing him to anyone nor selling the memoirs to a U.S. paper:
"Threaten with ending his £20 per month salary."

Hunt was not unaware of Crowley's apartment magick. The day
after a ritual on December 5, Crowley noted "Strange beings about."
When he recited *Liber Samekh* at night before the priestess, "she
saw a serpent with erect head issuing from the mouth of a crocodile.
Later, two serpents, one large, one small, chasing each other round
a disk of white light." On Friday, December 7, Marie "woke thrice
in the night, always seeing a Vase—a sacred oil lamp—and light and
book on which a serpent lay coiled." Kasimira, hardly unaware of
Marie, wrote that day to lawyer Eugene Shoecraft: Crowley was not
to claim publishing money from her; she couldn't even afford to stay
in Paris:

> He had many hardships in his life and he will find this time too
> the way to get out of it. I have no one to help me and I am only
> a woman. As to the question of marriage, I don't intend to marry
> Crowley or anyone, beside Crowley showed himself as a very vio-
> lent man and pulled my hair, so no woman would stand it . . .
> I was always straight to him and tried and did my best but he
> suspected me and misunderstood me most of the time. I wish
> him only the best and I am very sorry, when he is in trouble
> at present.[23]

Yorke arrived by train that day, forewarned Astarté would be there (she needed a dentist*), and there'd be theater in the evening with two actresses to supper, to advance plans for his play *The Three Wishes*.

The two actresses were Lily Lourioty and Suzanne Demars, and the supper party, which included magical ceremony and Marie's "sacred dances," lasted until 4:00 a.m. The theater trip was probably to Gaston Baty's 1928 production of Jean-Victor Pellerin's *Cris des Coeurs* (*Cries of Hearts*), at the Théâtre de l'Avenue (5 rue du Collisée; now demolished),

Fig. 19.17. Parisian poster for Strindberg's play Mademoiselle Julie *in January 1925, featuring Suzanne Demars and Lily Lourioty (lower left).*

---

*In her maturity, Lulu wrote a manuscript account of her early life, parts of which her son Eric Muhler was kind enough to read to me. Sometime between this period and the following spring, Lulu caught a train alone from Mory to Paris to meet her father. Contrary to arrangements, he was not at the station to greet her. While very resourceful, Lulu suffered immense anxiety. Fortunately, her fear was allayed by a kind couple who befriended her on the train. They put her in a taxi to the avenue de Suffren, whereafter she was taken out for entertainments, including a circus visit.

which starred both Demars and Lourioty.* Yorke left on the Sunday, holding the memory for the rest of his life of a collective dance and Egyptian chant in which everyone involved became uncannily aware of the presence of another, an invisible being, while a strangely dancing and fearless Marie dangled her limbs, like one possessed, for anxious seconds over fierce flames poked into a blaze in the apartment's fireplace.

The next day (December 9) Crowley received a call from an American lady: "I like her A.1," he noted. Specifics on a scrap of paper in the Yorke Collection:

Mrs Wm. E. Corey
Château de Vilgénis
Verrières-le-Buisson S.[eine]&O.[ise][24]

Mabelle Gilman Corey (1874–1960), divorced in 1923 from steel millionaire William E. Corey after a scandalous marriage in 1907, before which Mabelle enjoyed great success as musical comedy star in the States and in London. Marriage brought her a million dollars, jewels, and the Château de Vilgénis: her husband's gift. During the war, she'd let the château to the Red Cross as a U.S. officers convalescent home; espousing spiritual values, she disliked America for its noise and materialism.

The introduction came from Hunt, acting for King Alfonso XIII of Spain's cousin, disgraced Don Louis Ferdinand de Bourbon-Orléans, expelled from France in 1924 for drug dealing. It appears Hunt wanted Crowley to compile a faked horoscope to encourage rich divorcée Mabelle to marry Don Louis. Sensing skullduggery, Crowley "dismissed" Hunt on December 10, possibly without referring to the scam.

Curiously, a letter stamped with that date was sent from Paris's Prefecture of Police. The chief of the Première Bureau Cabinet was asked to send all available information on Aleister Crowley to the Service des Étrangers (Immigration), the service du Contrôle Britannique (British

---

*Lourioty was a comedienne; Suzanne Demars (born 1892), an accomplished actress who would star in movies *Les Derniers Vacances* (Roger Leenhardt, 1948) and *Le Point de Jour* (Louis Daquin, 1949). She first performed aged fourteen before enrolling at Paris's Conservatory of Music and Declamation in 1909. By 1922 she'd delighted critics with her voice and liveliness in Brussels and Paris. After 1925 her talent graced many plays at the Théâtre Montparnasse directed by Gaston Baty; Demars retired from the stage in 1968.

Fig. 19.18. Suzanne Demars and Lily Lourioty in Gaston Baty's 1927 French language production of American expressionist Elmer L. Rice's The Adding Machine *(1923).*

Fig. 19.19. Mabelle Gilman Corey (1874–1960) (Mrs. W. E. Corey), photograph ca. 1910–1915; George Grantham Baine Collection, Library of Congress.

Fig. 19.20. Château de Vilgénis when used by the Red Cross for convalescing U.S. officers during World War I, photographed by Sgt. R. Gallivan S.C., September 18, 1918.

Control Service—the Home Office) having indicated Crowley was an agent of German propaganda during the war, adding: "This foreigner actually resides in Paris." The immigration service chief signed the letter. The import of this communication will become clearer—and darker—in due course.

Hunt informed Yorke the next day (the eleventh) that despite all his efforts "on Crowley's behalf," it had always been a lost cause:

> That no publicity could be forced, that no paper in England wanted to touch anything connected with him, surely was no fault of mine.[25]

That same day, Regardie wrote to "C. de Vidal Hunt, Editor in Chief, Anglo-American Press Syndicates," requesting return of Crowley's materials. Hunt's reply to Crowley was childishly rude: "You *can* be funny after all . . . old bean"[26] On December 14, Crowley traversed the Parc de Vilgénis, 10 miles south of Paris, to Mabelle's château. It seems that chivalrous Aleister, ever keen to emancipate individuals from dishonorable marriages, advised Mrs. Corey to steer clear. Apprised of the encounter, Hunt was livid.

On December 16, Hunt dispatched what was effectively a blackmail

letter to Yorke, accusing Crowley of going to an old lady friend's château and behaving like a "discharged flunkey." Feeling morally compromised, Hunt indicated "safeguarding" his friends required

> [placing] the whole matter before the French Ministry of the Interior
> and the Sûreté Générale which will communicate with Scotland Yard,
> the editors of *John Bull* and the *Sunday Express* and all persons in
> England and America who have at any time been connected with him.
> The matter of my own hand in the spectacular rescue of Madame
> Kasimira Bass from Crowley's flat at 55 avenue de Suffren, Paris, as cor-
> roborated by Lawyer Church, together with the experiences in Tunis
> of Gérard Aumont, Sergeant in the 10th Company, 3rd Battalion,
> 28th Régiment de Tirailleurs Tunisienes, Caserne Serin, Lyon,* as well
> as his whole record as published in English and American newspa-
> pers will be submitted for investigation by the Sureté Générale, special
> department for foreign undesirables. Any defamatory letters against
> me or any defamatory actions on the part of Crowley against me will
> be followed by immediate criminal action.
>
> I am writing you this, my dear Yorke, because you should know. In
> London you looked happy and carefree. Here, after the fire hocus-pocus
> in Crowley's flat with the Creole 'priestess' and his unsuspecting secre-
> tary [Regardie], of which you told me, you seemed strangely nervous
> and oppressed. Can't you pull out of this thing? Is there anything I can
> do to help you? With all my best wishes. C de Vidal Hunt.[27]

Reconsidering the implications of his nuptial schemes, Hunt
appeared to backtrack on having Crowley investigated, informing Yorke
on December 19: "I am holding this decision in abeyance, however, pend-
ing further activities of the man, this halt being merely due to a desire on
my part to protect my friends, both here and in England, from the conse-
quences of unsavoury publicity."[28] In other words: "Don't squeal; or else!"

Crowley also addressed Yorke (December 20): "I admit that I was

---

*A letter to Yorke (January 5, 1929) describes Aumont pulling Hunt's leg with "a tale of
my [Crowley] raping a little girl in Tunis; and—this is where he really became funny—
and that his family put up enormous sums of money to hush the matter up. Hunt swallowed this hook, bait and sinker, and wrote off that idiotic letter to you under the
impression that he had some genuine information at last!" (YC OSD2, 151).

wrong about him [Hunt]. . . . Hunt was never playing a straight game at all. I don't know yet what it was, but I do know that it was crooked." He then related another scam that had inadvertently embroiled him in mid-April: "A lady [Madame Soutter] wanted to get into the movies. A man came to me and engaged me as an expert to go down to her little villa at Barbizon, on the border of the forest. I was to direct the taking of the test film, and I was to have 1000 francs and my expenses. So far so good. But what he told *her* was that I was the director of a wealthy film corporation, and that not only would I engage her as a star, but I would rent her place at Barbizon to have part of the films taken there." Of course, there was a "showdown" in twenty-four hours when the scam inevitably blew up: "that is the sort of thing that Hunt does." Hunt introduced him to Mrs. Corey "on some false pretence or other, I don't quite know what. However, we got on very well, and she then invited me to go out to lunch and see her place in the country last Friday. Then Hunt's manoeuvres started, and I really don't know what they were. [disingenuous?] The point was that Hunt had described Mrs. Corey to me in the grossest terms, which are quite unjustified . . . and I made it plain that I was not going to be a cats-paw in any crooked scheme. I cannot imagine that Hunt would be so asinine as to attract the attention of the Sûreté Générale to himself." Crowley said they'd better get on with publishing *Magick* and enclosed a quote from Paris's Lecram Press—while adding another nugget of wisdom for good measure:

> I don't wish to be mistaken for Mr. G. K. Chesterton, but I do think it may be upheld that purely rational people are of necessity insane. The universe is not a rational universe. It is the mere mechanism which is rational, and one can no more observe it or conduct life on lines of pure analysis than one can do so in so comparatively simple a proposition as a game of chess. I was boring Regardie only yesterday with a long lecture on the subject. A cynic might justifiably argue that a cash register itself operates business.[29]

Germer also received wisdom, sent on Christmas Day from the magus with gifts. Crowley here psychologizes the kabbalistic notion of "qliphoth," negative forces like waste generated in the process of creation: "They represent any discarded or outworn ideas. They represent vestiges of a previous state of being that hinder us in our present state. Just as the poor relations of the profiteer are liable to interfere with his social success. When we allow ourselves to be obsessed by Qliphotic conceptions we definitely retrogress and this process may be fatal in very much the same way as the normal process of metabolism in the human body is destroyed by the access of another process which is similarly a process of growth and decay, but of a more primitive type, such as cancer."[30]

Crowley was quick to kiss the past good-bye and greet the new year with optimism. He might have felt otherwise had he seen a letter of December 29 sent from the Ministry of the Interior to the Sûreté Générale, Central service of foreigners' identity cards, 7 rue Cambacérès. Newly appointed Minister of the Interior André Tardieu (1876–1945) had been informed a self-styled painter and writer called by the English press "King of Depravity," promoter of a religion of the god Pan, chased from England (*sic*), expelled from America (*sic*), from the Regency of Tunis (*sic*), Italy, and "apparently" from Germany, was living at 34 (*sic*) avenue de Suffren. Notorious for black masses (*sic*), drugs, and responsible for the deaths of several persons (*sic*), he not only edited several journals, or pornographic works (*sic*), but was an active propagandist for Germany, writing articles justifying the *Lusitania* sinking, the murder of Edith Cavell, and Zeppelin raids. The ministry required all information available on the foreigner and requested the prefect propose necessary measures. Signed for the minister by "Brisset," it was copied for the chief of General Information in January.

The year 1929 would be the year of the Great Crash—and Crowley was watched by Secret Chiefs. Someone had been playing with fire.

Fig. 19.21. André Tardieu (1876–1945), minister of the Interior 1928–29, three times French prime minister between November 1929 and June 1932.

TWENTY

Refus de séjour 1929

On New Year's Day, Crowley wrote to Yorke: "It is quite clear that Hunt was perfectly off his head when he wrote that stupid letter to you."[1] Plans to move to a cheaper studio better suited to magick in the rue Pergolèse fell through; the woman renting consulted lawyer C. V. Church for references. Crowley concluded the reconstruction effort was under "magical attack."

On January 8, the deputy director of the Prefecture of Police's General Information service (Cabinet 1ère Bureau) reported alleged wartime propagandist for Germany Crowley was unknown to the Prefecture's Garrisons and Foreigners service and the Sûreté Générale's immigration control and hadn't been located in the Seine département.[*] Three weeks later, the Prefecture's General Information service asked the Prefect's Cabinet to mount a search.

The plot thickened (in secret) when, on January 10,[†] "Brisset" signed another letter for the Interior Ministry (Directorate of the Sûreté Générale; central identity cards service) addressed to the Prefect

---

[*]From 1917 the Interior Ministry ran a central service for foreigners' identity cards. By the late 1920s, as the denomination "undesirable" peppered official texts and speeches, the ministry recommended surveillance and expulsion. Yorke heard from Crowley about government restrictions: the Bankers Trust was sacking U.K. or U.S. workers, while Les Ambassadeurs on the Champs-Élysées was told to replace a negro jazz band with French musicians who shouldn't make any noise! (YC OSD2, 157.)

[†]January 10, 1929, marked first appearance of Hergé's *Tintin,* in a Russian spy story in Belgium's *Le Petit Vingtième.*

of Police, saying American Mademoiselle Sarah Regardie had recently requested France's U.S. ambassador refuse a visa to her brother Israel Regardie, who intended working in Paris with Crowley, because Crowley was a harmful influence. The ministry was informed Crowley pretended Regardie was an employee, while Regardie paid him money. The ministry wanted precise information on Crowley's resources, Regardie's visa, and Regardie's actual whereabouts. Regardie's 1970 Crowley study, *The Eye in the Triangle,* attributed official interference to Sarah's having read about sex in his *Equinox* collection.

Meanwhile, Lulu wrote movingly from a farm at Mory near Ansauvillers on January 14:

> chér papa,
>
> J'ai reçue ta lettre hier, j'en été bien contente car j'aitait bien tourmante a la pensé de te savoir souffrant je désir de tout mon coeur que tu sais tout a fait guere.*

> Le 15. 1929.
>
> Toujours en attendant une petite lettre de vous vous embrase [*sic*] de tout mon coeur.
>
> Votre petite fille qui vous aime.†
Loulou Astarte²

On the sixteenth, someone called Millage sent Crowley "a Madame Sédir . . . widow of a well known French writer and occultist."³ Indeed, Martinist Paul Sédir (born Yvon Le Loup, 1871–1926) was Papus's close colleague in the kabbalistic Order of the Rose-Cross, Rite of Misraim, and Gnostic Church until embracing the Christian mysticism of "Love thy neighbor" and the search for the kingdom of God after

---

*"Dear papa, I received your letter yesterday, I was very happy because I was very tormented to think of you suffering I desire with all my heart that you know how to heal."
†"The 15th. 1929. Always waiting for a little letter from you embrace you with all my heart. Your little girl who loves you."

meeting Monsieur Philippe in 1897. Sédir left the kabbalistic Order in 1909 and founded Les Amitiés Spirituelles in 1920 (see *Occult Paris*). His widow was important Symbolist painter and printmaker Jeanne Jacquemin, born Marie Jeanne Boyer (1863–1938), friend of Lauzet, Mallarmé, Verlaine, Huysmans, Redon, Rodenbach, Saint-Pol Roux, Lorrain, Vallette, and de Gourmont of the *Mercure de France*—indeed all the people Crowley would have done well to have met *before* joining the Golden Dawn. Crowley reckoned he could probably enlist her to the cause and wanted to get Aumont in contact with her, while he concentrated on translating *Magick* into French.

On the day of St. Sulpice, January 17, a police inspector appeared at 55 avenue de Suffren. Crowley informed Yorke the next day: "I

Fig. 20.1. "Le Maître Philippe" (Faith healer Nizier Anthelme Philippe, 1849–1905, center) with faithful disciples and leading Martinists Papus (far left, he called Philippe "friend of God"), Marc Haven (left), Paul Sédir (right), and Pierre Bardy ("Rosabis," far right).

think Mr. Hunt has been skunk enough to carry out his childish threat."[4] Regardie reckoned it a magical attack against *Magick* appearing through Lecram at 26 rue d'Hautpoul. The inspector opened with questions about Regardie; they'd all need new identity cards. Why was Crowley called "King of Depravity"? "Did he take drugs?" "Why was he expelled from America?" Crowley gave exact details of change of hotel for the past year. Disconnected questions followed based on "nonsensical rumours." The inspector seemed interested in the Kabbalah. "People come to consult you, and what do you advise them to do?" Crowley said his "sheet-anchor was common sense," and he never advised anyone to break the law. The inspector became more polite, then genial, though bewildered: "For the first time in my life I don't understand at all what is being said to me." Crowley said he'd been trying for fifty years to "make myself clear, but nobody seems to benefit seriously from my endeavours." Puzzled by Crowley's not taking money for consultations, the inspector said he'd make a report and see Crowley again when he went to get his identity card. Crowley doubted anything "serious" would come of it but told Yorke he'd ask Church to join him at the prefecture the next day.

Crowley told Yorke on the nineteenth that Church wondered whether the Hunt "blackmail letter" could wind him into civil or

Fig. 20.2. Ground-floor entrance to 55 avenue de Suffren (present day).

criminal courts, while the "little man" at the Service des Étrangers, charmed by Crowley, "as good as admitted" Hunt was behind it, avidly seizing the "blackmail letter." Crowley realized his case's weak point was his "contre-espionage" articles during the war, but "by a special dispensation of Providence, though I must admit I was as mad as hell about what I considered the stupidity of the British propaganda, and was extremely anxious about the whole conduct of affairs in England, from the nonsense about 'business-as-usual' upwards and onwards, you cannot find a single word in all those articles which is derogatory to France."[5] He also reckoned Aumont would be an important witness to what really happened in Tunis. Crowley then fell ill again. Lulu wrote:

21 janvier [January] 29

Maney kises [sic] and thank you for the slippers.

—and Regardie wrote to Yorke: "The police, thank God, have now discovered that all these stories about us and our phallic orgies are nonsense. But in view of the remarkable sense of importance of, and the really disproportionate amount of idiotic ideas prevailing amongst the French 'police' [sic] they want you and Aumont to call at the Service des Étrangers next Monday to answer all sorts of asinine questions, which they could answer themselves, and to tell them about the 'unsuspecting secretary' and the 'King of Depravity.'"[6]

On Tuesday, January 29, during a long interview, the Chef de Bureau des Étrangers assured Aumont "Notre ami ne sera pas inquisite," that is, Crowley would "not be interfered with."[7]

The next day, the prefecture's deputy director and chief of General Information sent a highly inaccurate Crowley bio to the prefect of police, asserting Crowley's wife was dead, that he'd abandoned his daughter Lola, that he'd left Tunis for *Berlin* (his passport number, issued by the English Consul, was included), and returned to Tunis. His trip to the Riviera and French Alps was wrongly dated to 1927. Of excellent English parentage, he'd dilapidated his fortune and now had 2,000 francs at the Banker's Trust, Place Vendôme. He published several poems (!) and planned to publish in French with Aumont.

Mostly subsidized by Gerald Yorke (misspelled) of 9 Mansfield Street, London, Crowley addressed himself mainly to women who paid sums to learn magic, believing him a new god who wanted to reform all religions. "Therion" meant he was chief of all occult societies, and while he claimed expulsion from Italy was for writing against the government, it was because his secretary died during an occult séance, after which a pavilion was rented in Tunis for black masses. Police being advised, he was ordered to quit the pavilion. He occupied his time consulting magic works from India and Egypt. Regardie's visa was valid until November 1930 and was based on having a salaried job; Crowley knew Regardie from his voyage to America and wanted to make a new messiah of him. Current accommodation (at 2,800 francs per month) being unsuitable, Crowley sought a studio for black masses. The last black mass was December 14, 1928. After a hearty dinner for five or six (nearly all women), strong aphrodisiac liqueurs were served. Excited by odor of incense, they undressed and took white robes constellated with stars. Baptized as priestess of the cult, Ferrari made incantations, then the assistants indulged in a veritable orgy. Black masses occurred only when Yorke was in Paris. Someone said Crowley's cult rendered his wife mad, causing her death. He would declare her death necessary to serve the cause of black magic. Crowley's apartment contained 8 kilos of incense and cult ornaments, and numerous pornographic writings in English.

To sum up, Crowley, Regardie, and the woman Ferrari were individuals devoid of all morality, and an administrative measure of expulsion appeared necessary in their regard.

On February 1, 1929, Astarte Lulu's school teacher, Madame Philippe, wrote to Crowley. Lulu was doing her ten times table: "elle est très intelligente."[8] ["She is *very intelligent*."]

A week later, apparently oblivious to what passed among the chiefs, Crowley vacated to Fontainebleau for his health. Convinced Hunt and Kasimira conspired to "pull the legs" of the police, Crowley assured Yorke on February 13 that the prefecture had given them a "clean bill of health"; publishing *Magick* assumed priority: Lecram estimated 30 francs per copy (450 sold would cover costs), and Holroyd-Reece (see page 30) was due the next day to discuss American distribution. Opposition remained, however. On Saturday the ninth, while enjoying a "splendid walk" in Fontainebleau Forest, Marie, still in Paris, went to the cinema. Shadowed from the house by Kasimira, Crowley's ex-lover "accosted" her on an omnibus. From Kasimira's intimidating remarks, Crowley deduced a plot with Hunt. Kasimira knew he'd left for Fontainebleau; surely, she was watching the house. Malice in Kasimira's eyes unsettled Marie. Crowley believed Hunt a thief of sensationalist articles about him lent when still employed, for "the police say that they have them."[9] Wouldn't a summons scare Kasimira into good behavior and get Hunt off his back?

On Sunday, February 10, de Miramar arrived in Fontainebleau amid snow, rain, and hard frost. They performed the IX° for sexual energy. Results: "A1," but shocking weather on the Monday made walking impossible and gave Crowley a bad chill on the kidneys. They got back to Paris at 5:00 p.m. on the Tuesday (the twelfth): "Freezing like hell. Everything deranged."

Lulu wrote on February 14:

Chère papa,

. . . j'observerai les principes de la sagesse comme tu me la écrire je m'efforcerai d'être toujours bien sage et bien studieuse à fin que tu soit toujours content de moi.*[10]

On February 15, the Interior minister wrote urgently to the police prefect in rue Cambacères. The prefect's report conclusions were to be adopted without delay. Crowley, Regardie, and Marie-Thérèse Ferrari warranted forcible removal and would figure on the next prohibition circular. "Brisset" signed for the ministry.

Two days later, Yorke met Crowley's daughter Lola in London to ascertain if she'd meet her father. Seeking Uncle Gerald's advice, Kelly selected some of Crowley's books, asserting a man's works were part of him. One wonders *which* works Kelly chose. Anyhow, having seen them, Lola told Yorke that if they *were* part of him, she was sorry for the other part.

On February 27, Crowley informed Yorke that despite feeling ill, he'd

---

*"Dear papa, . . . I will observe the principles of wisdom like you write it to me. I will strive to be always very wise and well studious to the end that you are always happy with me."

gone out to see pictures by Edward Bright Bruce (1879–1943), whom he'd met at Cassis. Bruce, who'd recently left Italy over Mussolini, had abandoned a legal career for art in 1922. Crowley renewed acquaintance with art dealer and critic Martin Birnbaum (1878–1970), "a very wealthy and eminent New York Jew, who was, taking it all in all, a pretty good friend of mine."[11] They discussed Carry le Rouet where Birnbaum fancied investing. Crowley thought it "fair to assume that he respects me as an artist as well as personally and could be easily convinced that I have been rather badly treated." Leaving the next day for New York he could be contacted c/o J. P. Morgan & Co., Paris. Crowley suggested Yorke do so for assistance

On Sunday, March 3, Crowley, competing for the Coupe de Paris, drew against chess luminary, Odessa-born Vitaly Halberstadt (1903–1967), migrant to France from Russias's civil war. That same day Crowley's name appeared in Monseigneur Jouin's right-wing *Revue Internationale des Sociétés Secrètes* (International Review of Secret Societies), produced in Paris for continental distribution. *R.I.S.S.* propagandized about dark forces operating behind Masonic frontages, subverting true faith and order. Roger Duguet's "La querelle des Hauts Grades" ("The Quarrel of the High Grades," Masonic section, no. 9, pp. 217–29) referred to "Satanist" Aleister Crowley. Duguet dismissed the defense of "regular" Masons that "fringe orders" like the O.T.O. were "irregular," by asserting all Masonry was "irregular," there being no "regularity" beyond papal authority, Christ having regularized the Church. "In short," wrote Duguet, "like it or not, an Aleister Crowley exists; he is a Mason and chief of a branch of Masonry, just as regularly Masonic as Calvinism is Protestant without being Lutheran." Argument ensued as to whether Crowley was significant in Masonry; metaphysician René Guénon (1886–1951) denied he was. Crowley found it all absurdly amusing, as he did right-wing conspiracy theories in general. Important persons in power did not share Crowley's amusement. Crowley was marked, and it is possible that there was a covert link between the authorities' efforts to turn him out of the country and his name appearing in the rightist, politically motivated "International Review of Secret Societies."

A distinctly unamusing inspector arrived on Tuesday, March 5, summoning Crowley, Regardie, and Marie to the prefecture. Crowley, too ill, delayed until Friday. Their last visit having been "charming," Crowley thought it was merely to collect identity cards purchased on February 20. Regardie was told his card wasn't ready, and he couldn't take Crowley's without written authorization. When Regardie returned with authorization, he and Marie were handed a "refus de séjour," dated February 15 (the date the prefect received Interior Ministry instructions). Crowley's was delivered by an inspector in the afternoon. The prefecture insisted Marie and Regardie leave France on March 9. Refused entry to England on March 10, they returned to Belgium: Regardie was worried sick; Marie had enteritis.

American consul in Paris, William Earl de Courcy (1894–1981) informed the prefecture's immigration bureau chief on March 8 he wanted nothing more to do with the Regardie affair.

Crowley castigated Yorke next day for arguing against vigorous counterattack: "You have come to a moment in your life when you have to decide whether you are going to stand for truth and justice whatever it costs you or to keep on good terms with everybody, and let your principles slide." A doctor's certificate would give Yorke a few weeks to interview the ambassador and insist on a showdown.[12] Regardie and Marie, meanwhile, were lodged at the Hotel des Colonies, rue des Croisades (still open). Crowley advised Regardie on March 11:

> You might go and see Paul at the Palace Hotel. He used to be a night porter at the Berkeley [Hotel, Knightsbridge] London. He has a string of little country pubs, one of which might suit you while you vegetate—and *re-type the Memoirs.*[13]

Martha Küntzel addressed her "dear and revered Great Brother, beloved Master" from Leipzig on March 15: "It looks as if all the black magicians of the world had combined their efforts to hinder and annihilate you."[14] Undeterred, Crowley looked to high places, announcing to Yorke on the sixteenth he'd engaged Paul-Boncour, "one of the most celebrated and influential Avocats [advocates] at the High Court."[15] Trained in law, Republican Socialist Party reformer and Tarn département deputy Joseph Paul-Boncour (1873–1972) was chairman of the Chamber of Deputy's Foreign Affairs Committee, enjoying constructive relations with Interior Minister Tardieu. A big gun, Boncour would become prime minister in 1932. Crowley, with studied venom, tried to goad Etonian Yorke into a sense of shame for inaction, warning him the press wouldn't hesitate to trace him. "All Paris talking about the affair, and it should be over in London by the weekend at the latest. People will be pointing at you in Clubs and places where they play Bridge, and the only possible course for you is to hold your head high." Furthermore, Regardie informed him, English police were asking a lot of questions about Yorke. "This is why you are responsible for the whole trouble, because you gave Hundt his handle. You let him make you drunk and you babbled about invocations and Thoth and so on. I am quite aware that this is not a crime, but it is a handle on which to base a story of dark doings." Nevertheless, the "backstairs influence" of Boncour might see the refus de séjour annulled "at any moment." Additionally, the Chess Club president was to "have a word" with Sir William Tyrell, the ambassador. "We have got about a week to work on."[16]

Crowley tried all avenues, performing sex magick that day (March 16): "Lina!!!!!!!!! To help de M[iramar]. out of her trouble." Three days later he was able to send 1,000 francs to Brussels.

On March 18, the prefect of police sent a note to the Interior minister. The ministry's decision of February 15 to proceed with expulsion had been executed: Regardie and Ferrari left Paris on March 9, declaring London their destination. Paris's prefect of police was Jean Chiappe (1878–1940), good friend of André Tardieu (Tardieu presented him with the Knight's Cross of the Legion of Honour in February 1929), and supporter of anti-Masonic, anti-Semitic, xenophobic group Action Française. When Chiappe was dismissed in 1934, Action Française demonstrated to keep him.*

A stray "P.S." from March 19 to 26 informed Yorke that Crowley had "just seen lawyer"—probably one Denizot (see page 340).

Whole bubble burst! It's the mere political misunderstanding of 14 years ago [1914]. No "moral turpitude" or "black magick." Easy enough to clean up but may take a long while, and I'm upset about

---

*Nazi collaborator Chiappe, made high commissioner of France in the Levant in autumn 1940, was killed when an Italian fighter accidentally shot down the plane carrying him to Lebanon.

the exiles. The lawyer insists absolutely that I sit tight till the whole matter is cleared up. Please note that this has nothing whatever to do with the Police but with the Interior only. At the worst, I am merely like L.G. in 1900. You can help a good deal in clearing up this last point—since the rest is already dismissed as nonsense; but you can only do it by close consultation.[17]

"L.G." refers to politician Lloyd George whose vocal opposition to the Second Boer War in 1900 was dismissed as treacherous. When an angry mob disrupted a speech in Birmingham, he only escaped disguised as a policeman. Crowley's outspoken criticism of anti-German British propaganda in 1914 was taken for treason when it featured in his own counterpropaganda campaign against Germany in America.

On March 20, Yorke was apprised of Crowley's plan. First, an interview with the ambassador (this proved in vain). Second:

> . . . the intervention of Paul-Boncour, who has only to telephone the Prefecture to get the matter rescinded. But (2) will cost a lot of money—first payment £50, I gather—and the pretext is (like Tetragrammaton) one, one, and alone [?]. I must smash my detractors, make all public, show that the whole attack is base malice.
>
> To do this is easy, and incidentally, will vindicate your action before all the world. It is really in your best interests to do this. If not you would have to go all your life skulking around and saying "I know not the man." And all the cocks in Europe will crow at you. I think you ought to come over here this week-end and see various people who are working on my behalf. . . . Wire me if you're coming, I'll get on & work my bloody guns.[18]

That day, Astarte and her dog "monsieur Lénine [Lenin]" visited Crowley. The black dog was a gift from her father and either Marie or Kasimira. Lulu recalled in her mature years that the dog proved a painful embarrassment at Mory, where it was very unpopular with the women running the school. Mr. Lenin was eventually incarcerated in a kennel; Lulu recalled that the women disliked her; this may have been because Crowley couldn't be relied upon to pay the fees regularly. It's doubtful Lulu knew how little time was left ever to see her father again.

Her Aunt Hélène would take her to America in 1930 where Lulu doubtless grew accustomed to her aunt's utterly hostile view of Crowley.* The next day, Crowley saw another Helene, a Hungarian, for sex magick.

Crowley wrote to Germer on the twenty-second: "The blackmail business must be met by bribery. High-placed people are involved: so it will cost a lot. . . . We've got to win this fight. I'm sitting tight and keeping my head: sick, God knows, but who cares?"[19]

Finding what he took for Yorke's "stand-off attitude" morally disgusting,[20] Crowley compared it pointedly, and doubtless unfairly, to a card left by a man he'd known slightly since 1915. On it was an offer of help should he need it. The man "happened to be in New York (where I met him) just at the time when I was pretending to be pro-German, Irish rebel, &c. in the hope of getting a job in our Naval Intelligence, to whom I reported all I did and heard. And this morning he came round, and it turns out that he knows the Minister of the Interior very well indeed—translated all his books into English &c.† He also told me

---

*Lulu's son Eric Muhler informed the author that he was told that his Great-Aunt Hélène obtained custody over Lulu when Hélène demanded Crowley look from his apartment window to a figure by a lamppost in the avenue below. She said he was from Interpol and if Crowley signed custody documents, the inspector would stay outside, but if Crowley refused, she would summon him up to arrest Crowley. For so pressuring him, the family story goes, Crowley put an angry hex on Hélène that ultimately resulted, Hélène alleged, in a terrifying brush with electrocution from a lamp cable, which she only narrowly survived, leaving her scarred. Eric only discovered Crowley was his grandfather at age eighteen (he'd always believed Mr. Shumway of Connecticut was his grandfather). His mother (known as Mrs. Louise Shumway Muhler) told Eric that it was having experienced Crowley as a father that gave her authority to warn her son about the dangers of drugs (Eric chauffeured Jimi Hendrix to the Monterey Pop Festival in June 1967—and back to Jimi's hotel to pick up some forgotten lighter fuel, which Jimi famously applied to his guitar at the climax to the Jimi Hendrix Experience's tumultuous set). The main problems with Hélène's account as remembered are that Crowley was not accused of any crime so could hardly be arrested, while Crowley's letters of the time make it plain he was not afraid to go to prison over the refus de séjour affair, as it would bring him publicity, and he was sure, ultimate vindication, so long as he complied with police instructions. What Crowley lacked was cash to induce assistance from well-placed parties.

†British-born writer (Paris resident) Henry Noble Hall (1879–1949; O.B.E. 1929) was a senior journalist in the United States during World War I and from 1930 head of British propaganda in France for the British Council. He translated works by Interior Minister André Tardieu (1876–1945), in particular *France and America* (1925) and *The Truth about the Treaty* (1921).

that Cosgrave* was in Paris—the editor of N.Y. *Sunday World,* through whom I got my introduction to the U.S. Dept. of Justice as soon as America got into the War!"[21]

On March 23 or April 3,† Crowley instructed Yorke to return Martha Küntzel's gift of £2 ("Those old people need it too badly"), adding: "I'll expect you here Sat a.m. 6th April, and try to get the Minister's friend [Henry Noble Hall] to meet you at lunch. Then we can all combine a final Victory for next week. Please wire me that you are coming."[22]

Crowley was astonished at Yorke's lack of fight, practically accusing him of giving Hunt the ammunition by "babbling." Nor should he expect 666 to come to England. "I will go to Brussels to my poor friends, innocently expelled for my sake, and sink or swim with them. Don't worry about my finances. Read that Bible, hang it all! I may be fed by ravens, or there may be a cruse of oil which faileth not."[23] "It is absurd to talk of keeping your name out of all this. Too many people know you as my [backer?]. All they will say is Why doesn't he come straight out and fight, if he's innocent? Why does he hide behind Crowley? He has the money, and is the hidden spring of these atrocities?"[24]

Crowley was keen for Yorke to come over: "Please bring with you with the utmost care Hunt's original blackmail letter to you. he can hardly deny its origin, but we may as well have it in reserve. Prove that 'our hands are clean and our detractors are medieval lunatics.'"[25]

On Saturday, April 6, Yorke was in Paris, dining with Crowley and Henry Noble Hall, translator and former London *Times* war correspondent. The following Monday, Yorke departed while a Dr. Bianquin gave Crowley a ten-day certificate to remain in Paris, while a nurse arrived next day.

On Friday, April 12, at 5:55 p.m., an advance copy of *Magick in*

---

*John O'Hara Cosgrave (1866–1947), author and Sunday editor of the *New York World* 1912–1927). See *Aleister Crowley in America* regarding Cosgrave and Noble Hall.

†Regardie absent, and Crowley ill, Crowley's letters were no longer typed, or dated.

Theory & Practice arrived. "Victory!" declared Crowley, while Regardie wrote, more circumspectly, from Hotel à l'Étoile du Sud, 30 Boulevard Van Iseghem, Ostende:

> I certainly hope Hunt gets it in the neck, but as you say even if he does, will that influence the Minister of the Interior to protect his own neck and cancel his decree: I don't know. I wish I knew enough about practical magick; I'd send half a dozen bud-wills to him to try to change his mind, and also put the Four Great Princes of the Evil of the World on his track.[26]

Crowley wrote again to Yorke on April 15: "I hope you are in direct correspondence with Noble Hall about marketing *Magick*. The advance copy is very good: extremely few mistakes, and those unimportant."[27] Furthermore, "*Paris-Midi* is supposed to be publishing first article to-day,* giving the supposed facts; interview with me tomorrow &c. Their man phoned our Embassy and Consulate, and was told they'd never heard of me!!! You see the idea? They daren't say so. . . . That's where a man like Leopold [?] could come in, with one word in the right ear he could cause a free inquiry, and the whole bag of tricks would open, and exit the mangy alley-cat!"[28]

If ever a word did reach the Interior minister's ear, that ear was definitely closed. Crowley's time in Paris had run out. On Wednesday, April 17, he found himself "very tired and nervous" at the Hotel Metropole, Brussels. Summoning energy for a rite of sex magick with Marie, he dedicated it to "Success to our campaign and happiness in marriage."

Vain on both counts.

Aleister Crowley would never sleep another night in Paris, nor ever see daughter Lulu again.

The prefecture's Cabinet reported on April 17 that the object of a refus de séjour had left Paris, destination: Brussels and Ostende. An

---

*The first *Paris-Midi* article appeared on the front page the next day, April 16, 1929 (see chapter 1). Parts of the interview appeared in the *Birmingham Gazette* in England on April 17. In it, the prefecture denied to the newspaper that the refus de séjour was linked to espionage. Confident no witness would appear against him, Crowley demanded an open inquiry into charges of working as a German spy and being a black magician.

Fig. 20.3. Hotel Metropole, Place de Brouckère,
Brussels, Belgium.

immigration service report of April 29 noted that the minister of the Interior's letter of February 15 prescribing removal had been delayed in execution due to illness, noting that Crowley didn't himself appear to establish his departure. From information gathered, it followed he left Paris on April 17. His name was placed under observation in the "service des garnis" (garrison service for controlling migrants) and the commissaire of police.

TWENTY-ONE

The Last Time He Saw Paris
1929–1930

Raynes* of New York and Oxford, the foreign editor of the Literary Digest, during the war, a man of really remarkable intelligence and knowledge, always maintained that the persecution to which I was subjected—you must remember it dates from the time I left Cambridge or thereabouts—was due to the personal animus of some great English family.

CROWLEY TO YORKE; BRUSSELS, APRIL 23, 1929

Important business in Paris remained. Crowley hoped his "removal" would be canceled through lawyer Denizot. He told Yorke that French supporters needed "cash to hand round in the proper quarters."[1] Lecram Press had yet to print a run of *Magick,* there being no distribution, while Gérard Aumont in Tunis hadn't fulfilled his contract for a French translation, and Germer insisted Martha Küntzel's German translation was puerile. Then there was Lulu at Madame Mathonat's school in Mory, separated from mother and father (Ninette couldn't cope).

---

*Maitland Ambrose Trevelyan Raynes (1879–1944), WWI British intelligence asset; see *Aleister Crowley in America.*

Yorke left Brussels after a short visit on the twenty-ninth. Warned by Assistant Commissioner "A" of London's Metropolitan Police (Head of Special Branch), Lt. Col. John Fillis Carré Carter (1882–1944), to avoid Crowley, a letter of May 1 from WWI intelligence officer Everard Feilding confirming Crowley's defense against the treachery charge, assisted Yorke's rehabilitation campaign. Noble Hall advised Yorke to tell Carter the "spy tosh and moral stink" was a smokescreen for something too "dreadful" to think of.[2] Crowley suggested Yorke get Carter to invite him formally for dinner first week of June.[3] On the fourteenth Crowley informed Germer in Detroit it was France's *Interior minister* who'd intervened, taking advantage of alleged irregularity in identity cards of the inhabitants of 55 avenue de Suffren. "It is purely a backstairs business, and I have reason to believe, though I cannot be absolutely sure, that the British and American Embassies are at the back of it. . . . We don't understand what the English have against us, or against me. The police have assured Yorke that there is no possible charge on which they can prosecute me, and this is evidently the fact. What we suspect is the case is an intrigue of some powerful person or persons who dare not come into the open." Lawyer Denizot was confident a court action would favor Crowley because lawyer Maître Paul-Boncour was "one of the most powerful men in the country" with "every chance of becoming prime minister"[4] (true).

Meanwhile, Crowley moved to Hôtel Schlosser, celebrated barman Charlie Rainbow's converted country house with trout stream at Mortehan-Cugnon sur Semois, Belgian province of Luxembourg, 7 miles from the French border, whence he wrote to Yorke about Carter:

Now about Carter. Raynes . . . when I was in New York, was in touch with the head of the Belgian Secret Service. On one occasion he mentioned to me a Carter,* who, if I remember correctly, was being

---

*Carter joined the Indian Police Service, Burma (as lieutenant), 1905; Teng Yueh (Tengchong, Yunnan) is less than 40 miles from the Burma-China border. Consul George John L'Establere Litton (ca. 1867–1906) died suspiciously when Crowley was there Christmas–New Year 1905–1906; Crowley investigated, and reported it. A new consul was not appointed until 1908 (Whewell, "Legal Mediators: British Consuls in Tengyue," 112).

sent up to Teng Yueh [Tengchong] to replace Litton. I think I met
him on the road and exchanged a few friendly words. . . . The curious thing was that Raynes spoke of Carter as if he had something
against me, or such was my impression.[5]

Yorke's pencil note to this letter tells us Col. Carter paid for Crowley to
come to England from Brussels. They "dined together, A.C. and Carter
getting on well. Later he paid A.C. £50 for information about communist activities in Belgium, and both [Neville] Foreman and Regardie
through me for information about Co-Masonry and the Theosophical
Society and IR [Israel Regardie] joined [Co-Masonry] to supply information. GJY [Gerald Joseph Yorke]." Crowley wanted Carter to know his
views on Indian governance and suspicion that Annie Besant "wanted
to destroy British rule in India," and that T.S. funding for anti-British
propaganda was "extremely probable." Delighted to hear Feilding had
defended him, Crowley wanted Yorke also to consider "Achad [Charles
Stansfeld Jones, O.T.O.] knew positively of my relations with the
[U.S.] Department of Justice. When he was in New York (winter 1917)
I made a point of showing him a report to Palmer of the Department.
Also, he can testify that I told him to use all his authority with the
O.T.O. Lodge in Vancouver to get men to enlist (autumn 1915)."[6] He
also told Yorke he'd found a journalist he could trust: George Langelaan
(1908–1972), who worked for S.O.E. in WWII, wrote the story *The Fly*
(which served as the basis for the science-fiction movies of that title of
1958 and 1986), and who defended Crowley's clandestine role in WWI.

On May 20, Carter suggested dining with Crowley, asking Yorke:
"Would he mind my inquisitiveness?"[7] Next day Lulu sent "*many kises*"
(*sic*) to "Dear Beast," telling him about a boy of six who loved her and
wanted to marry. She said, "all right," which made him "very happy,"
and she had other little friends with nice mothers who let them play
in a garden full of flowers, and in a playhouse when it rained.[8] A stern
letter of the thirtieth from Lulu's school expressed great surprise at not
receiving fees for Lulu promised on the sixteenth. Further delay was
unacceptable.[9]

Crowley moved back to the Metropole ("the Rainbow has somehow faded"), where Denizot told him to "sit tight" (all was going well)
and where he was found by another "intelligent and honest" journalist,

Eugène Herdies of Belgium's Société Metaphysique. Herdies knew Feilding and Jules Courtier in Paris (see pages 258 and 260).[10] He then answered Carter's question about inquisitiveness from the Metropole on May 24:

> Please tell the boy bandit that I adore inquisitiveness and that I shall consider myself on my honour to tell him the whole truth about any matter that he likes to ask me about. I hope further that he will not object to a little inquisitiveness on my part. What baffles me in this whole affair is the psychology of the officials. However, we hope that the thing will be cleaned up.[11]

Crowley left Brussels for London at 8:00 a.m., Sunday, June 9, dining with salon hostess Gwendolen Otter in Chelsea, and seeing Augustus John on the eleventh after which, at 7:20 p.m., he met Col. Carter outside the Langham Hotel, Portland Place. They dined until 11:30. Crowley's diary comment: "All clear."

Crowley's trajectory now broke clear of French gravity as Carter and circumstance encouraged a new path. Writing to Yorke from Georgian House, Bury St., St. James's on July 23, Crowley couldn't understand why Yorke thought him in a hurry to take legal action in France; Denizot advised waiting a few weeks.[12] He was off to Leipzig with Karl Germer to marry Marie—*Carter's* condition for allowing her to Britain. Next day Crowley signed four contracts for Yorke's publishing syndicate, Mandrake, giving Yorke power of attorney.

Back from Leipzig, Crowley tried to arrange Lulu's coming to England. A letter from lawyers Field Roscoe & Co., 36 Lincoln Inn Fields, W.C.1, of August 7 revealed Ninette Shumway (née Fraux's) address: 45 avenue Leon Gambetta, Montroye [an error for Montrouge, a poor Parisian suburb south of Montparnasse], Seine.[13]

Having moved with Marie and Regardie to Ivy Cottage, Knockholt, Kent, Crowley wrote on November 7 to the Home Office, Whitehall, to request permission to adopt Astarte Lulu Crowley, informing the authorities that the "mother of the child has not been heard of for over 18 months." Letters addressed to her had not been opened. "I sent her to live on a farm in the Oise *département* of France. She is now flourishing and it is time to send her to a good school in England." He'd been informed by the Children's Court only children of British nationality could be adopted. Crowley continued:

> It is evidently necessary to the proper education of the child that she be placed at once under better influences in the country of her only available parent until she can acquire citizenship by residence, when the adoption can take place. I therefore respectfully petition you to allow her to come to England as an act of grace.
>
> I have the honour to be, sir, your obedient servant,
> Aleister Crowley[14]

A reply from Home Office official Norman Brook on November 20 asserted that discretion lay with immigration officers at point of entry. If Crowley were at the dock to receive her, all should be well. Yorke added a note to the letter: "When it came to the point, A.C. was unable to get hold of Astarte Lulu. Ninette her mother died, and no one knew where Astarte was." For reasons of his own, Yorke deliberately misled researchers on this subject. Ninette (born 1895) in fact lived in France until her death in 1989. Crowley was kept in the dark because Hélène Fraux believed Lulu's morals and general welfare would be imperiled if he knew anything at all. Crowley kept his feelings to himself.

THE LAST DASH

If things happen which people normally consider unpleasant it is simply another amusing incident in my career. All these things only have to be looked upon in perspective for their absurdity to become apparent.
ALEISTER CROWLEY,
KNOCKHOLT, JANUARY 9, 1930

In April 1930, Crowley went to Leipzig and Berlin with Germer (see *Aleister Crowley: The Beast in Berlin*). To encourage better reception for his Thelema Verlag publications, Germer arranged for Crowley to meet teacher, influential theosophist, and editor of *Hain der Isis* (1927–1932) Henri Clemens Birven (1883–1969) in Berlin. Birven, who had close contacts with survivors and followers of Paris's occult revival of the 1880s and '90s, was concerned about hostile propaganda concerning Crowley from the right-wing Catholic "International Review of Secret Societies." Seven months earlier, Germer had shared with Crowley Birven's suspicions about the refus de séjour:

> He [Birven] hinted that he knew who might be back of the Paris expulsion business. He seems to have made enquiries in Paris and seems to have excellent connections with high Police officials. I am also inclined to suppose that people around Oswald Wirth* might be involved. He [Birven] said that he talked about you with those people in Paris very seriously. That they refrained from arguing deeply, but remained rather silent, apparently not daring to answer him straight in his face. But that when getting home he received a letter with the strict instruction "Crowley has to be dropped." Of course, he is not letting himself be influenced by that.[15]

After persuading Birven that Thelema was not a "do as you please" anarchism but a rigid code of discipline, Crowley returned to London on May 7 to negotiate an abortive merger of Mandrake with Aquila Press for a London Thelema headquarters, before leaving for a motoring holiday through Germany, Czechoslovakia, and Austria with Germer and wife, Cora, from August 2 to 23. Exasperated by Mandrake's running out of money on August 27, Crowley, accompanied by new girlfriend, young artist Hanni Jaeger, whom he'd fallen for in Berlin (he split with Marie), took ship to Portugal to see poet Fernando Pessoa. Docking at Lisbon on September 2, Crowley was disturbed by Hanni's increasing instability. When Hanni left for Berlin on the nineteenth, Crowley launched an internationally reported suicide stunt with Pessoa and friends, with him apparently killing himself for love of Hanni at the Boca do Inferno (Hell's Mouth) near Cascais, as a publicity exercise to promote *Magick*.

Leaving the world wondering whether Crowley was at home in hell, he had to decide whether he might get away with taking the

---

*For Oswald Wirth (1860–1943), tarot and Freemasonry scholar, friend of Stanislas de Guaita and Papus, see *Occult Paris*.

Sud-Express through forbidden France to Paris. Departing Lisbon at 11:30 a.m. on Tuesday, September 23, 1930, he crossed the French frontier at 7:00 p.m. Avoiding police at the Gare d'Orsay, he alighted at the Gare d'Austerlitz at 7:25 p.m. on Wednesday, September 24. He took a taxi to the fine restaurant Lapérouse, 51 Quai des Grands Augustins, on the edge of the Latin Quarter.

Despite having visited only once since the war, he felt overwhelmed when staff recognized him "with joy!"—only saddened to hear old acquaintance, American painter Thomas Alexander Harrison (1853–1930), was terminally ill. Having been recognized, he risked arrest and feared observation at the Gare du Nord—some forty-seven years since first seeing the station with his parents.

He departed unhindered for Berlin at 10:55 p.m., crossing the French-German border at Aachen at 7:00 a.m. In his wallet: 700 francs (about $28).

Paris would never see 666 again.

Notes

Endnote Abbreviations

AC: Aleister Crowley.

OTOG: O.T.O. Archive, Germer–AC Letters.

YC: Yorke Collection, Warburg Institute. Citations are to folders in the collection including D1, D6, E4, E13, E19, EE1, EE2, NS4, OS22, OS38, OS39, OSB1, OSD2, OSD3, OSH3, OSH4, OSN4, S12 followed by page numbers or other identifying information.

CHAPTER TWO. ONE FLAME 1883–1898
1. William Breeze, email to the author, April 22, 2022.
2. Crowley, *Confessions,* 108.
3. YC EE1, vol. 1, December 4, 1896.
4. YC EE1, vol. 1, December 3, 1896.

CHAPTER THREE. THE ROAD TO AUTEUIL 1898–1900
1. "Notes of Travel 1898–1999," ed. Hymenaeus Beta, unpublished. Private collection.
2. YC EE1, vol. 1, October 28, 1899.
3. Crowley, *Confessions,* 188.
4. YC NS4.
5. Crowley, *A Magicall Diarie* 1899, ed. Hymenaeus Beta; unpublished. Private collection.
6. YC D6.
7. YC D6.
8. YC OS22, January 1902.

CHAPTER FOUR. TOWARD THE CITY OF LIGHT

1. Kelly, "Comments."
2. Jean Overton Fuller, *The Magical Dilemma of Victor Neuburg*, 116–17.
3. YC D6.
4. YC D6.
5. YC D6.
6. YC D6.

CHAPTER FIVE. PARIS, NOVEMBER 1902

1. Godwin, "Lady Caithness and Her Connection with Theosophy," 127–48.

CHAPTER SIX. OLD THREADS AND NEW 1902–1903

1. Crowley, *Confessions*, 334.
2. Crowley, *Confessions*, 335.
3. Haweis, "Reminiscences of Auguste Rodin."
4. Crowley, *Confessions*, 335.
5. Crowley, *Confessions*, 335.
6. Crowley, *Confessions*, 337.
7. Crowley, *Confessions*, 337.
8. Kelly, "Comments," 1.
9. Kelly, "Comments," 2.
10. Crowley, *Confessions*, 350–51.
11. YC D6 (undated).
12. Goff, *Eileen Gray*, 32.
13. Goff, *Eileen Gray*, 42, citing three letters from Eileen Gray to Auguste Rodin, December 1902, January 1902, and January 20, 1902, located in the Musée Rodin Archives.
14. Goff, *Eileen Gray*, 42, citing Bibliothèque Jacques Doucet, fonds Paul Léautaud, MS 24133, deux lettres de Paul Léautaud à Eileen Gray, Paris, February 24 and April 30, 1904.
15. Adam, *Eileen Gray*, 35.
16. Goff, *Eileen Gray*, 54–55.
17. Goff, *Eileen Gray*, 53, quoting Paul Henry, *An Irish Portrait* (London: Batsford, 1951).
18. Quoted in Goff, *Eileen Gray*, 55.
19. Quoted in Goff, *Eileen Gray*, 54.
20. Rault, *Eileen Gray and the Design of Sapphic Modernity*, 13–14, quoting Lady Kathleen Young Kennet, *Self-Portrait of an Artist*.
21. Rault, *Eileen Gray and the Design of Sapphic Modernity*, 14.
22. Rault, *Eileen Gray and the Design of Sapphic Modernity*, 14.
23. Goff, *Eileen Gray*, 31.

24. Crowley, *Confessions,* 555–56.

25. Crowley, *Confessions,* 556–57.

26. Kelly, "Comments," 3.

27. Kennet, *Self-Portrait of an Artist,* 168; reported November 4, 1918, quoted in Cavell, "Manliness in the Life and Posthumous Reputation of Robert Falcon Scott."

28. Cavell, "Manliness in the Life and Posthumous Reputation of Robert Falcon Scott," 538–64.

29. Duncan, *My Life,* 194.

30. Reported in Lees-Milne, *Midway on the Waves,* 141.

31. Kennet, *Self-Portrait of an Artist,* 89.

32. Cavell, "Manliness in the Life and Posthumous Reputation of Robert Falcon Scott," 538–64.

33. Crowley, *Confessions,* 356.

34. Crowley, *Confessions,* 356.

35. Goff, *Eileen Gray,* 34, drawing on Adam, *Eileen Gray,* 37.

36. Goff, *Eileen Gray,* 35.

37. Goff, *Eileen Gray,* 37.

38. Goff, *Eileen Gray,* 38.

39. Crowley, *Confessions,* 335–36.

40. Kelly, "Comments," 2.

41. William Breeze, email to the author, April 15, 2022.

42. William Breeze, notes to "Nina Auzias Stein" (lecture presentation), "Magick, Mysticism and Art" Conference, Academia Ordo Templi Orientis, Barcelona, June 24, 2018.

43. Edmund Fuller, *Journey Into the Self,* ix.

44. Edmund Fuller, *Journey Into the Self,* xi.

45. Edmund Fuller, *Journey Into the Self,* 25–29.

46. Edmund Fuller, *Journey Into the Self,* 22–24, 27.

47. Edmund Fuller, *Journey Into the Self,* 29.

48. Edmund Fuller, *Journey Into the Self,* 22.

49. Edmund Fuller, *Journey Into the Self,* 22.

50. Whineapple, *Sister Brother,* 275, 301.

51. Edmund Fuller, *Journey Into the Self,* 48.

52. Crowley, "Jeremiah in the Quartier Montparnasse," 713.

53. Wagner-Martin, *Favored Strangers,* 67.

54. Edmund Fuller, *Journey Into the Self,* 44.

CHAPTER SEVEN. WHERE SOUL AND SPIRIT SLIP 1903

1. YC NS4.

2. YC D6.

3. YC D6.

4. YC D6.

5. YC D6.

6. YC D6.

CHAPTER EIGHT. RODIN

1. Crowley and Rodin, *Le Dit de Rodin,* 114, citing letter located at Dept. of Rare Books and Special Collections, Princeton University, New Jersey.

2. Kelly, "Comments," on pages 222, 227, and 230–32 of the 1929 *Confessions.*

3. YC OSB1.

4. Crowley, *Confessions,* 339.

5. Crowley, *Confessions,* 339.

6. Haweis, "Reminiscences of Auguste Rodin."

7. André Murcie, introduction to *Le Dit de Rodin,* 9.

8. André Murcie, introduction to *Le Dit de Rodin,* 12.

9. André Murcie, introduction to *Le Dit de Rodin,* 15.

10. André Murcie, introduction to *Le Dit de Rodin,* 17.

11. André Murcie, introduction to *Le Dit de Rodin,* 18.

12. André Murcie, introduction to *Le Dit de Rodin,* 28.

13. André Murcie, introduction to *Le Dit de Rodin,* 28.

CHAPTER NINE. LE CHAT BLANC

1. Crowley, *Confessions,* 344.

2. Kelly, "Comments," 7, referencing unpublished proofs of *Confessions,* 754.

3. Crowley, *Confessions,* 349.

4. Maugham, *The Magician,* chapter 3.

5. Crowley, *Confessions,* 349.

6. Crowley, *Confessions,* 349.

7. Crowley, *Confessions,* 349.

8. Kelly, "Comments," 4, on (then) unpublished proofs of *Confessions,* 265.

9. Kelly, "Comments," 4 on Crowley's 1929 *Confessions,* 572.

10. Kelly, "Comments," 7, on (then) unpublished proofs of *Confessions,* 754.

11. Maugham, *The Magician,* chap. 3.

12. Kelly, "Comments," 5, on 1929 *Confessions* 2:350–54.

13. Maugham, "A Fragment of Autobiography," in *The Magician.*

14. Kelly, "Comments," 5, on 1929 *Confessions* 2:350–54.

15. Maugham, "A Fragment of Autobiography," in *The Magician.*

16. Maugham, "A Fragment of Autobiography," in *The Magician.*

CHAPTER TEN. I PIPED WHEN YOU DANCED

1. YC D6.

2. YC D6.

3. Crowley, *Confessions,* 371–72.

4. YC D6.

5. *The Journals of Arnold Bennett 1896–1910,* 168.

6. Bennett, *Paris Nights,* chap. 3, "Evening with Exiles."

7. Crowley, *Confessions,* 405.

8. Crowley, *Confessions,* 405.

9. Starr, "Aleister Crowley, Freemason!"

10. YC D6, 38; NS4, 43.

11. YC D6.

12. YC D6.

13. YC D6.

14. YC D6.

15. YC D6.

16. YC D6.

17. YC D6.

18. YC D6.

19. YC D6.

20. YC D6.

21. YC OSB1.

22. YC D6.

23. YC OSB1.

24. YC NS4, no. 38 (pages 4 and 5 only of a long letter).

CHAPTER ELEVEN. ADONAI 1907–1908

1. YC OSB1.

2. YC OSB1.

3. Crowley, *Confessions,* 573.

4. Crowley, *Confessions,* 575.

5. Crowley, *Confessions,* 583.

CHAPTER TWELVE. JOHN ST. JOHN, OR ALEISTER CROWLEY'S GREAT MAGICAL RETIREMENT, 1908

1. Aleister Crowley, "John St. John," *Equinox* 1, no. 1 (March 1909): suppl.

CHAPTER THIRTEEN. RAGGED AND WILDE 1909–1913

1. Crowley, *Confessions,* 570.

2. Kelly, "Comments," 7.

3. Crowley, *Confessions,* 594.

4. Kelly, "Comments," 7.

5. Crowley, *Confessions,* 595.

6. Jean Overton Fuller, *The Magical Dilemma of Victor Neuburg,* 73.

7. Crowley, *Confessions,* 669.

8. Kaczynski, *Perdurabo,* 235–36.

9. Lhombreaud, *Arthur Symons,* 17, 277.

10. Wilson, *Tate Gallery,* 101.

11. Monro, "Review of *Good Sir Palamedes.*"

12. Crowley, *Confessions,* 687.

13. Jean Overton Fuller, *The Magical Dilemma of Victor Neuburg,* 43–51.

14. YC S12.

15. Hamnett, *Laughing Torso,* 45.

16. Crowley, *Confessions,* 645–46.

17. Crowley, *Confessions,* 648.

CHAPTER FOURTEEN. FIERY ARROWS 1914

1. YC NS4.

2. YC NS4, letters AC–Cowie.

3. YC NS4, August 27, 1914.

4. YC NS4, September 7, 1914.

5. Crowley, *The Vision and the Voice,* 391.

6. Regardie, *The Golden Dawn,* 476–77.

7. Crowley, *The Vision and the Voice,* 359–60.

8. Fogel, *The Parchment of Circles,* 487–88.

9. Wheatley, *The Time Has Come,* 131–33; Wheatley, *The Devil and All His Works,* 276; Wheatley, introduction to Aleister Crowley, *Moonchild.*

10. Baker, *The Devil Is a Gentleman,* 302.

11. John McClure, "Literature and Less: A Page on Books of the Day," review of *Morrow's Almanack and Every-Day Book,* edited by Burton Rascoe, *Times-Picayune,* October 27, 1930.

12. YC NS4, letters AC–Cowie.

13. YC NS4, letters AC–Cowie.

14. YC NS4, letters AC–Cowie.

15. YC NS4, letters AC–Cowie.

CHAPTER SIXTEEN. SPIRITUAL POISON 1921–1923

1. Hamnett, *Laughing Torso,* 175.

2. YC D1.

3. YC D1.

4. YC OSH3.

5. YC OSH3.

6. YC OSH3.

7. YC OSH3.

8. YC OSH3.

9. YC OSH3.

10. YC OSH3.

11. Hamnett, *Laughing Torso,* 176.

12. YC D1.

13. YC OSH3.

14. YC OSN4, "Book of Oaths."

15. YC OSH4.

CHAPTER SEVENTEEN. I DIED 1924

1. Hamnett, *Laughing Torso,* 171.

2. YC OSH4.

3. Vogeler, *Austin Harrison and the English Review,* 97.

4. YC D1.

5. YC D1.

6. YC D1.

7. YC OS38.

8. YC OS38.

CHAPTER EIGHTEEN.
MAN IS A GAMBLER 1925–1927

1. YC OS39 memorandum bk addresses, drafts of letters 1925.

2. Bob Forrest, "Colonel Robert J. R. Brown and *Life's Echoes by 'Tis True!,*" Appendix 25 to Index of the Rubaiyat Archive on Bob Forrest's website, www.BobForrestweb.co.uk (accessed March 8, 2022).

3. OTOG.

4. OTOG.

5. OTOG, October 29, 1925, to Karl Germer.

6. YC OSN4, "Oaths," November 1925.

7. YC E19, Ninette Fraux–AC, 1925–28.

8. YC E19, Ninette Fraux–Dorothy Olsen.

9. YC E19, Ninette Fraux–AC.

10. YC E19, Ninette Fraux–Jane Wolfe.

11. YC E19, Ninette Fraux–"Astrid."

12. YC E19, Ninette Fraux–Jane Wolfe.

13. YC E19, Ninette Fraux–AC.

14. OTOG.

15. OTOG

16. OTOG

17. YC E19, card Ninette Fraux–AC.

18. OTOG, after September 22, 1927.

19. YC E19 (dated "Barbizon, le 18"; September 1927?).

20. OTOG.

21. OTOG, December 22, 1927.

CHAPTER NINETEEN. THE MORTAL KISS 1928

1. YC OSD2, AC–Yorke, February 25, February 27, March 29, 1928.

2. OTOG, February 28, 1928.

3. YC OSD2, AC–Yorke, May 25, 1928.

4. OTOG, May 31, 1928.

5. OTOG, June 6, 1928.

6. Sieveking, *The Eye of the Beholder,* 248.

7. YC OSD2, June 1928.

8. YC OSD2, AC–Yorke, August 2, 1928.

9. YC OSD2, 51, note on letter from Martha Küntzel, August 1, 1928.

10. YC E4.

11. YC OSD2.

12. YC E13.

13. YC OSD2, 61–62.

14. YC OSD2, 50–51.

15. YC E4.

16. YC E13, "Monday 28th 1928."

17. YC OSD2, 69, October 5, 1928.

18. YC OSD2, 77.

19. YC OSD2, 79, October 30, 1928.

20. OTOG, November 1, 1928.

21. YC OSD2, November 19, 1928.

22. YC OSD2, 104, November 28, 1928.

23. YC E4, December 7, 1928.

24. YC OS E2, 37.

25. YC E4, Hunt–Yorke, December 12, 1928.

26. YC E4, Hunt–AC, probably December 13, 1928.

27. YC OSD2, 133–34, Hunt–Yorke, December 16, 1928.

28. YC E4, Hunt–Yorke, December 19, 1928.

29. YC OSD2, 123, AC–Yorke, December 20, 1928.

30. OTOG, December 25, 1928.

CHAPTER TWENTY. REFUS DE SÉJOUR 1929

1. YC OSD2, 139.

2. YC E13.

3. YC OSD2, 163, AC–Yorke.

4. YC OSD2, 164–65.

5. YC OSD2, 166.

6. YC OSD2 176, January 21, 1928.

7. YC OSD2, 182, Memorandum of Events.

8. YC E13.

9. YC OSD2, 170.

10. YC E13, "14 fevrier 29."

11. YC OSD3, 197.

12. YC OSD3, 206.

13. YC NS 117.

14. YC OSD3, 231.

15. YC OSD3, 223.

16. YC OSD3, 223.

17. YC OSD3, 226.

18. YC OSD3, 218.

19. OTOG, March 22, 1929.

20. YC OSD3, 208.

21. YC OSD3, 209.

22. YC OSD3, 210 (undated).

23. YC OSD3, 215.

24. YC OSD3, 216.

25. YC OSD3, 221, Tuesday, March 19 or 26, or April 2.

26. YC EE2, April 12, 1929.

27. YC OSD3, 213.

28. YC OSD3, 213.

CHAPTER TWENTY-ONE.
THE LAST TIME HE SAW PARIS 1929–1930

1. YC OSD3, 227–28.

2. YC OSD3, 244, AC–Yorke, May 11, 1929.

3. YC OSD3, 246, May 13, 1929.

4. YC OSD3, 260, AC–Germer, Hotel Metropole, May 14.

5. YC OSD3, 249.

6. YC OSD3, 251–52.

7. YC EE2.

8. YC E13.

9. YC E13.

10. YC OSD3, 271, June 3, 1929.

11. YC OSD3, 256, AC–Yorke, Metropole Hotel, Brussels, May 24, 1929.

12. YC OSD3, July 23, 1929.

13. YC EE2.

14. YC EE2.

15. YC OSD3, 307, Germer–AC, September 13, 1929.

Bibliography

Adam, Peter. *Eileen Gray: Architect/Designer.* London: Thames and Hudson, 2000.

Baker, Phil. *The Devil Is a Gentleman: The Life and Times of Dennis Wheatley.* London: Dedalus, 2009.

Bennett, Arnold. *The Journals of Arnold Bennett* 1896–1910. Edited by Newman Flower. London: Cassell, 1932.

———. *Paris Nights and other Impressions of Places and People.* New York: George H. Doran, 1913.

Cavell, Janice. "Manliness in the Life and Posthumous Reputation of Robert Falcon Scott." *Canadian Journal of History* 45, no. 3 (Winter 2010): 538–64.

Churton, Tobias. *Aleister Crowley in America: Art, Espionage, and Sex Magick in the New World.* Rochester, Vt.: Inner Traditions, 2017.

———. *Aleister Crowley in India: The Secret Influence of Eastern Mysticism on Magic and the Occult.* Rochester, Vt.: Inner Traditions, 2019.

———. *Aleister Crowley: The Beast in Berlin; Art, Sex, and Magick in the Weimar Republic.* Rochester, Vt.: Inner Traditions, 2014.

———. *Aleister Crowley: The Biography.* London: Watkins Publishing, 2011.

———. *Deconstructing Gurdjieff.* Rochester, Vt.: Inner Traditions, 2017.

———. *The Golden Builders: Alchemists, Rosicrucians, and the First Freemasons.* York Beach, Maine: Weiser, 2005.

———. *Occult Paris: The Lost Magic of the Belle Époque.* Rochester, Vt.: Inner Traditions, 2016.

Coleman, Philip, Kathryn Milligan, and Nathan O'Donnell, eds. *BLAST at 100: A Modernist Magazine Reconsidered.* Leiden, Netherlands: Brill, 2017.

Conwell, Columbus C. *The Hymns of Homer: Translated into Verse from the Original Greek.* Philadelphia: Mifflin & Parry, 1830.

Crowley, Aleister. *The Book of the Law.* Newburyport, Mass.: Weiser Books, 1987.

———. *The Collected Works of Aleister Crowley.* 3 vols. Des Plaines, Ill.: Yogi Publication Society, 1974.

———. *The Confessions of Aleister Crowley* [Abridged]. Edited by John Symonds and Kenneth Grant. London: Routledge and Kegan Paul, 1978.

———. "Jeremiah in the Quartier Montparnasse." *Vanity Fair.* June 3, 1908.

———. *Liber TzBA Vel NIKH. Sub Figura 28. The Fountain of Hyacinth.* Edited by Steve Wilson. London: Iemanja Press, 1992.

———. *Moonchild.* Vol. 3 of *The Dennis Wheatley Library of the Occult.* With an introduction by Dennis Wheatley. London: Sphere, 1974.

———. *Oracles: The Biography of an Art.* Inverness: Society for the Propagation of Religious Truth, 1905.

———. *The Spirit of Solitude.* London: Mandrake Press, 1929.

———. *The Vision and the Voice, with Commentary and Other Papers.* With Victor B. Neuburg and Mary Desti. Edited by Hymenaeus Beta [William Breeze]. York Beach, Maine: Weiser Books, 1998.

Crowley, Aleister, and Auguste Rodin. *Le Dit de Rodin.* Translated into French by Philippe Pissier. Paris: L'arachnoïde, 2018. Originally published as *Rodin in Rime* (London: Chiswick Press, 1907).

Duncan, Isadora. *My Life.* New York: Boni and Liveright, 1927.

Fogel, Tuvia. *The Parchment of Circles.* N.p.: CreateSpace, 2015. Reprinted as *The Jerusalem Parchment,* Rochester, Vt.: Inner Traditions, 2018.

Fuller, Edmund. *Journey Into the Self: Being the Letters, Papers & Journals of Leo Stein.* Introduction by Van Wyck Brooks. New York: Crown, 1950.

Fuller, Jean Overton. *The Magical Dilemma of Victor Neuburg.* Oxford, U.K.: Mandrake, 1990.

Godwin, Joscelyn. "Lady Caithness and Her Connection with Theosophy." *Theosophical History* 8, no. 4 (October 2000): 127–48.

Goff, Jennifer. *Eileen Gray: Her Work and Her World.* Newbridge, Ireland: Irish Academic Press, 2015.

Hamnett, Nina. *Laughing Torso.* London: Virago Press, 1984.

Haweis, Stephen. "Reminiscences of Auguste Rodin." *Vanity Fair,* June 1918.

Hensley, Donald M. *Burton Rascoe.* New York: Twayne, 1970.

Kaczynski, Richard. *Perdurabo: The Life of Aleister Crowley.* Rev. ed. Berkeley, Calif.: North Atlantic Books, 2012.

Kelly, Gerald. "Comments on the 2 vols. of A.C.'s *Confessions* by his brother-in-law Gerald Festus Kelly. 1949," placed in Swiss cantonal archive by Annmarie Aeschbach of Swiss O.T.O., Stein, Switzerland: MC-41-D-03-18-07-14; Appenzell Ausserrhoden, Departement Inneres und Kultur, Amt für Kultur, Kantonsbibliothek, Landsgemeindeplatz 1/7, CH-9043 Trogen, www.ar.ch/kantonsbibliothek (in German). Kindly made available to me by Hymenaeus Beta (William Breeze), O.T.O.

Kennet, Kathleen Bruce Young. *Self-Portrait of an Artist.* London: John Murray, 1949.

Lees-Milne, James. *Midway on the Waves.* London: Faber and Faber, 1985.

Lhombreaud, Roger. *Arthur Symons: A Critical Biography.* Philadelphia: Dufour Editions, 1964.

Maugham, W. Somerset. *The Magician: A Novel Together with a Fragment of Autobiography.* London: William Heinemann, 1956.

Monro, Harold. "Review of *Good Sir Palamedes*" (by AC in *The Equinox*) in *The Poetry Review,* September 1912. Reproduced by 100th Monkey Press: www.100thmonkeypress.com/biblio/acrowley/articles/articles.htm.

Rault, Jasmine. *Eileen Gray and the Design of Sapphic Modernity: Staying In.* New York: Routledge, 2016.

Regardie, Israel, ed. *The Golden Dawn.* St. Paul, Minn.: Llewelyn, 1986.

Sieveking, Lancelot de Giberne. *The Eye of the Beholder.* London: Hulton Press, 1957.

Spence, Richard B. *Secret Agent 666: Aleister Crowley, British Intelligence and the Occult.* Port Townsend, Wash.: Feral House, 2008.

Starr, Martin P. "Aleister Crowley, Freemason!" Chap. 9 in *Aleister Crowley and Western Esotericism,* edited by Henrik Bogdan and Martin P. Starr. New York: Oxford University Press, 2012.

Vogeler, Martha S. *Austin Harrison and the English Review.* Columbia: University of Missouri Press, 2008.

Wagner-Martin, Linda. *Favored Strangers: Gertrude Stein and Her Family.* New Brunswick, N.J.: Rutgers University Press, 1995.

Wheatley, Dennis. *The Devil and All His Works.* New York: McGraw Hill, 1971.

———. *The Time Has Come. The Memoirs of Dennis Wheatley. Drink and Ink 1919–1977.* London: Hutchinson, 1979.

Whewell, Emily. "Legal Mediators: British Consuls in Tengyue (Western Yunnan) and the Burma–China Frontier Region, 1899–1931." *Modern Asian Studies* 54, no. 1 (2020): 95–122.

Whineapple, Brenda. *Sister Brother: Gertrude and Leo Stein.* London: Bloomsbury, 1996.

Wilson, Simon. *Tate Gallery: An Illustrated Companion.* Rev. ed. London: Tate Gallery, 1991.

Yorke, Gerald. *Aleister Crowley, The Golden Dawn and Buddhism. Reminiscences and Writings of Gerald Yorke.* Edited by Keith Richmond, with contributions by David Tibet, Timothy d'Arch Smith, and Clive Harper. York, Maine: The Teitan Press, 2011.

Index